The Rise of the Mongols

Five Chinese Sources

The Rise of the Mongols

Five Chinese Sources

Edited and translated, with an Introduction, by

Christopher P. Atwood, with Lynn Struve

Hackett Publishing Company, Inc.
Indianapolis/Cambridge

To students of the "Mongol Century," past and future.

For further information, please address
       Hackett Publishing Company, Inc.
       P.O. Box 44937
       Indianapolis, Indiana 46244-0937

       www.hackettpublishing.com

Cover design by E. L. Wilson
Composition by Aptara, Inc.
Cartography by Beehive Mapping, based on work by Wei CHEN

Library of Congress Control Number: 2021932944

ISBN-13: 978-1-64792-002-9 (cloth)
ISBN-13: 978-1-62466-990-3 (pbk.)

Contents

Preface

The idea behind this book originated in 1999, when I began to teach on the Mongol Empire at Indiana University. My introduction to Mongolian history was as a freshman at Harvard when I took Joseph Fletcher's Empire of the Mongols course in the fall of 1982. For that class, Professor Fletcher used no textbook, just primary sources in translation, and I was captivated. Part of the fascination was to see one people and one set of events, the Mongols and their conquests, through so many eyes: Persian, Chinese, Latin Christian, Armenian, as well as the Mongols themselves.

Seventeen years later, when I planned to teach a version of this class myself, I wanted to give students something like the same experience. But since taking Professor Fletcher's class, I had learned that there were many valuable, untranslated sources on the Mongol Empire, particularly in Chinese. Some of them were the earliest known descriptions of the new Mongol regime, and for that reason, if no other, they deserved attention. As part of my preparation for teaching, I began to translate several of the works included here, starting with Zhao Gong and his "A Memorandum on the Mong-Tatars" and continuing with Peng Daya and Xu Ting's "A Sketch of the Black Tatars" and eventually getting to Zhang Dehui's "Notes on a Journey." I also began working on the collection of biographies from the Mongols' Yuan dynasty, edited by the Chinese scholar Su Tianjue. Included in that collection was the bulk of Song Zizhen's "Spirit-Path Stele" written in honor of the famous scholar and reformer Ila Chucai.

At the time, however, my knowledge of classical Chinese and of the thirteenth-century context was still insufficient. A number of passages taxed my ingenuity. So, I turned to a senior colleague, Lynn Struve, professor of history at Indiana University, who had just completed a classic volume of translations on a similar period of turbulent transition: the seventeenth-century Manchu conquest of Ming China. Lynn had taught me in her Imperial China course, and now she went far beyond the usual demands of mentorship for a young colleague, generously going over every line with suggestions and queries. I took the suggestions and researched the questions as well as I could. Students began using the translations and seemed to be getting something out of them. Their questions and insights began to direct how I taught and understood these texts. Passages from the translations were even occasionally cited in print. For many years, however, I was occupied with other questions and texts. My earlier research had been on the twentieth century in Inner Mongolia, and it took a long time for me to feel that I was really conversant enough with the Mongol Empire to say that I had understood these texts. Meanwhile, I discovered the importance of other texts as well, particularly

Li Xinchuan's "Random Notes" which, written in 1216, constituted the earliest account of the Mongol conquests in any language.

In the summer of 2016, another colleague, Professor Sarah Schneewind at UC, San Diego, asked on the Facebook "Sinologists" group if anyone had some good readings to represent the Mongol Empire for a class she was planning that fall on Late Imperial China. I forwarded a few of my translations to her and was inspired when she said they deserved to be in print. She also suggested that Hackett Publishing, where she had published her book *A Tale of Two Melons*, might be interested in them. I was just then relocating to the University of Pennsylvania and, stimulated by her encouragement, decided finally to see about publishing these sources. I approached Hackett's senior editor Rick Todhunter at the Association for Asian Studies Annual Meeting, and we began corresponding in the spring of 2017.

Hackett proved entirely as efficient and encouraging an outfit as Sarah had said it would be. Rick had only one demand, that the relevant parts of Li Xinchuan's history, since his was the very first history to treat the Mongol conquests, had to be included. Meanwhile, for an "Introduction," I began to write up much of the explanatory material that I had used in my lectures to make sense of these translations. What would students want to know? What would they need to understand to make sense of these Chinese works on the early Mongol Empire? Years of discussion with students have helped me answer these questions.

Completing the Li Xinchuan translation, completing the untranslated parts of Ila Chucai's biographical inscription, and getting the long draft translations into shape took a fair amount of time. As I went back to some of the issues Lynn Struve had flagged so long ago, I knew that the newly translated and revised materials could also benefit from her revisions. When I sent them to her, I was deeply grateful that she agreed once again to go over the texts as carefully as if they were her own. The resulting translations would never have been started or brought to completion without her willingness to drop her own multifarious projects on the seventeenth century and assist me in bringing these stories of the thirteenth century to light. Her contribution went far beyond what could be acknowledged in a preface, and I was happy when she agreed to share credit on the title page of our translation. In the introductory material and commentaries that follow, the "we" refers to Lynn and myself; almost every footnote and every difficult reading was discussed at length between us.

Over the course of two decades, many others have also helped to polish and complete these translations. Particularly helpful in reading through the manuscript and consulting on some of the most difficult puzzles were the two Yuan-era specialists Professor Ma Xiaolin of Nankai University and Dr. Qiu Zhirong; we had known each other in China and I had invited them to come to the University of Pennsylvania as visiting scholars in 2019–2020. Professor Manling Luo of Indiana University also assisted Lynn on several difficult points. Equally helpful throughout were Hackett's three anonymous readers: Reader A gave many suggestions on the background and Chinese translation; Reader C repeatedly flagged issues which readers without Chinese training might find puzzling; and Reader B focused on keeping it simple, keeping it consistent, and not overthinking it—all important advice though sometimes difficult to follow simultaneously.

Before dealing with the translation, however, I had to deal with a number of discrepancies in the Chinese texts. Over the years, many scholars helped me secure copies of manuscripts and printed editions that assisted me in determining possible corruptions and alternative readings in the text. In addition to Ma Xiaolin, I would also like to thank Professor Lucille Chia, Professor Dang Baohai, Wen-ling Liu and the Indiana University Herman B. Wells Library, Professor Matsuda Kōichi, Professor Nakami Tatsuo, Professor Tachibana Makoto, Professor Ulaanbars (Qi Guang), Wang Han and the National Library of China, Dr. Wu Zhijian and the Zhejiang Library, Dr. Xu Quansheng, Zhou Qiao, and Zhou Qing and the Shanghai Library.

My reading of Zhang Dehui's "Notes on a Journey" was especially shaped by travel in Mongolia and Inner Mongolia. Here I would like to thank D. Gereltuv and Yo. Badral, owner-operators of the "Mongolia Quest" tour group in Mongolia, and H. Erhimbatu (West Üjümüchin) and Nahiya (Kheshigten) in Inner Mongolia for help on the ground. In discussing visual evidence, finding high-resolution images, and securing permissions, I benefited from the help, assistance, and advice of Professor Sakura Christmas, Professor Susan Huang, Eva-Maria Jansson and the Danish Royal Library in Copenhagen, Dr. Jin Lin and the China National Silk Museum, Professor Stefan Kamola, Cynthia Mackey and the Peabody Museum of Archaeology and Ethnology, Professor Egas Bender de Moniz Bandeira, Constance Mood and Christal Springer of the Fisher Fine Arts Library at the University of Pennsylvania, Dr. Eleanor Sims, Professor Eiren Shea, Robbi Siegel of Art Resource, Dr. Alla Sizova, Professor Nancy Steinhardt, Luvsantseren Tugstenuun, Enkhtsetseg Tuguldur, Yang Yuqing, and Vito Acosta. Dr. Chen Wei, now of the Beijing Architectural Design Institute, did the crucial first drafts of the maps.

Many persons helped me with difficult passages, oriented me to contemporary scholarship, and checked materials for me, particularly Professor Paul Goldin, Professor Yuri Pines, Dr. Stephen Pow, Dr. O. Sukhbaatar, and Dr. Brian Vivier. Members of Facebook's "Sinologists" group answered several queries with a characteristic mix of academic overkill and great senses of humor, especially Professor J. Michael Farmer, Professor Michael A. Fuller, Dr. David Porter, Professor Doris Sung, Professor Sixiang Wang, and doctoral students Simon Berger and Jiajun Zou.

Over the course of two decades many scholars and students have helped me in ways too varied to recall; without them I would not be the scholar I am today. I hope those not mentioned here will forgive my oversight. But here I would like to remember by name three mentors in the study of medieval Mongolian and the Mongol Empire: György Kara, Francis Woodman Cleaves, and Joseph Fletcher. Although I only studied under Professor Fletcher for two years before his untimely decease, without his Core Curriculum class Empire of the Mongols, this book would not exist. The responsibility for any errors is, however, mine alone.

And as always, in everything I do is Okcha. Thank you.

Chronology of Major Events

1114 Jurchen leader Akûdai of Manchuria rebels against the Kitan Liao dynasty and founds the Jin dynasty the next year.

1125 Akûdai's forces capture the last Kitan emperor; Kitan prince Daiši Lemya flees to Central Asia.

1127 The Jurchen Jin dynasty captures the Song capital, Kaifengfu, and conquers North China.

1141 Daiši Lemya wins the Battle of Qatwan and founds the Qara-Khitai empire in Central Asia.

1162 Possible date of birth of Temüjin (Chinggis Khan).

1187 The Muslim armies of Saladin (Salah al-Din) recapture Jerusalem from the Crusaders.

1196 Temüjin (Chinggis Khan) and his patron, Ong Khan, join the Jin in an attack on the Tatars.

1203 Temüjin (Chinggis Khan) overthrows Ong Khan and begins the unification of Mongolia.

1204 The Fourth Crusade sacks Constantinople, beginning the Latin Empire of Byzantium.

1205 The first Mongol invasion of the Tangut Xia.

1206 Chinggis Khan is enthroned; the Song dynasty attacks the Jin dynasty.

1209 The Uyghurs surrender peacefully to the Mongols.

1210 Muhammad, Sultan of Khwarazm, defeats the Qara-Khitai at Talas.

1211 The Mongols invade the Jin dynasty in North China.

1217 Muqali is appointed viceroy in North China.

1219 The Mongols invade the Sultanate of Khwarazm in Central Asia and Iran.

1227 The Tangut Xia dynasty is destroyed; Chinggis Khan dies.

1229 Chinggis Khan's son Öködei Khan is enthroned.

1230 Ila Chucai begins a new program of taxation in North China.

1234 The Song dynasty and the Mongol Empire cooperate to destroy the Jin.

1235 Öködei Khan orders armies against Eastern Europe and the Song dynasty.

1240 Abduraqman is appointed head of taxation in North China.

1241 Öködei Khan dies; his widow, Töregene, serves as regent.

1251   Möngke Khan seizes power from Öködei Khan's descendants.

1258   The Mongols, led by Möngke Khan's brother Hüle'ü, conquer Baghdad, ending the Abbasid Caliphate.

1259   Möngke Khan dies while campaigning near Chongqingfu; the Mongol Empire breaks up.

1260   Qubilai Khan is enthroned in Shangdu and moves the Mongol Empire's center of power to North China.

1276   Mongol armies enter Hangzhou; the Southern Song dynasty falls.

1294   Qubilai Khan dies; Mongol armies evacuate Dai Viet (Vietnam).

1347   The Black Death begins attacking the Black Sea and Mediterranean ports.

1351   The Red Turban Rebellions begin against Mongol rule in China.

1368   The Mongol dynasty is expelled from China.

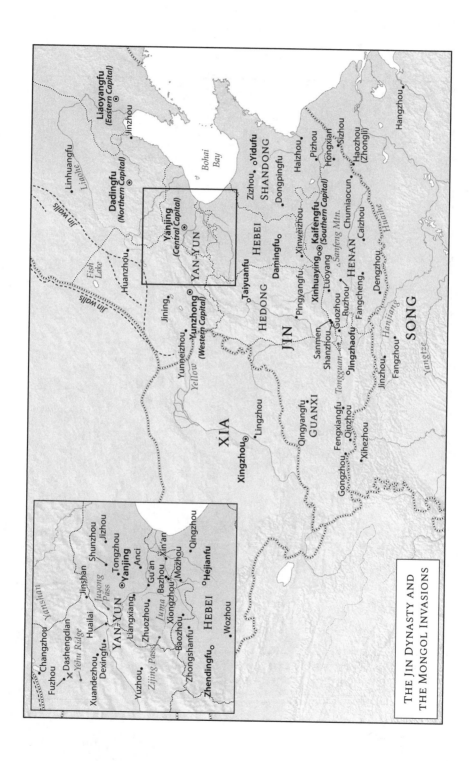

THE JIN DYNASTY AND
THE MONGOL INVASIONS

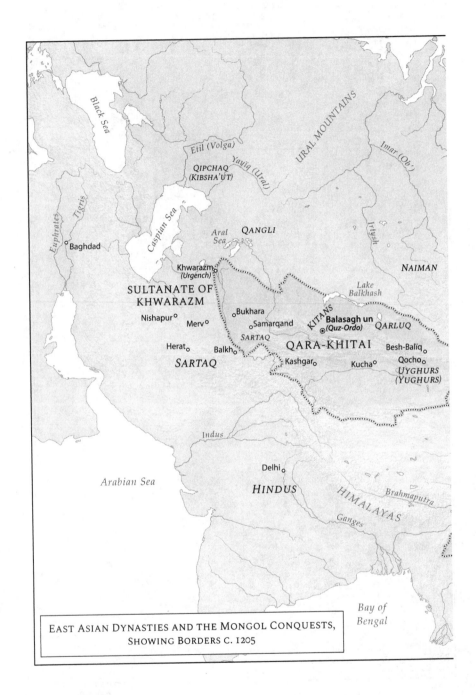

EAST ASIAN DYNASTIES AND THE MONGOL CONQUESTS,
SHOWING BORDERS C. 1205

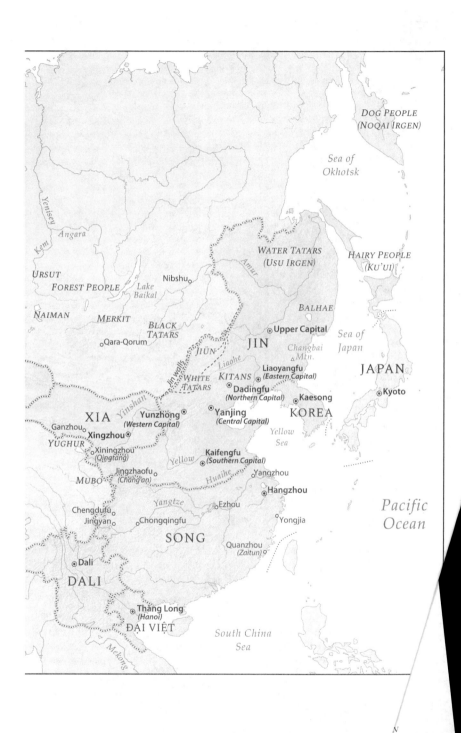

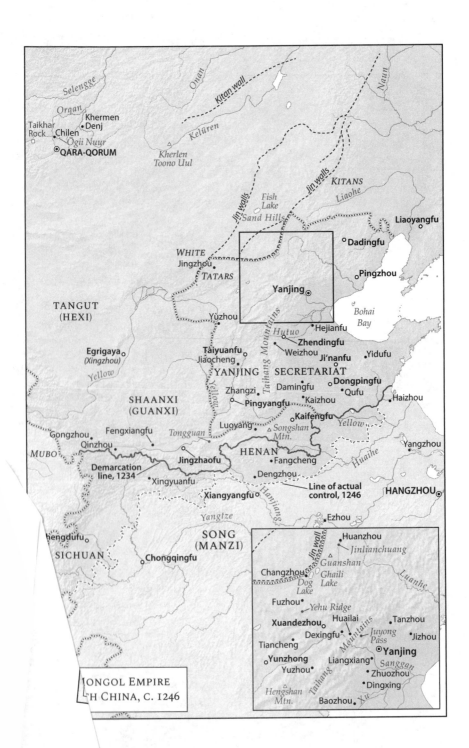

Selengge
Onan
Kitan wall
Naun
Organ
Khermen
Denj
Taikhar
Rock
Chilen
Kelüren
ÖGII NUUR
QARA-QORUM
Kherlen
Toono Uul
Liaohe
KITANS
Liaoyangfu
Jin walls
Fish
Lake
Dadingfu
WHITE
Jingzhou
Sand Hills
TATARS
Yanjing
Pingzhou
TANGUT
(HEXI)
Yuzhou
Bohai
Bay
Hutuo
Hejianfu
Taihang Mountains
Zhendingfu
Egrigaya
(Xingzhou)
Taiyuanfu
Jiaocheng
Weizhou
Ji'nanfu
Yidufu
Yellow
YANJING
SECRETARIAT
Zhangzi
Damingfu
Dongpingfu
Yellow
Pingyangfu
Kaizhou
Qufu
SHAANXI
(GUANXI)
Luoyang
Kaifengfu
Haizhou
Gongzhou
Fengxiangfu
Tongguan
Songshan
Mtn.
Yellow
Yangzhou
Qinzhou
HENAN
Huaihe
MUBO
Demarcation
line, 1234
Jingzhaofu
Fangcheng
Xingyuanfu
Dengzhou
Line of actual
control, 1246
HANGZHOU
Xiangyangfu
Hanjiang
Yangtze
Ezhou
hengdufu
SONG
(MANZI)
SICHUAN
Chongqingfu

MONGOL EMPIRE
TH CHINA, C. 1246

Jin wall
Huanzhou
Jinlianchuang
Guanshan
Changzhou
Ghaili
Lake
Luanhe
Dog
Lake
Fuzhou
Yehu Ridge
Huailai
Tanzhou
Xuandezhou
Dexingfu
Juyong
Pass
Jizhou
Tiancheng
Taihang Mountains
Yunzhong
Yuzhou
Liangxiang
Yanjing
Sanggan
Zhuozhou
Hengshan
Mtn.
Baozhou
Xu
Dingxing

Introduction

As thirteenth-century historians never tired of pointing out, the Mongol Empire burst out of nowhere to take over almost the entire "known world" of Afro-Eurasia. The anonymous Russian chronicler of Novgorod city is only the most emphatic in writing: "The same year [1224], for our sins, unknown speakers came, whom no one exactly knows, who they are, nor whence they came out, nor what their language is, nor of what race they are, nor what their faith is; but they call them Tatars."[1] To Muslim and Christian writers this sudden rise from obscurity to dominance was a sure sign of divine intervention and a reminder of the role of unpredictable fortune in human affairs. The rise of these Tatars, as the inhabitants of Mongolia were generally known to the people they conquered, took place far enough away that little reliable news reached historians writing in Persian, Armenian, Arabic, or Slavic languages about how it happened. Like the famous European travelers John of Plano Carpini, William of Rubruck, and Marco Polo,[2] they had to gather oral traditions current among the Mongols and their conquered peoples in order to piece together the story of their rise. Legends abounded and agreed-upon facts were few.

Eventually, however, Muslim historians gained access to the traditions of the Mongols themselves, full of concrete details and mostly quite realistic. Writing in the service of the Mongol khans of the Middle East at the beginning of the fourteenth century, the great Persian historian Rashid al-Din combined previous Persian and Mongolian histories and commentaries into his *Compendium of Chronicles*, which became the authoritative account of the rise of the Mongols not just for Persian and Arabic readers, but also, after the eighteenth century, for European readers as well.

Through his work, the Mongolian traditions of Temüjin, who assumed the imperial name Chinggis (misread by early European scholars as "Genghis") Khan, became the storyline of Mongolian origins. And when the *Secret History of the Mongols*, written in the mid-thirteenth century and indirectly one of Rashid al-Din's major sources, was recovered by careful scholarship and translation in the twentieth century, this Mongolian story became all the more dominant. The "virgin birth" of his distant ancestress, Alan the Fair; Temüjin's harsh childhood and upbringing by his heroic widowed mother, Ö'elün; and the souring of his childhood friendship with Jamuqa: all of these tales became the history of where Mongols came from. It all culminated with the lurid tales told by Persian histor

---

1. Michell and Forbes 1914, 64, with modifications following the footnotes. What is tra here as "race" is *plemia*, which in Imperial Russia became the standard term for "tribe anthropological sense.

2. See Dawson 1955; Jackson 2009; Polo 2016.

Chinggis Khan, personally named Temüjin (1162?–1227).

of the great duel between Chinggis Khan and the Khwarazm-Shahs ruling Central Asia and Iran and the sack of cities like Bukhara and Samarqand from 1220 on.

Sidelined by this way of telling the rise of the Mongols were the stories recorded by historians and border officials writing in Chinese. Of course, many of the Chinese stories of the rise of the Mongols were very similar, if not identical, to those told farther west. In the Chinese tradition, as in the Persian, the Mongol tradition based on the *Secret History of the Mongols* eventually came to play a dominant role. The *Yuanshi*, or "History of the (Mongols') Yuan Dynasty," even though it was compiled by the following Ming dynasty, took its main story line for the first five Mongol khans from material originally written in Mongolian.

But a number of other writings about Mongol history conveyed a very different picture of the rise of the Mongol Empire. Mongolia is much closer to China than it is to Persia or Europe, and generals and officials along the border had filed innumerable reports over the centuries describing developments in Mongolia and their responses. Sadly, the vast majority of those reports on the rise of the Mongol Empire were stricken from the historical record by historians working the Mongols' Yuan dynasty. But in South China a number of such works were served outside the official archives and have been copied and recopied until present.

nce the Mongols began their conquest of North China, increasing numbers inese generals and local strongmen rallied to their standard. The earliest efectors to the Mongol cause were barely literate, if at all, and left no record they saw their new lords. But after 1215, when the Jin's Central Capital ng (present-day Beijing) fell to the Mongols, literate officials joined the banner and began to leave records of their hopes and dreams in Mon-e. In those records, it was the agonizing Mongol campaigns in North m 1211 to 1234, not the great expeditions against far-off Central Asia, tRussia, which marked the high point of the drama of conquest. Once cived military struggle to pacify North China ended in Mongol victory, par in Mongol service labored patiently and persistently, but with only s, to get the now-triumphant empire to transition to a peacetime footing. Their writings thus were part of an ongoing policy debate, intended both to encourage like-minded officials that their efforts were not in vain, and to publicize arguments that might be used to convince the Mongol rulers that reform was in their own interest.

This volume offers a selection of five important works that together detail the rise of the Mongol Empire in Chinese eyes. Three of them were written by officials of South China's Southern Song dynasty (1127–1279). This dynasty had lost North China to the Jurchens, an earlier invading people from Manchuria. But even restricted to the Yangtze Valley and the ports on China's southeastern coast, the Southern Song built a highly urbanized, commercial economy; indeed, some have seen South China at this time as the world's first truly modern society. Officials of the Southern Song observed the Mongol conquest of their Jurchen rivals' Jin dynasty in North China with a mixture of schadenfreude, astonishment, and increasing

Öködei Khan (1186–1241), second emperor of the Mongol Empire.

apprehension. Two of these sources date from the time of Chinggis Khan himself (r. 1206–1227) and are the earliest known descriptions in any language of the rise of the Mongols. The third dates from the time of Chinggis Khan's son and successor Öködei Khan (r. 1229–1241) and gives the earliest detailed description of Mongolian administration in the territories they conquered.

The fourth and fifth accounts translated here come from officials in North China who were writing in the service of the Mongol rulers. Both come from the time of Qubilai Khan (Marco Polo's "Cublai Caan"), whose rule from 1260 to 1294 marked a new phase in the empire's history. Yet both deal with the perio before his enthronement as Great Khan. The first of these is a biography of ʃ Chucai (1190–1244), who became a model reformist official under Öködei Khɛ but whose work was abandoned after his death. Song Zizhen's biography of Chucai, written in 1268, offers both a program for the Qubilai-era reforms under way and a warning about the forces that might derail them. The final translated in this volume is the account of how a minor North Chinese ɑ Zhang Dehui (1194–1274), went to visit Qubilai in Mongolia. At the timɾ visit, Qubilai was not yet khan, just one of the several hundreds of Chinggiʃ grandsons who were wondering what to do with the world their grar conquests had put in their hands. In addition to his description of the prince's nomadic life in Mongolia, Zhang Dehui left a record of the conversations he had with the young Qubilai about Confucius, Mongol administration, and the nature of ritual and good government.

Together, these accounts offer a view of the early Mongol Empire very different not just from those of Muslim and Christian travelers and chroniclers, but also from the Mongol tradition embodied in the *Secret History of the Mongols*. Two examples will suffice to illustrate this difference. In the *Secret History of the Mongols*, North China's Jin dynasty (1115–1234) is only a distant presence on the horizon during Chinggis Khan's rise to power. Mongol rulers in his father's and grandfather's generations fell victim to the Jin dynasty's alliance with hostile Tatars. At one point, in 1196, Chinggis Khan cooperated with the Jin in a campaign against those same rival Tatars. But apart from those isolated events, the *Secret History* and accounts derived from it mention no interaction of Chinggis Khan's family with the Jin dynasty before his invasion began in 1211.

The two earliest accounts in this anthology record a very different picture. In his 1216 history, the second volume of his *Random Notes from Court and Country since the Jianyan Years*, Li Xinchuan records that up until the very year of his attack, Chinggis Khan actually paid annual tribute to the Jin dynasty. This history and Zhao Gong's 1221 "A Memorandum on the Mong-Tatars" tell how the Mongol attack on the Jin dynasty was preceded by complex political maneuvers with the White Tatars and the Jiün (Ch. *Jiu*)—mixed-origin nomadic auxiliaries who patrolled the frontier with Mongolia on behalf of the Jin court. These diplomatic efforts to win over Inner Mongolian allies of the Jin hardly appear in the Mongolian telling. According to Zhao Gong, Chinggis Khan had even spent ten years as a captive in Jin territory, an episode about which the *Secret History of the Mongols* is completely silent.

The texts included here likewise offer a very different picture from the Mongolian or Persian sources regarding the administrative reforms in North China under Öködei Khan. In the *Secret History*, these reforms were instigated by the n himself, as part of the natural evolution of Mongol rule. The Persian his- n 'Ata-Malik Juvayni treats the change from Chinggis Khan's severe and nspiring punishments to Öködei Khan's mild and clement forgiveness as a estation of God's dual nature of punishment and mercy. Where officials are ned by name, they are always Muslim ones from Central Asia, sent to rule n China.

 hinese writers, however, whether in service to the Mongols or to the rival Song dynasty, those reforms are associated inextricably with the great fficial Ila (Ch. Yelü) Chucai. Although his name is not even mentioned an, Muslim, or European sources, the great biography written by Song 268 and intended to be inscribed on a stele by his "spirit-path" or s his tomb, treats him as the mainspring of the reforms. Muslim officials sp ud Yalavach, lauded by Persian historians, appear in Song Zizhen's sig e only at the end, as bit-part villains who ruined Ila Chucai's far- uch a eulogistic source could easily be accused of bias, but the

Southern Song writers Zhao Gong, Peng Daya, and Xu Ting, who had no reason to support his cause and who—in Xu Ting's case, at least—knew him personally, spoke very highly of his abilities.

Yet even the Southern writers doubted the degree to which any Chinese official, even one as able as Ila Chucai, could reform Mongol rule. To them, the Mongol regime was irreformable. This difference between the Southern Song writers and the Chinese writers in Mongol service warns us not to expect any generic "Chinese" point of view in these sources. Political loyalty was more important than ethnicity in determining viewpoints. But the simple fact of viewing the Mongol expansion not from the west, but from the south, gives all Chinese writers a very different set of names and events to emphasize. And as the reader will see, all of the writers shared a significant set of allusions and expectations that derived from their education in the Chinese literary tradition.[3]

Reading these sources and comparing them to the Persian, European, and Mongolian sources is thus a fascinating illustration of the multiplicity of historical viewpoints on a single world-historical event. These Chinese sources paint a very different picture of the Mongol Empire. Partly this is a matter of inclusion or omission of persons, places, and incidents or even outright errors. But perhaps the most interesting moments of comparison come when the Chinese literary tradition and the specifics of the North and South Chinese interaction with the Mongol Empire visibly shape how the writers paint the commonly accepted picture of the empire. Whether it is Mongol treatment of the captive cities, the taxation policy, or the personalities of the empire's leaders, these sources give us a panorama that has not been often seen before in English-language studies of the Mongol Empire.

The Rise of the Mongols in the Eyes of the South

China and the Rise of the Mongols

The most important fact about the Chinese world during the rise of the Mongols was its internal divisions. The great Han and Tang dynasties had not only ruled the lands inhabited by the Han (ethnic Chinese) people but also held sway over large areas inhabited by non-Chinese peoples in southwest China, Inner Mongolia, Manchuria, and Central Asia, as well as parts of today's Vietnam and Korea. The Tang dynasty broke up in the wake of the catastrophic Huang Chao Rebellion (874–884). From that time until the rise of the Mongol Empire, ethnic Chinese dynasties not only were unable to dominate the rest of East Asia, they were also unable to unite all the lands settled by Han Chinese.

North China first saw a series of short-lived dynasties that constituted the Five Dynasties period (907–960). Of these five, four were founded by men from the

---

3. See Appendix §2.1 (p. 185) for a table arranging the major allusions and their sources chronologically.

so-called Shatuo, a mixed people who had coalesced on the borders of Inner Mongolia and China's Shanxi Province. The core of the Shatuo people was a house of Turkic-speaking commanders whom the Tang had allowed to relocate from Central Asia to Shanxi as a reward for their loyalty. In the chaos of the Huang Chao Rebellion, those commanders fought for the Tang dynasty. Joining in their army and adopting their identity were Sogdians (Iranian-speaking Central Asians from what is now Uzbekistan and Tajikistan), as well as Tatar pastoralists from the Mongolian plateau. This mixed people adopted the Turkic language of the leading house, but many had the deep eyes, high noses, and full beards that Chinese identified as typical of "Westerners."[4]

With the fall of the Tang dynasty, Shatuo commanders joined the melee and founded several short-lived dynasties in North China. In the rise and fall of these unstable regimes, local kingdoms in Vietnam, Yunnan, and South China broke away from control of the generals in the North China plains. Eventually a northern warlord of Han or ethnic Chinese background, Zhao Kuangyin, was able to reunify the most important parts of North and South China and found the Song dynasty (960–1127).

Although the Song dynasty was vastly wealthier and more populous than its neighbors, it remained hemmed in throughout its existence by powerful non-Han neighbors. In the far south and southwest the kingdoms of Dai Viet (northern Vietnam) and Dali (in modern Yunnan Province) successfully eluded Song control. Korea, under the new Goryeo (Koryŏ) dynasty, controlled most of the peninsula and engaged in cultural and economic commerce with the Song dynasty. In northwest China and adjoining areas of Kökenuur, Inner Mongolia, and Central Asia, petty kingdoms established by Turkic-speaking Uyghurs controlled the sparsely populated oases, high mountains, and desert-steppe territories.

The Uyghurs had ruled a vast empire based in Mongolia from 742 to 847. This empire had allied with the Tang, supplying the Tang with strong military support in return for favorable terms in the trade of horses for silk and cash. Their palace in central Mongolia had a vast golden roof visible for miles and the capital city of Orda-Baliq was surrounded by cultivated fields. But internal unrest and increasingly severe weather, culminating in the terrible winter of 839–840, devastated the kingdom. The tributary Qirghiz to the north revolted and sacked the Uyghur capital; members of the Uyghur imperial family fled to what is now Inner Mongolia, Gansu Province, and Central Asia, where they adapted to the local environments and either settled down as a ruling class over oasis farmers or continued a seasonal round of mobile pastoralism.

Most formidable of all the enemies of the Song were the Kitans, another pastoralist people who established an empire that repeatedly humiliated Song armies. The Kitan's Liao dynasty (907–1125) claimed to be a "Middle Kingdom" just like China and a successor to the Tang. Based in what is now southeastern Inner Mongolia, the Kitans built up an empire that included not just their own heartland, but also Manchuria, most of Mongolia proper, and several prefectures

---

4. On these racial stereotypes, see Abramson 2008, 87–89. On the Shatuo, see Atwood 2010.

along North China's border with Inner Mongolia. The most important of these prefectures were Yanjing (present-day Beijing) in the North China plain and Yunzhong (present-day Datong) over the mountains to the northwest in Shanxi Province. The Kitan conquest provoked a strong reaction from the Song dynasty leaders who repeatedly attempted to regain this formerly Chinese territory until a final Kitan victory forced them to sign the treaty of Chanyuan in 1005. In this treaty, the Song court acknowledged the Liao as an equal state and relinquished its claims to fourteen disputed prefectures, including Yanjing and Yunzhong.

The Kitans spoke a language of the Mongolic family, but one different enough to be incom-

Kitan groom leading a horse, c. late 11th century.

prehensible to Mongol speakers. The Liao emperors traveled their realm in a constant circuit, pausing to hunt, hawk, and fish according to the seasons. A Song envoy in 1075 described the imperial court as follows:

> There were [only] three buildings in total. . . . The rest were felt tents, several tens of them, all facing east. Pillars of pine marked the front of the court, and a man holding a placard reading *gemen* [that is, the gates to the imperial precinct] stood between the pillars. East of them were six or seven tents that housed the Secretariat, the Bureau of Military Affairs, and Visitors' Bureau. Further east was a single felt tent, and next to it were parked six felt covered wagons. There was a big banner in front of them that read: "Ancestral Temple." All of this was in the wild grasslands.[5]

At the same time as the Kitans housed Chinese-style administrative offices in felt tents or yurts, they also built sedentary forts in the lands of Mongolia that they ruled. Zhang Dehui saw the ruins of such forts in Mongolia, and several have since been excavated.[6]

---

5. Pursey 2019, 178. "Bureau of Military Affairs" may also be translated as "Privy Council."

6. Most impressive, although not seen by Zhang Dehui, is the Kitan Liao pagoda of Kherlen Bars on the Kherlen River; see Steinhardt 2016. Recent research also demonstrates that the

The balance of power between the Kitan Liao and the Chinese Song dynasties was temporarily upset by the rise of another ambitious regime led by a non-Han pastoral people, the Tanguts. The Tangut people had originated from the eastern valleys of the Tibetan plateau, around present-day northwestern Sichuan and southeastern Qinghai. Their language was not Tibetan, however, but Miñag, the only historically documented language of the Qiangic family; linguists are now describing other languages of the family along the eastern edges of the Tibetan plateau.[7] During the Tang dynasty, certain Tangut chiefs fled the expanding Tibetan Empire and in return for pledging loyalty were allowed by the Tang to move with their people to the pastures of northern Shaanxi and the Ordos area in southwestern Inner Mongolia. As the Song rose to power, some Tanguts paid them tribute, while others were less submissive. In 982, a Tangut chief, Li Jiqian, defied the Song and began to build up a kingdom. In 1028, his son conquered the Uyghur kingdom of Ganzhou and in 1038, his grandson declared himself the ruler of the Xia Empire, usually called the Western Xia in scholarly literature.[8] Like the Kitans, the Tanguts also devised a new script to write their previously unwritten language. After a series of wars, the Western Xia settled into a subordinate position in the Liao-Song-Xia trilateral relationship. Domestically, they viewed themselves as an independent empire, but in diplomacy with the Song and the Liao, they accepted an inferior position as a vassal kingdom.

A much more serious upset to the status quo came with the rise of the Jurchens. Jurchen speakers lived dispersed in the forests and along the rivers of Manchuria. Most villagers carried on small-scale farming and raised pigs and cattle, but their real wealth came from trading northern products to the Kitans, Koreans, and Song Chinese: sable and other furs, ginseng, river pearls, falcons, and even more exotic products like walrus ivory sourced from the Bering Sea. The rise of the Kitans subjected them to a rigorous tribute regime in which these products were extorted by military force. As is briefly recounted in Li Xinchuan's account, a man claiming Korean origin and named Akûdai (Ch. Aguda) led a Jurchen revolt in 1114 against the Kitan rulers. His revolt met with astonishing success and soon he and his new dynasty, the Jin or "Golden" dynasty, made an alliance with the Song, aiming to divide up the Liao territory between them.

What followed was one of the greatest fiascos of Chinese foreign policy. According to the treaty with Akûdai, the Song and the Jurchens would each contribute

---

Kitan built a wall roughly along the northern frontier of present-day Mongolia. By contrast, the Jin dynasty's frontier was along the border of Inner Mongolia with present-day Mongolia. See Shelach-Lavi et al. 2020; and Shelach-Lavi, Honeychurch, and Chunag 2020.

7. The Qiangic family is part of the larger Sino-Tibetan (or Tibeto-Burman) language family. But whether the Qiangic family is more closely related to Burmese, Tibetan, or Chinese or is its own separate branch is currently disputed. The family is named after the Qiang, the only people in the language family currently recognized as a separate ethnic group in China today. The other speakers are usually considered for official purposes as part of the Tibetan ethnic group and use Tibetan or Chinese for writing, although their languages are quite different from either.

8. The designation as "Western Xia" or Xixia distinguishes them from China's legendary first dynasty, the Xia.

to the conquest of fourteen coveted prefectures. Yanjing would fall to the Song in return for the Song paying a subsidy to the new Jurchen regime. The Song commanders assumed that the Liao's Han (ethnic Chinese) population was panting for liberation and made little allowance for serious opposition; they found out too late that the Han of the fourteen prefectures would not rebel against the Liao dynasty in which they had played a valued role. In the end, with a combination of diplomatic truculence and military weakness, the Song stumbled into a war with the victorious Jurchen Jin, one which ended in total failure for the South. By 1127, the Song emperor Huizong and his family had been captured and deported to the Jurchen homeland in Manchuria. The Jin dynasty eventually added to its territory all of North China up to the Tangut border, although it ruled the Chinese lands for a while through a Chinese collaborator, Liu Yu (1073–1146), rather than directly.

This sudden Jin victory could not re-create the stable three-cornered diplomatic system that had existed between the Song, Liao, and Xia dynasties. A member of the Song dynasty's imperial Zhao family escaped to Hangzhou in South China where he established the Southern Song dynasty (1127–1279). Eventually the Treaty of Shaoxing in 1142 made a temporary peace between the Jin and Southern Song dynasties. The Huaihe River was set as the boundary, leaving North China to the Jin, which the Southerners had to acknowledge as the dominant state. But the legacy of resentment between the two states was a standing invitation to ambitious men on both sides to revisit the issue. From 1161 to a second peace treaty in 1165, the Jin tried to conquer the South. Forty years later, from 1206 to 1208, the Southern Song launched a war to recover the North. Both wars were failures, but the last attempt by the Song to drive the Jurchens out of North China took place just as Chinggis Khan was being enthroned in Mongolia. It thus contributed crucially to distracting the Jin from the rising threat to the north.

Even more destabilizing for the Jin frontier were the repeated Kitan rebellions that broke out on the empire's Inner Mongolian frontier. The Jurchen rise was so sudden that they scarcely had any time to adjust to their new position as rulers. Moreover, although the Jurchens traditionally raised horses in their forest clearings and riverside settlements in Manchuria and fought their initial campaigns from horseback, they soon found that only the steppe Kitans of Inner Mongolia, with their vast herds, could supply the horses and riders they needed. Thus, the Jurchens had no choice but to conscript the subjugated Kitan horsemen as a core part of their army, employed both in the north against the Tatars of the Mongolian plateau and in the south against the Southern Song. A massive mobilization of Kitans made in preparation for the 1161–1165 war against the Song sparked a widespread rebellion from 1159 to 1163. Another smaller rebellion took place in 1183 in response to Jin campaigns against the Tatars in the North. When Chinggis Khan launched his invasion of the Jin, both Kitan disaffection and Jurchen fear of it were crucial advantages in weakening the Jin armies.[9]

---

9. On the Kitans under Jurchen rule, see Jagchid 1988, 34–48.

Kitan rebellions were stimulated by the continued existence of a Kitan empire in Central Asia. Although the Jurchen armies captured the last emperor of the Liao in 1125, there were many members of the imperial Ila house still at large. One of them, known as Daiši Lemya, or "the Grand-Preceptor Scribe," fled north to Mongolia where he rallied the Tatars of Mongolia to his cause. But rather than directly confront Jin power, he prudently moved his army west, proclaiming himself Gür-Khan or "universal ruler" of a new Kitan Liao dynasty in 1131, and he set his capital at Balasaghun (Quz-Ordo) in what is now northern Kyrgyzstan. In 1141, the new dynasty crushed the armies of the Seljuk Turks to the west and conquered the area of what is now Uzbekistan. The new Qara-Khitai Empire, as it was called in Persian and Arabic sources, drew tribute from all the local rulers in Central Asia: the Buddhist Uyghur kingdom to the east in Besh-Baliq and Qocho, Kucha and Kashghar in the southeast, the kingdom of the Muslim Qarluq Turks to the northeast, and the great cities of Bukhara, Samarqand, and Khwarazm in the west. The Qara-Khitai emperors continued to meddle in Mongolia and inspire rebellions in the Kitans' Inner Mongolian heartland, but in the end, they never returned east.[10]

Mongolia and Its Frontiers before the Rise of Chinggis Khan

In Mongolia itself, the fall of the Kitan Empire liberated the local Tatar rulers from Liao control to found their own kingdoms. The Tatars first appear as one of the subject peoples in eastern Mongolia during the Second Türk Empire that ruled Mongolia from 682 to 744. During that time and during the following Uyghur Empire (742–847), most of the herders in Mongolia spoke a Turkic language. But the Tatars were the vanguard of a Mongolic-speaking advance from eastern Inner Mongolia into the steppes of Mongolia, which by the time of Chinggis Khan had made the eastern half of Mongolia Mongolic speaking. At the same time, as the Tatars absorbed many Turkic speaking peoples in Mongolia they became heavily Turkicized in their speech and political ideology.

Already in the thirteenth century, the people of Mongolia had a sense of their plateau as a single sociopolitical space bounded by the Qara'un-Jidun (present-day Hinggan) Range to the east and the Altai Range to the west. But during the rise of Chinggis Khan, this area was not a linguistic unity: the eastern half was Mongolic-speaking and the western half Turkic-speaking. Bilingualism was very common, however, and differences in language between Turkic and Mongolic speakers had little or no significance for politics. In the words of the later *Secret History of the Mongols* they were all *isgei tu'urghatan*, "those living in walls of felt."[11]

Modern scholars have generally pictured the political landscape of Mongolia at the time of Chinggis Khan according to the picture painted in Mongolian

10. On the Qara-Khitai and their empire, see Biran 2005.

11. *Secret History of the Mongols*, §§203, 205–6.

sources written in the time of the empire. As these sources looked back to the pre-imperial past, they described the "Tatars" as a relatively small group along the border of present-day eastern Mongolia and the Inner Mongolian Autonomous Region. In central Mongolia, these sources spoke of the Kereyit kingdom, while a sprawling Naiman kingdom, divided into two parts ruled by rival brothers, stretched from western Mongolia as far as western Siberia. The Mongols themselves and the Merkit appeared as two hostile, warring coalitions of petty chiefs. Among all these

Standing archer, showing classic Mongol hat, braids, cummerbund, boots, and accessories, from a Mongol-era illustrated encyclopedia.

groups, the "Tatars" alone distinguished themselves as allies of the Jin dynasty, which appears in these records as only a distant presence.

These names—Kereyit, Naiman, Merkit, or even Mongol—appear rarely if at all in the earliest accounts of the early Mongol Empire translated here. In these accounts, the people of the Mongolian plateau are *all* Tatars, with at most further divisions into "Black" and "White" and "Raw" and "Cooked." To a large degree this is simply because the authors had very little information on Chinggis Khan's early life. Even the information they did have is curiously irreconcilable with what we know from the Mongolian sources. Zhao Gong writes that Chinggis Khan's father was a *paiza* chief, a commander of merely ten men, named Gie-leu. How this can be reconciled with the rising young prince of a noble lineage named Yisükei presented in the *Secret History of the Mongols* and other later Mongolian accounts is a mystery.

Yet the designation found in the Song sources of the people of the Mongolian plateau as all "Tatars" was probably in some sense accurate. Although terms like Merkit, Mongol, and many others do appear in Chinese sources, they designate only very minor groups found in long lists of chiefs rallying to Daiši Lemya or enrolled as tributaries of the Jin dynasty. Tatar, or its Kitan synonym Chubugh (Ch. Zubu), was the correct general term for all of these petty chiefs, one that was only rejected later by Chinggis Khan's dynasty, which took the name "Mongol" from its own house and made it the name of a whole people.[12]

---

12. This name was also applied to the language of Chinggis Khan's empire. Technically speaking, therefore, to speak of "Mongolian language" before the unification under Chinggis Khan is anachronistic; the language at that time was actually called Tatar.

Although modern scholarship has shown that Kitan is a relative of the Mongolian language spoken by Chinggis Khan, Li Xinchuan thought the Mongols were more related to the Jurchens. The Jurchen language, however, was a Manchu-Tungusic language, not of the Mongolic family and hence not very similar to Mongolian, although it probably sounded close enough to Chinese ears. Li Xinchuan thought them related, however, due to the hypothesis, which modern historians have tended to accept, that the Mongolic-speaking Tatars moved onto the Mongolian plateau not from the Kitans' land of southeastern Inner Mongolia, but from farther north in the Amur and other river basins of Manchuria. This was also the original land of the Jurchens, and many Mongolic-speaking peoples may indeed have lived in fairly close proximity with the Jurchens and followed a similar lifestyle.[13]

A further confusion that affected both Li Xinchuan's and Zhao Gong's accounts was that between the "Mongol" of the empire and the "Monggus" kingdom established in the Amur valley more than a century earlier.[14] Due to the similarity of the first syllable "Mong," it appears that some Song border experts tried to see the Mongol Empire as a new and revived successor of the long defunct Monggus kingdom. In their way of life, as described by Li Xinchuan, the Monggus appear to be classic "Water Tatars," that is, people whose way of life was adapted to life in the Amur River basin, including fish-skin clothing and a raw fish diet. But both Zhao Gong and Li Xinchuan noticed that the Mongols themselves acknowledged no such connection. It is likely that while the *names* Monggol or Monggul and Monggus may have a common origin, the two regimes actually had nothing to do with one another.

Within the category of "Tatar," the Song authors distinguished the "Black" and "White" and "Raw" and "Cooked." Both Li Xinchuan and Zhao Gong use these terms and give some idea of their meaning, but they leave certain aspects unclarified. The terms "Black" and "White" evidently meant "North of the Gobi" and "South of the Gobi," respectively. Although "black" in many Turco-Mongolian contexts meant "common" or "vulgar," among the Kitans it had the connotation of both "northern" and "powerful." For this reason, when Kitans needed to designate their own people as opposed to Han Chinese and other subjects, they proudly called themselves Qara Kitat, "Black Kitan."

In this scheme, "Black Tatars" designated those Tatars, mostly Mongolian speaking, north of the Gobi Desert; in the terms used by the later Mongolian histories, the "Black Tatars" were the Kereyit, Merkit, and the pre-imperial Mongols proper. The "White Tatars," by contrast, designated the people known in Mongolian accounts as the Öng'üt: descendants of the Shatuo who had founded regimes in North China during the Five Dynasties. As shown by archaeological

---

13. See Ratchnevsky 1966.

14. The known references to this kingdom span from year 1083 in the late Kitan Liao to 1147 in the mid-Jurchen Jin dynasty. The full version of the name in Chinese transcription varies from *Měnggǔzǐ* to *Mánggǔzǐ* to *Měnggǔsī*, all of which come from an original that may be reconstructed as *Monggus*.

remains and short inscriptions, they were Turkic speaking and in the middle of the eleventh century had converted to the Christianity of the Church of the East—something mentioned in none of the early Chinese sources.

The terms "Raw" and "Cooked" were part of a centuries-old Chinese viewpoint in which Chinese influence was viewed as "cooking" the "raw" non-Chinese barbarians. The "Raw Tatars" were those who had the least Chinese influence on them and thus were the most "savage" and "barbarous"; "Cooked Tatars" were those who appeared civilized in Chinese eyes—by which was meant both superficial conformity of dress and adornment and a deeper deference to Chinese political authority. Since those south of the Gobi were closer to China, the "White Tatars" were considerably more "cooked" in Chinese eyes while the "Black Tatars" tended to be the "raw" ones. In the sources translated here, being "cooked" refers primarily to customs and practices, but it also had a very practical meaning of delivering either taxes or military service to the dynasty.[15]

In his attempt to explain to his Southern readers the origins of the Mongols, Li Xinchuan pointed in two different directions. On the one hand, he linked them to the ancient people of Manchuria. Those ancient people had split into a Northern Black River people and a Southern White Mountain people. Geographically, the Black River here is the Amur River in northern Manchuria, and the White Mountain is the Changbai "Ever-White" or Baekdu "White Headed" mountain on the southern border of Manchuria with North Korea. But black was also the color of the direction north and the element water in the Chinese system of "Five Phases" (*wǔxíng*) and the idea of northern, black, and martial Jurchens along the river and southern, civilian, and white Koreans on the slopes of the mountain to the south was one that somewhat paralleled the distinction of Black and White Tatars.[16] On the other hand, Li Xinchuan was also aware of the Tatars along the Yinshan Mountains in what is now southwestern Inner Mongolia. Those Tatars were known to Song diplomats and became the ancestors of the later "White Tatars" or Öng'üt.

Thus, during the rise of Chinggis Khan, the people who would later be called Mongols lived in contact both with the powerful political regimes around them and with other pastoralist and foraging peoples to their east, west, and north. To the south and east were people known as the Jiün (Ch. *Jiǔ*).[17] This term included

---

15. Thus, we read in the *Jinshi* ("History of the Jin") about the early Jurchens under Kitan rule: "Those in the south who were counted in the census by the Kitans were called 'Cooked Jurchens'; those in the north who were not counted in the Kitan census were called 'Raw Jurchens'" (*JS* 1.2). Similarly, the *Songshi* ("History of the Song") writes about the Tanguts on their northwestern frontier: "Their clans were scattered, the big ones numbering a thousand households, the small ones numbering a hundred households. From Yizhou . . . as far as Lingzhou and Xiazhou all had [such Tanguts], each one with their own chiefs. The ones obedient to the dynasty were called 'Cooked Households' and the rest were called 'Raw Households'" (*SS* 492.14.151).

16. However, white was associated not with the south, but with the west in traditional Chinese correlative thinking.

17. This Kitan word is attested in many different Mongolian spellings. It appears as Jüin in the *Secret History of the Mongols*. The final *-n* is a plural suffix.

the "Cooked" or "White" Tatars, as well as a potpourri of other peoples living in what is now Inner Mongolia: Tatars, Kitans, Öng'üt, Uyghurs, and even Tanguts. What they had in common was that they patrolled the frontier that bordered on the "Raw Tatars," first for the Kitan Liao dynasty and then for the Jurchen Jin. Although the Jin dynasty eventually built a series of walls along the frontier, roughly along the present-day border between Inner Mongolia and independent Mongolia, socially the boundaries between the Jüin and the "Raw" Tatars beyond the frontier were quite fluid. They attended each others' festivals, intermarried, and, when dissatisfied with their Kitan or Jurchen overlords, might ally for political or military action. Linguistically, a kind of Mongolian was probably coming to be their lingua franca. Zhao Gong's account of the Jüin shows how essential their support was to the rise of Chinggis Khan. Once the Chinggisid dynasty was established, the former Jüin peoples were rapidly sorted, with those who allied early with the conqueror becoming integral parts of the new Mongol elite. The others were divided out into less favored roles as "Tatars," "Kitans," or "Tanguts."

To the north and east of Mongolia were the "Forest Peoples" (*Hoi-yin Irgen*) and the "Water Peoples" (*Usun Irgen*). Each came with their stereotyped clichés—skis and reindeer for one, fish-skin clothes and raw fish diet for the other—and both were seen as easy pickings for the nomad khans. Their lands were sources for valuable goods: furs, pearls, and even walrus ivory from the Arctic Ocean and Bering Sea. Peoples of the Mongolian plateau had long been traveling down the major rivers—the Irtysh, Ob', Yenisey, Angara, and Amur—to secure these goods by trade or violence.

Beyond Mongolia's natural western frontier of the Altai Mountains, the Mongolic-speaking Raw Tatars were also in regular social contact with Turkic-speaking mobile pastoralists. But these Turkic-speaking nomads tended to gravitate toward other regimes and other cultural influences. In eastern Turkestan, the Qara-Khitai or "Black Kitan" Empire held sway over the Uyghur, Qarluq, and other petty Turkic-speaking kingdoms. Beyond them, in what is now central and eastern Kazakhstan, were the Qangli nomads, while to their west from western Kazakhstan along the steppe grasslands as far as the Caucasus, Crimea, the Carpathian Mountains, and the Slavic lands were the Turkic-speaking nomads variously known as the Qipchaqs, Cumans, or *Polovtsy* (Russian for "Pale Ones").

These Turkic nomads had cross-cultural ties not just with "Raw Tatars" in Mongolia but also with the Islamic dynasties to their south. The most powerful Islamic dynasty at this time was the Khwarazmian Empire, centered on the oasis of Khwarazm, south of the Aral Sea and on the left bank of the Amu Darya River.[18] The rulers originated among the Turkicized inhabitants of the oasis but intermarried extensively with the Qangli potentates to the north in the Kazakhstan grasslands. The growing Khwarazmian Empire at first paid tribute to the powerful Qara-Khitai, thereby winning a free hand for expansion to the south and west. In 1210, the Qara-Khitai Empire was shaken by an irruption of refugees from Mongolia fleeing the rise of Chinggis Khan and

---

18. Khwarazm is also written as Khorezm in Russian. It is Xorazm in modern Uzbek.

the Khwarazmian ruler threw off Qara-Khitai rule. His regime thus reached the apex of its power less than a decade before Chinggis Khan's invasion.

Up to 1210, the Central Asian oases felt the sway of either the Khwarazmian or Qara-Khitai regimes. These Central Asian oases had originally been settled by people speaking Iranian and Tocharian languages and following Indian religions, especially Buddhism. But by the time of Chinggis Khan, the combined processes of Turkicization and Islamization had divided the Central Asian oases into the three zones. To the southwest, in Samarqand and Bukhara, the inhabitants had long since converted to Islam, but ethnically they were still Persian-speaking Tajiks. To the northeast, in the oases of Turpan and Besh-Baliq, the Uyghur kingdom was Turkic speaking but still Buddhist. In between, in the northwest oasis of Khwarazm and the central oases of Khotan and Kashghar, the townspeople and farmers were Turkic-speaking Muslims.

Whatever their language or religion, these oasis people were all quite similar in their culture and way of life. They dominated the caravan trade in Mongolia and North China,

A statue of a court vassal, probably a Turkic bodyguard, at a Khwarazmian or Seljuk court, twelfth to early thirteenth century.

and Chinese writers described them as a stereotypical mercantile diaspora people: clever, hardworking, and eager for profit. Uyghurs also served as scribes for petty kings on the Mongolian plateau, which eventually led the Mongols under Chinggis Khan to adopt the Uyghur script for writing Mongolian. Chinese writers tended to see all oasis people as "Uyghurs," although more careful observers understood that the genuine Uyghurs were a subset of those "Uyghurs" and used different terms for them. As is described on pp. 26–27 ("Tatars," "Turkestanis," and "Westerners"), the earlier Chinese words for "Uyghurs" gradually morphed into *Húihúi* and became a Chinese term designating Muslims as a religious community. But this process was not complete by this time.

Legitimacy and the Dynastic "Script"

In this context of multiethnic regimes all struggling to establish a stable pecking order, legitimacy was the implicit concern of all our authors. The strange Mongols and their rise were of great interest to them, of course, but ultimately, they were most worried about how the upsurge of the Mongols would reshuffle the order of legitimacy in the world of East Asia, a world where literary Chinese was the written language of choice.

In terms of political loyalty, these writings fall into two camps. In the first camp lie those writings by Southern Song scholars and officials: Li Xinchuan, Zhao Gong, Peng Daya, and Xu Ting. For them, the key question was how the rise of the Mongols would shake up the existing balance of power between the Southern Song dynasty, confined to the Yangtze River valley and China's southeastern coast, and the rival Jin dynasty ensconced in China's traditional northern heartland of the "Central Plains." Writers in the second group, including Zhang Dehui and Song Zizhen, had already made their choice to support Chinggis Khan and his descendants as the new rulers of the East Asian world. For them, the question was how to induce the Mongol khans to play the expected role of enlightened emperors, entrusting the business of rule to good officials trained in the Confucian canons. These two different stances are crucial to understanding their writings.

Good Barbarians and Bad

For the four writers who owed their loyalty to the South, the rise of the Mongols was just one in a long series of disturbing events to the North and not the most alarming, at least at first. The one big fact these Southern Song writers found almost impossible to ignore was what Zhao Gong called the "one hundred years of the Jin caitiffs' military might." The key question was: What would the impact of the rising Mongols on this hated Jin regime be? Could the Mongols be played off against the Jurchens' Jin dynasty, allowing the Southern Song to recover the North? Would the Mongols consent to pay tribute and acknowledge the Song emperor as the true suzerain of all East Asia? These were the questions with which the writers initially approached the Mongol invasions of the North.

Since the nineteenth century, Chinese attitudes toward non-Han "barbarians" have often been seen as governed by "Sinicization." From this viewpoint, China is seen as an open civilization, welcoming barbarians, but only as long as they embrace Chinese cultural and ethical norms. What one finds in these sources, particularly in the account by Zhao Gong, however, is a very different attitude, one that found a place for "barbarians," but only as long as they *refused* to assimilate and remained pristine in their simplicity.[19]

The key to this paradox was that Chinese ritual and ethical norms were inextricably connected with state-building. Barbarians like the Kitans or Jurchens who embraced Chinese norms such as rituals between ruler and vassal; the distinction between given, personal names and courtesy names; the proclamation of accurate imperial calendars and year slogans; and the promulgation of formal court

---

19. Our interpretation here builds on that of Shao-yun Yang 2015. Yang emphasizes how Chinese theories of geography and *qi* (the psychophysical stuff that determines how a being acts) were deployed more often to *avoid* "civilizing" the "barbarians" than to promote their incorporation into the Chinese world.

dress—such barbarians were engaged in state-building. And any state-building while the Song dynasty's Zhao family was still on the throne was necessarily seen as hostile by the Song. Thus, the Jurchens were hated rivals precisely because they had successfully assimilated Chinese political culture and hence were able to fashion a new dynasty that could plausibly rival the Southern Song.

At least at first, however, the Mongols seemed blessedly innocent of such dreams. They appeared uninterested in adjusting the movements of the sun and moon into an accurate calendar, in distinguishing given names from courtesy names, in using Chinese graphs to write, or in constructing an administration with a proper panoply of titles. As such, they were not fundamentally threatening to the Southern Song dynasty's imperial legitimacy. Back when it ruled the North, the Song dynasty had attempted to overthrow the Kitans' Liao dynasty with the similarly barbarous Jurchens. Although this attempt had backfired badly, it is likely that some Southern observers hoped to pursue a similar plan with the Mongols.

Li Xinchuan, who appears to have put his account of the Mongol invasions of the North together from around 1214 to late 1215, with some further notes added in late 1216 or early 1217, did not entirely dash such hopes. Although his account highlighted the brutality and destruction of the Mongols' invasion of the North, he emphasized that the Mongols probably did not intend to rival the Southern Song: "The Tatars are only motivated by greed and in the beginning had no far-reaching plans." He includes an account of a peculiar embassy that the Mongols attempted to make to the South in February 1214. They crossed the border and presented a map to the border officials as a sign of submission in an effort to get Song help against the Jin. The Song court responded to this unauthorized interaction at the border by placing a temporary embargo on contact with the Mongols. However, Li Xinchuan's account sketched a potential rivalry between the more honest and upright Temüjin (Chinggis Khan) who had retreated back to Mongolia and Samuqa whom he portrayed as a greedy and ignorant adventurer. Samuqa was the Tatar whom Temüjin had left in charge of North China and Li Xinchuan's account implied that war in North China was likely to continue. In this situation, given that the Tatars were "crude and uncouth, without any distinction between lord and vassal," Samuqa's allegiance to Temüjin could not be taken for granted; a wise Song policy might explore an alliance with Temüjin and attempt to widen his rift with Samuqa.

Whether by coincidence or in response to Li Xinchuan's account, Southern Song frontier officials soon traded in their embargo for a chance to fish in the troubled waters of North China. When the Jin moved their capital south of the Yellow River to Kaifengfu[20] in 1214, many people in the areas north of the river felt the court had given up on defending them from the Mongols. Feeling abandoned and left to their own devices, they launched a number of insurrections. In Shandong Province, "Red Jacket" (*Hóng'ǎo*) rebels rose up against the Jin government, seizing

---

20. For reasons explained on pp. 35–36, we find it helpful to include the *-fu* and *-zhou* suffixes for upper-level and lower-level prefectures, respectively. The prefectural level was basic level of administration in Chinese-style regimes at this time.

a number of county and prefectural seats. Soon a kaleidoscope of rebel forces were confronting each other and the generals of the Jin and Mongol regimes, all trying to reestablish order under their own auspices. One such rebel, Li Quan, submitted in 1218 to the Song in return for recognition as an army commander and a supply of grain. For almost a decade thereafter, the Song backed Li Quan and other rebel warlords in Shandong and Hebei. Not until April 1227, when Li Quan surrendered the Shandong city of Yidufu to Mongol armies under the commander Daisun, was a fragile peace reestablished in North China.

In the midst of these proxy wars, the Song opened direct diplomatic relations with both the Mongol court in North China, headed by the viceroy Muqali, and with Chinggis Khan, then campaigning against the Khwarazmian sultan in Central Asia. Zhao Gong's 1221 account of the Mongols reflects this newer, more intense Song engagement with the Mongols. Zhao Gong still saw many hopeful signs of "barbarism" among the Mongols. His picture of Mongol customs had many positive aspects: a continuing crudity of institutions, a directness and simplicity that would make them easy partners to deal with, and a strange resemblance in their dress and methods of divination to the practices of China's ancient sage dynasties. Yet Zhao Gong already noticed alarming signs that Jin "caitiffs" had begun to teach the Mongols the basic elements of Chinese-style state-building; from his Song perspective, such civilizing influences could only be corrupting.

The joint accounts of Peng Daya and Xu Ting show a final stage in this process of growing knowledge of, and disillusionment with, the Mongol conquerors. Peng Daya visited the Mongols in 1233, at a time when the Mongols had finally secured what Chinggis Khan had advocated on his deathbed: an alliance with the Southern Song to destroy the final remnants of the Jin dynasty. Despite unexpected defeats under the new khan Öködei, Mongol armies had finally broken into the Jin dynasty's last refuge in Henan Province without Song help. But famine brought on by the Jin generals' scorched-earth policies and by Mongol plunder made it hard to continue final operations against the Jin. The Song frontier commanders were flush with grain, however, and after negotiations, a well-stocked Song army joined the Mongols in December 1233 as they besieged the Jin emperor in his final capital of Caizhou (present-day Runan). On the morning of February 9, 1234, the two armies stormed the city as the last Jin emperor hanged himself.

The end of the Jin dynasty snapped the fragile ties that bound the Mongol and Song courts together. The Song armies seized the remains of the last Jin emperor so as to desecrate them in the Song dynasty's ancestral temple in Hangzhou. The agreement with the Mongols partitioned Henan between the two sides. But the Song court was unable to resist the lure of revanchism, and after the Mongol armies withdrew, they promptly tried to seize the entire province. By the time of Xu Ting's mission to the Mongol court in 1235–1236, Mongol armies were counterattacking and the Southerners were once again trying to extract themselves from a war they had unwisely provoked.

Compared to that of Zhao Gong, the combined account by Peng Daya and Xu Ting was far better informed but also much more hostile to the Mongols. The vastly greater level of information is evident in the lists of the commanders and

officials. Li Xinchuan had named only a few Mongols and in so doing even confused two major Mongol commanders, Samuqa and Muqali. Zhao Gong named
many Mongol officials, but he lists several people who cannot be easily identified as well as names that must simply be mistakes. The names of Mongols and
their officials and commanders listed by Peng Daya and Xu Ting, however, are
all easily corroborated in other sources, especially because their transcription of
non-Mongol names into Chinese graphs is much more precise and accurate than
Zhao Gong's.

Although the Mongols were still seen as being radically deficient in culture,
it was clear enough to both envoys that the Mongol regime had no intention of
paying tribute to the Song. Although the Mongols were not yet "caitiffs" (a term
of abuse still reserved for the Jin), all of their titles and imperial positions were
now prefaced with the damning label *wěi* or "bogus."[21] At times Peng and Xu
could still express admiration for Mongol honesty, directness, and battle prowess,
all stereotypical traits of both barbarians and northerners. But especially for Xu
Ting, it was important that his Song readers understand the gravity of the Mongol
threat and yet not be too overwhelmed by the prospect of Mongol invasion. Thus,
Xu repeated the menacing threat of Ila Chucai, "You [Song people] are relying
only on the Great River, but if the horse hooves of our [Mongol] dynasty need to
go up to the heavens, they will go up to the heavens; if under the seas, they will go
under the seas." But Xu also was careful to criticize the impression that Peng Daya
gave of an unbeatable Mongol menace, saying, "We cannot just exaggerate the
Tatars' strength while forgetting the principle of being responsible to strengthen
ourselves." With this statement, near the end of Peng and Xu's account, Xu Ting
renounced any Song hopes for accommodation and instead called on the South to
turn again to stubborn resistance.[22]

The Dynastic Script

For those classically trained scholars in Mongol service, however, the issues were
quite different; that the Mongols would build a new state was a given, and their
main concern was that they do it right. For them, there were no valid alternative models of rule. For them, what we see as the conventions of "Chinese" rule
were simply the basic preconditions of moral and effective leadership in any
state. In Song Zizhen's admiring biography, Ila Chucai tells Öködei with absolute confidence that "wherever there is a kingdom or a family, all have followed

---

21. In other contexts, *wěi* might be translated as "forged," "fabricated," or at best as "artificial."
This practice of labeling putatively illegitimate governments as "bogus" has continued into modern times. The "Manchukuo" regime founded by the Japanese army in 1931–1945 is regularly
designated as "bogus Manchuria" in Chinese, and during the Chinese Civil War of 1945–1949,
the Communist side regularly referred to the "bogus constitution" of the Nationalist side. Further parallels with delegitimizing phrases such as reference to Israel as "the Zionist entity" are
not hard to find.

22. On the evolution of Song attitudes toward the Mongols, see Garcia 2012.

the [Confucian] teaching of the Three Fundamental Bonds and Five Constant Virtues without exception, just as Heaven has the sun, moon, and stars." Yet, Ila Chucai and the authors Zhang Dehui and Song Zizhen all took service with the Mongols at a time when the conventions of Chinese rule had not been fully adopted. They thus needed to rehearse their Mongol sovereigns in a well-known script in which successful war leaders received honors, taxes, and stable rule in return for agreeing to follow Confucian precepts.

This Chinese "script" of dynastic state-building had been pioneered in the foundational works of imperial Chinese history, the *Shiji* or *Records of the Grand Historian* by Sima Qian (ca. 145–86 BC) and the *Hanshu* or *Book of the Han Dynasty* by Ban Gu (AD 32–92). Elaborated over subsequent centuries of historical writings, this script was a version of the cyclical theory of imperial rise and fall that was shared by premodern thinkers as diverse as Herodotus (ca. 484–425 BC), the Persian historian of the Mongols 'Ata-Malik Juvayni (AD 1226–1283), and the famous Tunisian historian Ibn Khaldun (AD 1332–1406).[23]

Like these thinkers, Chinese historians of the dynastic cycle assumed that dynasties arose periodically from, and declined eventually back into, periods of chaos. Under conditions of hardship and depopulation, bands of hardy and eager fighters formed around charismatic leaders. Such a period of chaos would only end when one leader, luckier and abler than the rest, finally conquered "the civilized world" and brought the strife to an end. Once peace was restored, the new dynasty would begin to develop increasingly sophisticated institutions. Ultimately, however, as generations passed, the dynasty would be weakened by its very sophistication as taxes increased and the solidarity of the ruling class broke down. In the end, domestic rebellions and foreign invasion would shatter the dynasty's mandate to rule and a new dynasty would coalesce around one of the generals fighting over the ruins.

For Chinese historians, the oldest and most typical example of this script was the rise of the Han dynasty (206 BC–AD 220). This dynasty was founded by Liu Bang (256–195 BC),[24] a famously crude but eminently teachable peasant. It was to him that the Confucian official Lu Jia first enunciated the famous aphorism that Ila Chucai would later quote to Öködei: "Although the world may be won on horseback, it cannot be governed on horseback." Horseback here was no reference to the Mongols as nomads but an allusion to the inevitable predominance of the military in founding any dynasty.

Indeed, the one occupational group that, according to this script, could not and in fact did not supply dynastic founders were the scholar-officials who had custody over the script. Whether because they had assimilated the moral imperative of loyalty, or because their training rendered them unable to effectively command the loyalty of armed men, Confucian officials never established new dynasties.[25]

---

23. Raaflaub 1987; Irwin 2018.

24. His posthumous temple name was Han Gaozu or "Supreme Founder of the Han."

25. The one great exception was Wang Mang's Xin "New" dynasty (AD 9–25) that briefly interrupted the four-century rule of the Han dynasty. Wang Mang was an official who used both

Thus, the central problem in each new dynasty was how to handle the relation between the founding military coterie on one hand and the realm's professionally trained literati on the other. Such military coteries were bound not by ethics or universal ideals, but solely by loyalty to the leader, a loyalty based on kinship, local ties, and gratitude for past benefits. But once the conquest was finished, the great danger was that the military coterie would continue to rule in the old particularistic fashion by which they had come to power, turning the whole world over to their kinsmen, hometown boys, and camp followers.

It was this possibility, first and foremost, that the literati were guarding against when they offered their services to the victorious new emperor. In so doing, they were by no means defenseless. While fighting as one commander among many, the ruler's position had only been first among equals. With the restoration of peace, however, the literati could offer him a very attractive deal. With court ritual they would elevate the new emperor above his kinsmen and old war comrades, making him an unquestioned sovereign to whom all would have to kowtow. In return, all they asked was that the emperor create new offices to tax and administer the war-ravaged land, and that he staff them not with his old cronies from the war band, but with literati trained in the art of ruling by the Confucian canons.

The benefit of employing such officials was twofold: first, as men schooled in proper administration, they would replace inefficient and sporadic plunder with systematic taxation at moderate rates. Revenues would increase even as the burdens on the people abated. Second, these officials in their training had imbibed the principle of loyalty to the throne, and in any case as timid civil officials were most unlikely to foment rebellion or sedition. Thus, the emperor's throne became more secure. As long as he employed professional literati he could rely on their backing against rebellious former comrades or rival kinsmen of his own family.

In following this script there was nothing essentially different for the literati about civilizing a vulgar and semiliterate peasant like Liu Bang, a brutal and cynical warlord like Cao Cao (ca. AD 155–220), or a barbarian chieftain like Akûdai or Chinggis. Since the fourth century, Chinese cultural leaders had been following this script not just with domestic commanders but with foreign conquerors as well. Superficially, this process has been described as one of Sinicizing the foreign rulers and the "barbarian" war bands they commanded. However, to talk about Mongol conquerors being Sinicized implies that to the scholar officials there was something called "Chinese culture" which non-Han conquerors lacked and which had to be imparted to them.

In fact, as Shao-yun Yang has pointed out, the formal doctrine of Chinese thinkers had no concept of "culture" in the modern sense of a common set of values shared by educated elites and uneducated masses alike.[26] Instead, for

---

Confucian rhetoric and his position as an imperial in-law to first control and then usurp the Han throne. In response to this gross violation of the script, later historians like Ban Gu excoriated him as the ultimate hypocrite.

26. See Yang 2019, 7–15.

them, what we might subsume under "Chinese culture" was conceptually divided between, on one hand, various habits and customs of the common people, called *fēngsú*, which had no moral value, and, on the other, *lǐ* or ritual propriety, which had supreme moral significance and could only be mastered through a specifically Confucian education.[27] The process of training a commander with Mongol *fēngsú*, or customs, in the proper exercise of *lǐ*, or ritual propriety, necessary for good rule was essentially the same as training a Chinese peasant rebel or bandit chief to see the need for Confucian proprieties. A rebel or bandit may have been born Han, but his *fēngsú* or customs and habits had to be transformed just as much as those of a Kitan, Jurchen, or Mongol khan.

Song Zizhen's "Spirit-Path Stele" for Ila Chucai is one of the most powerful portraits ever drawn of a humane man saving the world by transforming military into civilian rule. The Song envoys Zhao Gong, Peng Daya, and Xu Ting described Chucai as a man of tremendous talents, even as they lamented that he was strengthening a rival to the Song. Song Zizhen in the text of stele never doubted, any more than did Chucai himself, that Chinggis Khan and his descendants were the dynasty that Heaven had chosen to reunify the civilized world. But precisely because his loyalty never wavered, both Ila Chucai and Song Zizhen were able to confront with clear eyes the enormous magnitude of their task. The existence of the script gave Chucai the confidence to take the long view. With Chinggis Khan, he bided his time, resorting to astrological subterfuges and tales of miraculous, talking, horned beasts.

But when Öködei took the throne, Chucai felt the new ruler was ready for the full curriculum and began to "advance the teachings of the Zhou dynasty and of Confucius." Near the end of his life, alas, Öködei, allured by the revenues promised by greedy tax farmers, lost sight of good government. After his death, Chucai had to revert to the old astrological tricks he had used to control Chinggis Khan to control Öködei's widow and the regent Töregene. He may have seemed defeated when he died, but the scholars he had saved from the wreckage of the Jin dynasty were to continue in the same direction, reaching a new highwater mark of reform under Öködei's nephew Qubilai (r. 1260–1294).

This task, however, was not an ethnic one. The word "Mongol" appears only twice in Song Zizhen's spirit-path stele text. Rather than being "Mongols" who conquered "China," Song Zizhen labels them as "Northerners" who have conquered the "Central Plains"—peripheral, yes, but not qualitatively alien. When Chinggis Khan tried to forge a particularistic, ethnic link with Chucai as a Kitan, saying that the Mongols had taken revenge on behalf of their Kitan cousins against the common Jurchen foe, Chucai rejected the very idea that such ethnic rivalries could motivate a scholar-official. Loyalty was determined by reading the

---

27. In Zhang Dehui's account, he divides this category of *fēngsú* into two. The first is "local conditions" or *fēngtǔ*, meaning both the environmental conditions and the human practices adapted to them. The second is "traditional customs" (*xísú*), that is, one not so directly tied to the environment.

signs of Heaven, and ethics were determined by the words of the canons: neither was ethnic.

In practice, however, the dynastic script's lofty indifference to cultural particularities was hard to maintain. The ancient Confucian philosopher Mencius (372–289 BC) argued that everyone had within them the sprouts that if properly cultivated could ripen into the virtues of a sage. The implication was that the division between everyday customs and ritual propriety was relative, not absolute. But was this really true of Mongols and nomads? Certainly, many literati of North and South China could hardly see them as potential sage rulers. A deeper argument was needed to assure skeptical literati that the Mongols had within their own customs or *fēngsú* the sprouts of ritual propriety.

In his "Notes on a Journey," Zhang Dehui, one of the Jin scholar-officials rescued by Ila Chucai from the destruction of the Jin state, made just that argument. Elsewhere in his biographical literature were recorded his conversations with the young prince Qubilai, then just one of the many grandsons of Chinggis Khan in the empire, on how to rule. But in his "Notes on a Journey," Zhang focused not on the conversations, but on the ritual calendar that he had observed during his year with Qubilai's camp as it nomadized through the heart of Mongolia. This description demonstrated that Qubilai's naïve simplicity was already being cultivated by the practice of ritual—ritual that could be the germ of Confucian virtues. Qubilai was thus teachable, and Zhang recommended him to his colleagues as the hope of the Mongol dynasty. Through many such conversations, Qubilai would slowly build up a following among the officials in North China; in the end they would give him crucial backing that would allow him to seize power and enthrone himself as great khan in 1260.

Even then, however, for scholar-officials like Zhang Dehui and Song Zizhen it was still hard to say if the new khan could quickly learn the script and perform genuine Confucian governance. The biggest problem was not the Mongol aristocrats or their nomadic customs, but rather the peoples variously known as Uyghurs, Turkestanis, or Westerners. Unlike the Kitan Liao or Jurchen Jin, the Mongol conquest elite had access to the services of literate bureaucrats, moralists, scholars, merchants, and tax farmers from cultures alien to the scholar-officials trained in the Confucian canons: Persian-speaking Muslims, Buddhist Uyghurs, Christian Öng'üt (White Tatars), and eventually Tibetan Buddhist lamas and even Italian merchants like Marco Polo.

Already in Song Zizhen's spirit-path stele, it was these rivals who tempted the well-meaning but easily befuddled Öködei to depart from the Confucian program. In Qubilai's time, as well, and even to the end of the Yuan dynasty, these rival literati with their rival scriptures and administrative practices would deny the Confucian literati the monopoly on advice to the khans that they considered their due. Written at a time when the hold of Confucian literati on Qubilai's heart was slipping, Song Zizhen's encomium was a warning to Qubilai and his court of what could happen if such rival teachings were allowed to interfere with the cherished program of peaceful dynastic evolution. Ultimately Qubilai too, like Öködei, would rebel against the lines he was being fed and try to put on a different performance, one the Confucian literati neither understood nor approved. Song Zizhen and Zhang Dehui's works would remain as eloquent and melancholy reminders of Confucian dreams endlessly deferred, all the way to the fall of the dynasty.

Caitiffs and Calendars: Some Conventions of Chinese History Writing

Every translation from Chinese into English must negotiate the equal and opposite perils of misleading paraphrase and unintelligible fidelity. The extreme brevity and reliance on classical allusion that Chinese writers strove for, as a mark of good style, cannot be exactly reproduced for readers who lack the same store of allusions. Even beyond that difficulty, imperial Chinese history writing took for granted a whole slew of ideas and practices that readers not deeply immersed in the Chinese historical experience will find mystifying. These include not just administrative titles and institutional structures, but seemingly simple matters like the management of calendars and ways of designating rulers. We have done our best to handle these difficulties with a combination of slightly expanded translation at some points and footnotes at others.

Here we discuss at greater length the conventions, terms, and practices that a reader unfamiliar with Imperial Chinese history writing is likely to find strange or difficult. Many of these conventions and terms, like "caitiff" and "memorial" are widely used by Sinologists but probably unfamiliar to broader audiences. In some cases, such as dealing with different and concurrent dating systems supported by different dynasties, or often inaccurate Chinese renderings of foreign words, we have had to invent our own conventions to deal with situations not often encountered in Sinology.

"Barbarians" and the "Civilized World"

One of the most notorious of the conventions in Chinese historical and geographical writing is the use of a variety of words usually translated as "barbarian" to refer to all non-Chinese. Since the 1860 Treaty of Tianjin, which explicitly prohibited the Chinese government from using the term *yi* ("barbarian") to refer to the British and other European and American powers, this usage has been cited as evidence for a deep-seated and distinctive Chinese ethnocentrism. Indeed, the Chinese have used a wide variety of terms for "them" folks outside China, a diversity mirrored by a similarly wide variety of terms for the "us" inside China. In recent decades there has been considerable debate about whether all of these terms are truly derogatory, whether there were earlier periods in Chinese history that were more cosmopolitan, and finally whether Chinese viewed non-Chinese as inherently inferior or simply lacking proper cultural training.[28] In comparative perspective, however, the Chinese viewpoint was not all that unusual; the Roman and Byzantine empires, for example, adhered to the dogma of universal emperorship and preferred, if at all possible, to treat all outside peoples as either contumacious barbarians or docile allies.[29]

It would be far from the truth, however, to view all these Chinese writers as blinded by ethnocentrism. Readers will observe that the sources in this collection have rather diverse views. Even though two Song diplomats, Peng Daya and Xu Ting, for example, chose to combine their accounts, Xu Ting takes a clearly more hostile line against the Mongols than does Peng Daya. And those sources written in the service of the Mongols are firmly committed to the idea that the Mongols do indeed have Heaven-endowed virtues and that with proper training they can become able rulers.

"Caitiffs"

Our authors loyal to the Southern Song dynasty do use a certain number of stereotypical terms for non-Chinese. The most hostile is *lŭ*, a term which we have translated as "caitiff," following Sinological convention. Derived from the same Latin word that gives us English "captive," the word is defined as "a base, cowardly, or despicable person."[30] Paul Kroll's authoritative dictionary defines this *lŭ* as "1. to take captive, capture"; "2. prisoner, captive" with a submeaning as "slave"; and "3. caitiff, recreant; term of contempt used for military enemies, esp. Outlanders."[31] The term is clearly derogatory, but it does not refer to non-Chinese in general; rather it targets those who were hostile to the writer's own Chinese regime. Indeed, as the reader will notice, this term is used by Song writers not for the truly nomadic and utterly alien Mongols, but rather for the heavily sinicized Jurchens who had occupied North China and driven the Song dynasty to take refuge in South China. Only in the Ming dynasty (1368–1644), when the Chinese had driven out the Mongols and faced them as a foreign enemy across the Great Wall, did the Mongols then become the Chinese writers' archetypal *lŭ* or caitiff. A "caitiff" then is not just a "barbarian" but a feared and hated barbarian who threatens the security of the dynasty.[32]

---

28. See Shao-yun Yang 2019, especially 7–15, for a discussion of those questions.

29. Obolensky 1971, 272–77. In this context, the relationship of the East Roman Empire first to the Persian Empire and then to the Arab Caliphate was *mutatis mutandis*, remarkably like that of the Song first with the Liao and then with the Jin. In both cases, the correlation of forces was such that the two sides had to recognize each other as equals but continued to hold all other peoples in the world as subordinate to one or the other. See Ostrogorsky 1959, 14–15; Chrysos 1978, 70–71.

30. Merriam-Webster at merriam-webster.com/dictionary/caitiff.

31. Kroll 2015, s.v. *lŭ* (283a).

32. As Reader C has pointed out, the nuance of "caitiff" in Old French is slightly different. It had more of a sense of contempt and less of fear than *lŭ* carried in Chinese. The combination of fear, loathing, and contempt that this term generated for Song writers and officials can be more closely compared to the Nationalist Chinese use of "Communist bandits" for the mainland

"Ethnics" and "Barbarians"

By comparison, the terms *fān*, *hú*, and *yí* express not so much political hostility, although that might be implied, but rather cultural difference. *Fān* originally referred to a "paling, hedge, or bulwark," and then to those living in such regions, that is, border people. Unlike *lǔ* it was used as a rule for people who were politically part of the empire, but who were not ethnic Chinese in origin. Indeed under non-Han dynasties like the Tangut Xia and Kitan Liao this term could even be used for the ruling ethnic group. Clearly it did not necessarily express either political hostility or overt cultural contempt. However, its use did enclose a kind of bland ethnocentrism in which all those who were not Chinese were thus a kind of undifferentiated mass. We thus translate it as "ethnics."

Hú, which originally meant "beard," emerged in the third century BC as a word for nomads on the Chinese border. By at least the sixth century AD, it came to be used for Sogdians, a sedentary people hailing from medieval Uzbekistan who spoke a language of the Iranian family and formed a powerful trade diaspora in China and elsewhere. We usually translate it as "barbarians" although in some contexts "nomad" or "Sogdian" might be better.

Yí and *mán* were two of four different terms used in ancient China to designate various peoples whom the emerging Chinese people came to view as alien, even before the unification of the Chinese lands themselves. The *yí* were to the east, the *mán* to the south, and the *róng* and the *dí* to the west and north. The graphs used to write them encoded ideas about them. The *yí* and *róng* graphs contain weapons and encode the perennial Chinese idea that foreigners are crudely militaristic and rely only on force. *Dí* contains the "dog" radical and codes the idea that northerners are like animals and *mán* contains the "insect" radical, coding the idea that foreigners in the hot, pestilential south were like bugs. *Yí* and *róng* are thus best translated as "barbarians" and *dí* and *mán*, with their animalic or even insect-like implications, as "savages."[33]

"Tatars," "Turkestanis," and "Westerners"

Classical terms such as *yí* were only occasionally used, however, in the texts translated here. Instead, for the Mongols, the general term used was "Tatars" (*Dádá*); for those to the west of China, from Central Asia to the Middle East and beyond, the general term was what we have translated as "Turkestanis" (*Húihú*) or "Westerners" (*Húihúi*). *Dádá* is the Chinese transliteration of the term "Tatar," which was the name of certain nomads who appeared in Mongolia from the late seventh to early eighth century AD. Probably speaking a language similar to what would later be called Mongolian, they increased in numbers after the fall of the Türk and Uyghur dynasties that ruled Mongolia until 847. By the tenth century, nomads

---

Chinese government or the American government's worldwide mobilization against "terrorists" after September 11, 2001.

33. On classical terms for non-Han or non-Chinese, see Wilkinson 2000, 710–12, 724–27.

speaking Mongolian-type languages and dialects were dominating in the plateau, and "Tatar" became the general term for all the people living there. When Chinggis Khan rose to power, he decreed "Great Mongol State" to be the name of his empire, but outsiders continued to call them "Tatars" or, in the case of the Latin Christians of Europe, distorted the name to "Tartars."

"Turkestanis" (*Húihú*) and "Westerners" (*Húihúi*) are two different stages on the path by which a word that originally meant the Uyghur nomads of Mongolia eventually came to be China's designation for mostly urban Muslims in China. The Uyghurs were originally a group of Turkic-speaking nomads living in northern Mongolia. Probably pronouncing their name at first as *Huyghur*, they were called *Húihú* or *Húihé* in Chinese.[34] In AD 840, in the aftermath of climate stress, a massive snowstorm and attacks by rival nomads, the capital was sacked and members of the ruling dynasty fled east, south, and west. Those who fled west took refuge in the oases of what is now eastern Xinjiang. Thus, they occupied the famed "Silk Roads" connecting the oases from China's western outpost of Dunhuang through Turkestan into the Middle East. As a result, Chinese slowly came to designate all the western oasis peoples, with their stereotypical high noses, deep-set eyes, and thick beards, as *Húihú*, meaning no longer just Uyghurs, but all those broadly "Western" or racially Caucasian-featured people in Turkestan and the Middle East, regardless of language or religion. New terms were coined in Chinese to represent the Uyghurs proper.

As Chinese perspectives widened along with the Mongol Empire and as more such Turkestanis migrated into China, the term *Húihú* was simplified into *Húihúi* by just repeating the first syllable. During most of the Mongol Empire, this term was used to translate the Mongolian *Sarta'ul*, itself an ethnic term used to designate oasis dwellers with more or less Caucasian features. During the succeeding Ming dynasty (1368–1644), the Uyghurs were finally converted to Islam and the descendants of the Westerners in China proper who had not converted to Islam gradually assimilated into the surrounding population. Thus, *Húihúi* eventually came to be used in China as a term exclusively for Muslims, particularly those Muslims subject to the dynasty. In the Mongol dynasty, however, this was not yet true, and the sources speak of "*Húihúi* Jews" and "*Húihúi* Hindus." Given the gradual evolution of the term as China's perspective broadened, we therefore translate *Húihú* as "Turkestanis" and *Húihúi* as "Westerners." In the later sense, *Húihúi* corresponded to the more literal *Xīyù*, literally, "the Western Region" or more idiomatically, "the West"; Mongol-era scribes used sometimes *Húihúi* and sometimes *Xīyù* to translate Mongolian *Sarta'ul*.

"Chinese," "Han," and the "Civilized World"

Just as there were several ways to refer to those outside, so were there also many ways for Chinese to refer to themselves. The oldest were *Huá* or *Xià*, either alone or in

---

34. *Húihú* and *Húihé* are the modern Mandarin pronunciations. In the pronunciation of the Tang era (AD 618–907) both words were pronounced in Chinese roughly as *Khwei-ghor*.

combination. With their connotations of "civilized" (*huá*) and "grand" (*xià*) as well
as "Chinese," these were the favored terms used by classically trained literati to
draw a distinction between themselves and the "barbarians." Where *Xià* appears
in these reports, we translate it as "Chinese." But much more commonly used in
these sources are certain terms that would come to designate "China" and "ethnic Chinese" today. To designate their own realm, the Song sources as a rule use
Zhōngguó. This binome, or combination of two graphs, traditionally translated as
"Middle Kingdom," originally meant something like the "Central Lands." It is,
however, the modern word for "China," so we have translated it throughout simply as "China." For "ethnic Chinese," that is, the people who claimed the Chinese
language and cultural traditions as their own, the usual term in these sources
is *Hàn*. Originally designating the Han dynasty (206 BC–AD 220), China's first
enduring imperial state, it is used today to designate the majority ethnic Chinese
as distinct from the fifty-five official ethnic minorities in China. Since the term is
used today and is familiar to those with some knowledge of China, we have left it
untranslated as "Han."[35]

But even before the rise of the Mongols, many areas inhabited by Han Chinese
were no longer part of the political *Zhōngguó* (China). Song men looking north
across their border saw many lands that were once their own territory now controlled by Jurchen rulers from Manchuria. Rather than call those lands also *Zhōngguó*, they generally called them either *Zhōngyuán*, "the Central Plains" or *Hàndì*,
"Han lands." "Central Plains" was an old phrase for the broad flat alluvial plain
around the area of Henan Province; our sources use it, however, simply as a synonym for North China as a whole. "Han lands" is self-explanatory—the lands
inhabited by Han Chinese—but the phrase was used particularly for lands settled
by the Han which had fallen under the rule of non-Han peoples like the northeastern Jurchens or the northwestern Tanguts.[36]

Chinese writers who served the Mongols, however, preferred to use a much
more ideologically ambitious word to designate the lands inhabited by the Han.
Rather than "Central Plains" or "Han lands," they distinguished the Chinese part
of the empire—the part that could and should be ruled according to the principles
of Confucianism—as *tiānxià*, literally, "All under Heaven." It would be a mistake
to take this phrase too literally, however. The emphasis was not on Heaven as
the physical firmament, but on Heaven as the commanding will that ordained
good government. "All under Heaven" was the world that was susceptible to the
civilizing forces of just rulers who had received Heaven's mandate. In this sense,
tiānxià corresponds to "the civilized world" or sometimes "the whole society"—all
areas and inhabitants that were worth considering. In this sense, the reader of
Song Zizhen's biography of Ila Chucai will often see *tiānxià* explicitly juxtaposed
with "the West"; both might be under the rule of the Mongol emperors, but only

---

35. Note however that when referring to language and writing systems, we use "Chinese" not
"Han."

36. On Chinese terms for themselves, see Wilkinson 2000, 95–96, 132.

the Han lands were part of the "civilized world," susceptible to the full civilizing influences of the Confucian program.

Moons and Slogans

One of the ways in which the legitimacy of such heavenly ordained rulers was shown was in the ordering of time. In Western Eurasia, calendars were decided by religion. Christians followed the purely solar Julian calendar and dated years from the birth of Jesus. Muslims followed the purely lunar calendar prescribed in the Qur'an and counted years from Muhammad's emigration from Mecca to Medina. Jews used a mixed lunar-solar calendar and counted years from the creation of the world described in Genesis. In East Asia, however, the state, not religion, governed the passing of time.[37]

Moons and Solar Terms

Like the Jews, the East Asian realms followed a mixed lunar-solar calendar, one in which the months were naturally observable moons, with the first day being always a new moon and the fifteenth always a full moon. But since twelve such natural lunar months add up to a little over 354 days, the Lunar New Year slides back about eleven days each year. Purely lunar calendars, like the Muslim one, do not adjust for this, and hence the Islamic New Year over time cycles through all the seasons. But the East Asian calendars, like the Jewish one, inserted extra months, called intercalary moons, into the year roughly every three years in order to keep the New Year always roughly within the same time frame. The details varied due to the precession of the equinoxes and other complications, but during the time of these translations, East Asian rulers always kept the Lunar New Year sometime between January 15 and February 15.[38]

Since East Asian months were natural months, not the arbitrary slices of time as in a purely solar calendar, we call them "moons" not "months." East Asian moons are numbered, rather than having specific names, and people sometimes translate phrases like *éryuè* or *sānyuè*, literally, "second moon/month" and "third moon/month," as "February" or "March." But since the equivalence is variable, we have avoided such misleading terms. Instead we have borrowed a leaf from contemporary Mongolian practice by numbering the moons with Roman numerals. We then insert in parentheses the roughly corresponding month in the Gregorian calendar for that particular year, so that readers may have a sense of where in the progression of seasons the event fell. Thus, for example, under year 1214, Li Xinchuan writes, "In the autumn, moon VIII [September–October], the Tatar armies once again besieged Yanjing." As for year equivalents, we have

---

37. On East Asian calendars, see Wilkinson 2000, 170–72.

38. Earlier in Chinese history, during the Han dynasty, for example, the Lunar New Year fell about ten days later on average, roughly between January 25 and February 25.

converted the years to the current Christian era used internationally. It should be understood, however, that due to the different New Year's date, the equivalence is not exact.[39]

Since the moons varied in their correspondence to the progression of the sun through the constellations, Chinese astronomers, agronomists, and other scientists found it useful to have another, purely solar system for their specialized purposes. Careful observers like Peng Daya, for example, when remarking on the Mongolian weather would sometimes key their observation to either the twenty-four "solar terms" (*jiéqi*), that is, periods of roughly sixteen days, or to the "eight nodes" (*bājié*), designating the solstices, equinoxes, and the beginning of the four lunar seasons.[40]

Although the broad principles of the calendars were common knowledge to all in the Chinese cultural sphere, the right to proclaim a calendar with specific dates for a new year and a decision of when to intercalate an extra moon were prerogatives of the legitimate emperor. All those under the emperor's sway used his calendar, including tributary kings like those of Korea who might otherwise have almost complete autonomy. Proclaiming the New Year was thus an attribute of sovereignty; "to grant (some kingdom) the standard calendar" was a common way to refer to extending the imperial sway.[41] Chinese writers tended to assume that those outside China could not possibly have a calendar, since they did not have the principles of legitimate government. They repeatedly wrote of the Mongols, for example, who "until recently" only recognized the greening of the grass and had no exact calendar; that same comment appears in the Ming dynasty as in the Song and in both cases is known to be false.

Year Slogans: Legitimate and "Bogus"

Even more clearly marking imperial allegiance was the system of dating the years. Like most ancient monarchies, the East Asian kingdoms and empires dated events by the years of the ruler's reign. But since the Han dynasty, East Asian rulers had been going one step further, at crucial moments proclaiming *niánhào*, literally, "year-signs," from which the whole realm would then date the subsequent years. The term *niánhào* is usually translated as "regnal years" or "reign titles" or some other such abstract title. But in practice they were transparently political slogans, like Warren Harding's "Back to Normalcy" or Franklin Roosevelt's "New Deal" in American politics, intended to galvanize public opinion and gloss over inconvenient realities. A new emperor would always proclaim a new such slogan either at the beginning of his reign or at the first new year after his enthronement. But prior to the Ming dynasty (1368–1644), a new slogan might be proclaimed even in the middle of a given reign sometimes to celebrate a major achievement and sometime to change the emperor's luck after a major disaster.

39. For the months or moons of Chinese calendars, see Wilkinson 2000, 179–80.

40. For the solar calendrical terms, see Wilkinson 2000, 185–86.

41. See, for example, Shao-yun Yang 2015, 396, 397.

Thus, when the emperor of the Jin dynasty, ruling North China, was in the midst of the first great Mongol invasion, he hoped to change his luck by proclaiming that the year beginning February 5, 1212, would not be the "Great Peace (*Dà'ān*) Year 4" but rather, "Exalted Felicity (*Chóngqìng*) Year 1." Soon the "Felicity Exalted" seemed not to be working in light of another defeat by the Mongol armies, so the next year, in the fifth moon, "Felicity Exalted Year 2" was changed to "Perfect Calm (*Zhìníng*) Year 1." Three months later, however, the emperor was killed in a bloody coup, and the new emperor had to rename the year yet again, this time as "Immaculate Blessing (*Zhēnyòu*) Year 1." We have here translated the slogans to illustrate their often ludicrously aspirational character, but in practice translations vary and have not been standardized. Consequently, when such "year slogans" are mentioned, we have given them in their Chinese names, followed by the year in Arabic numbers: thus *Chóngqìng* 1, rather than "Felicity Exalted 1," *Zhìníng* 1, rather than "Perfect Calm, Year 1," and so on. A table of all the year slogans mentioned in these translations, with their meanings, is given in Appendix §2.6 (p. 190).[42]

As one might imagine, such slogans were the prerogative of sovereignty and their use denoted loyalty to the emperor proclaiming them. But a Southern Song writer telling the history of the hostile Jin dynasty in North China often could not avoid using the Jin dynasty's year slogans, however distasteful the need to use them might be. In that circumstance, the writer could demonstrate his loyalty to the Southern Song perspective by adding the word *wĕi*, "bogus" or "fabricated," to the slogan. Thus Li Xinchuan, in reporting the events in North China, first gives the date according to the Jin year slogans, usually with the redeeming "bogus" attached, and then gives it according to the Southern Song year slogans.[43]

Sixty- and Twelve-Year Cycles

There was, however, a politically neutral way to refer to years, and Li Xinchuan uses that also: the sexagenary cycle. This cycle was formed by juxtaposing ten heavenly stems (*tiāngān*) with twelve earthly branches (*dìzhī*). Running both sequences simultaneously created sixty unique combinations that were used to number both years and days. This system, dating back to the Bronze Age, was one of the first elements in the early Chinese writing system and was not tied to any political regime. It could thus be used as a non-political way of denoting years, so long as it was clear from context which sixty-year cycle was in question.[44] In our translation, such dates are given the form of the "stem" and "branch" terms

---

42. Most bilingual dynasties, such as the Kitan Liao and the Jurchen Jin, proclaimed such year slogans in both of their languages, Kitan and Chinese for the Liao, Jurchen and Chinese for the Jin. Although Qubilai Khan began proclaiming year slogans in 1260, he and his successors used only Chinese. The Manchu Qing dynasty from 1616 to 1912 proclaimed such year slogans in three languages: Manchu, Mongolian, and Chinese.

43. On year slogans, see Wilkinson 2000, 180–82.

44. On the sexagenary cycle, see Wilkinson 2000, 175–79.

separated by a slash with the Christian-era date given in brackets, thus, for example: *gēng/chén* [1220].

Sometime during the Han dynasty, the twelve earthly branches came to be identified with twelve animals, producing the famous "Year of the Mouse," "Year of the Cow," "Year of the Tiger," and so on, often called the "Chinese zodiac." This system proved vastly more "user friendly" than the full sexagenary cycle, especially for non-Chinese, and it was soon adopted and used by Türks, Tibetans, Uyghurs, Mongols, and many others. During the Mongol Empire, the Mongols used only the twelve-year animal cycle for dating events, something noted by Zhao Gong in his account.[45]

Court and Country

One of the most difficult aspects of traditional Chinese histories is the extraordinary range of titles and ranks in the central government. As explained in many of the accounts here, the simplicity, not to say crudity, of Mongol administration means that relatively few such titles appear here. In translating titles, we generally followed Charles Hucker's *A Dictionary of Official Titles in Imperial China* (1985), which renders the names mostly based on the actual functions. Readers seeking to know more about a particular title may look up the English name in this dictionary. Still, given the complexity of the titles, a summary of the generally expected form of government in China at the time may help orient readers.[46]

Offices and Examinations

All the dynasties of China in the twelfth century, whether Song, Liao, Xia, or Jin, inherited a system in which the emperor ruled principally through a civil bureaucracy. In the original Tang dynasty version of this system, the top level of the civil bureaucracy was organized into the "Three Departments" (*sān shěng*), in which the Department of State Affairs (*Shàngshū shěng*) conducted the everyday business, and the Secretariat (*Zhōngshū shěng*) advised the throne and coordinated policy making. (The third, the Chancellery, or *Ménxià shěng*, quickly declined in importance and does not appear in the sources translated here.) Over time, administration tended to be simplified into a single *shěng*, designated either as the Department of State Affairs or more commonly as the Secretariat, handling both routine paperwork and communication with the throne. This unit oversaw the civil bureaucracy, supervising the functionally specialized "Six Boards": of personnel, revenue, rites, war, punishments, and public works.

The Secretariat was headed occasionally by a single "Director" (*lìng*) or more often by dual left and right "Grand Councilors" (*chéngxiàng* or *xiàng*) or "Managers"

---

45. On the twelve-animal cycle, see Wilkinson 2000, 183–84.

46. Readers seeking a more detailed picture may also wish to consult the introductory essays surveying the Song, Liao, Jin, and Yuan systems of government in Hucker 1985, 40–69.

(*píngzhāng*). The Kitans in their language used the title *seng'un* from the Chinese term of address "Lord Minister" (*xiànggōng*); under Kitan Liao influence this title was widely used in the North through the tenth to fourteenth centuries. Ranking below the "Grand Councilors" or "Lord Ministers" were "Vice Grand Councilors" (*cānzhèng*), and a further panoply of aides, all in left and right pairs. When there were dual top officials, the left was, according to Chinese tradition, the senior one, while the Mongols ranked the right as senior.[47]

In addition to the line officials of the civil bureaucracy, there were two other major units. Military affairs migrated to a separate privy council (*Shūmì yuàn*), which handled actual operations and relegated routine matters of recruitment and logistics to the Board of War under the Secretariat. The censors in the Censorate (*Yùshǐtái*) supervised officials in the other two branches, impeaching them when they detected malfeasance—real, imagined, or fabricated. In addition, the palace staff was always a vast organization with a large force of palace guards under the direct control of the emperor's intimates.

By the twelfth century, all the Chinese-style dynasties were recruiting a large part, although not the absolute majority, of their officials through the famous examination system.[48] Theoretically, this led to the dominance of a classically trained body of scholar-officials who implemented Confucian ideas of governance. Persian and European visitors to China under the Mongols did not often notice the Confucian ideological underpinnings, but they were amazed by how status and salaries were attached to positions, rather than inherited rank, and how promotion was governed by regular performance reviews.

Yet as one may gather from reading Zhang Dehui's memories of serving the Jin dynasty, even before the Mongol conquests, the role of such upwardly mobile officials was much larger in theory than in reality. In the North, ruled by the non-Han Jurchen people from Manchuria, princes of the imperial family and nobles of other great Jurchen families dominated the top levels of government. And under the Mongols, as Song Zizhen's encomium for Ila Chucai shows, Chinese officials faced rivals of other ethnic origins. Classically trained officials often felt they were mere window dressing for a government really dominated by powerful princes, generals, and financial operators.

Hereditary Privileges and Emergency Organizations

Another way in which Chinese governance departed from the ideal type of purely rational bureaucracy envisioned by Max Weber is in the granting of certain hereditary privileges and aristocratic titles to generals and officials.[49] These

---

47. On these terms, see Hucker 1985, §§3733 (*lìng*); §§483, 2303 (*chéngxiàng~xiàng*); §4699–4700 (*píngzhāng*); §2331 (*xiànggōng*); and §§6868, 6872 (*cānzhèng*).

48. Miyazaki 1981 gives a vivid picture of this system's workings; Elman 2000 gives an up-to-date scholarly picture.

49. Herlee Creel 1964 long ago argued that the Chinese state, as early as the Han dynasty, precociously exemplified the Weberian ideal of bureaucracy. Although Creel's position would hardly

titles were granted both to members of the royal family and to figures who were prominent in the dynasty's founding. The highest-ranking titles were named after larger regions designated with a single Chinese graph, nominally connected to a traditional region, such as "Prince of Yue" or "Prince of Zheng." (Yue was the traditional name for the far south of China and Zheng was the traditional name for a region in Henan Province.) Slightly lower in status were two-graph titles designating smaller place names less redolent of tradition, such as "Prince of Dongdan." (Dongdan was the name for a region in Manchuria.) These titles carried salaries, at least nominally collected from the named region, but only under the Mongol Empire did such princes actually supervise the area concerned.

Those not related to the imperial family by blood or marriage could be posthumously granted lower titles based on moral qualities, such as the "Duke of Civil Preferment," which Ila Chucai's father bore. Such titles, while not officially heritable, did come with privileged consideration for the titleholder's descendants. During their lives, however, the top three officials in the government were often granted the titles "Grand Preceptor," "Grand Mentor," and "Grand Guardian," collectively known as the "Three Dukes" (*Sān Gōng*).[50] These titles were primarily honorary, although they often carried substantial stipends. "Grand Preceptor," or *Tàishī*, was also commonly granted as a title to threatening foreign rulers who needed to be mollified. In that form it became known among the Mongols and was bestowed by Chinggis Khan on his viceroy in North China, Muqali.

Apart from these regular and titular offices, ad hoc units were created to deal with rebellions or invasions. If an emergency broke out in a particular province or region, then largely autonomous "mobile" (*xíng*) versions of the central secretariats and privy councils could be created to command civil and military resources in the area until the rebellion or invasion was suppressed. Later on, under the Mongols, these "mobile" secretariats were maintained even after the conquest and formed the embryos of provincial governments in later dynasties. Other official titles connected with either suppressing rebellions or fighting on the frontier included "Pacification Commissioner" (*Xuānfǔshǐ*) and "Bandit-Suppression Commissioner" (*Zhāotǎoshǐ*). Since Chinese political theory, like that of imperial Rome, held that "barbarians" could have no legitimate reason to resist the Chinese throne, any military action by unconquered foreign people like the Tatars was treated as illegal "banditry." Thus, the "Bandit-Suppression Commissions" in the Jin dynasty of North China were actually frontier military commands intended for conducting offensive and defensive actions against the "barbarian" "bandits."

---

be fully accepted today, there remains a tendency to exaggerate the rational and bureaucratic aspects of Chinese governance, partly because they are the best documented.

50. Chinese traditional government inherited several titles from the Zhou dynasty (1046–256 BC), which were eventually systematized into an artificial hierarchy of five ranks. Traditional Sinology matched these five ranks with the five feudal ranks found in European history, thus translating *gōng* as "duke," *hóu* as "marquis," and so forth. These equivalences, however, are purely conventional and should not be taken too seriously. A *gōng* was the highest of these titles and was originally used for the patriarch of a lineage, as a posthumous title for any lord, or for a member of the royal family serving as chief official under his relative, the king. See Pines, 2020.

Prefectures, Counties, and Capitals

The local administration system in China at this time was based on the prefecture. Prefectures, of which there were about 185 in North China's Jin dynasty, were centered on walled cities. Depending on their importance, prefectures were called either *zhōu* (ordinary prefectures) or *fŭ* (metropolitan prefectures); within each designation prefectures were also ranked as upper, middle, or lower, depending on population and tax receipts. The tax-paying population of these Jin-dynasty prefectures ranged from well over a million in the prefectures of present-day Beijing and Kaifeng to less than ten thousand along the Inner Mongolian frontier. Prefectures with about 100,000 taxpayers were most common. All of the *fŭ* prefectures and some of the *zhōu* prefectures had garrison armies that served as the dynasty's basic territorial military.

Under each prefectural jurisdiction were from three to ten counties (*xiàn*); each county seat was also supposed to be walled, but had no resident military force. Above the prefecture was the "route" or *lù*, which had a regional military command seated in a *fŭ* prefecture and which supervised on average about fifteen prefectures. Alongside the routes was a system of "capitals," designated by direction: central, northern, southern, eastern, and western, and—for the Jin dynasty—an additional "Upper Capital" (Shangjing) in the ruling Jurchens' ethnic homeland. Of these "capitals," only one actually functioned as a seat of government; the other capitals were in effect high-level, strategically important "route" commands, in which a viceroy (*liúshŏu*)[51] supervised civil and military officials. In the Jin dynasty, the Central Capital or Zhongdu (in modern-day Beijing) was the seat of the imperial court and the main center of government up to the initial Mongol invasions. In 1214, after making a temporary peace with the Mongols, the Jin court fled south of the Yellow River to their Southern Capital, in present-day Kaifeng, Henan Province. Other such capitals that appear in these sources include the Western Capital, seated at modern Datong, which supervised the Tatar frontier, the Northern Capital (now a ruin in southeastern Inner Mongolia), and the Upper Capital in the Jurchen heartland near modern Harbin.

This hierarchy of jurisdictions meant that cities in China had a multiplicity of designations. At each level—capital or route, prefecture, and county—walled cities had a particular name. Thus, the same walled city could be called the Western Capital (Xijing), Datongfu (Metropolitan Prefecture of Datong), or Yunzhong County. Each one of these units had their administrative seat within the walls of the city now called Datong. Moreover, since each dynasty had a different arrangement of capitals and military route commands, the higher-level names changed with each dynasty. Thus, in the Liao dynasty (907–1125) the "Southern Capital" (*Nánjīng*) designated modern Beijing, in the Song Dynasty (960–1127) it designated what is now Shangqiu in Henan Province, and under the Jin dynasty (1115–1234) it designated present-day Kaifeng, also in Henan Province. The Ming dynasty

---

51. This title is translated as "Regent" in Hucker 1985, §3813, but we have translated it as "Viceroy" to avoid confusion with *jiānguó*, which also appears in these translations and is translated as "Regent" as well in Hucker 1985, §840.

(1368–1644), after the fall of the Mongols, placed their "Southern Capital" south of the Yangtze River at the great city today called Nanjing. Similar changes occurred in many of the route designations.

Given the potential confusions, we have adhered to the following basic principles:

1. For prefectures, we have added the *fǔ* or *zhōu* as part of their name. Thus, we write "Taiyuanfu," not "Taiyuan Prefecture," and "Zhuozhou," not "Zhuo Prefecture." The *fǔ* versus *zhōu* designation gives important information about the significance of the place in the administrative hierarchy and so is added for the reader.[52] This practice also follows the universal practice of non-Chinese medieval writers who wrote about China.

2. The Jin dynasty panoply of capital names (Central Capital, Southern Capital, Western Capital, etc.) occur rarely enough that we have chosen to translate rather than transcribe their names.

3. The main regional terms found in the sources—"Shandong," "Hebei," "Henan," and "Shaanxi"—correspond roughly to the modern provinces of China. "Shanxi," however, is found as "Hedong."

4. The "Central Capital" of the Jin or Zhongdu was traditionally called Yanjing, and its "Western Capital," or Xijing, was traditionally called Yunzhong. The areas around these two cities, on the northern frontier of traditional Han settlement, are often abbreviated in these sources to their first syllables, Yan or Yun, but we write them out to avoid confusion.

5. Classical Chinese words are monosyllabic and in their modern pronunciation are quite short and simple by the standards of many other languages, including English. The usual practice of eliminating tone marks in personal or place names further simplifies them. In our experience, students who are not familiar with Chinese find it easier to remember bisyllabic names. Thus, where a geographical term is monosyllabic, we generally transcribe it with its following classifier word as well. Thus, we write "Tongguan Pass" for *Tóng guān* and "Hengshan Mountain" for *Héng shān*, rather than Tong Pass or Heng Mountain.

6. Chinese is a tonal language. In not a few cases prefecture names differ only in their tones—for example, "Wèizhōu 魏州" and "Wēizhōu 威州." In those cases, we have distinguished the main word by tone markers, thus "Wèizhou" and "Wēizhou." The same practice is followed with easily confused surnames, such as Shí 石 vs. Shǐ 史.

---

52. Chinese usage sometimes does and sometimes does not add the prefecture name. Where it does not, we omit the word "prefecture" in the English translation. Where the Chinese does add the prefectural term, we add the word "prefecture" as well. Thus, if the Chinese has simply "Jing" then we translate it as "Jingzhou" rather than "Jing." But if the Chinese has "Jingzhou," then we translate it as "Jingzhou Prefecture," rather than just "Jingzhou" or "Jing Prefecture." Although technically repetitive, we find this usage clearer and easier to follow in English.

7. For this reason, where we have needed to refer to specific graphs, either in discussing possible corruptions in the text or in explaining the nuances of our translation, we have used the proper tone marks to distinguish what would otherwise be homonyms. For proper nouns and titles of books, however, we have followed general practice and omitted the tone marks. All of the graphs may be found in the glossary of "Chinese Names and Terms" (Appendix §3.1 [p. 193]).

Names and Styles

Names in East Asia give the surname (family name) first, then the given name—the opposite name order from that in European languages. Thus, for the Chinese general Liu Bolin, Liu is his family name, and Bolin is his given name. However, persons are generally referred to in histories not by their family names but by their given names. In the sources, Liu Bolin appears first with his full name but subsequently only his given name is used.[53]

Courtesy, Childhood, and Ladies' Names

Chinese men with pretensions to culture, however, did not normally use their personal names (*míng*) in upper-class social interactions. Instead they adopted "courtesy names" (*zì*) which would serve as their term of address in all polite situations. Well-known writers might even have another title, a *hào*, that is, a "style" or pen name, and some intellectuals accrued multiple sobriquets, often from the names of their studios or places of residence. Thus, the famous scholar-official Ila Chucai appears in the sources written during his lifetime more often under his courtesy name, "Jinqing," than under his personal name, "Chucai."[54] It was only in purportedly objective sources—such as dynastic or local histories, censuses, examination lists, or genealogies, or after death—that persons were referred to by their *míng*. Distinguished figures might be granted posthumous honorific titles by the court, but such names were used only in highly formal, mostly commemorative cases.

While Chinese generals like Liu Bolin were at most semiliterate and thus appear only by their personal names or *míng*, the Song envoys were surprised to see that even persons as exalted as the Mongol emperor used the same name they were given by their parents as a child. It is presumably for this reason that Zhao Gong, Peng Daya, and Xu Ting all believed that the personal names of Mongol leaders like Temüjin, Muqali, and Öködei were mere "childhood names" (*xiǎomíng*), and that Mongols in general only had such childhood names. In fact,

---

53. On Chinese family names, see Wilkinson 2000, 96–98.

54. It is not a coincidence that the more anti-Mongol Xu Ting preferred to designate Ila unceremoniously as "Chucai," while the less anti-Mongol Zhao Gong and Peng Daya politely used his courtesy name, "Jinqing."

Chinese "childhood names" refer to babyish nicknames, and the names the Mongols bore corresponded rather to *míng* or personal, given names.[55] But the absence of a system of courtesy names was merely one more way in which the Mongols seemed to lack the basic prerequisites of civilization.[56]

Chinese women were even less likely to use their personal *míng*. Once respectably married, they were generally referred to solely by the surnames of their families of birth. Unlike with men, their personal names were not normally recorded even after death. Thus, in Ila Chucai's biography, for example, his living wife and his deceased mother appear solely as "Su *shì*," i.e., "[woman of the] Su surname," and "Yang *shì*," i.e., "[woman of the] Yang surname," respectively. As a result, the *míng* or names of women, even those given biographies in the major histories on account of their chastity, exceptional maternal virtue, or other distinguishing feature, are, more often than not, completely unknown. We render X *shì* as "the lady *née* (born as) X."[57]

Speaking of Emperors

For emperors, the rules governing personal names were yet more complex.[58] Whether of Han Chinese or foreign origin, all dynasties were based on a lineage of a single surname.[59] Thus the emperors of the Song dynasty had the surname Zhao. Emperors of course had given names, just like all other persons. The emperor of the Song dynasty during the rise of Chinggis Khan was named Zhao Kuo. When he died childless in 1224, a distant relative from the imperial family succeeded him; he had the same surname Zhao, and the personal name Yun. However, once an emperor ascended the throne, his personal name was taboo to his subjects; the emperor's personal name was thus often referred to his "taboo" (*hùi*) or "name subject to taboo" (*mínghùi*). Beyond not referring to the emperor by his name, even using the graphs of his name in other contexts could be seen as disrespectful to the imperial majesty and hence tended to be avoided. Even after his death, the deceased emperor's name was taboo as long his dynasty held the throne.

---

55. This practice of referring to non-Chinese names as "childhood names" had already become common in the Kitan Liao and Jurchen Jin dynasties. Biographies from that time treat the ethnic names of Kitan and Jurchen figures as unofficial, childish nicknames, while their Chinese names were treated as "(real) names" (*míng*).

56. On the diversity of Chinese names, courtesy names, and sobriquets, see Wilkinson 2000, 98–101, 102–5.

57. On women's names in Imperial China, see Wilkinson 2000, 101–2.

58. On imperial titles and names, see Wilkinson 2000, 108–10.

59. Although this fact might seem obviously true of all dynasties, the Chinese case was a bit different from that of many other dynasties elsewhere in that descent through the female line was absolutely unheard of, while descent even from very distant collateral male lines was not considered a break of continuity in the dynastic line. Thus, even when very distant cousins whose ancestry was barely traceable were put on the throne, the dynastic continuity was considered unruptured, yet succession to the throne by a son of the emperor's daughter was unthinkable— let alone succession by a daughter herself!

Thus, a search of Li Xinchuan's lengthy history of the Song dynasty up to his time will not find a single instance of the emperor's personal name "Zhao Kuo."

In place of his personal name, an emperor after his death was referred to by his temple name, that is, the title by which he was known in the dynasty's temple for ancestor worship. Each emperor, like every family head in China, was expected to maintain a shrine where his ancestors, male and female, were enshrined with their names written on "spirit tablets." Each dynasty thus maintained such a temple in the imperial city where their officials worked. In the temples, all the deceased emperors in good standing and their chief consorts were enshrined with "temple names" (*miàohào*). Emperors' temple names were made by choosing one of a small number of modifiers to attach to either the word *zǔ*, "founder" (used only for one or two of the most important emperors in any dynasty) or *zōng*, "ancestor" (for the rest).[60] These temple names usually followed a stereotypical set of dynastic roles—the great founder who established the empire, the cultured ancestor who established institutions, the accomplished ancestor who perfected the institutions, and so on.[61]

Thus, when the Mongol Empire under Qubilai Khan got around to creating an ancestral temple and enthroning the previous Mongol emperors, Chinggis Khan was enthroned as the "Great Founder" (Taizu) and his son Öködei was enthroned as the "Great Ancestor" (Taizong). Qubilai himself, after his death, was enthroned as the Shizu or "Renovating Founder"; Qubilai and Chinggis were the only Mongol emperors considered important enough to be given temple titles based on *zǔ*, or "founder." Since these titles were conventional, most of them are found in multiple dynasties, making it necessary to repeat the dynasty name to distinguish, for example, one Taizong from another. Thus, Öködei would be known as Yuan Taizong (i.e., Taizong of the Mongols' Yuan dynasty) to distinguish him from emperors such as Tang Taizong (r. 626–649) of the Tang dynasty. For most Chinese dynasties, these "temple titles" are the most common way to refer to emperors. For the Mongol Empire, however, names like Yuan Shizu or Yuan Taizong for Qubilai or Öködei are unfamiliar to readers and misleading because they seem to be a Chinese language *name* rather than a *title* with a meaning. For the Mongol Empire, we have thus translated the titles, rather than transcribed them.[62]

---

60. Anyone honored after death, whether emperor or eminent vassal, was also granted a *shì* or posthumous title. A posthumous title would be a longer phrase, but also one that referenced in stylized fashion the emperor's accomplishments. Thus, Chinggis Khan's posthumous title was *Shèngwǔ huángdì*, which could be variously translated as "Holy Martial Emperor" or "Peerless Warrior Emperor."

61. The only exception would be if an emperor were either the last emperor of the dynasty or were overthrown in a coup d'état by another member of the family. In the first case, the following dynasty would grant him an honorary title to signify that new dynasty now had the authority to give titles. In the second case, the deceased emperor's whole reign might be seen as a mistake, and rather than be enshrined in the temple of sovereigns, he would be excluded from the ranks of imperial ancestors and granted some lesser title.

62. For a list of these posthumous temple titles and their meanings for the Jin dynasty and the Mongol rulers up through Qubilai, see Appendix §2.2, §2.3, p. 187.

After an emperor's death, such posthumous temple names would be inserted into Chinese-language sources on his reign regardless of any resulting anachronism. In the case of the Mongols, where during much of the early empire no such system of taboos was in place, this anachronism sometimes becomes glaring. Thus, near the end of Song Zizhen's "Spirit-Path Stele," Ila Chucai is reported as saying to Öködei's widow shortly after Öködei's death: "This old vassal served the *Great Founder* and the *Great Ancestor* for more than thirty years and has certainly never turned his back on the dynasty." But the italicized titles "Great Founder" and "Great Ancestor" actually translate Chinese-style temple names not created until several decades after this conversation reportedly occurred. At the time, the "Great Founder" would have been called "Chinggis Khan" and "Great Ancestor" "the Qa'an,"[63] meaning Öködei, the titles these two emperors bore during their lifetimes. To mark the reality that such titles were inserted subsequently into records written under the Mongol Empire, we have put the translated title in small capitals (for example, GREAT FOUNDER).[64]

At the other end of the spectrum, Southern Song annalists and border commanders writing about the troubles of the Jin dynasty were more than ready to show their contempt for the rival regime by using the tabooed personal names of the Jin emperors. For them the problem came when, for clarity's sake, they sometimes felt it necessary to use the same temple names used by their loathed Jin-dynasty antagonists. In such cases, as with the year slogans, they might preface it with the word *wěi* or "bogus."

First and Third Person

It should be noted that although three of these accounts—Zhao Gong's, Peng Daya and Xu Ting's, and Zhang Dehui's—are records of personal travels, all of them are written in the third person. This impersonality is helped by the fact that in classical Chinese if the subject of a sentence can be assumed, it need not be stated. Thus, when Zhang Dehui's account of his travels begins, in translation, "We proceeded north in response to the summons," there is in fact no word for "we" in the original. And when he continues, "So I turned my head and addressed my traveling companions," again, the "I" and the "my" had to be supplied in translation. Occasionally, for emphasis, the author refers to himself by name as "[Zhao] Gong" or "[Xu] Ting." In such cases, we have matched the emphasis by writing "I, Gong" or "I, Ting."

In the "Spirit-Path Stele," we find numerous conversations between the minister Ila Chucai and his rulers, first Chinggis Khan, then Öködei Khan, and finally Öködei's regent Töregene. These conversations are governed by imperial

---

63. This title, an alternate form of "khan," was first widely used by Öködei for whom it became a sort of personal title as well.

64. We borrow this practice from English Bible translations in which the Hebrew name of God, the famous *Yahweh* (often pronounced Jehovah) is routinely replaced by "Lord" in small capitals (LORD).

etiquette: the speaker refers to himself as *chén*, or "vassal,"[65] while referring to his ruler as *bìxià*, literally, "below the stairs [of the throne]."[66] The emperor should properly refer to himself as *zhèn*, an archaic word for "me"; if he is being respectful and polite he will refer to his minister as *qīng*, an archaic word for "minister" or "liege."[67] One can trace the quality of Ila Chucai's relations with his rulers through the presence or absence of this language. We have tried to render these terms in readable language based on English royal etiquette: *chén* as "your servant," *bìxià* as "Your Highness," *zhèn* as the royal "We" or "Our," and *qīng* as "Our liege."

Foreign Sounds and Graphs

The sources translated in this volume were written in Chinese and record the rise of a people, the Mongols, who spoke a language that is not just unrelated to Chinese but also radically different in its sound and syllable structure. Not surprisingly, one of the most difficult problems for the original authors was how to write Mongolian names using the Chinese script. This problem is all the more complex for the translator, who has to juggle the original Mongolian sounds, the Chinese graphs used to record those sounds, and English conventions of spelling.

Chinese is written with graphs each of which usually has a fixed pronunciation and a distinctive meaning, though some have alternate readings with alternate meanings. (A few graphs in Chinese are used almost entirely for their sound, such as *ā* 阿 or *hā* 哈.) Each graph is pronounced as a single syllable, and classical Chinese is formed with mostly monosyllabic words. But the early Mandarin vernacular spoken at the time of these sources had many two-syllable words. Etymologically, such words had often come into existence by combining two older one-syllable words. In any case, whether etymologically correct or not, two-syllable words were always written by combining single-syllabic graphs matching the sound and meaning of the two syllables. When writing words of non-Chinese origin, however, graphs were often combined without any regard to the meaning.

Sino-'Barbarian' Glosses

Since each graph represents a complete Chinese syllable, only those sequences of sounds found in Chinese could be easily represented by this method of direct representation. The Chinese rules of syllable structure were quite restrictive; at the end of a syllable, for example, the only consonants allowed in thirteenth-century

---

65. This is often translated as "minister"; however, it applies to anyone serving the ruler, whether in civil or a military capacity.

66. The idea is that the speaker does not dare to address the ruler directly but instead is speaking to the ruler's intimate servant who serves "below the stairs" of the throne.

67. See Wilkinson 2000, 104, 108–9.

Chinese were *m*, *n*, and *ng*.[68] Mongolian syllables, by contrast, could also end in *l*, *b*, *k*, *q*, *r*, *s*, or *t*. A Mongolian syllable like the *-gis* in *Chinggis*, the name of Chinggis Khan, thus could not be directly represented in Chinese, but had to be approximated, either by combining one syllable with *gi-* and another with *-si* or else by just dropping the final consonant.

Eventually, certain conventions were developed to render Mongolian names as Chinese graphs. Certain graphs such as *sī* 思, *ér* 兒, and *lè* 勒, for example, came to be used more or less exclusively to represent the consonants *-s*, *-r*, and *-l*, respectively, at the ends of syllables. These and other conventions significantly improved the ability of Chinese scribes to represent Mongolian names. But such conventions took time to develop and were followed mostly by those scribes working in Mongol service; they were not used by writers of the Song or even by writers like Zhang Dehui who, although in Mongol service, did not have much interest in exactly representing Mongolian names. Thus, of the sources translated here, only the eulogy for Ila Chucai generally follows a consistent system for representing Mongol names.

For a translator into English, how to represent these Chinese versions of Mongolian names is a real challenge. The simplest way would be to phonetically Romanize the Chinese graphs using the English alphabet according to the standard Pinyin system, with the Mongolian name given in a note or in brackets if need be. The problem is that such bracketing would be needed in virtually all cases, and the text would soon bristle with strange Chinese doppelgangers of almost every Mongolian name. Moreover, the pronunciation of Chinese graphs in the thirteenth century varied significantly from that of today, creating additional complications. Let us take the name "Chinggis." It is written with the Chinese graphs 成吉思, which if written in Pinyin would be "Chengjisi." The resemblance to "Chinggis" is only distantly visible. However, in the thirteenth century, those same graphs were actually pronounced "Ching-gi-sï." Moreover, since the final graph *sī* was always used for *-s* at the end of a syllable, a moderately informed Chinese reader of the time would actually know to read it not as "Chengjisi" but rather as something very close to Mongolian "Chinggis." Given these facts, it is unnecessarily confusing to transcribe 成吉思 as "Chengjisi" when it is actually a good representation of Mongolian "Chinggis." Thus, where the Chinese transcription follows the known rules for transcribing Mongolian we simply write the name as it is usually written in English—thus not "Chengjisi" or even "Chinggisi," but just "Chinggis."

More difficult are cases where the author uses a nonstandard—or just plain wrong—transcription of the Mongolian. Let us take, for example, the way Zhao Gong refers to two of Chinggis Khan's sons. One he names as 約直 and the other he names as 天婁. If we transcribe these names with Pinyin, they are Yuezhi and Tianlou. We know, however, that these refer to Jochi and Tolui. How should they be written in English translation? If we write Yuezhi and Tianlou we give a

---

68. Later, in modern Mandarin, only *-n* and *-ng* were allowed, and all syllables ending in *-m* were merged with those ending in *-n*.

seriously exaggerated impression of Zhao Gong's mistake, because much of the divergence from the correct Mongolian is created either by changes in Chinese pronunciation since the thirteenth century or by certain conventions for representing Mongolian syllables with Chinese graphs. The name Yuezhi was actually pronounced like "Yo-ji" in the thirteenth century, and the *-ji* in this case could be used to represent *-chi*. Hence Zhao Gong's version would be read by an informed Chinese reader as something like "Yochi," differing from the correct Mongolian "Jochi" only in one interesting particular: *Y-* for *J-*. Similarly, "Tianlou" would be pronounced in the thirteenth century roughly as "Tien-lèu"; it was a further convention of representing Mongolian words that *-ie-* could represent *-e-* and that *-n* at the end of a syllable could represent *-r* or *-l*, especially if the syllable following began with that sound. Thus "Tianlou" could be understood by a Chinese reader as something close to "Telleu," which is not the same as, but certainly closer to, the correct Tolui. For these unorthodox transcriptions, then, our practice is to give the author "the benefit of the doubt" and give the name in the closest form to the correct Mongolian that the author's Chinese would allow. In the glossary (Appendix §3.2 [p. 200]), readers will find all the names with their Chinese graphs, the thirteenth century reading, and the modern Mandarin reading.

Other Alien Languages

The Mongols of course were not the first people who spoke an alien language to rule China. In the centuries before Chinggis Khan's rise, members of several different language families established dynasties in North China:

1. The Shatuo (also known as White Tatars or Öng'üt) spoke a now extinct eastern dialect of Turkic;

2. The Tangut spoke a now-extinct language of the Qiangic branch of the Tibeto-Burman family;

3. The Kitan spoke a now extinct language of the Mongolic family;

4. The Jurchens spoke an early dialect of Manchu.

Names and terms in Kitan and Jurchen appear frequently in these sources. Like Mongolian, these languages were multisyllabic and had a different syllable structure from Chinese. Since the Kitans' Liao and the Jurchens' Jin dynasty both had bilingual officialdoms, they also created a similar set of conventions for adapting Chinese graphs for recording Kitan and Jurchen words and names. (The Jurchens appear to have taken over more or less unchanged the system for recording Kitan words in Chinese graphs.) Unlike Mongolian, however, this system is not as well understood, and traditionally scholars have simply used modern Pinyin to write their names. Recently, however, research on deciphering the Kitan script has made considerable progress. We have thus taken pains to give Jurchen, Kitan, and other names in their original non-Chinese forms. This approach has the advantage of reproducing more accurately the impact that these documents had, particularly on Song dynasty readers. They picture a North China ruled by differing groups of fundamentally alien, non-Chinese peoples among whom the Mongols were simply the latest and most successful conquerors.

Imperial Surnames of the Kitans and Jurchens

A few more specific comments on the names of the Kitan and Jurchen imperial families may be in order. The Kitan imperial family used two different words for their imperial surname, Ila and Yêrud. *Ila*, which was probably the original term, appears to mean originally "stallion" and by extension "messenger, standard-bearer, warrior." *Yêrud*, which was probably adopted later as a more exclusive term, is related to the Kitan adjective *yêruwun*, "flourishing, prosperous."[69] Ila was written in Chinese as "Yila" and Yêrud was written as "Yelü." Due to the Chinese language's phonemic constraints, the two ended up looking much more similar to each other in Chinese than they were in the original Kitan and thus were often confused.

Even after the fall of the Kitan Empire, members of the Ila~Yêrud family continued to be well-known. Most prominent in these sources is the great official whose personal name was Chucai, and whose courtesy name was Jinqing. During his life, Chucai always used the form Ila (Ch. Yila), as can be seen from his "Account of a Journey to the West" (*Xiyoulu*) and from the consistent usage of contemporaries such as Zhao Gong, Peng Daya, and Xu Ting.[70] But his son Zhu preferred the more exclusive Yêrud name, and presumably at his urging, Chucai's posthumous eulogists, Li Wei and Song Zizhen, writing in Chinese named him "Yelü," and that usage prevailed in later sources: Yelü Chucai. Here we generally follow the Kitan form of the name Ila as he used it in his life, but we use the Chinese "Yelü" when specifically citing Song Zizhen's classic spirit-path stele.

The Jurchen Jin dynasty's imperial surname is also found in medieval sources in Jurchen, Mongolian, and other languages in a number of different forms: most often Wongian, but also Wonyan, Wongyon, or even Ongging. In later Manchu, the name appears as *Wanggiyan*. In fact, it appears to be not a Jurchen name at all, but a Sino-Kitan one, formed by adding a Kitan suffix to the Middle Chinese *ong*, "king, prince, sovereign" (modern Mandarin *wáng*). The Wongian were thus the "royal" or "kingly" Jurchen. The Chinese graphs 完顔 chosen to render this name during the Liao-Jin period are read in modern Mandarin as *Wányán*. In our translations, we give them throughout in the most common Jurchen form, Wongian, precisely to emphasize the surname's foreign, non-Chinese character.

---

69. On *Ila* and its meaning, see de Rachewiltz 1974, 191–98. On *Yêrud*, see Kane 2009, 37, 45, 191; Shimunek 2017, 67, 198, 318. György Kara (personal communication, February 16, 2018) suggests that the Kitan word is a cognate of Mongolian *ira'u(n)*, "melodious, agreeable."

70. For *Xiyoulu*, see de Rachewiltz 1962, 18, 43–44 n. 32. The biography of Chucai's father in the *Jinshi* is also written with the Ila surname; see *JS* 95.2099–101.

Selections from *Random Notes from Court and Country since the Jianyan Years*, vol. 2

By Li Xinchuan of the Southern Song

The following excerpts form the earliest known history of Chinggis Khan's conquests in any language. They were written in the years up to 1217, just as the conqueror's initial lightning forays into North China were yielding to deadlock and before he turned to the conquest of Khwarazm and Islamic Central Asia. The material on Chinggis Khan is part of the second volume of Li Xinchuan's two-volume unofficial history of the Southern Song dynasty, Random Notes from Court and Country since the Jianyan Years *(i.e., since 1127).*

Li Xinchuan (1167–1244, courtesy name Weizhi) was born in Jingyan County in southern Sichuan (today under the administration of Leshan Municipality).[1] His father, Li Shunchen, had passed the Southern Song's highest and most prestigious examination, the palace examination (jìnshì) in 1166. In 1179, he had received appointment as a court official in the "temporary" Southern Song capital of Hangzhou; he died in 1182. Li Xinchuan attributed his interest in history to the times in his early teens when he accompanied his father to the imperial archives and to meetings with famous officials. Unlike his two brothers, who both passed the palace examination, Li Xinchuan only sat for the examinations once, in 1196, and was not successful. Instead he devoted his life to writing the history of his own dynasty, the Southern Song; later in his life, in 1225, he was rewarded with a position as a court historian.

The Random Notes from Court and Country since the Jianyan Years *(Jianyan yilai chaoye zaji) was the most popular and widely read of the many histories he wrote. Most of his other works were too detailed and specialized to achieve a wide audience, although their accuracy has always been valued by professional historians. The two volumes covered the periods from 1127–1202 and 1202–1216, respectively. Within that basic structure, the work was organized topically—the first volume had 521 separate sections and the second volume had 264 sections, both volumes organizing their sections under thirteen themes. These themes illustrate the wide range of Li's interests: the emperors, imperial sacrifices, rituals, policies, court politics, politics in the provinces, anecdotes, random events, official organization, recruitment of officials, taxation, military, and border defense. In keeping with Li Xinchuan's reputation as a historian, the accounts translated here stand out for their political and military detail, careful attention to chronology, and dispassionate treatment of dramatic events.*

---

1. On Li Xinchuan and his work as a historian, see Chaffee 1993, Xu Gui's preface to the modern edition of *Jiaynyan yilai chaoye zaji*, and his biography in the *Songshi* (*SS* 438.12,984–86).

The accounts translated below are parts of §251 and §252 and the whole of §253, found in the second volume's chapter on "Border Defense, part II." The first story under the "Border Defense" rubric is a history of the disastrous war waged by the Southern Song in 1206–1208 to regain the North. Li Xinchuan and his father, like most classically trained Southern officials, had been eager revanchists. The catastrophic failure of their resulting war of choice, which Xinchuan went over in detail in the chapter "Border Defense, Part I," seems to have chastened him, giving a strong sense of how overconfidence can result in disastrous undertakings. It is noticeable that in his account of the Tatar invasions and the Jin court's move of their capital southward, he is very cautious about encouraging the Song court to take advantage of the difficulties of the Jin regime.

Unlike other records translated here, and unlike the other chapters in his Random Notes, *the sections from Li Xinchuan are based neither on personal histories nor on court archives. There is no evidence that Li Xinchuan ever crossed the frontier into Jin- or Mongol-occupied North China, and it was that lack of personal experience that probably led him to conclude: "Distant affairs cannot be known completely; a summary has been recorded here for the time being." Yet it is impressive how accurate a picture he was able to paint of the very complicated events there. His critical sense enabled him, for example, to immediately reject the work of historical fiction,* Record of the Southern Transfer *or* Nanqian lu *(attributed to Zhang Shiyan), which misled many other historians.*

Probably his primary source were intelligence reports submitted by Song envoys who paid regular visits to the Jin court on ceremonial occasions, such as the Lunar New Year or imperial birthdays. In his account of how "The Tatars Cross the Frontier" (§253, pp. 61–62), he refers to a mission which the Mongols sent to the Southern Song border commander in Haozhou in February 1214, and it appears from his account that he had access to the border officials' report on that incident. Elsewhere, in §85, reporting on affairs in his home province of Sichuan, he writes:

> *In the fall of* xīn/wèi *[1211], the court sent Director Yu (given name, Rong) on a mission to the North to offer felicitation on [the Jin emperor's] so-called Ten-Thousand Autumns Festival. But [the Jin capital] Yanjing was already being menaced by the Mongols and they had no time to receive the envoy. After reaching Zhuozhou prefecture, Director Yu returned home.*[2]

He then records how another envoy in the fall of gŭi/yŏu *(1213) was forced to turn back at Wozhou Prefecture because of a coup d'état in the Jin court, and how the following New Year's mission was turned back at the border station at Xuyi. The court concluded that the Jin dynasty was in serious trouble and temporarily closed the border.*[3] *A few pages later, he implies that Associate Administrator An, stationed in Xingyuan (present-day Hanzhong City) along the Sichuan frontier was a source of information*

---

2. Li Xinchuan, *Jianyan yilai chaoye zaji*, vol. 2, 10.665. The Jin emperor's birthday fell in moon VIII.

3. Li Xinchuan, *Jianyan yilai chaoye zaji*, vol. 2, 10.665. The refusal to welcome the Song envoy in *gŭi/yŏu*, VIII, is mentioned as well in the *JS* 13.295.

about the relocation of the Jin court from Yanjing in the north to Kaifengfu in the south in the summer of 1214.[4] *Undoubtedly it was from these types of reports that he drew his information.*

According to its preface, Li Xinchuan completed his second volume in Jiading 9, or year bǐng/ zǐ, *VII, that is, July–August 1216. In his section on the Western Xia, the last event is dated to the summer of 1214, and in his section "The Jurchens Move South," the last event reported is the fall of Yanjing in May 1215. His section "The Tatars Cross the Frontier" probably also concluded originally with the fall of Yanjing. The following account, however, of the Mongol expedition from Tongguan Pass to Xinghuaying must have been added after he completed his final preface, since Jin dynasty annals date events of this expedition from moon VIII,* bǐng/zǐ *(September 8, 1216) to moon XI,* yǐ/yǒu *(December 16, 1216).*[5] *It is likely that Li Xinchuan derived his account of this expedition, the "Flowery Cap Army," and the rebel activities in Shandong from a single source, which he added into his text sometime after he had written his preface, probably early in 1217. This Shandong report, along with a Western Xia document that he also mentions at the end of the section, gave Li his first information about the famous Mongolian commander Muqali, information which he was unable to integrate into his account, leaving that task for Zhao Gong a few years later.*

Li Xinchuan's history does not emphasize the Tatar invasion of North China as some unique catastrophe. After the lengthy discussion of the Song–Jin war, and the three sections on the Tatar invasion and the Jin and Western Xia's response to it, he continues with eleven more narratives about border defense, all focused on the Sichuan region's western and southern frontier. Together these eleven narratives added up to over forty pages in the modern printed edition, compared to the ten or so pages he devoted to the Tatar incursions in the North. If the Tatar conquests raised an unprecedented challenge to the Song, it was not yet obvious to one of the dynasty's greatest historians.

§251. The Jurchens Move South

The Complete Story of the Jin Dynasty in Five Generations and Eight Lords

The Jin dynasty first established imperial titles in the time of Wongian Min;[6] down to the present ruler Xun, it has had a total of five generations with eight lords. The dynasty lasted for ninety-eight years before it began to decline.[7]

---

4. Li Xinchuan, *Jianyan yilai chaoye zaji*, vol. 2, 10.667.

5. *JS* 14.319–21.

6. Wongian (Manchu Wanggiyan) was the surname of the Jurchen emperors; see the Introduction, p. 44. Min is the Chinese name of the founding emperor more usually known by his Jurchen name, Akùdai.

7. Here Li Xinchuan is counting from 1118, the date of Akùdai's imperial proclamation, to his own year of 1216. See Appendix §2.2 (p. 187), "Emperors of the Jin Dynasty."

Their land was at the foot of the Changbai Mountains,[8] on the northeastern frontier of the Kitans at the source of the Yalu River, which probably was the land of the ancient "Sushen" clan. In the Han Dynasty [206 BC–AD 220] they called themselves "Yilou,"[9] during the Northern and Southern dynasties [ca. AD 386–589] they called themselves Murkit, in Sui-Tang times [581–907] they called themselves Marghat, and only reaching the Five Dynasties [907–960] did they begin to call themselves Jurchens.[10] During the time of their ancestors, they used to communicate and exchange greetings [with the dynasties of China]; later they submitted as vassals of the Liao.[11] The earliest progenitor of the Wongian family was Zhipu.[12] He was a Silla man who fled from Silla to the Jurchens; the Jurchen chiefs elected him as their leader.[13]

The position passed through seven generations to Min, [under whom] they first became mighty; he was the so-called Akûdai.[14] In Jianzhong-Jingguo 1 [1101], the Liao ruler Tianzuo was enthroned.[15] He was unspeakably dissolute and cruel, so Akûdai rebelled against him. (It was in Zhenghe 4, VIII [September 1114].) Undertaking military action year after year, he seized over half of the Kitan land. In Chonghe 1, VIII [August–September 1118], Akûdai first called himself an emperor; since his rivers produced gold, he therefore called the dynasty the Great Jin ["Great Golden"] and proclaimed the year Tianfu 1 (year *wù/xū* in the sexagenary cycle [1118]).[16]

---

8. Changbai or "Ever-White" Mountains are a range of mountains in Manchuria and North Korea. Its most famous peak, also called Changbai in Chinese and Baekdu in Korean, is a dormant volcano with a lake in its crater situated on the Sino-Korean border. It was worshiped in the Qing dynasty (1644–1912) as the seat of the Manchu people and is also both the legendary origin of the Korean people as well as the birthplace of the current North Korean regime.

9. "Sushen" and "Yilou" are modern Mandarin readings; the ancient reading of these graphs has been reconstructed as Siuk-dins and 'Ip-lio, respectively (see Schuessler 2009). Not enough is known about them to say for sure whether their language or culture were in fact ancestral to the later Jurchens.

10. Murkit and Marghat are two successive versions of what appear to be the same name of roughly the same people, living along the Amur and Sungari Rivers. That they were at least in part the ancestors of the later Jurchen people is widely accepted. Their names are pronounced as *Mulgil* and *Malgal* in Korean and *Wùjí* and *Mòhé* in modern Mandarin, and appear as Moukri in a Greek source from the East Roman Empire (see Atwood 2014c). The Murkit-Marghat along the Amur River had a common way of life focused on fish products from the river, but they spoke a wide variety of languages, undoubtedly including an early form of Jurchen.

11. The Liao was the dynasty established by the Kitan people, ruling Manchuria, most of Mongolia, and the Yanjing-Yunzhong area of North China from 907 to 1125.

12. As mentioned above, the Wongian family was the imperial clan of the Jurchen Jin dynasty.

13. Silla emerged as a petty kingdom in southeast Korea in the mid-fourth century. The kingdom eventually unified most of the Korean peninsula in 676 and ruled until 935.

14. This is the Jurchen reading of his name; in Chinese transcription it is Aguda.

15. Tianzuo or "Heavenly Legacy" (r. 1101–1125) was the posthumous title granted by the Jin to the last Liao emperor.

16. On the sexagenary, or sixty-year, cycle, see the Introduction, p. 31; it was a relatively apolitical way of dating.

Cai Jing and Tong Guan heard of this and recruited men to sail over the sea on a mission to him.[17] They formed a pact to make a pincer attack on the Liao, whereby the Yanjing area would be returned to us. In the winter of Xuanhe 4 [1122], Tong Guan made an incursion on Yanjing, but was defeated by the Liao. In moon XII of that year [January 1123], Akûdai entered Yanjing. In spring, year 5 [1123], Wang Fu concluded a treaty with Jin by which we would pay annually gold and silks worth 500,000 taels, and goods worth 1,000,000 strings of copper cash,[18] while also requesting to get back the territory of six prefectures, including Yanjing and Jizhou. Akûdai approved it. On *yǐ/chǒu* day of moon V [June 8, 1123], Akûdai died at the age of fifty-six. (He had been on the throne for six years.) His posthumous title was "Emperor of Primal Might,"[19] and his temple name was Taizu ["Great Founder"].

Akûdai had eight sons who were not enthroned. Enthroned was his younger brother Sheng; he was the so-called Ukimai.[20] Sheng was enthroned and he proclaimed the year Tianhui 1. (Year 1 was *gǔi/mǎo* [1123].) In year 7 [1125], spring, Tianzuo of the Liao was captured by the Jin men. In moon XII of that year [January 1126], he then invaded our capital. In the spring of Jingkang 1 [1126], our court sliced off three strategic areas of Hedong and Hebei, made a treaty with them, and they returned. That winter, they came back again, and our capital fell. In the winter of Shaoxing 4 [1134], Sheng died at the age of sixty-one. (He had been on the throne for twelve years.) His posthumous title was "The Cultured and Ardent Emperor" and his temple name was Taizong ["Great Ancestor"].

He had eight sons who were not enthroned. Enthroned was Akûdai's grandson . . .

> *There follows a listing of all of Akûdai's and Ukimai's sons and a number of other major Wongian princes with their positions. This survey of Jurchen imperial genealogy and succession was primarily intended to enable his Southern Song readers to follow the imperial succession and the subsequent year slogans of their northern rival. We have thus omitted it here; the most important genealogical links may be found in the "Genealogy of the Jin Dynasty" in Appendix §2.4 (p. 188). The few events mentioned include the Jin prince Liang's murder of his emperor and seizure of the throne; his moving the capital to Yanjing (present-day Beijing), which was renamed as the Central*

---

17. Cai Jing (1047–1126) was a civil official, and Tong Guan (1054–1126) was a eunuch commander. Both served the Song dynasty, which at the time was hoping to "rescue" the Han area of Yanjing-Yunzhong from Kitan rule. Both were later blamed for the fiasco of the Song dynasty's alliance with the rising Jurchen Jin against the Kitan Liao dynasty and were executed in 1126.

18. A tael was both a traditional unit of weight, measuring about 1.4 ounces, and a monetary unit of value, equaling the value of a tael of pure silver. See the tables of weights and measures in Appendix §2.7 (p. 192). Chinese currency systems were also based on copper coins, which were assembled into strings of cash by being tied through the square hole in the center of the coins. One string of cash with 1,000 coins conventionally equaled a single silver tael in monetary value, although strings usually had fewer than the nominal number of 1,000 coins in them.

19. *Wǔyuán huángdì* 武元皇帝.

20. This Kitan or Jurchen name of unknown meaning is also found as "Ukima."

*Capital (Zhongdu); his unsuccessful invasion of the Southern Song; and his own death
at the hands of his generals while campaigning in Yangzhou. Liang (who was denied
canonization in the dynastic temple and is known to history as the Prince of Hailing)
was succeeded by his cousin Yong, the Prince of Ge. Li Xinchuan writes of him:*

Yong conducted himself with humanity and generosity and did not undertake
military actions; the Northerners called him a "Little Yao or Shun."[21] [His grandson and successor] Jing was enthroned and in *gēng/xū* [1190], he proclaimed the
Mingchang slogan. The slogan was changed to Cheng'an in *bǐng/chén* [1196] and
to Taihe in *xīn/yǒu* [1201]. In Taihe 6 [1206], North and South engaged in battle,
and after two more years, Jing died at age forty-one; it was on Jiading 1, XI, *bǐng/
chén* [December 29, 1208]. (He had been on the throne for twenty years.) His temple name was Zhangzong ["Model Ancestor"].

At first when Jing was to be enthroned, the Princes of Yue and Zheng both
expressed their resentment.[22] Jing summoned the Prince of Zheng and murdered
him (in Shaoxi 4, XI [December 1193]). The Prince of Yue had two sons. The
elder was titled Prince of Ai, and his mother was a royal concubine from the Zhao
family. The Prince of Ge[23] had loved him and bestowed on him a covenant cast in
iron. Jing hated him, but did not dare to kill him. The Prince of Ai made use of
living in the Upper Capital[24] to rebel, and the Prince of Yue was then executed by
Jing (in Qingyuan 1, V [June–July 1195]).

Jing died without any sons,[25] and only Yunji was still alive out of all Yong's
sons. Jing's favorite palace attendant, Palace Gateman Li[26] transmitted his last
command to Sahal, the Assistant Director of the Right in the Department of
State Affairs, and they jointly enthroned him. The Prince of Ai at the time was in
the Central Capital;[27] Yunji suspected that he might start a coup and imprisoned
him in Zhendingfu. He appointed Sahal as Grand Preceptor and Director of

---

21. Yao and Shun were two ideal emperors in China's mythical ancient history. Their purported
program of rule, based on apocryphal texts of the Warring States period and preserved in the
Confucian canons as the *Exalted Documents*, may be seen in Legge [1865] 1991, 1–51.

22. The Prince of Yue, whose personal name was Yunsheng, was the eldest son of Yong, the
emperor Shizong or the "Renovating Ancestor" of the Jin dynasty. The Prince of Zheng, personally named Yundao, was Yong's third son and held command of the Wuding Army. Jing was
the son of Yungong, Yong's second son and crown prince, who died before his father.

23. This was the title of Shizong before he ascended the throne; as a Song man, Li Xinchuan
preferred not to use his imperial title.

24. That is, Shangjing, in the symbolically important, but geographically remote, Jurchen homeland. Its ruins are not far from the modern city of Harbin.

25. This is not actually true, if sons by concubines are included. Congyi, who is mentioned
below, was a son of Jing by a concubine.

26. "Palace attendant" is *nèishì* 內侍; "palace gateman" is *huángmén* 黃門. The first is a general
term for palace eunuchs, the second a more specific title held by eunuchs in the palace service.
See Hucker 1985, §§4237, 2841.

27. That is, Zhongdu, usually called Yanjing in these sources. It was the main capital of the Jin
and located in the southwestern corner of present-day Beijing.

the Three Departments, and enfeoffed him as Prince Shen.[28] The next year he proclaimed year Da'an 1 (year 1 was *jǐ/sì* [1209]), which in *rén/shēn* [1212] was changed to Chongqing, and in *guǐ/yǒu* [1213] was changed to Zhining.

While Jing had been on the throne, Yunji was ordered to go to Jingzhou Prefecture[29] and receive the presentation of tribute from the Black Tatars. He saw that their prince Temujin was fierce, arrogant, and disrespectful and feared that he would cause calamity on the frontier. He wanted to go back and tell Jing to eliminate him, but it so happened that Jing had died of disease.

In Da'an 3 (year *xīn/wèi*; our dynasty's Jiading 4), spring, moon III [April–May 1211], as the Tatars came in to pay tribute, Yunji dispatched heavily armed soldiers to bivouack in the area "behind the mountains"[30] planning to attack them by surprise at the presentation grounds, and to then lead troops on a deep raid. He learned that someone in the caitiffs'[31] Jiün armies had called on the Tatars and warned them about the matter. The Tatars were suspicious and did not yet believe him. But when the informant came back again, the Tatars sent a man to spy out the truth. They then delayed and did not present tribute.

In the autumn, on the night of VII, 18 (day *dīng/mǎo*)[32] [July 27, 1211], the Tatars suddenly arrived; they battled with the Jin at Huihe River for a full three days with no decisive victory or defeat.[33] Temujin selected three thousand crack cavalrymen to charge and break their lines. The Jin army fell into chaos, and Temujin personally followed up his advantage with his main army.

Yunji sent orders posthaste to the Western Capital's Viceroy[34] He-Šire Zhizhong, to lead a large army to meet the enemy at Dashengdian. Zhizhong was a veteran general who understood military affairs and was good at battle.[35] Since

---

28. On the offices and titles mentioned in this paragraph, see the Introduction, pp. 32, 34.

29. The correct official graph for the prefecture was *jìng* 淨 (see e.g., *JS* 24.566), but Li Xinchuan uses the homonym *jìng* 靖, while Zhao Gong uses another homonym *jìng* 靜.

30. This phrase, "behind the mountains" (*shānhòu* 山後), is to be understood with the speaker facing south toward the Jin capital Yanjing (modern Beijing); it thus refers to the area north of the mountain ranges sheltering the capital. In modern times this is the northwestern Hebei and Chakhar area of central Inner Mongolia. In the Jin times this area was divided into three prefectures: Changzhou, Huanzhou, and Fuzhou, known as the "the prefectures behind the mountains."

31. Ch. *lǔ*: this derogatory Chinese term here refers to the Jurchens and their regime. See the Introduction, p. 25. But it is remarkable how little Li Xinchuan actually uses this term and other derogatory terms for the Jurchen regime, compared to other Southern Song writers.

32. The text here actually has *dīng/yǒu* 丁酉, but the eighteenth day of moon VII is actually *dīng/mǎo* 丁卯, so we have followed the corrected date. Such copyists' errors in the sexagenary cycle dates are quite common.

33. These Jin troops were under the command of Hûša, of the imperial Wongian surname, whose Chinese name was Chengyu. See his biography in *JS* 93.2065.

34. The Western Capital or Yunzhong is present-day Datong in northern Shanxi. The Jin adopted the Song system of multiple capitals; those outside the central capital, where the emperor usually stayed, were ruled by "viceroys" (Ch. *liúshǒu*). These viceroys held both civil and military powers and could operate outside their seat, as here.

35. Zhizhong is his Chinese name; in Zhao Gong's account, he appears always under his Jurchen name as Hûšahû. See his biography in *JS* 132.2832–39.

the enthronement of Yunji, he often had felt alienated, and at this point he was not willing to battle forcefully. Those under him observed this and consequently they suffered a great defeat. Zhizhong fled back with a hundred horsemen. Yunji was furious and dismissed him.[36]

The Tatar armies reached Cuiping Gap, and the Jin suffered another great defeat.[37]

On IX, 14 [October 22], they attacked Fengshengzhou Prefecture[38] and two days later sacked it. They advanced to Yehu Ridge and Yunji again sent an army to meet them, using carts to form a battle line, only to be greatly defeated again.[39]

In moon X [November–December], the Tatar armies reached Jìnshan[40] County, sixty-five miles[41] distant from Yanjing.

In Chongqing 1 (our dynasty's Jiading 5), spring, moon I [February 1212], the Tatar soldiers reached Juyong Pass. The senior general Wongian Fuhai abandoned the pass and took to his heels. Yunji long had been miserly, so his officials did not obey orders. Yunji discussed going himself to the Southern Capital (that is, Kaifengfu)[42] with an honor guard of 5,000.[43] It happened that five hundred men of the honor guard spurred each other on, vowing to meet the enemy with death before dishonor, and killed several hundred of the Tatar soldiers. The Tatar soldiers did not dare advance, and they asked some of the villagers they had captured, "How big is this army?" The villagers duped them saying, "Two hundred thousand." The Tatars, frightened, thus gathered up their troops and retreated.[44]

---

36. The Battle of Dashengdian must be the same as the battle known in sources derived from Mongolian-based accounts as the Battle of Huanrzui ("Badger's Mouth"). In this battle, we know that Zhizhong (Hûšahû) was the commander. The battlefield was north of Yehu Ridge, and as the northernmost of the great Jin-Mongol battles, was often mistakenly seen as being part of the early initial advance that led to the Battle of Huihe River. A consideration of all the sources, however, indicates that it took place at the end of the campaign season, when the Mongols had retreated and were being pursued by Jin forces under Zhizhong (Hûšahû). Although much briefer, Zhao Gong's chronology seems more accurate than Li Xinchuan's in this regard.

37. This account appears to be a continuation of that on the Battle of Huihe River.

38. This name of this prefecture had actually been changed in 1209 to Dexingfu, under which it appears in Peng and Xu's "Sketch," p. 124, and in Zhang Dehui's "Notes," p. 165.

39. Actually, Yehu Ridge, called *Hünegen Daba'a* or "Fox Pass" in Mongolian, is north of not just Fengshengzhou (Dexingfu) Prefecture but even the Huihe River and Cuiping Gap. Thus, the Tatars could not have "advanced" to Yehu Ridge. But such a reference would fit much better the circumstances of Battle of Dashengdian/Huanrzui. Thus, this sentence is probably another misplaced reference to the Battle of Dashengdian/Huanrzui, one that took place later, in February 1212, at the end of the campaign, after the Tatars had made their final retreat back to Inner Mongolia. The Jin armies were then ordered to advance and pursue the Mongols as they retreated north through the Yehu Ridge. They were then defeated as stated here.

40. The text here mistakenly has Jinshan 晉山, a homonym for the correct Jinshan 縉山.

41. Lit., 180 *lĭ.* See the tables of weights and measures in Appendix §2.7 (p. 192).

42. The Jin dynasty's Southern Capital had been the Song's main capital when they still held most of the North. Kaifengfu was its prefectural name, both under the Song and the Jin.

43. Here and below, "honor guard" translates *xìjūn* 細軍, lit., "precisely trained or excellent army."

44. This retreat from the plains outside the Jin capital of Yanjing was probably not the end of the story. Other sources indicate that the Jin armies under Zhizhong (Jurchen name Hûšahû)

In the autumn of Zhining 1 (our dynasty's Jiading 6), moon VII [July–August 1213], the Tatar soldiers came back to the region behind the mountains. The chief military commander Wongian Fuking[45] met the enemy but was defeated, and Yunji demoted him. In moon VIII [August–September], Hû-Šire Zhizhong was recalled as Vice Marshal on the Right, commanding 3,000 men of the special forces to go out and engage the enemy.[46] On day 20, or *wù/zǐ* [September 6], they marched out from Yanjing.

Previously, the Vice Marshal on the Left, Nanping, had pandered to Yunji's idea, and cancelled the system of military rewards; the common soldiers were enraged about it.[47] Zhizhong, following on the popular sentiment of indignation, wanted to depose Yunji, and so turned his troops around claiming to them that he would execute Nanping. On day 24, or *rén/chén* [September 10], the army arrived outside Donghuamen Gate. Zhizhong summoned Nanping to come for a council of war and stabbed him to death with his own blade.[48]

When the court heard of the incident, they closed all the gates. Zhizhong summoned Jinshou,[49] commander of the honor guard, and said to him, "I came here solely to execute a rebellious vassal;[50] I have no intention to rebel." Soon after, when the honor guard all came to rescue the emperor, Jinshou commanded them to stop. The soldiers were cowed by Zhizhong's prestige, and none dared make a move. Only Wongian Šanggian, commander of the Guanxi Heroes' Army, came leading five hundred men from his unit, but they were all killed by the special forces.[51] Impressed by Šanggian's valor, Zhizhong summoned Šanggian's father,

pursued the retreating Mongols north and tried to engage them at Yehu ("Wild Fox") Ridge and instead were soundly defeated. This was the famous Battle of Dashengdian or Huanrzui.

45. Fuking's Chinese name was Chenghui; he appears in Song Zizhen's "Spirit-Path Stele" as Wongian Chenghui.

46. Here and below, "special forces" translates *wǔyì jūn* 武藝軍, lit., "army of martial arts," referring to military forces that have received special training.

47. Nanping was a Jurchen, of the Tukdan surname. Scattered references to him in *JS* 13.296, 99. 2190, 2197, and 132.2836 add that he was not just a vice marshal but also prefect of the capital city, and hence a crucial figure who had to be eliminated if Zhizhong's coup was to succeed. Nanping's brother, Tukdan Ming, was prefect of the strategic Zhendingfu (see also his brother's brief biography in *JS* 120.2628).

48. The *Jinshi* says that Zhizhong personally speared Nanping as he rode out the gate and that once Nanping fell to the ground, his confederate Jinshou then cut off his head (*JS* 132.2836).

49. Li Xinchuan treats Jin as his surname and Shou as his name, but he was actually of the Jurchen Tukdan surname. (It is not known if he was any relation to Tukdan Nanping.) According to the *Jinshi*, Jinshou was much more closely involved in the coup than Li Xinchuan portrays him. In that account it is Jinshou whom Zhizhong sends to summon Nanping. Jinshou's assistance in the coup was rewarded with money and with the position of prefect and commander in Dongpingfu (see *JS* 13.297 and 132.2836–38).

50. "Vassal" or *chén* was the usual Chinese term for all of those who served the sovereign. It is often translated as "minister," although the term was also used, as here, for military officers as well as civilians. See Hucker 1985, §392. The relation of *chén* or vassal with the *jūn*, "sovereign" or "lord," was one of the fundamental social relations in Confucian ethics.

51. Guanxi is the area of what is now central Shaanxi, around Xi'an city. The Guanxi Heroes Army (*Guānxī dàhàn jūn* 關西大漢軍) was a volunteer unit outside the regular military structure.

Fuhai, and ordered him to persuade Šanggian to submit. Šanggian shouted out, "This old bandit wants to rebel against the court. How could I surrender to him?" and continued to fight with all his might. From morning to noon, he killed several tens of people with his own hands before dying with several arrows in his body. The blood from the soldiers and civilians killing each other filled the place.

Zhizhong then advanced to attack Donghuamen Gate. Yunji sent his son the Prince of Jiang to stand under the gate with an imperial proclamation calling on anyone to kill Zhizhong—even if a commoner he would be appointed prefect of Daxingfu[52] and hereditary commander of a battalion.[53] Neither soldier nor civilian responded. Zhizhong was about to set a fire to burn down the gate, but Haju,[54] the general guarding the gate, opened it up and Zhizong led his troops to the palace. The bodyguards all scattered. Zhizhong advanced as far as the Hall of Great Peace[55] when Yunji caught sight of Zhizhong and shouted out in the distance, "Where did the Sacred Lord order his vassal to go?" He replied, "Just back to the old residence!"[56] Yunji retreated into the empresses' chambers and asked them to go out with him together, but the empresses held him back, "If we go out, we'll be killed!" Zhizhong saw that he did not come out for a long time and so sent soldiers in to seize him. Yunji with his wives and children were all imprisoned together in the old residence.[57] Zhizhong then summoned Tamjêma, the eldest son of Xun (Prince Feng), to hand over the imperial seal to him.[58] On the night of day 26, or *jiǎ/wǔ* [September 12], Zhizhong deputed a palace attendant, Supervisor Li, to murder Yunji in his office.

On IX, 9, or *bǐng/wǔ* [September 24], the Prince Feng arrived at Yanjing, and Zhizhong led all the officials to welcome and do obeisance to him on the road.

---

52. Daxingfu was the prefecture that administered the Jin dynasty's Central Capital (Yanjing). The position would thus be equivalent to the mayor of the empire's capital city. The position was vacant because the previous office holder, Tukdan Nanping, had just been killed by Zhizhong (*JS* 13.296, 99.2197, 132.3836).

53. "Battalion" here translates *qiānhù jiā* 千戶家 or "Thousand-Household family." A *qiānhù* (written in Jurchen as *cengkû* or *minggan*) was a militia unit consisting of a thousand families. The Jurchens were all organized into such militia units, so to be appointed to such a position was to be made a member of the dynasty's Jurchen elite.

54. Haju is a common Jurchen name, and a number of such officials with that name were holding office in the capital around this time. We cannot positively identify this Haju with any of them.

55. Ch. *Dà'ān diàn* 大安殿.

56. "Old residence" is Ch. *jiùfǔ* 舊府. Yunji is referring to himself in the third person as the "Sacred Lord"; his rhetorical question is intended to point out that Zhizhong is acting completely outside imperial orders; Zhizhong's reply is cryptic, but seems to be a reference to the first office he held as a young man when he served as part of the bodyguard to the crown prince in the palace (*JS* 132.2832); in that sense, he was just returning to his "old residence" in the palace.

57. Again, this seems to be a reference to part of the private quarters, perhaps of the crown prince.

58. Xun (then titled Prince Feng) was the one whom Zhizhong planned to enthrone as the new emperor, but Xun was not in the capital at the time. Tamjêma, Xun's son, was in the capital, however. So, in order to show his sincerity, Zhizhong handed over the seal to Tamjêma pending Xun's arrival to ascend the throne.

He was then enthroned as emperor, proclaiming Zhenyou 1. Yunji was posthumously demoted to the Commandery Marquis of Donghai, while Zhizhong was appointed as Grand Preceptor, Chief Military Commander, and Director of the Three Departments, and was enfeoffed as Prince of Ze.

The Tatar soldiers reached Zijing Pass, seventy miles[59] from Yanjing. Zhizhong wanted to lure their soldiers south to Zhuozhou and Yizhou,[60] so he gathered his troops to attack them. The Tatars sacked Zhuozhou and Yizhou, and reaching the western bank of the Zaohe River, they wanted to cross the bridge. Zhizhong just then had a foot malady and presided over the battle while sitting in a cart, yet the Tatars suffered a great defeat.

The next day they engaged in battle again. Zhizhong's ulceration was so severe he was unable to go out; he dispatched Left Army Supervisor Geuki with 5,000 Jiün soldiers to hold them off.[61] As Geuki did not arrive in time, Zhizhong wanted to behead him. But considering Geuki's previous merits, Xun gave an imperial order that he be spared the death penalty. Zhizhong increased the number of his soldiers, and ordered him to go out again, saying, "If you win, then your crime will be redeemed; if you lose, then you will be executed without pardon." Geuki went out and battled from dusk until daybreak. Suddenly a big north wind arose, blowing stones and raising sand, so that they could not lift their faces. The Tatars took advantage of the wind to unleash fire and charge to the attack; Geuki's army totally collapsed.

Thinking to himself that he would certainly be killed by Zhizhong, Geuki thus led his Jiün army to surround Zhizhong's office, broke into his bedchamber, and killed him. He then withdrew and went to Yingtianmen Gate to await his punishment; it was X, 15, or day *xīn/hài* [November 28]. Since Geuki held the power over the troops, Xun did not dare punish him. Rather, he took into custody all those who had followed Zhizhong in killing those who crossed him, and killed them.

At this point, the Tatar ruler left his great chief Samuqa behind to besiege Yanjing [as he] personally led troops to ravage the prefectures of Hedong, Hebei, and Shandong. By the spring of Zhenyou 2 (our dynasty's Jiading 7 [1214]), the Tatars had sacked over ninety prefectures before regrouping their forces back at Yanjing. The Jin ruler Xun generously bribed Temujin and gave him Yunji's fourth daughter, Missy,[62] in marriage. He also sent Left Grand Councilor and Chief Military Commander, Wongian Fuking, with him as hostage. The Tatars thereupon returned.

---

59. Lit., 200 *li*. See the tables of weights and measures in Appendix §2.7 (p. 192).

60. The direction is actually not south, but northeast. Li seems to have misunderstood the position of Zijing Pass.

61. Geuki was a Jurchen general of the Juhung surname; his biography is in *JS* 106.2339–46.

62. Ch. *Xiǎo jiějie* 小姐姐. Li Xinchuan treats this as a name but, as he must have known, it is actually just a term of address for unmarried girls. *Xiǎojiě* is a general term for younger, unmarried females and *jiějie* means elder sister; so *xiǎo jiějie* perhaps means "the youngest of the older daughters." Li, being Chinese, knew it was not her name, but simply wrote down what was reported. Her Jurchen name was Yali (Ch. Yanli).

Henan Route Commander-General Pusan Siging[63] memorialized,[64] requesting that the capital be transferred to Kaifengfu and Xun approved it. He made Vice Grand Councilor Xu Ding[65] his commissioner to arrange lodging places along the road. Xun's nephew Congyi, Prince Huo, remonstrated, "The tombs of the ances-tors, the ancestral temple, the altars of soil and millet, the offices and storehouses— all of them are in Yanjing. How can it be right to just abandon them?" Xun said, "Yanjing is short on grain and cannot meet the needs of the court, the officials, and the armies. Now we are going temporarily to the Southern Capital. If, after one or two years, the grain stores are plentiful, then it will not be too late to return." Congyi begged to personally supervise the move, but Xun did not agree. Congyi became sick with worry and indignation. He died on V, 10, or *jiǎ/xū* [June 19].[66]

On day 18, or *rén/wǔ* [June 27], the Jin ruler set out from Yanjing through the Lizemen Gate, passing by Zhuozhou, Baozhou, and Zhongshanfu prefectures on southward. Reaching Zhendingfu, he stayed a few months. Setting out again and reaching Damingfu Route, he crossed the Yellow River at Xinwèizhou Prefecture to reach Kaifengfu, where an amnesty was proclaimed for the whole realm.

In the autumn, moon VIII, the Tatar armies once again besieged Yanjing and divided up the soldiers to descend on the districts and prefectures of the Central Plains.[67] They also sent messengers to Kaifengfu demanding compensation for their army in gold, silver, and the like; Xun gave it all to them. The next year, on V, 2 or *gēng/shēn* [May 31, 1215], the Tatars sacked Yanjing; the Chief Military Commander Wongian Fuking cut his throat and died.[68]

---

63. Pusan Siging (d. 1217) was a Jurchen military official; for his biography, see *JS* 101.2230–2233. Li Xinchuan's current text gives his name as Pusa Qijin 蒲撒七斤; he appears in the *Jinshi*, however, as Pusan Qijin or with his Chinese given name Duan. *Púsān* 僕散 was the transcription of Pusan, the Kitan version of the Jurchen surname Fusan. At the time, however, it was virtually a homonym of *Púxiān* 蒲鮮, which was the Chinese version, via Kitan, of another Jurchen surname Fusen. It is likely that Li Xinchuan originally wrote *Púsān* 蒲散, which was later corrupted by scribes to *Púsā* 蒲撒, written very similarly. Although *Qījīn* appears to be just a Chinese name meaning "seven catties," Persian versions of the name show that it was actually read in Jurchen as "Siging."

64. In the Chinese bureaucratic system, *zòu* 奏 were "formal policy statements submitted to the ruler" (Kroll 2015, s.v. *zòu*, 632b). This term as a noun and a verb is conventionally translated as "memorial" or "to memorialize."

65. Xu Ding (d. 1226) combined both hereditary status (he was the son of a Han grand coun-cilor) and scholarly achievement (he passed the highest level of the examination system in 1188). See his biography in *JS* 108.2373–84.

66. Congyi's Jurchen name was Alin and he was a son of the Jǐng (Zhangzong) by a concubine. See *JS* 93.2057.

67. Ch. *Zhōngyuán*; these are the plains around the lower Yellow River and by extension the entire heartland of North China.

68. It is likely that the original draft ended the narrative here and then went directly into the summary paragraph "The Jin have had ninety-eight years from when Akûdai was proclaimed emperor . . ." Li Xinchuan seems to have added the following notice about the "Flowery Cap Army" sometime in 1217 when a members of that army from Shandong began sending envoys to the Southern Song dynasty.

There was a clerk in the Board of Revenue, Guo Zhong, who was from Yuzhou Prefecture. He led soldiers and civilians from behind the mountains to attack the Tatars and drove them out. Jin people later called his force the "Flowery Cap Army."[69]

The Jin have had ninety-eight years from when Akûdai was proclaimed emperor and they have lost their country. Hedong and Hebei having been harrassed by the Tatars, Shandong has rebelled. The Jin are blocked off in the east by the Yellow River and in the west by Tongguan Pass. Their territorial situation is increasingly cramped, so in their plans they cast covetous eyes on the Huaihe and Hanjiang valleys to the south. Indeed, the sprouts of war are rising again. (In the recently circulated *Record of the Southern Transfer*, the descriptions are full of errors. It must be a forgery written by a Southerner, so I have not used it.)[70]

§252. The Western Xia Knock at the Passes

In the following brief chapter, Li Xinchuan lists the successive sixteen reigns of the Tangut kingdom from the late Tang to his own time, together with a few major events of the kingdom's rule. Up to the Jurchen conquest of the North, the Xia were a major foreign policy irritant for the Song. Then Tangut relations with the Southern Song were cut off, but the chapter concludes with a few notes on how the Mongol invasions were resulting in a renewal of ties:

Previously, after the Jin annexed the Liao lands, [the Tangut ruler] Qianshun[71] served them very conscientiously. The Jin followed the old example of the Liao and enfeoffed him as the King of Xia and the Xia annually brought tribute for a hundred years up to the present.[72] In Jiading 2 [1209], the Xia began to be attacked by the Tatars, and they sent messengers to the Jin to ask for assistance. The Jin ruler Yunji had recently been enthroned and was not able to aid them. As the Tatars

---

69. Ch. *Huāmào jūn* 花帽軍. Guo Zhong was later given the Jurchen imperial surname Wongian as a mark of honor, and he appears in the Jin dynasty history as Wongian Zhongyuan; see his biography in *JS* 103.2265–68. The discrepancy in his given name, either Zhong or Zhongyuan, may be a mistake on Li Xinchuan's part, or may be explained by Zhong being his given name and Zhongyuan his courtesy name.

70. Ch. *Nanqian lu*. This work survives today in a MS with an attribution not to a Southern Song writer, but to a Jin one (see Zhang Shiyan 1996). The source is obviously a completely fictional romance, but surprisingly, Zhao Gong in §3 of his "Memorandum" (see p. 76) also refers to it as a potentially historical source. Li Xinchuan would have been appalled to know that some time after the fall of the Jin dynasty, an anonymous historian at the Mongol court even combined this work with Li Xinchuan's text to create a new version of Jin dynasty history. See Yuwen Maozhao 2011. We thank Jiajun Zou for his assistance in identifying this work and for forwarding to us a scanned copy of the facsimile edition.

71. Qianshun was the personal name of the Tangut ruler with the posthumous temple name of Chongzong ("Exalted Ancestor"; r. 1086–1139).

72. This estimate includes the period of Xia relations with the Liao Empire.

reached Xingzhou and Lingzhou[73] before returning, the Xia resented [the Jin failure to help]. The Jin also were afflicted by the Tatars, and as their power declined more and more, the Xia kingdom revolted, proclaiming Guangding ["Radiant Security"] 1 in the spring of *xīn/wèi* [1211]. In Guangding 4 [1214] their Left Privy Councilor and Supreme Bandit-Suppression Commissioner on the Tibetan Route, Wanqing Yiyong, ordered the ethnic monk Gambo Babo[74] to present two wax-sealed messages[75] to Dangchang Fort in Xihezhou Prefecture wishing to ally with our dynasty for a two-pronged attack to recover our former territory. The Area Commander-in-Chief of Ethnic Troops Fu Yi forwarded it to his superiors.[76] This was in Jiading 7, VII [August–September 1214]. Dong Renfu, who had just entered Sichuan, did not report it to the court, and consequently, intelligence about the caitiffs was cut off.[77]

§253. The Tatars Cross the Frontier

The Complete Story of the Mong Kingdom:[78]

The ancestors of the Tatars were of the same race as the Jurchens, both probably descendants of the Marghat. The latter's kingdom was called Murkit in the Yuan Wèi, Qi, and the Zhou eras [i.e., 386–581]; by Sui times [581–618] it was called

---

73. Xingzhou and Lingzhou are present-day Yinchuan and Lingwu in Ningxia Province; Xingzhou was the capital of the Tangut kingdom. They were known as Egrighaya (or Erighaya) and Dörsekei (or Dörmekei), respectively, in Mongolian.

74. "Ethnic" here is *fān*, a relatively neutral term meaning "non-Han," particularly those in a westerly direction. Gambo Babo combines the Tangut title *gambo*, with the common Tibetan name man's name *dPa'-bo*, "hero."

75. A "wax-sealed message" (Ch. *làshū* 蠟書, lit., "wax message") was a type of message that was wrapped up in a wax ball, so that the envoy could not open it without it being known. The envoy would have to present it to the intended recipient and deliver his own oral message without knowing the contents of the written message. If the oral and written messages diverged, or if the wax was tampered with, the recipient would know the envoy was untrustworthy.

76. As above, "ethnic" here translates *fān*. About these ethnic soldiers, the *Songshi* or "History of the Song" writes, "Among the Qiang barbarians of the Northwest, the tribes have no internal unity. Those who defended the border passes were called 'Cooked Households' and the rest were called 'Raw Households'" (*SS* 191.4750). Fu Yi belonged to one such "Cooked Household," serving the Song as a border soldier, and was probably of Tangut origin. His Han name indicates that even if he was not Han, he was well integrated into Han society.

77. Dong Renfu is mentioned elsewhere as an official assigned by the court to Sichuan; see Li Xinchuan, vol. 2, §83, 661. "Caitiffs" as a rule should be the Jin, but it is perhaps referring to the Mongols here.

78. When Li Xinchuan uses the graph *méng* alone, he is implicitly conflating two different names that he will mention below: "Monggus" (Ch. *Měnggǔsī*) and "Mongol" (Ch. *Měnggǔ*). We have therefore simply transliterated the term as Mong, and not attempted to distinguish the two. Although the graph 蒙 is read as *méng* in modern Mandarin, it was read as *mong* in thirteenth-century Chinese and we spell it as such here.

Marghat.[79] The latter's land was 2,100 miles[80] straight northeast from Chang'an[81] and bordered on the sea to the east. They were separated into scores of tribes with names like "Black River," "White Mountain," and the like.[82] The "White Mountain" ones were originally vassals of Goguryeo,[83] but when the Tang wiped out Goguryeo, their survivors were incorporated into Balhae;[84] only the "Black River" ones maintained their territory intact. When Balhae flourished, the Marghat all submitted to them. Later they were attacked by the Qai and the Kitan, and the tribes split up. Those living on the upper reaches of the Huntong River were called Jurchens (the Huntong River is the Yalu);[85] they are remnants of the "Black River" race.

Those of them living in the Yinshan Mountains[86] called themselves the Tatars and during the late Tang and the Five Dynasties had frequent contacts with China. They each repeatedly paid tribute in the reigns of both Song Taizu and Taizong,[87] in all cases coming by way of Lingwu. But with Li Jiqian's rebellion, all ties were cut off and there was no further contact.[88] Consequently they were

---

79. The Yuan Wèi, Qi, and Zhou dynasties were all in North China. They were ruled by an elite of mixed para-Mongolic Tabghach and ethnic Chinese officials, with the emperors being of non-ethnic Chinese origin. (The Zhou here is not to be confused with the classic Zhou dynasty of China's pre-imperial past.) The Sui dynasty was founded by an ethnic Chinese general who seized power from the last Zhou emperor and proceeded to reunify China in AD 589.

80. Lit., 6,000 *li*. See the tables of weights and measures in Appendix §2.7 (p. 192).

81. Chang'an is the modern city of Xi'an in Shaanxi Province. It was the capital of many ancient and medieval Chinese dynasties.

82. The "Black River" is now called the Amur River, and the "White Mountain" is the Changbai "Ever-White" or Baekdu "White-Headed" Mountain on the Sino-Korean border.

83. Goguryeo (also spelled Koguryŏ) was a kingdom originating along the banks of the Yalu River, along the borders of present-day Liaoning Province in China and North Korea. The kingdom's start is conventionally dated to 37 BC. In later centuries the kingdom dominated the area of southeast Manchuria and northern Korea until its destruction by the Tang dynasty in AD 668. The kingdom used Chinese in writing. Evidence of the vernacular language used is scarce and ambiguous. Korean historians, however, have always treated this kingdom along with Silla as one of the early Korean dynasties. Its name in an abbreviated form, Goryeo (Koryŏ), is the origin of the English "Korea."

84. Balhae (in the Korean reading; Bohai is the modern Mandarin reading) was a kingdom ruling the area around northeastern Korea, eastern Manchuria, and the Vladivostok area of the Russian Far East, lasting from 698–926. Like Goguryeo, this kingdom used Chinese for official purposes; the vernacular language is not clear, but may have been related to Korean.

85. Li Xinchuan is confused about the river names. The Huntong is not the Yalu, but rather the Chinese name for the Sungari River in central Manchuria, known today as the Songhua River.

86. By mentioning the Yinshan Mountains in west-central Inner Mongolia, Li Xinchuan is suddenly shifting his focus far to the west.

87. Song Taizu ("Great Founder") and Taizong ("Great Ancestor") were the posthumous names of the Song dynasty founder Zhao Kuangyin (r. 960–976) and his successor and brother Zhao Kuangyi (r. 976–997).

88. Li Jiqian (963–1004), from a family of Tangut commanders in the Shaanxi-Inner Mongolia border area, served under the Song. In 982, when he learned of Song Taizong's plan to dismiss

subjugated by the Kitans. Song Shenzong[89] once wanted to make use of the road through Qingtang[90] to summon them to submit, yet in the end he was unable to reach them.

The Tatars are all brave, fierce, and good at warfare. Those closer to the Han lands are called "Cooked Tatars"; they grow sorghum and millet, using flat-bottomed earthenware pots to boil those grains for food. Those farther away are called "Raw Tatars"; they live by bow hunting alone and use neither [metal] weapons nor armor, their arrowheads being made solely of bone.[91] That is because their land does not produce iron. Though the Kitans maintained contact with them through peaceful trade, the ban on exporting iron to them was very strict. When the Jin took over Hedong, they discontinued use of tin-alloy coins, and when they arrested Liu Yu, they also discontinued iron coins. Consequently, the iron coins of Shaanxi and Hedong all came into Tatar hands, and they began to make weapons in a big way, so that their kingdom became increasingly powerful.[92]

At the time, the Jin men were in their golden age, and the Tatars presented annual tribute, so the Jin created the Northeast Bandit-Suppression Commissioner to handle them in unified fashion. It was when the Prince of Wei [r. 1208–1213][93] ascended the throne that Temujin first rebelled and titled himself Emperor Chinggis. All of Shandong, Hedong, and Hebei[94] was despoiled although they were unable to hold them.[95]

---

his family from office, he led a revolt and in 990 enthroned himself as the king of Xia. His revolt was the beginning of the rise of the Tangut Xia dynasty.

89. Song Shenzong was the sixth Song emperor and reigned from 1067 to 1085. Shenzong or "Divine Ancestor" is his posthumous name; his personal name was Zhao Xu.

90. Present-day Xining city in Qinghai province.

91. On this distinction of Raw and Cooked, see Zhao Gong's "Memorandum," pp. 72–73, and the Introduction, p. 13.

92. This sentence refers to various currencies briefly used during the tumultuous rise of the Jin and the expulsion of the Song from North China. Chinese currency was traditionally based on round copper coins with square holes. In the frontier, however, special coins of iron or tin were commonly issued to fund military operations. Large-scale iron coinage, for example, was used in conjunction with the Song's military buildup against the Tangut Xia dynasty in Shaanxi (von Glahn 2016, 233; Peng 1994, vol. 1, 332). When Cai Jing (mentioned on p. 49) was trying to recover the Yanjing-Yunzhong area for the Song, he also circulated coins of copper-tin alloy in the Hedong area (Peng 1994, vol. 1, 344). Similarly, after the Song had been driven out of North China, the Jin set up a Han Chinese general, Liu Yu, as their puppet ruler in North China. He minted his own so-called Fuchang coins from 1130 to 1138. When the Jin dynasty abolished his regime and extended their rule over all North China, Liu Yu's iron Fuchang coins were demonetized (Peng 1994, vol. 2, 464, pl. lxii.6). However, Li Xinchuan's claim that the demonetization of these coins allowed the Tatars to subvert the embargo on the export of iron to the Mongolian plateau is questionable; in practice the quality of such iron coins was deliberately altered through alloying to make them unusable for utensils or weapons (Peng 1994, I 344–45).

93. Prince of Wei was Yunji's title before he became emperor.

94. Lit., "the two He's."

95. At this point, Li Xinchuan inserts an episode that appears out of place. We have indented this passage to mark it as in some sense parenthetic. The passage gives the story of the

On the night of Jiading 7, I, 9 or *jiǎ/xū* [Feb. 19 or 20, 1214[96]], at the third drum watch,[97] from the northern bank at Wutuanpu in Zhongli County (Haozhou Prefecture), three horsemen crossed the Huaihe River coming southward.[98] When the Military and Naval Inspector Liang Shi asked why they had come, the three men produced a pouch of documents and a map painted on silk, saying they had been sent by Chinggis, the Prince[99] of the Tatars, to present a map and request military aid.[100] The next day, the prefect learned of it and dispatched Li Xing, a commander-general of crack troops, with a party to say that, without a directive from the court, the prefecture did not dare to accept the items, and a directive was given to dismiss them. The day after that, the horsemen were met at Chumiaogang,[101] and then sent off on rafts to leave. Before this, Yang An'er—Li Quan's father-in-law—had gathered soldiers and rebelled when he saw that the caitiffs' regime[102] was falling into chaos. Yang had ravaged Shandong, relying on the mountains and seas to advance and retreat unexpectedly. The Tatars, having besieged Yanjing but failing to take it, had sent soldiers to ravage the area of Shandong where the bandits often rose up in response to them. The Tatar force that reached Ji'nanfu dispatched thirty-seven cavalry to protect those three men on their approach to our frontier. They later sent 300 soldiers to escort them, passing Pizhou Prefecture and seizing boats to cross over the Yellow River, then heading westward. Once they got to Haozhou

---

first—unsuccessful—attempt by the new Mongol state to open relations with the Southern Song. It appears to be placed here, whether originally or in a later draft, as a way of illustrating how the events that follow might have become known to the Southerners.

96. The date is given in two ways, by the number in the month, and by the day as numbered in the sixty-year cycle. The date is, however, contradictory, with the ninth of the first moon being February 20 in the Gregorian calendar, while the *jiǎ/xū* date is February 19.

97. The third of the five watches of the night, thus from around 1:00 a.m. to 4:00 a.m.

98. Near present-day Fengyang city in Anhui Province. The Huaihe River was the northern frontier of the Southern Song territory, marking its border with the Jin Empire.

99. Here the term is *wángzǐ* 王子, or "prince," in its literal meaning as "son of the king." The title is of course lower than the imperial one that Chinggis normally claimed. Was Chinggis Khan diminishing his titles deliberately to appeal to the Southern Song or was this how his status was referred to in Southern Song official reports?

100. Ch. *nàdì qǐngbīng* 納地請兵, lit., "present land and request soldiers." To present a map of one's territory was a classic gesture of submission in East Asian politico-military etiquette.

101. Chumiaogang or "Chu Temple Dike"; this is probably at or near the present-day Chumiao-cun "Chu Temple Village" in Huaiyuan County, Anhui Province. Here we follow the suggestion of Ma Xiaolin and Qiu Zhirong to emend *zhūmiàogāng* 諸廟堽, "various temples and dikes," to Chumiaogang, "Chu Temple Dike." Chu was a minor deity often worshiped by boatmen. We may assume that at the time this was a well-known local place near the ferry dock where the horsemen were entertained politely before being sent back.

102. Ch. *lǔrén*: this derogatory Chinese term refers to the Jurchens and their regime. See the Introduction, p. 25.

Prefecture, their road was cut off and they were unable to return. They hid out among Hongxian County's Bailu Lakes.[103] After three days, the county sent men to detain them and remand them to Sizhou Prefecture. Some people said of those three men that one was a Tatar interpreter, one was the Jin dynasty's associate administrator of Mozhou Prefecture who had been captured, and one was a Han fellow. As a consequence, the border officials were warned that if any similar cases should occur in the future, [the interlopers] should be driven off, and that violators would be subject to military law. Moreover, such incidents were to be reported to the court. At that time, Temujin truly had become very powerful. Even so, he still lived in his old country. He established a mobile secretariat[104] in the Yanjing-Yunzhong area and ordered his great vassal Samuqa to manage it; he is the so-called Grand Preceptor and Prince of State. His great general is called Qamuli.[105]

There was also a Mong kingdom to the northeast of the Jurchens. The Tang called them the Mong'u tribe, the Jin also called them Mong'u, as well as calling them Monggu.[106] The people did not cook their food, could see in pitch dark, used shark skin[107] for armor, and could deflect flying arrows. They began to rebel in the early Shaoxing years [1131–1162] and the Chief Military Commander Zongbi campaigned against them year after year but was unable to quell them. (Zongbi was also called Uju, the so-called Fourth Prince.) In the end he was unable to suppress them, so instead he divided up his troops to occupy the strategic points and bought them off generously. Their chief also usurped the title "Ancestral

---

103. This lake cannot be identified, but the terrain is crisscrossed by rivers and canals and dotted with lakes left behind by the periodic flooding of the Yellow River. The three men presumably took refuge on an island in one such lake.

104. Ch. *xíngshěng* 行省, or "mobile secretariat": this institution later became the origin of Chinese provincial administrations. See the Introduction, p. 34.

105. This name is probably a corruption of "Muqali," whose reign as viceroy in North China is described at length in Zhao Gong's account. The modern texts here have *Hābùr* 哈布爾, which is an exact transcription of Mongolian "Qabul." But there is no Qabul known in the Mongol administration at this point. (Qabul Khan was Chinggis Khan's great-grandfather and cannot be in question here.) Since the transcription of Qabul uses graphs that were very characteristic of the "rectification" of graphs used to transcribe Mongolian and Manchu names ordered by the Qianlong emperor (r. 1735–1796), we suspect that the text originally had *Hémóulǐ* 合謀理, which appears below at the end of this chapter as a version of Muqali's name, but with the *hé/qa* and *móu/mu* syllables reversed. We have thus chosen to treat it the same way here, pending verification with a genuine pre-eighteenth-century text.

106. The full version of these names was Monggus, with a final -*s* as a plural.

107. Fish skins were a famous part of the dress of the peoples in Amur River and Sakhalin Island (Levin and Potapov 1964, 689, 706, 723, 725–26, 741, 752, 770). For images of such clothes and films of their manufacture, see the websites "Nivkh Fish Skin Robe" and "Skin Clothing Online—Nationalmuseet." Salmon is the usual material, however; shark skin is not known to be used for clothing.

Emperor." By the time of the Jin ruler Liang [1149–1161],[108] they had long since been a border menace along with the Tatars. The Mongs having invaded the Jin kingdom, they took Kitan and Han women as wives and concubines. The children born susequently were no longer entirely like the Mongs, and they gradually began to cook their food. At this point, the Tatars consequently called themselves the "Great Mongol State," and the border officials called them Mong-Tatars. Yet the two kingdoms were situated to the east and west of one another, with several thousand *li* between them[109]; it is unknown why they were given the same name.

In this golden age of the Jin kingdom, they established the Northeast Bandit-Suppression Commission to guard against the Mong'u and the Koreans, and the Southwest Bandit-Suppression Commission to subordinate the Tatars and the Western Xia in a unified fashion. The area later occupied by the Mong'u was where Ukimai, when he was establishing the dynasty, built twenty-seven militia forts. Yet the Tatar frontier borders on Linhuangfu Prefecture to the east, neighbors on the Xia to the west, in the south stretches to Jingzhou Prefecture, and in the north reaches the kingdom of the giants.[110] They have neither walls nor moats, nor houses, nor mansions, but instead make felt tents for which they choose dwelling places that have the most beneficial water and grass. They neither plow nor spin, but cut skins for fur coats and use oxen and sheep as staple foods. The people are all cunning, determined, and fond of killing. Ignorant of the lunar calendar, they simply take each greening of the grass as one year. They also have no writing. Whenever they transfer troops and horses, they plait grass to indicate the rendevous and have people transmit this by relay, as fast as a shooting star. Or they break sticks as tallies and carve several marks on them, each party receiving one half. When the deployed army is met, the tallies are matched for verification.

The so-called "Raw Tatars" are also divided into White and Black.[111] The present-day Temujin is a Black Tatar; along with the White Tatars, they were all subject to the Jin. Every year their kings would go themselves to the tribute-presentation grounds on the Jin frontier and personally pay their submission. The Jin would reciprocate with bestowals according to how their behavior was assessed; they would not allow them to cross the border.[112]

In Mingchang 1 of the Jin ruler Jing (year *gēng/xū*, our dynasty's Shaoxi 1 [1190]), the younger brother of the king of the White Tatars, Sesui, murdered

---

108. This is the emperor known to history by the title Prince of Hailing; he was considered a usurper by later Jin emperors and denied canonization in the imperial temple.

109. A *li* is a little over a third of a mile. See the tables of weights and measures in Appendix §2.7 (p. 192).

110. This is the mythical Buddhist northern continent of Uttarakuru.

111. On this distinction of White and Black, see Zhao Gong's "Memorandum," p. 72, and the Introduction, p. 12.

112. "Allow" could be interpreted as "compel" here; however, from Zhao Gong's "Memorandum," p. 84, one may surmise that being allowed to cross the frontier and trade in China was a welcome opportunity, which the Tatars resented being deprived of.

his elder brother and took the throne in his place. Sesui's son Baisbo[113] was two years old at the time. The Jin men took him back to their country and had him fostered in the family of a Black River battalion commander.[114] In the spring of Taihe 7 (year *dīng/mǎo*, our dynasty's Kaixi 3 [1207]), when [the younger brother of] Sesui[115] came to Huanzhou[116] Prefecture to pay tribute, the Jin took advantage of his not being on his guard, got him drunk, and murdered him.[117] They restored Baisbo as king and sent him back to his kingdom. Earlier, when Baisbo was in the Black River battalion commander's family, he had been pleased with the commander's daughter, and at this point he wanted to take her as his wife. But Jing did not accede to it. Baisbo, resentful and angry, defected to the Black Tatars.

In this way the Black Tatars became increasingly powerful. Having gradually unified the clan lands, they then raised a great army and attacked Hexi.[118] Within several years all the districts and prefectures of Hexi had been sacked. They even forcibly carried off a bogus princess of the Xia kingdom in departing, and the Xia actually had to serve them as vassals.[119]

In the spring of Da'an 3 (year *xīn/wèi*, our dynasty's Jiading 4 [1211]), Temujin came to pay tribute. The Jin ruler Yunji was going to ambush him, but the plan was detected. That autumn, the Tatars first went into rebellion. In the spring of Chongqing 2 (year *guǐ/yǒu*, our dynasty's Jiading 6 [1213]), he then attacked Yanjing. That autumn, Yunji was murdered. (For details on the events above, see the chapter "The Jurchens Move South.") Temujin then left Samuqa to keep Yanjing under siege and then marshaled the forty-six campaign commanders of the surrendered Han army under Yang Boyu and Liu Bolin and combined them with the Tatars' great army. Dividing into three routes, they attacked and took the

---

113. Li Xinchuan's text has *Báibōsī* 白波斯 throughout, but all the parallels prove beyond a doubt that he, or more likely an early copyist, mixed up the order of the second and third graphs. *Báibōsī* is thus a mistake for *Báisībō* 白斯波, i.e., Baisbo (the *sī* is being used for a final -*s*). We have thus restored the correct form throughout. This is the Baisbu of Zhao Gong's account.

114. Lit., *qiānhù jiā* or "a thousand-household family." A *qiānhù* (written in Jurchen as *cengkû* or *minggan*) was a militia unit consisting of a thousand families.

115. The text reads simply "Sesui" but one must assume "younger brother" was omitted.

116. The text here has mistakenly substituted the homonymous Chinese graph *huán* 環 for the correct *huán* 桓.

117. Li Xinchuan was unaware of the background here. Mongolian sources, such as the *Secret History of the Mongols*, record that Sesui's younger brother Ala-Qush in 1204 had opened diplomatic relations with Chinggis Khan, then unifying Mongolia. This was part of a larger unrest among the Inner Mongolian people after 1206 described in Zhao's "Memorandum," p. 84. It was undoubtedly the prospect of the White Tatars going over in a block to Chinggis Khan that led the Jin to put him to death.

118. Hexi, or "West of the River," refers to the area of Gansu Province west of the Yellow River. It is commonly used to refer to the Tangut or Western Xia kingdom.

119. Chinggis Khan invaded the Xia in 1205 and again in the winter of 1207–1208. The Tangut princess was married to Chinggis Khan after the third campaign in the autumn of 1210.

prefectures and towns of Hebei, Hedong, and Shandong. Boyu had been a clerk in Yuzhou prefecture; Bolin had been an archer from Jining County.[120]

At this time, since all their soldiers had been transferred to defend the zone "behind the mountains," the routes in the Central Plains had no military protection. Villagers everywhere were drafted as soldiers and sent up onto city walls to defend them. The Tatars drove their family members onto the attack, and fathers and sons and older and younger brothers would often shout out to each other from afar in mutual recognition. For this reason, the people had no will to fight, and all the walled towns that the Tatars reached surrendered at the first drum roll. From moon XI in the winter of Zhenyou 1 (Zhenyou 1 was the same as Chongqing 2; it is Zhining 1 [1213]) to moon I of spring, Zhenyou 2, in all they sacked over ninety prefectures; not a single place they passed escaped being wasted and destroyed. For several thousand *li* across Hebei, Hedong, and Shandong, the massacre of the people was almost total. Gold, silk, lads, lasses, cattle, sheep, horses, and other livestock: all were rolled up like a mat and carried off. Houses and cottages were burned down, the walls and ramparts became deserted ruins! Only Damingfu, Zhendingfu, Qingzhou, Yùnzhou, Pizhou, Haizhou, Wozhou, Shunzhou, and Tongzhou Prefectures had troops who maintained a solid defense and could not be sacked.

In moon II, the Tatars returned back to Yanjing. Yanjing's grain supplies were depleted, and four or five out of ten soldiers and civilians died of starvation. The Jin ruler Xun dispatched men to negotiate peace. Temujin's demands were exorbitant: a princess of theirs, with an escort of 10 generals and a 100 man honor guard; a princess's entourage of 500 man- and maidservants; 3,000 items of clothing in multi-colored silk embroidery; 3,000 carriage horses; gold, silver, pearls, jade, and such. He also asked that Left Grand Councilor Wongian Fuking serve as hostage. Xun agreed to everything. When Temujin sent his people to select the girl, there were seven princesses available, but only Yunji's young daughter, Missy,[121] stood out as elegant and intelligent, so she was given to him. Xun was even ordered to do obeisance from a distance in the direction of the Tatar's country; Xun did not dare refuse. And since Samuqa had besieged Yanjing for a long time but had never taken captives or plundered, Temujin wanted that army to be rewarded with gold and silk. Xun agreed to this, too, and the Tatars thereupon returned.

Juyong Pass is almost forty miles[122] northwest of Yanjing. The road passes through a narrow gorge, and the several tens of thousands of soldiers defending it wanted to wait for the Tatar army's return and attack them there. But Wongian Fuking, who was there in the Tatar army, transmitted the Jin ruler's command that, since peace had already been negotiated with the Tatars, unauthorized military moves were not permitted. So no one dared take action. Once the Tatars

---

120. Yang Boyu is not otherwise known; Liu Bolin and his son Liu Heima became important generals in Mongol service; see Zhao Gong's "Memorandum," p. 79, and Peng Daya's "Sketch," p. 124.

121. Ch. *xiǎo jiějie*. This is a family term of address, not a name (see note 62, p. 55).

122. Lit., 110 *li*. See the tables of weights and measures in Appendix §2.7 (p. 192).

had gone through the pass, before heading home they took the several tens of thousands of young adult lads and lasses whom they had looted from Shandong, Hebei, and Hedong and killed them all, before finally wending their way home. It was moon III of that year.

In moon V, the Jin ruler Xun moved the capital to Bianjing.[123] The Tatars heard about this and said, "To move right after making peace—this shows they are suspicious and still harbor resentment. They purposely talked peace only as a means to forestall us." In the autumn, moon VIII, they again led troops to attack the counties and prefectures of the Central Plains. In the winter, the Jiün army of Yanjing went into revolt and besieged Yanjing together with the Tatars. In the spring of Zhenyou 3 (*yǐ/hài*; our dynasty's Jiading 8 [1215]), a relief army of 50,000 from Dongpingfu reached Anci; they met a Tatar army and collapsed without a fight. An army of 80,000 from Damingfu reached Gu'an but also collapsed and scattered. Only an army of 40,000 from Zhendingfu, having rendezvoused with 10,000 soldiers from Baozhou and Zhuozhou, engaged the Tartar army at Fort Xuanfeng for two whole days, until their grain ran out and they were defeated. From that time, there was no communication in or out of Yanjing. In moon V, Yanjing was sacked.[124]

In Shandong great hordes of bandits rose up. Yang An'er was originally a tanner in Zizhou Prefecture. During the Taihe years [1201–1208] of the Jin ruler Jǐng, he killed a man and became a fugitive from the law. He became a bandit in the Taihang Mountains with over a thousand followers. Jǐng got him to surrender with a summons; in substitution for the death sentence he was banished to the Upper Capital. With the Tatar incursions, the Jin made him a vice commander-general and ordered him to recruit an "Ever-Victorious Army" of 3,000 men to meet the enemy in battle. His army was defeated and scurried off, his men returning to Shandong where they regrouped. When the Jin launched a punitive campaign against them, An'er put out to sea with several of his followers and was killed by the ship's sailors.[125]

Another was "Hao the Eighth," whose name was Hao Yi. In the spring of Zhenyou 2 (year *jiǎ/xū*; our dynasty's Jiading 7 [1214]), he occupied Shandong and rebelled, usurping the dynastic title Great Qi, and proclaiming Shuntian 1.[126]

---

123. This is Kaifengfu, south of the Yellow River, the Southern Capital of the Jurchens.

124. It is likely that the original draft ended the narrative here, and then went directly into the summary paragraph beginning, "It is true that the Tatars are only motivated by greed . . . ." Li seems to have added the following sundry bits of information about the Shandong bandits, the "Flowery Cap Army," the Mongol expedition through Tongguan Pass, Zhang Fu, Zhang Jin, and Xiao Wu'anu sometime in 1217 based on information shared by Shandong rebels when they began sending envoys to the Southern Song dynasty.

125. Yang An'er died in 1214; his band was taken over by his younger sister, Yang Miaozhen or "Fourth Lady" (*sì niángzi* 四娘子). She eventually married another Shandong man, Li Quan (1190–1231), and they merged their bands. She and Li Quan submitted first to the Song (1218) and then to the Mongols (1227). See Wu 2002.

126. Shuntian, or "Obedient to Heaven."

The Jin men dispatched the "Flowery Cap Army"[127] and he was captured alive and publicly dismembered in Kaifengfu.

Another notorious bandit was Liu Erzu. His daughter, Miss Liu, also gathered several tens of thousands of followers, but they were all smashed by the "Flowery Cap Army."[128]

In the fall,[129] the Tatar army crossed the Yellow River from Hedong and attacked Tongguan Pass. They were unable to take it that way, so they went round-about via small roads in the Songshan Mountains in a dash to Ruzhou Prefecture. When they met mountain streams, they would quickly interlock their iron lances and join them to make bridges for crossing. Thus, Tongguan Pass was lost. The Jin ruler recalled the "Flowery Cap Army" from Shandong posthaste. In moon X, the Tatar armies got as far as Xinghuaying, seven miles[130] from Bianjing, but the "Flowery Cap Army" attacked and defeated them. The Tatar army then took Tongguan Pass again. At the Xijin Ford in Sanmen, they took advantage of the Yellow River freezing over; strewing ashes over it, they led the troops to cross over back to Hedong. Since then, they have not invaded Henan again.

The Jin ruler then appointed Manager of Government Affairs Xu Ding as grand marshal, with a special mandate to defend the passes and suburbs. Yet, [to the northwest] among the prefectures in Shaanxi there were also ones that had been sacked. To the south of Yanjing, only in a few prefectures like Xiongzhou and Bazhou in the area long ago called the Three Passes, with its deep obstructions of dikes and moats, were the Tatars unable to enter.[131] Two Jin generals, Zhang Fu and Zhang Jin, occupied the Xin'an Military Prefecture[132] to defend the place (Yanshan Mountain being sixty-five miles[133] to the north).

There was also the Liaodong Pacification Commissioner Xiao Wu'anu, originally a man of the Liao. Exploiting the chaos among the Jurchens, he proclaimed himself an emperor. With his base in the seven routes of Liaodong, he has aimed

---

127. This was the army of volunteers from the North China-Inner Mongolian border commanded by Guo Zhong, who is referred to in the account of "The Jurchens Move South," p. 57.

128. Liu Erzu was killed in 1215. There is no corroboration about his daughter; "Miss Liu" (*Liú Xiǎojiě*) may be a confusion with Yang An'er's sister Miaozhen (see note 125, p. 66), or may be another woman leader in this movement.

129. Although the text implies that the year was 1215, it was actually 1216, and thus one of the latest events recorded in this work.

130. Lit., 20 *lǐ*. See the tables of weights and measures in Appendix §2.7 (p. 192).

131. These dikes and moats were situated along the Juma and Nanyi Rivers, which cut east to west across the North China plain. This system of waterways and forests had been the Song's old defense line against the Liao (Chen 2018; Zhang 2016; Tackett 2008) and the system was now reconstructed to hold off the Mongols. This resistance in Xin'an continued into the reign of Öködei Khan and is mentioned in Song Zizhen's "Spirit-Path Stele."

132. "Xin'an Military Prefecture" (Xin'anjun) was its name during the eleventh century when it was the center of the Song's defense system against the Kitan armies. After the Jin conquered the North it was demoted to an ordinary county.

133. Lit., 180 *lǐ*. See the tables of weights and measures in Appendix §2.7 (p. 192).

Temple scene from a mural in a Jin-era Buddhist monastery illustrating the most splendid architecture of the period.

to lead his troops and take over the Yanjing, Yunzhong, Hebei, and Hedong areas.[134] The Tatars have not been able to destroy him.

It is true that the Tatars are only motivated by greed and in the beginning had no far-reaching plans. After they sacked Hebei and Hedong, the wasteland stretched a thousand *lǐ* with all signs of habitation wiped out. The grandeur and beauty of Yanjing's palaces were the crowning achievement of ancient and modern times. When the Tatars saw them, they were so stunned and frightened they did not dare look up. Yet not long afterward the fires set by the undisciplined soldiers were not extinguished for over a month. At first the money and material that they amassed was of no use to them, to the point that silver was used to make horses' troughs and gold to make liquor jars—the biggest of these taking several thousand taels.[135] Their customs are crude and uncouth, without any distinction between lord and vassal. Samuqa's residence even has golden ornaments and

134. In the original "Yan, Dai, Wèi, Jìn." These are the classical names for areas in North China; we have translated according to that sense.

135. This would be roughly several hundred pounds. See the tables of weights and measures in Appendix §2.7 (p. 192).

an imperial[136] bedstead and his footrest is a golden stool. His extravagance and presumptuousness are such as this, and his requisitions and censures never end; the people of Yanjing suffer greatly under him.

After the Jin ruler Xun had moved south, he sent messengers repeatedly to sue for peace, but these efforts were not heeded even as the bribes paid to the Tatars did not cease. Temujin sympathized with Xun's attitude and wanted to come to terms. But Samuqa was ashamed of still having no military achievements and adamantly resisted doing so. Temujin said to him, "It's as if I had caught all the water deer in my hunting ground and only a single rabbit was left. For so many years you have not been able to catch it, so now you ought to let it go." Samuqa did not agree and sent a man to tell the Jin ruler, "If you desire to negotiate peace, then abandon your imperial titles and acknowledge yourself a vassal; then we will enfeoff you as a prince." But the Jin officials in turn would not agree. When someone spoke to Xun saying he wished with his death to wipe out the empire's disgrace, Xun's indignation also was aroused.

Distant affairs cannot be known completely; a summary has been recorded here for the time being. (Temüjin[137]: in a Xia document, this is what is known as Temujin. Samuqa: Shandong people[138] sometimes call him Mohulo, and sometimes Qamuli, but I do not know which is correct.[139] It is also said that of the three people who were sent by the Tatars to cross the Huaihe, one of them was the Hebei scholar Zhang Sanshen.)

---

136. "Imperial," lit., *long*, "dragon."

137. Temüjin: here the published text has *Tèmòjīn* 特默津, which was the officially approved version of Chinggis Khan's name in Chinese from the transcription reforms of the eighteenth-century Qianlong reign on. It is most unlikely that Li Xinchuan originally wrote this; we have assumed that the official Qianlong-era orthography was used because Li's original text had the official Mongol-era orthography for the ruler's name in Chinese, which was *Tiěmùzhēn*. To represent that "official" usage in the translation, we have used the most correct, scholarly spelling of his name.

138. These "Shandong people" are most likely some of the above-mentioned Shandong bandits who in 1217 began to send envoys to the Southern court, sharing information on the situation in the North in order to entice the Southern Song to support them.

139. Li Xinchuan here has confused Samuqa Ba'atur with Muqali who in 1217 would be declared the Prince of State and is described at length in Zhao Gong's "Memorandum." The form *Móhóuluó* appears in Zhao Gong. *Hémóulǐ* is an obvious error for *Móuhélǐ*; that name too appears in Zhao Gong, with the graphs in the correct order. But since the same error in the order of the graphs appears above, in the account of the abortive Mongol mission to the Song, it likely dates back to Li Xinchuan's original text. We have thus written it in the Mongolian fashion, but with a similar transposition of syllables to simulate the effect the name would have on an informed reader such as Zhao Gong.

A Memorandum on the Mong-Tatars

By Zhao Gong of the Southern Song

The following work is the earliest known general description of the Chinggisid Mongols and their customs in any language. Many Chinese and Mongolian sources incorporate earlier material and Li Xinchuan accurately summarized envoys' reports, but this is the only eyewitness source on the empire that actually dates from the time of the founding itself. Internal evidence of this text indicates that it was written in 1221, by a person with the given name Gong who was an ambassador from the Southern Song regime in South China to the Mongols then ruling North China. Although the work is based on the author's own observations, it is written in the third person. The author refers to himself several times as Gong and twice as "our [i.e., Song] envoy."[1]

Tao Zongyi (1316–1403), by copying this work into his reading notes around 1370, preserved the only copy of it during the tumultuous Yuan-Ming transition. His original must have been anonymous, but Tao assumed that the envoy with the given name Gong must have been the famous Southern Song general Meng Gong (1195–1246). The twentieth-century scholar Wang Guowei, however, showed that the chronology of this account is inconsistent with the general's known biography. After combing through Song dynasty sources, he found that one Zhao Gong, holding the minor office of "Consultant to the Account Keeper of the Campaign Commander," had been independently dispatched north to Mongol-held territory in the year xīn/sì *(1221) by Jia She, the Southern Song dynasty's "Huainan East Circuit Military Commissioner," an important frontier military official. This minor official Zhao Gong undoubtedly was the author of this record.*[2]

Gong's account is mostly based on his personal observations. He traveled from the Song frontier north to Yanjing (modern Beijing) and back, without ever seeing the Mongolian steppe in person. He cites a number of documents, although more to back up his claims about changes in the dating systems and to verify which Han officials were in power than to discuss their content. He also cites one now lost work, Li Daliang's Zheng Meng ji, *on the Jin campaigns against the Monggus kingdom, written in the mid-twelfth century. Li Xinchuan also cites Li Daliang's work, and it is likely that the resemblances between Zhao Gong's account and that in Li Xinchuan's* Random Notes from Court and Country since the Jianyan Period *stem from that common reading.*

---

1. Ch. *wǒ shǐrén* 我使人. The passages with his name we have translated as "I, Gong" while the latter passages we have translated as "I [or "me"] as Song envoy"

2. See Wang Guowei 1962, 459–61.

The Chinese name of the work, Meng-Da beilu, *is literally the "A Memorandum³ on the Meng-Da."* Měng *is the first syllable of Chinese* Měnggǔ *for "Mongol(s)" and* Dá *is the first syllable of Chinese* Dádá *for "Tatar(s)." At first glance, it would thus be about the Mongol-Tatars and that is how previous translators have rendered it. But Zhao Gong uses* Měng *throughout as an abbreviation not for* Měnggǔ *"Mongol," but for* Měnggǔsī *or Monggus, the name of the defunct Amur valley kingdom that Li Xinchuan and other early Southern Song observers tried to link to the Mongols, even as they could not help but realize the differences. The one instance Zhao does use* Měnggǔ, *in a citation of the empire's official Chinese language usage, he is clearly taking it, too, as an abbreviation for* Měnggǔsī *or Monggus. To preserve the ambiguity between "Monggus" and "Mongol" we thus translate the title not as a "Memorandum on the Mongol-Tatars," but as a "Memorandum on the Mong-Tatars."*

§1. Establishment of the Kingdom

When the Tatars first arose, their location was northwest of the Kitans and their lineage stemmed from a separate branch of the Shatuo.⁴ Hence they have not been heard about in past historical periods. There are three branches of them, called the White, the Black, and the Raw.⁵

Those called the White Tatars⁶ have a slightly more delicate appearance, and in character they are respectful, cautious, and filial. At funerals for a mother or father, they slash their faces and weep, and whenever I rode alongside any one of them who did not look repulsive but whose cheeks had scars from knife cuts, if I asked, "Are you a White Tatar?" he would say "Yes." Whenever they take Chinese⁷ lads and lasses as plunder, they teach them and then send them home. In their conversations with people they show human feeling. At present in the kingdom of the descendants of this tribe the princess Beki of the Tatar lord Chinggis has power over affairs. The vice-commissioner who recently came to our Song

---

3. What we translate here as "Memorandum" is *bèilù* 備錄 or "record prepared [against loss]." This seems to be an early forbear of the late imperial Chinese term *bèiwàng lù* 備忘錄, lit., "record prepared against forgetting," i.e., a "memorandum." We thus use "memorandum" for *bèilù* as well, a translation that fits the position of the recorder and the nature of the record.

4. The Shatuo were a mixed Turco-Sogdian people who settled in the area of present-day Shanxi Province in North China. See the Introduction, p. 6.

5. Zhao Gong here mixes two different ways of classifying the Tatars: White vs. Black, and Raw vs. Cooked. On these distinctions see Li Xinchuan's discussion of the Tatars (pp. 60, 63) and the Introduction, pp. 12–13.

6. The White Tatars are known elsewhere as the Öng'üt or Önggüd. Zhao Gong is correct to describe them as descendants of the Shatuo. Their country is referred to as Tenduc by Marco Polo, from Tiande (pronounced Tendok in Middle Mandarin) Military Prefecture in Inner Mongolia. See Polo 2016, §74 (62).

7. Ch. *Zhōngguó*, "Middle Kingdom" or "Middle Realm." On this term, see the Introduction, p. 28.

to pay respects, Subqan, is a White Tatar. Whenever I would ride alongside him, Subqan would make courteous conversation, and when receiving expressions of sympathy, he would say, "Enduring hardship is not praiseworthy. Please take no note of it."

Those called Raw Tatars are very poor; moreover, they are crude and incompetent. They can only mount their horses and follow along with the rest.

The present emperor Chinggis and his generals and great ministers are all Black Tatars.

On the whole, the Tatars are not very tall, the tallest not exceeding five feet and three or four inches,[8] nor are they plump or fleshy. Their faces are broad and vertically have compact cheekbones. Their eyes have no upper fold, and they grow extremely little facial hair, so their appearance is rather ugly. The Tatar lord Temujin differs in that he is of noble bearing with a broad forehead and long whiskers and cuts a heroic, robust figure. Now called Chinggis, he is the son of the *paiza* chief Gie-leu[9]—a "*paiza* chief" in this country being the chief of ten men.[10] As he is now the lord who established the kingdom, so, borrowing the title, they call him "Emperor" Chinggis. With his campaigns to the east and his conquests to the west, his country has become very powerful.

§2. The First Rise of the Tatar Ruler

The present Emperor Chinggis was born in year *jiǎ/xū* [1154]. Originally his country had no sexagenary cycle dating, so now, it is easier to base one's record on what they they say [their birth year was] than to tell their actual ages.[11] In their custom, each time the grass grows green is one year, so if someone asks one of them his age, he says how many times the grass has greened. Also, once when I asked one of them what month and day he was born, he laughed and replied, "I never knew it in the first place, nor can I remember how many springs and autumns it has been." Whenever they see a full moon, they consider it one month, and if they see that the greening of the grass is very delayed, only then do they know that this year has an intercalary month.

Chinggis, when small, was taken prisoner by men of the Jin and held as a slave.[12] Only after more than ten years did he escape and return; thus, he has

---

8. Lit., one *chǐ* and two to three *cùn*. See the table of measurements in Appendix §2.7 (p. 192).

9. Chinggis Khan's father was named Yesükei; what this name "Gie-leu" (modern Mandarin *Jiélóu*) represents is a riddle.

10. A *paiza* chief was called that due to the tablet or badge of authority or *paiza* that they carried. See Peng and Xu's "Sketch," pp. 112, 113. For the number of men under his command, the Zhang, Fu₃, Uang, and Shen MSS have "thousand" (*qiān* 千) while the Zhao, Niu, and ζ texts read "ten" (*shí* 十). We follow the latter texts. (For these terms for the texts, see p. 180.)

11. On the Chinese sexagenary, or sixty-year, cycle, see Peng and Xu's "Sketch," p. 105, and the Introduction, p. 31.

12. All accounts of Temüjin's rise agree that he spent time in captivity; they disagree, however, on who the captors were. Zhao Gong here says he was held by the Jin dynasty, while William of

a thorough knowledge of Jin affairs. His character is both brave and bold. His largeness of spirit can encompass a great following. He reveres Heaven and Earth and values loyalty. The name "Temujin" which circulates is his childhood name.[13] He has never had a surname, nor does he have a legal name subject to taboo.[14] In recent years, as certain Jurchen officials who defected to him have been employed, they have borrowed the title and called him "Emperor Chinggis." Some say that "Chinggis" is a translation of the phrase "Endowed by Heaven."[15]

§3. The Dynastic Title and Year Slogan[16]

Neighboring the Tatar country to the south are the Jiün clans, to the east and the west are the Shatuo and other tribes.[17] In olden times there was the Monggus kingdom, which during the Jin people's bogus Tianhui years [1123–1137], also once harassed the Jin caitiffs, causing them distress.[18] The Jin caitiffs at one point engaged them in battle, but later they made peace with them by presenting gold and silk. In Li Daliang's *Zheng Meng ji* ["Notes on Campaigns against the Mong"],[19] it says, "A Mong man[20] once changed the year slogan to Tianxing and called himself the Great Founder, the Primal and Luminous Emperor."[21] The

---

Rubruck (§26.2) says he was captured by the Tangut kingdom. The Mongolian accounts, however, say he was captured by rivals in Mongolia, either the Tayichi'ut or the Merkit.

13. On the confusion over "childhood names" found also in Peng and Xu's "Sketch," see the Introduction, pp. 37–38.

14. Ch. *mínghùi* 名諱. The use of a Chinese man's *míng* or legal name was avoided by those subordinate to him, an avoidance that was particular strict for emperors, where it was called a *hùi* or taboo. See the Introduction, p. 38.

15. Ch. *tiāncì* 天賜.

16. Chinese emperors proclaimed "year slogans," which their subjects would use for dating. See the Introduction, pp. 30–31.

17. On the Jiün, self-governing auxiliary troops under the Jin dynasty, see §10 "The Campaigns and Conquests," p. 84, and the Introduction, pp. 4, 13–14. On the Turco-Sogdian Shatuo, see §1 "Establishment of the Kingdom," p. 72, and the Introduction, p. 6.

18. Southern Song writers regularly used *wěi*, or "bogus, fabricated, forged," and *lǔ*, or "prisoner, captive, slave, caitiff," to refer to Jin dynasty institutions and people. See the Introduction, pp. 19, 25, 31, 40.

19. This work is quoted occasionally by Li Xinchuan, but has not survived. The author's name here is given as Li Liang, but Cao Yuanzhong (p. 6r) has identified his correct name as Li Daliang. Native to Xiongzhou Prefecture's Guiyi County, he was the son of a military official of the Song dynasty. Father and son surrendered together to the Jin, and Li Daliang went on to hold office under the Jurchens.

20. When Zhao Gong and Li Xinchuan use the single graph *měng* alone, they are implicitly conflating the term "Monggus" (Ch. *Měnggǔsī*) mentioned above and the name "Mongol" (Ch. *Měnggǔ*) mentioned below. We have therefore simply translated the term as Mong, and not attempted to distinguish the two.

21. Tianxiang is "Restored by Heaven." His title in Chinese is *Tàizǔ Yuánmíng huángdì* 太祖元明皇帝. Both *Tàizǔ*, "Great Founder," and *Yuánmíng huángdì*, "Primal and Luminous Emperor," are

present-day Tatars, however, are very simple and barbarous and have almost no institutions. I, Gong, have often looked into that statement, and learned that even the remnants of the Mong were ravaged and eliminated long ago. In general, whether northern regimes extended a thousand *lĭ*[22] or only a hundred *lĭ*, they rise and fall with no regularity.

When the present-day Tatars first arose, they had absolutely no writing, so whenever they issued orders or dispatched envoys back and forth, they count on their fingers to remember things.[23] When serving as envoys, they do not dare to add or subtract even a single word from their message; this is their country's custom. As their customs are so simple and since the Turkestanis[24] are their neighbors, with whose country they carry on barter and trade along the Two Rivers,[25] down to the present the documents that they use themselves in communicating with other countries are all written in Turkestani graphs, which look like Chinese musical notation for the flute.[26]

In the last two years, because Jin dynasty officials who defected or surrendered had nowhere else to survive and wanted to make themselves useful to this new regime, they began to teach them writing for intercourse with the Jin, actually using Chinese graphs. In the spring of last year, in all the documents that I, Gong, saw in circulation, they still used the term "great court"[27] and named the years simply "rabbit year" [1219] or "dragon year" [1220].[28] Only last year did they

---

typical posthumous titles (see the Introduction, p. 39). For a barbarian prince to take such titles while still alive would strike literate East Asian scholars, Jin or Song alike, as a ludicrous ritual solecism.

22. A *lĭ* is a little over half a kilometer or a third of a mile.

23. All the MSS here have *kèzhĭ* 刻指, "cut their fingers"; however, this must be a scribal error for *dǎozhĭ* 倒指, "count on their fingers," which is also said to be a practice of the Mongols in Peng and Xu's "Sketch," p. 105.

24. "Turkestani" here is Ch. *Húihú*. Originally meaning the Uyghur Empire in Mongolia, it later evolved into *Húihúi*, and after the Mongol period came to mean "Muslim." Here we translate it as "Turkestani"; see the Introduction, p. 27.

25. Zhang, Fu₃, Uang, and Shen MSS here read *Xīhé* 西河 "Western River" while Zhao, Niu, and ζ texts read as *Liǎnghé* 兩河 "Two Rivers." With Thomas Allsen (1989, 93), we prefer the reading of *Liǎnghé*, but our interpretation of the "two rivers" differs. He takes this as a reference to the Chinese regions Hebei, i.e., "North of the [Yellow] River" and Henan, i.e., "South of the [Yellow] River," but since the Jin dynasty still controlled both sides of the Yellow River at this time, this is implausible. Instead we think this is more likely a reference to the two rivers Onan and Kelüren that defined Chinggis Khan's homeland in Mongolia.

26. "Turkestani graphs" here is a reference to the Uyghur script that was adopted by the Mongols to write their language.

27. Ch. *Dàcháo* 大朝; this term commonly appears on decrees and coinage of the early Mongol Empire as a term for the state. It also appears on the Mongols' Islamic coinage as *al-Ūrdū al-Ā'zam* "the Exalted Ordo." *Ordo* or "tent palace" is the Mongolian mobile court; the original, however, is plural: *Yekes Ordas* or "Great Ordos" (Whaley 2001, 5–8).

28. Gong's point here is that the Mongols, in addition to not yet using proper "year slogans," used only the twelve-animal cycle and not the full sexagenary, or sixty-year, cycle. See Peng and Xu's "Sketch," p. 105 and the Introduction, pp. 31–32.

change and call it *gēng/chén* year [1220], and what they now call *xīn/sì* year is the present one [1221].[29]

In addition, the Mong were admired as a brave nation and therefore the dynasty was titled the "Great Mongol State"[30]; this is also something that the fugitive Jurchen high officials taught them. I, Gong, saw the Acting Emperor, Muqali, and he always said he was of "we Tatars," and all these great ministers and marshals always refer to themselves as "we Tatars";[31] they do not know what this "Mong" word refers to.[32] Whatever name they use for their kingdom, whatever year name they use, and whatever writings they circulate, it is all solely what the fugitive ministers, who know writing and apply forced analogies, have taught them. According to the *Record of the Southern Transfer*,[33] it is written that the Tatars issued a proclamation to the Jin dynasty dated "ninth year of the dragon and tiger"; this is wrong. In my humble opinion, to change or delay the yearly sequence certainly is something that the ministers who deserted from the Jin caitiffs taught them. To choose their imperial birthday as a celebration—still more certain it is they would have to teach them how to start the year count over upon establishing a new year slogan.[34]

§4. The Crown Princes and Princes of the Blood

The brothers in Emperor Chinggis's family were four in all, and Chinggis is the eldest. The eldest of the imperial younger brothers died in battle long ago.[35] The

---

29. In official use, the Chinese always used the ten heavenly stems and twelve earthly branches together, and used only the ancient names *zǐ*, *chóu*, *yín*, etc., the animal names of the twelve "earthly branches." The animal cycle names are used only informally, never in government documents. When writing Mongolian, however, the Mongols used only the twelve-animal cycle through the end of the dynasty, even for official documents.

30. Mongol here is *Měnggǔ*; this is the standard Chinese way to transcribe the Mongolian word *Mongghol* "Mongol." However, *Měnggǔ* works just as well, if not better, as an abbreviation of the name "Monggus," which Zhao Gong mentions above, and that is obviously how he took it. The statement is thus more logical in the Chinese than it can really be made to sound in English.

31. The blockprinted ζ text reads simply *wǒ* 我, "we," but the Zhao, Niu, Zhang, Uang, and Shen MSS read *wǒ Dádá* 我韃靼, "we Tatars."

32. Since, as Zhao Gong has already stated, the term *Yeke Mongghol Ulus*, or "Great Mongol State," was already in use as the official title of the new empire, the "Mong" which they did not know must have been the Monggus kingdom mentioned at the beginning of this section.

33. Ch. *Nanqian lu*. On this historical novel, also mentioned by Li Xinchuan, see note 70 (p. 57) to Li Xinchuan's chapter of the Jurchens (end of his §251).

34. The text of this last sentence is certainly corrupt. To make minimal sense of it, we have emended the *zhuàn* 撰, "compose, compile," of all codices to the similarly written graph *xuǎn* 選, "select, choose." There is probably also a missing verb phrase as well, but that cannot be so easily reconstructed.

35. Chinggis Khan's eldest full brother was Jochi Qasar (b. 1164?), whose last known event was the 1213–1214 campaign against the Jin dynasty. But the reference to an early death could also

second imperial younger brother, named Belgudei Noyê,[36] is known to be in the empire. The third imperial younger brother is named Temuge Otchin. Those whom he has assembled are mostly his own men and horses, and he is good in battle with many achievements to his credit.

Chinggis has a very large number of sons. The eldest, Biyin, died in battle attacking the Western Capital at Yunzhong during the defeat of the Jin dynasty.[37] The second son now is the Senior Crown Prince, named Yochi, the Third Crown Prince is named Okodai, the Fourth is named Telleu, and the Fifth is named Longsun. All of them were born of the primary empress.[38] Below them are ten or so others, who are sons of concubines. There are seven daughters of his, and the eldest princess is named Ojin Beki,[39] who has now been given in marriage to Imperial Son-in-Law Botu. The second princess is Ariq Bayin[40] who is commonly called Lady Beki and who was previously given in marriage to a fugitive official of the Jin dynasty, Baisbu.[41]

---

be a reference to his second oldest younger brother, Qachi'un (b. 1166?), who appears to have died even before Chinggis Khan had completed the unification of Mongolia.

36. *Noyê* is Zhao Gong's rendering, probably influenced by Kitan, of Mongolian *noyan*, "commander." The text has only *Nuó*, but originally must have read *Nuóyē* 那耶.

37. The Western Capital or Yunzhong is modern Datong in northern Shanxi province. The site of the capital was also known as the county of Yunzhong, and the prefecture of Datongfu. There is no record of any son of Chinggis Khan dying at Yunzhong, but Chinggis Khan himself was struck by an arrow during an unsuccessful siege of the city in the autumn of 1212 (*YS* 1.16).

38. This list of Chinggis's five sons by his primary empress presents several problems, soluble and insoluble. Yochi (modern Ch. *Yuēzhí* < Yo-ji), Okodai (the text has *Ādài* 阿戴, which is an error for **Ākědài* 阿可戴 < Okodai), and Telleu (modern Ch. *Tiānlóu* < Tienleu for **Telleu) are obviously Jochi, Öködei, and Tolui, in very approximate transcription. Insoluble are the following problems: Why is Cha'adai missing? And who are the otherwise unknown Biyin (< Bayan? Bigin?), who supposedly died at Yunzhong, and Longsun, whose name is not even Mongolian? *Lóngsūn* 龍孫 means "dragon's grandson"; since the dragon is the imperial symbol par excellence, has a Chinese title for one of Chinggis's grandchildren been misunderstood as a name of one of his sons?

39. The blockprinted ζ text reads *Āqí Biēyè* 阿其 鼈拽; the Zhao, Niu, Zhang, Uang, and Shen MSS read *Āzhēn Biēyè* 阿真 鼈拽. Wang Guowei had already divined *zhēn* as the correct reading for the second graph; *Āzhēn*, or Ojin in the Yuan pronunciation, represents the name Qoajin, in a form with an omitted *Q-* (see Pelliot 1944). *Biēyè* must represent Mongolian *Beki*, "princess" and we emend the text to *Biējǐ* 鼈撆, which was pronounced Bie-ki in Yuan Chinese.

40. Zhao Gong here has confused Ariq Bayan, who was the previous wife of Ala-Qush Digit-Quri, with Alaqai Beki, who was the Chinggisid princess first promised to the Öng'üt regent Ala-Qush Digit-Quri and then, when he was killed in a coup d'état, given to his nephew, Baisbu. See Atwood 2014b, 522, 531–32 n. 43, 45–46. For Bayin, we follow the ζ text's reading of *Bǎiyīn* 百因, and not the various corruptions such as *Bǎiguó* 百国 (Zhao, Zhang), *Bǎimù* 百目 (Uang, Shen), or *Bǐguó* 比國 (Niu). The correct text's *Bǎiyīn* is a fairly accurate transcription of Turco-Mongolian *bayan*, "rich."

41. Nephew of the Öng'üt vassal of the Jin Ala-Qush Digit-Quri (*digit-quri* was a title of a frontier chief), who went over to Chinggis Khan and was promised Chinggis Khan's daughter Alaqai Beki as his bride. Before the marriage could be consummated, however, he was killed by the Jin (see the account of Li Xinchuan, where he appears as Baisbo). Baisbu was his native name; his Chinese name was Zhenguo, pronounced as Chingüi or Šingüi. After Chinggis Khan conquered

He died, so she lives as a widow,[42] managing the affairs of the White Tatar kingdom and reading the canons every day. She has several thousand lady-officials who serve her, but all the decisions about campaigning and executions come from her personally. The third princess, called "Fivey,"[43] has been given in marriage to the son of the imperial maternal uncle who is Director of the Department of State Affairs.[44] In addition there are numerous grandsons, whose names are not yet known.

§5. The Generals and Meritorious Ministers

The one most outstanding in honor is their Grand Preceptor, the Prince of State, Moqlei,[45] which is his childhood name. The people in China address him as Mohulo, and in his edicts and conferments he is called Muqali. These are variations resulting from heavier or weaker sounds in the northern and southern pronunciation.[46] Known as Commander-in-Chief Entrusted with the Civilized World's Cavalry and Infantry, Grand Preceptor of the Mobile Secretariat, and Prince of State, he is a Black Tatar. For the past ten years, he has been campaigning to the east and punishing to the west, inspiring awe in both barbarians and Chinese.[47] All the great affairs of the conquest are decided by him personally, so he is called the Acting Emperor and in all his clothing and institutions he uses the rituals appropriate to a Son of Heaven. He has an elder brother called Jilger Noyê,[48] who has 1,000 cavalrymen himself, but holds no office. He has two younger brothers, the older of whom is called Moge, and is known to be in the

the Jin, he put Baisbu/Chingüi on the throne and married Alaqai Beki to him. See Atwood 2014b, 522–24 and 531 n. 40.

42. Alaqai may have been alive in 1237 when Peng Daya and Xu Ting wrote their account (see their "Sketch," p. 123). Baisbu had died by 1219, leaving behind one son by Alaqai, named Negüdei. Alaqai later married a cousin of Baisbu, but survived him as well; after 1237 Negüdei became ruler over the White Tatars.

43. Ch. *āwǔ* 阿五. *Ā*- is a personal prefix, indicating familiarity and a junior position.

44. The "imperial maternal uncle who is Director of the Department of State Affairs" is Alchi Noyê, as mentioned below. Although Alchi's sons did marry princesses from the imperial family, they were grand-daughters, not daughters, of Chinggis Khan. But he did have an adoptive son, Chikü, who married Chinggis Khan's daughter Tümelün; she is probably the one meant by "Fivey." See Atwood 2014/2015. On the Department of State Affairs, see the Introduction, p. 32.

45. The ζ text and the manuscripts all read *zhú* 助 for the last syllable, but we follow Wang Guowei's emendation to *lèi* 肋.

46. The three versions are *Mòhēilèi*, *Móhóuluó*, and *Móuhélǐ*, which correspond to a Mongolian original of Moqlei, Mohulo, and Muqali, respectively. The latter two of these versions are also mentioned here by Li Xinchuan. In Mongolian, the name was officially pronounced as "Muqali," but often as "Moqlai." On honorary titles such as "Grand Preceptor" and "Prince of State," see the Introduction, p. 34.

47. "Barbarians and Chinese": *Yí-Xià*. On these terms see the Introduction, pp. 24, 26, 27–28.

48. The codices reflect a reading of Ch. *Jìlǐgē-nuó* 計里哥那, but *jì* 計 (Yuan pronunciation, *gì*) should be emended to *zhī* 汁 (Yuan pronunciation *jì*), and *nuó* should be emended to *nuóyē*. "Jilger" is probably Mongolian *chilger* "slender."

bodyguards around Chinggis. The second is Daisun Gui-Ong,[49] who constantly follows as an attendant there.[50] The Prince of State always harangues the generals and officers in his unit like his own brothers, only addressing them by their childhood names, and not allowing them to use any other. The Prince of State only has one son, named Bo'ol.[51] He has a handsome appearance and deportment, and does not approve of shaving in the *pójiāo* style, but only wraps around a cloth for a turban and wears tight clothes.[52] He can speak the languages of several countries.

After him one called Grand Mentor Tugha is now[53] Duke of State; his reputation is second to Mohulo.[54]

There is also Jebe, whose office is also very elevated; he currently follows Chinggis, supervising his heaviest troops.

After him is Alchi Noyê, who at present has been entrusted as Director of the Department of State Affairs, and is the younger brother of Chinggis's primary empress. Under him are over 10,000 cavalry soldiers, and those he commands are rather law-abiding. The Tatars themselves say that those who follow the Prince of State are all bad, while those who follow the Director of the Department of State Affairs are all good.

After him is one called Liu Bolin, who is from Yunneizhou Prefecture in the Yanjing area.[55] Previously, he served as a chief commanding the troops of the Jin; he then fled and surrendered to the Tatar lord. He has a son who is extremely brave, and when the Tatar lord Temujin's eldest son died in battle, he then had

---

49. The title *Gūiwáng* 歸王 is a mistaken Chinese back translation of the Mongolian *Güi-Ong* or *Güyeng*, itself a version of the Chinese *Guówáng* 國王, "Prince of State." Daisun's title was actually the lower-ranking "Commandery Prince" (*Jùnwáng*; Hucker 1985, §1800).

50. The account here agrees more or less with that of *YS* 119.2929, in which Muqali is the second of five sons. Daisun, the third son and Muqali's younger brother, is the by far the best known of the other brothers (see Rashiduddin 1998/1999, 41, 228, 278; *YS* 119.2936, 2942, 148.3506). Although Zhao Gong implies that Daisun was in the West with Chinggis Khan, other sources show that he was in North China at the time. Persian sources also mention a brother of Muqali and Daisun commanding a thousand, but do not give his name (Rashiduddin 1998/1999, 228); this is presumably Zhao's "Jilger." Moge may correspond to the Buqa, said in the *Secret History of the Mongols* (§§137, 226–27) to be Muqali's younger brother and to have served in Chinggis Khan's bodyguard. But Möge itself is a well-attested Mongolian name and the *Secret History*'s account of Muqali's family is obviously incomplete.

51. On Bo'ol (1197–1228), see his biography in *YS* 119.2936–37.

52. The *pójiāo* 婆焦 style was one used for children in the Song dynasty; it involved shaving most of the head and leaving three tufts. See §12, "Their Customs," p. 87. Thomas Allsen (1997, 76–77) notes how this description of Bo'ol shows Middle Eastern influence on his and possibly other Mongols' clothing and hairstyles.

53. Emending the *ér* 兒 of all the codices to *xiàn* 見.

54. This is Ila Tugha(n), who with his brother Aqai was one of Chinggis's early Kitan supporters in northern China. See §6, "The Ministers in Office," p. 80, and his biography in *YS* 149.3532. On these hereditary titles, see the Introduction, pp. 33–34.

55. On Liu Bolin, see his biography in *YS* 149.3515–16. Yunneizhou is near modern Höhhot, in modern Inner Mongolia. The Yanjing area here includes all the lands along the mountains between Inner Mongolia and North China.

his eldest son's consort marry Bolin's son.[56] In capturing Yanjing and other places along with the Tatars, he has earned extremely great merit. In the past Bolin was enfeoffed as a prince, but recently he is in retirement in his home, and his son serves as the viceroy for the Western Capital prefecture.

After him is one called Lord Minister Dage, who is from a Jiün[57] family, and is known to be the viceroy of Yanjing.[58]

After him is Jabar, a Turkestani, who is already old but in Yanjing holds office together with Dage.[59] In Yanjing and vicinity there are Marshal Jilar,[60] Marshal Shĭ,[61] Marshal Liu,[62] and very many others. All have armies and horses under them and take orders from Prince of State Mohulo.

§6. The Ministers in Office

The principal Grand Councilor, Grand Preceptor Togha [error for Aqai], is the elder brother of Grand Mentor Tugha, who was originally a Jurchen and is

---

56. This son of Liu Bolin should be Liu Heima; on him, see "Sketch," p. 126. Mongols practiced the levirate marriage, by which a man's widows were inherited as wives by his younger brothers or son (with the exception, of course, of the son's own mother). By inheriting this prince's wife, Liu Bolin's son, Liu Heima, would thus be favored like a son or younger brother of this eldest son of Chinggis Khan. (On the problem of this supposed eldest son, see §4 "The Crown Princes and Princes of the Blood," p. 77.) Unfortunately, we have no corroboration or further information on this marriage of Liu Heima.

57. We follow Wang Guowei in reading *Jiŭ* 糺 for 乚, Zhang and Shen's *jì* 紀 or Zhao and Niu's *jì* 記.

58. His real name was Šimei Hiêmdêibu and he was the son of the Kitan Šimei Ming'an, who led the mass defection of the Jiün soldiers to Chinggis Khan in 1214. See his biographical notice in *YS* 150.3557. Zhao Gong calls him "Lord Minister Dage (Ch. *Dàgě xiànggong* 大葛相公) as if Dage were his personal name, but his title is given as "Big Brother of the Mobile Secretariat" in Peng Daya (see p. 124). Apparently, Zhao Gong confused *Dage* "Big Brother" with *Dage* as a name.

59. On Jabar Qoje (Mongolian, from Ja'far Khwaja), see *YS* 120.2960–61. He was a *sayyid*, or a descendant of Muhammad.

60. Jilar was a Kitan of the Kitan's former consort-lineage, Šimei. While escorting the Jin emperor south from Yanjing to Kaifengfu in the spring of 1214, he led his men into mutiny against the Jin and joined the Mongol cause. The 乚, Zhang, and Shen MSS read *Zhĭchánr* 紙蟬兒, while the Zhao and Niu MSS read *Zhĭlièr* 紙蹓兒. Both are corruptions of *Zhĭlàr* 紙蠟兒.

61. This is Shĭ Tianni, a Han landlord in the Yanjing area who joined the Mongol cause with his local militia in the winter of 1213–1214. He was killed in a mutiny against Mongol control in 1225, but his brother Shĭ Tianze quickly avenged his death and went on to become the highest-ranking Han commander in Mongol service. See Shĭ Tianni's biography in *YS* 147.3478–81.

62. Since the famous Liu Bolin has already been mentioned, Zhao Gong may be referring here to Liu Min, who was picked up by the Mongol army in 1212 as an abandoned child at the age of twelve. He quickly mastered the Mongolian language and soon caught the eye of Chinggis Khan himself. At the time, however, he was following Chinggis Khan's army on the Western Expedition and did not become a major figure in the Yanjing area until 1223. See his biography in *YS* 153.3609–11.

extremely cunning. The two brothers both came to serve the Tatar lord as generals and ministers.[63]

After him is the Grand Councilor of the Tatars *Zúliè-Duóhé*,[64] and there is also the Jurchen Grand Councilor Siging,[65] but the names of the rest of them were not ascertained. Generally, they are all fugitive Jurchen officials. According to what's going around, Bai Lun[66] and Li Zao are the chief ministers. But at present I only know of one place where it is written, "Bai Lun led soldiers to this place," and at present I still do not know if he is alive or dead.

Right now, Ila Jinqing, a Kitan, is in Yanjing. Having passed the examinations, he now handles documents as palace writer.[67] There are also Yang Biao, the minister of the Board of Personnel, and Yang Zao, the viceroy for their Northern Capital.[68] I, Gong, have seen before the Prince of State two office directors, right and left. When envoys arrive, the two men interpret what they say for him. They are former Jin prefects, and are Jurchen.

§7. Military Management

The Tatars are born and grow up among saddles and horses, so warfare comes naturally to them. From spring to winter, they go hunting[69] every day; that is their livelihood. Thus, they have no infantry; their whole army is cavalry. They muster

---

63. Tugha's elder brother was actually named Aqai, not Togha—the latter name is obviously just a different transcription of Tugha's name itself. They were not Jurchens but Kitans of the former imperial surname, Ila. On Ila Aqai, see *YS* 150.3548–50. At this time, he was following Chinggis Khan in the Khwarazm campaign.

64. There is no Tatar (Mongol or Öng'üt) civil official to which this name can be even remotely matched. There are variants in the MSS particularly of the second graph, but absent any identification, it is impossible to tell which one is correct.

65. Although the graphs are not the same, this should be the Jurchen right vice marshal who surrendered to Chinggis Khan with Tongzhou. See the *YS* 1.18. There his name is written as *Qījīn* 七斤 (i.e., "Seven Catties") or *Tsi-gin* in the Yuan-era reading; here it is *Qījīn* 七金 (i.e., "Seven Gold"), or *Tsi-gim* in the Yuan-era reading. However, his name is written as Siging in the Persian of Rashid al-Din, and we have following that spelling here.

66. This name is written as "Bai Lun 白倫" in the Zhao, Niu, and Shen MSS and as "Bai Jian 白儉" in the ζ, Zhang, Fu₃, and Uang codices. We follow the former reading.

67. This is the official usually known in history as Yelü Chucai, due to the influence of Song Zizhen's "Spirit-Path Stele," which uses that version of his name. However, Ila (Ch. Yila) is the Kitan surname that Chucai used in his own lifetime. Jinqing is Chucai's courtesy name, that is, a name adopted by the person in his adulthood, which was commonly used in both formal and informal contexts. See "Spirit-Path Stele," p. 136. As mentioned in Song Zizhen's biography, the examinations he passed were those of the Jin dynasty.

68. That is, *Běijīng*. This is not to be confused with modern Beijing, the "Northern Capital" of Ming, Qing, and present-day China. The Jin dynasty's Northern Capital was near modern Ningcheng, on the border between the Inner Mongolian Autonomous Region and Liaoning Province.

69. Ch. *zhúliè* 逐獵. This refers to large-scale battue hunting, in which the animals of an entire region are driven into a great circle and then killed at leisure.

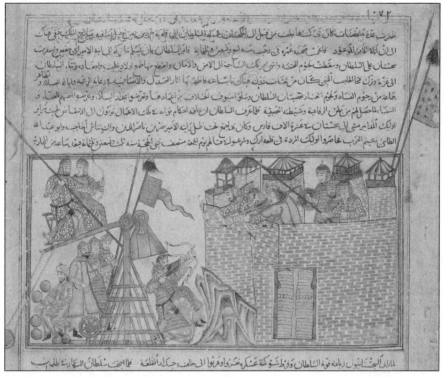

Siege with engines and sappers from a Mongol-era Persian manuscript.

several hundreds of thousands of men in arms without any writing at all; they proceed by transmitting orders [orally] from the marshals to the chiliarchs to the centurions to the *paiza* chiefs.

Whenever they attack a big walled city, they first assault the surrounding small towns, and take its people as plunder in order to supply [a levy of] people to be driven about. For this they send down orders saying: every cavalryman must willingly take ten people captive. When the number of people is sufficient, then each one is forced, from morning to night, to bring specified amounts of grass, firewood, soil, or stones—the slow ones being killed. They force them to fill up moats and ditches until they are level, or else use them to dig saps,[70] artillery pits and such, not sparing the lives of several tens of thousands of people. Thus, in no city they attack is the wall not broken.

When the city is taken, they execute them all without caring who is young or old, ugly or fair, rich or poor, obedient or rebellious, and never have the least

---

70. Ch. *édòng* 鵝洞, lit., "goose caves." Items used in siege warfare were often prefaced with the word "goose"; thus, the biography of Zhang Rou (*YS* 147.3476) records that the general "commanded He Boxiang to make 'goose carts' [*échē* 鵝車 or mantlets] and dig a hole under the wall." On medieval sieges in East Asia, see Franke 1974.

mercy. When they draw close to the enemy, if anyone does not follow orders, even the most honored must be executed. Whenever a city or fortress is taken and there is plunder, then they divide it into equal shares, and everyone, from the highest ranks to the lowest, leaves one share as tribute for Emperor Chinggis, whether there is a lot or a little. With whatever is left, they do an extra distribution to each according to rank, and those grand councilors and so on in the northern desert who did not come on campaign also receive shares.

Before every campaign or conquest, plans are laid between the third or fourth moons and circulated throughout their territories, and then again on the fifth of the fifth moon, they hold an assembly with feasting and plan together against whom the campaign will be that fall. Then everyone returns to his territory to avoid the summer heat and raise their livestock. When the eighth moon comes, they all gather at Yanjing and then set out.

§8. Horse Management

The Tatar country is abundant in water and grass—good for sheep and horses. When their horses have grown one or two years, they ride them hard on the grasslands and train them, yet they raise them to three years before using them as mounts again. Because they train them as colts, that is why they do not kick or bite. A hundred thousand can make up a herd, but they are quiet with no neighing or whinnying. After the horses are dismounted, it is not necessary to hobble or tether them, as they still do not run away, their nature being so fine and good. During the day they do not taste fodder; only when evening falls are they put to pasture, choosing fields according the greening and the withering of the grass. At daybreak they are saddled and mounted, without receiving any beans, chestnuts, or the like. Always when the men go to war, each has several horses, and each day they rotate using one horse as a mount. Thus, their horses do not become weary or exhausted.

§9. Staple Foods

The land of the Tatars has plentiful water and grass—good for sheep and horses. They live only by drinking mare's milk to slake their hunger and thirst. The milk of a single mare can satisfy three people. Whether going out or staying home, they only drink mare's milk or slaughter sheep as food. So anyone in the country who has one horse must have six or seven sheep, and they say that if you have a hundred horses, you must have a flock of six or seven hundred sheep. If the sheep for eating are exhausted when they go on campaign in China, they shoot rabbits, deer, and wild boars for food, so when an army of several hundred thousand are camped, they do not raise any smoke from kitchen fires. Recently, they have seized as slaves people from China who must eat grain to feel full, and therefore they seize rice and wheat as plunder; upon pitching camp, they additionally boil gruel and eat it. Their country also has one or two places where black broomcorn millet grows, and they also boil this to make gruel.

§10. The Campaigns and Conquests

At the time when the Tatars were in their own country, during the Jin caitiffs' Dading years [1161–1189], there was a rumor in Yanjing and in the Kitan areas that said: "The Tatars come nigh, the Tatars go away, they'll chase His Lordship[71] 'til he has nowhere to stay." Chief Ge, named Yong,[72] by chance heard this rumor and said in alarm: "This certainly means the Tatars will bring calamity to our country." He sent out emergency orders to the farthest wastes that troops should go out to exterminate them. Every three years he sent soldiers toward the north to kill and destroy, called it "thinning the ranks." Even now, people in the Central Plains all can remember this, saying, "Twenty years ago, what family was there in Shandong or Hebei that did not buy a Tatar as a little slave or maid?" These were all ones brought back as captives by those armies. Among the present-day great ministers of the Tatars, there are many who at that time were taken prisoner and brought to the Jin kingdom. Moreover, every year when their country would come to present tribute, the Jin would receive their ritual offerings outside the passes and then dismiss them, not even allowing them to cross the frontier. The Tatars fled away to the sandy deserts, and the hatred of the Jin entered into their marrow. When the bogus emperor Zhangzong [r. 1189–1208] was enthroned during the Mingchang years [1190–1195], he no longer commanded the killings. Consequently, the Tatars little by little returned to their original country, begetting sons and bringing them up.

Zhangzong, named Jǐng, who also considered the Tatars a calamity, built a new long wall north of Jingzhou Prefecture[73] and had the Tangut Jiün people defend it. When the Tangut Jiün began to rebel, [the Tatars] made an alliance with[74] the Iladu[75] Jiün, the Muden Jiün, the Me Jiün, and the Hiuden Jiün, and they rebelled together.[76] The Jin dispatched soldiers to pacify them, and the Jiün men scattered, fleeing to surrender to the Tatars. Moreover, there was a man of the Tian family

---

71. Ch. *guānjiā* 官家, an old colloquial term for government authorities, officials, or the emperor. Here is it referring to the Jin emperor.

72. The Jin emperor Yong (Jurchen name Uru); his posthumous temple title Shizong means "Renovating Ancestor" (r. 1161–1189). He held the title Prince of Ge before his accession to the throne. The ruler's personal name and pre-imperial title were taboo to his own subjects and their use by Zhao Gong underlines his loyalty to the Southern Song.

73. The correct official graph for the prefecture was *jìng* 淨 (see e.g., *JS* 24.566), but Zhao Gong uses the homonym *jìng* 靜, while Li Xinchuan uses another homonym, *jìng* 靖.

74. Reading *liánjié* 連結 with Zhang, Fu₃, and Uang, as opposed to Zhao and Niu's *jiélián* 結連, Ç's *jié* 結, and Shen's *lián* 連.

75. Reading *Yéládū* 耶剌都 with Cao's edition (23v) for the codices' *Jíládū* 即剌都. This form alternates in Jin-era sources with *Yíládū* 移剌都.

76. These names are given in their Jurchen forms. Muden appears in empire-era Persian and Mongolian sources as Megüden or Me'üden and the Hiuden appear as the Küiden. (*Den* is a plural suffix.) Not all of the Jiün actually rebelled. In 1216, the Me still fighting for the Jin were renamed the Kayê Alin ("Kayê Mountain") army, the Muden were renamed the Kangġa Alin ("Kangġa Mountain") army, and the Hiuden were renamed the Sahalian ("Black [River]") Army. See *JS* 24.570.

among the Turkestanis, with a wealth of valuables, who carried on an immense amount of trading and commerce while traveling through Shandong and Hebei. He told the Tatars everything about the abundance of people and goods there, and, like the Jiün, persuaded them to organize troops and come in to plunder.[77]

Temujin, indignant over their bullying and insults, for these reasons, invaded the frontier; the frontier prefectures were all conquered and their people killed. The caitiffs in Yanjing said about the Tatars, "Our country is like the sea, your country is like two handfuls of sand, how could you shake us?" The Tatars to this day, young and old, can all remember these words. The caitiff ruler and ministers first became alarmed when they captured the Western Capital. Devoting all the crack troops in the country, they put Marshal Hûsahû in command of 500,000 infantry and cavalry to meet and attack them, but the caitiffs suffered a great defeat.[78] Again they scoured Shandong, Hebei, and other places for 300,000 men and horses, including those of the imperial escort guard, and ordered Geuki to be commander-in-chief. Again, they were defeated and thereupon were driven by the Tatars to the very the walls of Yanjing.[79] This was the battle that exhausted one hundred years of the Jin caitiffs' military might, leaving [their armies] crushed and broken, defeated and dispersed—almost finished. Their dynasty then declined. Thereafter, as the Tatars encircled all of the prefectures of Hebei, Shandong, the Yanjing area, and elsewhere, none of the caitiffs dared to blunt their thrust.

---

77. This Turkestani of the Tian family has generally been identified with Chinqai (Mo. Chingqai, from Chinese Zhenhai); see Buell 1993, 98; Buell 1994, 169. He appears in Islamic sources as a Christian Uyghur, but is said in the *Yuanshi* to be a Kereyit. However, his mercantile and espionage activity fits better with early history of Jabar Qoje, who is said to have spied out the Jin realm for Chinggis Khan under the cover of trading; see *YS* 120.3960 and Juzjani [1881] 1995, 954. Given Zhao Gong's confusions about personnel, that Jabar is mentioned elsewhere seems hardly to exclude the possibility that he may be referred to again here.

78. This account refers to two different events: 1) Hûsahû as viceroy in the Western Capital, Yunzhong, marched out to battle the Mongol invaders in their first invasion in the winter of 1211–1212. Defeated near present-day Jijiazhuang in northwestern Hebei, he fled to the Jin capital at Yanjing rather than return to Yunzhong (*JS* 13.294, 132.2834). This left Yunzhong undefended and it may have been occupied by Mongol forces briefly. 2) When the Mongols retreated at the end of the campaign season in February 1212, he was ordered to assemble a large army and pursue them. They met in battle north of Yehu Ridge, and Hûsahû's army was totally defeated at the Battle of Huanrzui ("Badger's Mouth"). Hûsahû is the Jurchen name of the general known in Li Xinchuan's history by his Chinese name, Zhizhong. See his biography in *JS* 132.2832–39.

79. This battle is variously dated to *gǔi/yǒu*, VII (July–August 1213) or Zhining 1, VIII (August–September 1213); see *YS* 1.16 and *JS* 106.2340. Similarly, some sources designate the battle site as Huailai County (cf. *JS* 106.2340–41), while others put it in neighboring Jinshan County (*YS* 1.16). Marshal Geuki shared command with Wongian Gang, who took most of the blame from the defeat (*JS* 98.2181). A lower, but still probably also exaggerated, figure of 100,000 men is given for the size of their army in the *Jinshi* (*JS* 106.2340–41). After that defeat, the Jin armies fled to Juyong Pass; corpses were said to have littered the ground for forty *li* (Chen 2010, 20.5r).

§11. The System of Offices

The Tatars inherited the system of the Jin caitiffs, setting up like them offices such as directors or overseers, directors of the department of state affairs, left and right

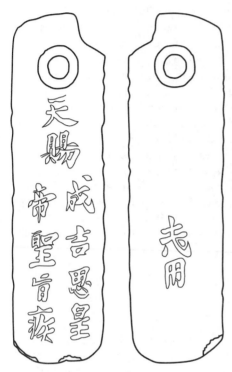

An early paiza from Chinggis Khan's time with Chinese (left) and Kitan (right) inscriptions.

grand councilors, and left and right managers of governmental affairs; they also established a grand preceptor, marshals, and so on.[80] As for the gold *paiza*s which they wear on the waist, those ministers ranked first in honor bear one with two tigers facing each other, calling it a "fighting-tigers gold *paiza*."[81] On it is written in Han graphs: "By edict of Emperor Chinggis, endowed by Heaven, the bearer is plenipotentiary."[82] Next in rank is the plain gold *paiza*, which reads: "By edict of Emperor Chinggis, endowed by Heaven, an urgent matter."[83] Next in rank below that is the silver *paiza*, with the same writing.[84] Like the imperial rescripts and other documents that Chinggis also issues, this is something that the deserted ministers of the Jin caitiffs have taught them. Those who are dispatched to supervise the common people are called "heralds"; those ministers who control the prefectures are all called "military

---

80. Zhao Gong gives here a potpourri of bureaucratic, honorific, and military titles dating back to the Han dynasty. On these titles, see the Introduction, p. 32–34.

81. Ch. *hǔdòu jīnpái* 虎鬭金牌. As Wang Guowei observed in his commentary, this is an error for the phrase *hǔtóu jīnpái* 虎頭金牌 or "tiger-head gold *paiza*" commonly found in Mongol-era sources (cf. Haneda 1936, 85–86).

82. *Tiāncì Chéngjísī Huángdì shèngzhǐ, dāng biànyí xíngshì* 天賜成吉思皇帝聖旨，當便宜行事.

83. *Tiāncì Chéngjísī Huángdì shèngzhǐ, jí* 天賜成吉思皇帝聖旨，疾.

84. A number of such *paiza* (Mo. *gerege*) have been excavated. The text given here was used on postal *paiza*s that enabled the wearer to use the post roads, and differed from the ones carried by officials as mark of their status (Dang 2001). Three more or less complete *paiza*, and one fragmentary one, have been found with exactly the same Chinese inscription for a second-ranking postal *paiza* as recorded by Zhao Gong. On the reverse of both is an inscription in Kitan with graphs that appear to mean "urgent" or "posthaste." One in gilt bronze and one in gilt silver were found in the Chengde area, and another in gilt silver was found in Yanshan County, Hebei; they range in length from 21.7 to 20.1 centimeters. See Dang 2001, 34–35; Dang 2003, 7–8; Shi 2000; Li 2000; Haneda 1936; and the website "Chingisu kōtei seishi haishi."

commissioners"; the valiant men who wait on them right and left holding bows and arrows are called "imperial bodyguards."[85]

§12. Their Customs

The Tatars slight the aged and love the strong. In their customs, they do not carry on personal conflicts. On the first day of the first moon, they always worship Heaven, which they do also on the fifth of the fifth moon. This is a result of their dwelling permanently in Yanjing and inheriting the Jin delight in exchanging gifts and drinking at banquets. Whenever Moqlei returns home from a campaign, his wives, each serving successively as the mistress of the ceremonies day after day, prepare wine[86] and ready drink for feasting, and those below them all do likewise.

It is their custom to not wash their hands much, and if, after snatching at fish or meat, if their hands are greasy, then they wipe them on their robes. They never take off their clothes for washing even to the point that they fall apart. The women commonly paint their foreheads with yellow powder, passing on through the generations this old Han[87] style of makeup, which has not been changed to the present. From the heights of Chinggis down to the citizens, the men all shave in the *pójiāo* style, similar to how small boys in China are left three tufts of hair. When the one on the front fontanelle has grown a little, then they trim it; the hair of the two lower ones on each side they twist together into small horns and let them hang to their shoulders.[88]

A girl (left) and a boy (right) showing Mongol hairstyles from a Mongol-era illustrated encyclopedia.

85. In Chinese, these three terms are *xuānchāi* 宣差, *jiéshǐ* 節使, and *hùwèi* 護衛. None of them became part of the later Yuan official nomenclature. *Xuānchāi* or "herald" was mostly used in the Jin dynasty, while *jiéshǐ* or "imperial commissioner" had been used since the Tang, but soon fell out of use in the Mongol era. *Hùwèi* or "imperial bodyguard" was mostly used in the Liao; the distinctive Mongolian guards or *keshikten* were translated as *sùwèi* 宿衛 or "Palace Guard."

86. Ch. *jiǔ* 酒. Often translated "liquor" or "wine," this term normally refers to undistilled liquor brewed from rice, millet, sorghum, or other grains. It is normally served warm; the closest thing to it in a Western bar today would be Japanese sake.

87. Here meaning the Han dynasty (206 BC–AD 220).

88. The "Treatise on the Five Phases" in the *Songshi* or "History of the Song" noted the vogue of these styles:

§13. Military Uniforms and Equipment

Chinggis's honor guard sets up a pure white banner so he may be recognized; apart from this he has absolutely no other flag or pennant, though his parasol also stands out by using red and yellow. His seat is a folding chair with a gilt dragon head; the Prince of State has one that uses silver here and there, and by this one can distinguish them.[89] Chinggis's saddle also is decorated with a coiling dragon of bright gold, as is that of the Prince of State. The present Prince of State sets up only a white banner—with nine tails and a black moon in the center—which is

Wooden saddle-tree with gold plating, front and back, from a Mongol-era tomb.

During the time of Emperor Lizong [r. 1225–1265] boys shaved their hair, but always left a tuft of hair that looked a little larger than a string of cash to the left of the top of the head, which they called *piāndǐng* 偏頂 ['leaning crown']. Or else they left it on the forehead and tied it up with silk fabric, which looked like the style of *bójiāo* 博焦 ['spreading scorch']; sometimes they called it *bójiǎo* 鵓角 ['pigeon horn'] (*SS* 65.1430; cf. Zhou 1984, 294).

As the above citation, with the addition to the term here of *pójiāo*, 'old lady scorching,' makes clear, the style is described with various graphs of totally different meaning but all with the pronunciation of roughly *bojiao* (the *pojiao* version found in the text would be pronounced *bojiao* in Song times). It thus seems possible that the term is a transcription of a non-Chinese term, and the style may have even become popular in the Southern Song due to Mongol influence, particularly as the *Songshi* text seems to see *bojiao* as a Mongol style imitated by Southern Song boys. See also Peng Daya and Xu Ting's "Sketch," p. 113, where this style is called *bójiāo*. Zhou Xibao's history of Chinese clothing and ornament illustrates this style (Zhou 1984, 308, figs. 7, 8, 9, 10).

89. The seats as described here can be seen on the seated "human-stones" (*khün chuluu*) found in Shiliin Gol League in Inner Mongolia and Mongolia's Sükhbaatar Province.

displayed when his forces set out on campaign. Below him, the marshals alone are allowed to have one banner each. The Prince of State has just one drum, which is used for battlefield deployment. Their saddle bridges are made of wood and are extremely light and ingenious. Their bows must have greater than a picul of tension,[90] their arrows use the wood of dune willows for the shaft, and their daggers are very light and fine and are curved.

§14. Those on Assignment

Those on assignment among them are called "heralds," and when those who come from the seats of the emperor or the Prince of State pass nearby, all those in the districts or the seats of the chiefs controlling the soldiers come out to pay their respects. Regardless of the officials' exalted or base rank, the heralds formally treat all the officials, regardless of rank, as their equals. They pass through the lancet arches and sit in places of honor in the prefectural offices. The prefects, having personally knelt down to greet them in the suburbs, then lodge them within the offices of the prefectural hall.[91] They entertain them with drums and pipes, banners and pennants, and singsong girls, and they see them off and come out to meet them beyond the suburbs. Whenever they see a horse, they trade their own for it, and even those who travel with them may all exchange horses, which they call "riding a station horse,"[92] after the idea of the ancient courier relay.[93] Recently when I arrived at the Prince of State's seat, everywhere the rites and formalities on meeting were very simple and the words and speeches very direct. Moreover, they said, "Your Great Song has a good emperor and good grand councilors." Generally speaking, their character is honest and simple, much like the manner of very ancient times. It is a pity that now the fugitive ministers of the Jin caitiffs have educated them, boring through their primitive simplicity,[94] ruined their naïveté, and made them detestable by instructing them in treacherous plots.

---

90. Ch. *dàn* or "picul," standardized in the Song and Yuan at 167.5 pounds.

91. Lit., "yellow hall" (*huángtáng* 黃堂), from the color prefectural offices were traditionally painted.

92. Ch. *chéng pūmǎ* 乘鋪馬.

93. Many of these same abuses are described in Song Zizhen's "Spirit-Path Stele" under year *dīng/yǒu* [1237].

94. The term here translated "primitive simplicity," *hùndùn* 混沌, is also used for the primitive chaos before the world was formed. Zhao Gong here alludes to a famous allegory in the classic Chinese philosopher Zhuangzi:

> The emperor of the South Sea was called Shu [Brief], the Emperor of the North Sea was called Hu [Sudden] and the emperor of the central region was called Hundun [Chaos]. Shu and Hu from time to time came together for a meeting in the territory of Hundun, and Hundun treated them very generously. Shu and Hu discussed how they could repay his kindness. 'All men,' they said, 'have seven openings so they can see, hear, eat, and breathe. But Hundun alone doesn't have any. Let's try boring him some!' Every day they bored another hold, and on the seventh day Hundun died (Watson 1964, 95).

§15. Worship and Sacrifices

Whenever they conduct divinations to tell good or bad luck—about attacking or retreating, killing or conquering—they take sheep scapulae and strike them with a red-hot iron hammer. They then look at the resulting cracks for omens in making decisions on great matters; it is similar to tortoise-shell divination.[95] Whenever they drink wine, they first make a toast. Their custom is to reverence Heaven and Earth most of all. In any affair, they must first call on Heaven, and when they hear the sound of thunder, they feel fear and dread and do not dare to go out on campaign, saying it is "Heaven crying out."

§16. The Women

Their predominant custom, when setting out on campaign, whether noble or base, is to take their wives and children along, and they themselves say they use them to guard the baggage, clothes, money, goods, and that sort of thing. Their women are solely in charge of setting up of the felt tents and loading and unloading saddles and other things from the carts and pack animals; they are extremely capable on horseback. What they wear looks like the Daoist costume in China. All the wives of their chieftains have *gùgū* hats.[96] Pieced together with iron thread, these have the form of a bamboo armrest,[97] being a little more than three feet in length. They are decorated either with dark purple[98] brocade and embroidery or with pearls and gold. On top of that, there also is a single stick, which is decorated with purplish velvet. They have robes with large sleeves, like crane-feather overcoats[99] in China, which are broad and long enough to trail on the ground, so when they walk two slave girls mind the train. Men and women sit together in no particular order, and it is not forbidden even for them to toast and urge each other to drink. When I went north to that country, I met personally with the Prince [of State] who then commanded me to drink wine, and his wife, Princess Naiman,[100] as well as the attending concubines, eight in all, who sat with us together in a

---

95. In the earlier Chinese dynasties, such as the Shang (ca. 1600–1046 BC) and the Zhou (1046–256 BC), tortoise shells and cow scapulae were heated and omens taken from the cracks.

96. Ch. *gùgū* 顧姑 (more usually written *gùgū* 故姑) is an ancient borrowing from a proto-Mongolic version of the word *kököl*, which in later Mongolian came to mean forelock (on a person), flowing mane (on a horse), or crest (on a bird). The genuine medieval Mongolian name of this headdress is *boqto~boqta* (see Kara 1990, 285, s.v. "bokto[q?]"). See Peng and Xu's "Sketch," p. 101; Shea 2020, 81–84.

97. Ch. *zhú fūren* 竹夫人, lit., "bamboo wife," defined as a large pillow-shaped piece of bamboo ware, used as an arm and leg rest in bed during summer.

98. Ch. *hóngqīng* 紅青, lit., "reddish black." This seems to mean "plum-colored"; see Allsen 1997, 17.

99. Ch. *hèchǎng* 鶴氅. The crane was the sign of immortality in China, so crane feathers symbolized the Daoist aspiration for immortality.

100. Ch. *Làimán*; many Chinese dialects read *l*- for *n*- and vice versa. The Naiman were a kingdom in western Mongolia that was conquered by Chinggis Khan in 1204; this princess may be from that area.

Empress Chabui (ca. 1225–1281), Qubilai Khan's principal wife, wearing a boqto hat.

mixed group. Whenever they feast with wine, men and women always share the same mats. Those who were called concubines all had dazzlingly white complexions and beautiful faces. Four of them seemed to be noble-born court ladies of the Jin caitiffs, and four were Tatars. Four of the concubines were especially beautiful, and those most favored by the prince wore barbarian clothes and barbarian headdress only.[101]

101. "Barbarian" here is Ch. *hú*. It is hard to tell if it means "northern nomad" or "western oasis dwellers" here, although Allsen (1997, 77), believes it is a reference to the adoption of Middle Eastern clothing. See the Introduction, p. 26 on this term.

§17. Banquets, Dance, and Music

When the Prince of State goes out on campaign, he also has girl musicians accompany him, taking along seventeen or eighteen beautiful girls who are extremely intelligent and clever. Most of them pluck a fourteen-string instrument to play "grand official" music and other pieces, and their clapping in time is very soft, their dances very exotic. In the custom of the Tatars, the host holds out a platter of jade cups to urge the guests to drink. If the guest leaves but a few drops, the host will not accept the cup back. Only when he sees that the person has drunk it all is he happy.

If they play polo,[102] it is only with twenty or so horsemen. They don't use many horses because they hate the noise and excitement it makes. Once when a game was over, the prince sent people to come and invite me to him, as Song envoy. He said, "Today we played polo, why didn't you come to play?" and I replied, "I did not hear that your lordship had sent a decree inviting me, and therefore did not dare to come." The Prince of State then said, "Having come into our country, you are a member of the family, and so whenever there is a feast, or a polo match, or we have a ring hunt or go out hunting individually,[103] you should come to have fun. Why do you still insist that someone come to call you over with an invitation?" At that he laughed out loud and made me drink six cups of wine as forfeit. Everyday, they do not end their banqueting until everyone is roaring drunk. Moreover, every time they drink wine, it is their custom that those who sit next to each other should, after tasting, exchange cups. If one's counterpart holds the cup with one hand, it means that I must taste a mouthful, and only then will he dare to drink. If he holds the cup in both hands, then he wishes to switch cups with me; I have to drink his wine to the bottom, and moreover pour wine to toast him. This made it easy to get drunk.

Whenever they see a foreign guest talk uproariously, make noise, and act rudely in a drunken state, or else vomit or fall asleep, then they are very happy and say, "The guest gets drunk, so his heart is one with ours, without any difference." On the day when I, as Song envoy, parted from them, the Prince of State admonished those accompanying me, saying, "Whenever you come to a good walled town, stay a few days longer. If there is good wine, drink it, or good tea and food, eat it, or a good flute or a good drum, blow it or bang it." What he meant by a good walled town is good prefectures and counties.

---

102. Lit., "hit the leather ball" *jījū* 擊鞠. Medieval polo, as in Central Asian buzkashi today, is played with a calf or goat carcass with the head, bowels, and two of the limbs removed.

103. This refers to the two different types of hunting practiced by the Mongols and other Central Eurasian peoples. In the ring hunts (Ch. *dǎwéi* 打圍; Mongolian *aba*), vast numbers of people are organized to surround a particular area and drive the game into a steadily tighter circle. What is called "individual hunts" here (Ch. *chūliè* 出獵; Mongolian *ang*) is more like the typical hunting practiced today. See Allsen 2006, especially 26.

A Sketch of the Black Tatars

By Peng Daya and Xu Ting of the Southern Song

*Peng Daya accompanied the Southern Song dynasty envoy Zou Shenzhi in late Jan-
uary or early February of 1233 on an unsuccessful mission to the Mongolian court.
Later Peng Daya served the Southern Song as the "Vice Circuit Military Commissioner" for Sichuan, winning praise for his determined defense of the area—in particular Chongqingfu Prefecture—against Mongol attacks that began in 1236. He also
went on another mission to the Mongols in 1240 after this account was written. His
stalwart defense measures and the strong fortifications he built at strategic points were
credited with delaying the Mongol conquest of the region by twenty years, although
those who suffered his intolerance of inefficiency accused him of taking bribes. He
summarized his own accomplishments with the following inscription: "On such-and-
such date, defending official Peng Daya built this as the empire's western gate," which
he had carved on Chongqingfu's city wall. He also had it carved within the temple to
the legendary counsellor Zhuge Liang, who in the third century had made Sichuan the
base for an attempt to restore the old Han dynasty against the rival Wèi dynasty of the
Cao family in the north.*

*By contrast, nothing is known about Xu Ting except what we read in this account:
that as an ambassador from the court of the Southern Song dynasty's Emperor Lizong
(r. 1225–1265), he traveled to the Mongolian court in 1235–1236 and had an audience with Öködei, and that on returning home he met Peng Daya, whereupon the two
envoys agreed to combine their written accounts. The present text, consisting of Peng
Daya's basic account with Xu Ting's commentary, was completed on April 27, 1237.*

*Peng Daya's description comes first, follow by Xu Ting's comments; the latter are
indented and followed by ".1" et cetera in the numbering.*

A Sketch of the Black Tatars

1. The kingdom of the Black Tatars (that is, the Northern Chanyu),[1] is titled "Great
Mongol" (*Měnggǔ*). In the land of the sandy desert is Mongol Mountain, and in
the Tatar language silver is called *měnggǔ*.[2] The Jurchens named their kingdom

---

1. "Chanyu" is the Chinese reading of the title for the ruler of the "Xiongnu," the first great
nomad empire of Mongolia known to history. It probably represents original *Darqa*.

2. Peng Daya is a bit confused. Chinese *Měnggǔ*, with its Yuan-era pronunciation *mong-gu*, was
used as the transcription of *Mongghol* (i.e., Mongol). But also sounded very similar to *mönggü(n)*,
the Mongolian word for silver.

the "Great Gold" (*Jīn*), and therefore the Tatars have named their kingdom the "Great Silver."[3]

2. Their ruler who first usurped the title of "emperor" was named Temujin in his childhood, and the title he usurped was "Emperor Chinggis." The present ruler's childhood name[4] is Ukudei, and there are eight [others in his regime] who by circumstance have usurped high titles.

3. His sons are called Köten, Köchü, Qashidai (who has been declared the bogus "heir apparent" and has studied Chinese writings with his teacher, Secretary Ma), and Qarachi.[5]

4. His grand councilors[6] are four men, called Alchidai (a Black Tatar, full of schemes, and decisive),[7] Ila Chucai[8] (courtesy name, Jinqing, a Kitan, also designated the "Vice-Director of the Secretariat"), Niêmha Cungšai[9] (a Jurchen, also designated "General")—together these three administer Han affairs together— and Chinqai[10] (a Westerner), who specially administers Western[11] affairs.

> 4.1. Ting: When I visited the steppe, Alchidai was already no longer serving as Grand Councilor, and Niêmha Cungšai had followed the bogus "heir apparent" Köchü on a southern campaign. The next year Köchü died and Alchidai replaced him, so Niêmha Cungšai continued by assisting the latter. Ila and Chinqai, titling themselves "Lord Ministers

---

3. The idea of a "Gold Mountain" in Manchuria and a "Silver Mountain" in Mongolia appears to go back to the Kitan Liao dynasty. "Gold Mountain" (Jīnshan) was the name for the present-day Great Hinggan Range, as well as the name of a town on its eastern slopes near present-day Qiqihar city in Heilongjiang. Liao annals also show a mountain and a branch of the Tatar people in the Mongolian plateau called Hümüs, from Turkic *kümüš* "silver." See *LS* 2.20 (=69.1082), 30.355, 36.430, and 46.765. Unfortunately, this mountain cannot be identified; it was probably in the eastern part of the plateau.

4. On this confusion over "childhood names" found also in Zhao Gong's "Memorandum," see the Introduction, pp. 37–38.

5. Qarachi is probably an error for Qarachar. Öködei's eldest son, Güyük, is missing from the list, probably because he was campaigning far off in the West at the time.

6. Ch. *xiàng* 相. This is an abbreviation for *chéngxiàng* or "Grand Councilor." See the Introduction, pp. 32–33.

7. Presumably the same as the Alchidai mentioned on p. 123.

8. This is the famous Ila (Yelü) Chucai, whose "Spirit-Path Stele" is translated in this volume. During his life, Ila Chucai always used his surname in the form Ila, not Yelü.

9. Niêmha Cungšai, a member of the Jin aristocracy, had originally been delivered to the court of Chinggis as a hostage (probably in 1214) and served in the bodyguard, or *keshikten*, as a scribe (*bichi'echi*). While serving at a feast he once courageously remonstrated against Öködei's excessive drinking. See his biography in *YS* 146.3465–66.

10. This is the Uyghur reading of his name, which was derived from the graphs pronounced in modern Mandarin as *Zhènhǎi*.

11. "Western" and "Westerner" here is *Húihúi*. Although this term later came to mean "Muslim," in the Yuan era it was used for all people from the West with a more or less "Caucasian" appearance. See the Introduction, p. 26. In fact, Chinqai was a Christian of Uyghur background.

of the Secretariat,"[12] administer all the country's affairs. Chinqai does not handle only Western affairs. The Tatars do not have the designation of "Grand Councilor"; they merely call such men *bichi'echi*, which means "clerk" in Chinese. They have merely been placed in charge of issuing documents.

5. Their land is outside of Juyong Pass (more than thirty-five miles northwest of Yanjing), where the terrain gradually gets higher and broader until leaving Shajing (Tianshan County, almost thirty miles),[13] and then it is flat and wide in all four directions and desolate to the horizon.[14] Far off there may occasionally be a mountain, which at first seems high and lofty, but when one gets closer it turns out to be only a sloping hill; in general, it is all sand and stones.

    5.1. Ting: The sand and stones that I observed were also never very large, only bits of sand and small stones, nothing more.

6. Its climate is crystal cold, without the four seasons or eight nodes of the year,[15] such that there is no thunder to "awaken the insects."[16] In the fourth and eighth moons[17] it often snows, the weather showing little change, and in nearer places north of Juyong Pass like Guanshan Mountain, Jinlian Valley,[18] and so on, it still snows even in moon VI.

---

12. Ch. *Zhōngshū xiànggōng* 中書相公. On this term see the Introduction, p. 33.

13. "Thirty-five miles" is lit., 100 *lĭ*; "almost thirty miles" is lit., 80 *lĭ*. See the tables of weights and measures in Appendix §2.7 (p. 192).

14. The town of Shajing or "Sand Well" was later the site of a route command (*zŏngguǎnfǔ*) under the Mongol Yuan, and its remains are in present-day Honggor *Sumu* in Dörben Heühed Banner (Siziwangqi) in Inner Mongolia's Ulaanchab League.

15. Ch. *bājié* 八節. These "eight nodes" designate the two solstices, two equinoxes, and the first days of the four seasons. Seasons are measured not by the solstices and equinoxes, but by the phases of the moon, with the first day of the first, fourth, seventh, and tenth moons being the beginnings of spring, summer, autumn, and winter, respectively. See the Introduction, pp. 29–30, on Chinese calendars.

16. "Awakening of Insects" (*jīngzhé* 驚蟄) is the third of the twenty-four "solar periods," each named after an expected feature in the weather or biological world. It lasts from approximately March 5 to March 19. In Mongolia, thunderstorms and lightning strikes only occur from May to August, with a peak in July. In South China, however, thunder begins in March or even February, although it also peaks in the summer. See Doljinsuren and Gomes 2015; Zheng, Sun, and Wei 2010.

17. Roughly May and September; see the Introduction, p. 29, on Chinese calendars.

18. *Jīnliánchuān* 金蓮川 or "Golden Lotus Valley" designates the upper Luan River valley; it was known in Mongolian as *Altan Ke'ere* or "Golden Steppe." (Ch. *chuān* 川 normally means "stream" or "valley." In Chinese of the Mongol Yuan period, however, it was treated as the equivalent of Mongolian *ke'er* "steppe" and is so to be understood in this name.) *Guānshān* or "Official Mountain" here should be the present-day Naobao Mountain (peak 1,539 meters above sea level), which overlooks the upper Luanhe River valley in the eastern part of Taipusi Banner (south-central Inner Mongolia). There was another Guanshan, however, in western Inner Mongolia.

6.1. Ting: On my return trip from the steppe I spent the night at the foot of Yehu Ridge.[19] On exactly the fifth day of the seventh moon, when I got up in the early morning, it was so extremely cold that both my hands and feet froze.

7. Their country's "crop" is wild grass, which begins to green in moon IV, becomes lush starting in moon VI, and in moon VIII withers again. Apart from grass, there is nothing else at all.

8. They herd cattle, horses, dogs, sheep,[20] and camels. The sheep are barbarian sheep,[21] with fine wool and tails broad like fans. Han sheep they call *gulü*.[22] Their camels include two-humped ones, one-humped ones, and no-hump ones.[23]

8.1. Ting: The cattle I observed on the steppe were all purely yellow oxen [i.e., not buffaloes, or yak crossbreeds] about the same size as those of Jiangnan.[24] They are great at walking, so, as they are not used for ploughing or field work, they are employed solely for hauling carts. Most do not have their noses pierced.

9. The yurts[25] (that is, felt tents) in which they live have neither walls nor roof beams; they move them to follow the grass and water, never staying for long. The Tatar ruler moves his abode to follow the great hunts, and all the bogus officials and subordinates accompany his moves, which they call "breaking camp." Cattle, horses, or camels are used to pull their carts, on which it is roomy enough to sit or recline, so they call them "tent-carriages." The four corners of such carriages are made by either planting poles or joining boards, which [things] they use to

---

19. Yehu or "Wild Fox" Ridge is over 2,000 meters above sea level and marks the watershed between waters flowing south through North China into the Bohai Gulf and those flowing north through Inner Mongolia into landlocked Central Asian basins.

20. Ch. *yáng* 羊; in Chinese, this term includes, unless otherwise specified, both sheep and goats.

21. "Barbarian" here is *hú*, a term that in this period referred particularly to western oasis dwellers. See the Introduction, p. 26. These fat-tailed sheep were called *Sartaqchin qonin* or "Western sheep" in Mongolian.

22. As the commentator Li Wentian first recognized, the term *gǔlü* 骨律, which Peng Daya misunderstood to be a Mongolian term, is the misheard Chinese term *gǔlì* 羖䍽. This term was used in the Jurchen- and Mongol-era North China to designate goats or billy goats (Mo. *ima'a* or *uquna*), not sheep; see Xu 2014, 16–18; Kuribayashi 2012, 123; Mostaert 1977, 63. Peng Daya was probably more used to the Southern term *shānyáng* (lit., "mountain sheep") for goats.

23. Native Mongolian camels are certainly two-hump or Bactrian camels, but one-hump camels or dromedaries must have been introduced from the Middle East. It is unclear what "no-hump" camels are, unless Peng Daya was confused by the tendency of Bactrian camels' humps in the summer to become mere flaps of skins that flop over on their sides.

24. Jiangnan or "South of the River" refers particularly to the area around the present-day cities of Shanghai, Suzhou, and Hangzhou.

25. Ch. *qiónglú* 穹廬, lit., "domed hut." This was the original Chinese term for Central Eurasian mobile dwellings covered with felt, dating back to the time when the Han dynasty faced the pastoralist Xiongnu Empire.

Two archaic-style yurts housing relics attributed to Chinggis Khan, Ejen-Khoroo Banner, Ordos, Inner Mongolia, 1932.

show their reverence for Heaven. These so-called victual carts are dispatched in groups of five, looking like columns of ants as they wind along, extending out for five miles,[26] with the distance horizontally from left to right reaching half of that length. When they find water then they stop, calling it "setting up camp." The leader's tent faces south and monopolizes the front rank; next comes those of his concubines and serving women, then of the bogus escorts and guards, and then of the bogus officials and subordinates. Wherever the Tatar ruler's hunting tents are located is always called "the *ordo*." His Golden Tent (its pillars are made of gold, hence the name), where the bogus imperial ladies are amassed with the resident populace,[27] is alone called "the great *ordo*." Its place is in a bend of a slope or hill in order to cut down the force of the winds.[28] As when the Han emperors move their temporary courts, so with them there is no permanent stopping place.[29] They simply move on, whether it be after a month or a season.

---

26. Lit., fifteen *li*. See the tables of weights and measures in Appendix §2.7 (p. 192).

27. Ch. *jùluò* 聚落, lit., "settlement, town, village." We know from many other descriptions that the vast numbers of people traveling with the Great Ordos made them seem like a whole town, even though they were in fact mobile and living in tents.

28. The word used for "bend" here (Ch. *juǎn'ā* 卷阿) is an allusion to a stanza in the *Canon of Odes* or *Shijing*, China's most ancient collection of lyrics. The stanza alluded to describes the court of a good lord, "Through a bend in the hillside / A gust of wind comes from the south. / All happiness to our lord, / We come to sport, we come to sing, / To spread his fame" (Waley 1960, 183; cf. Legge [1871] 1991, 491). See the ode *Juǎn'ā* in Book III.ii.8. We would like to thank Prof. Ma Xiaolin, Dr. Qiu Zhirong, and Michael A. Fuller for their assistance on this point.

29. It is unclear whether this refers to the Han as a dynasty, or the Han as meaning ethnic Chinese in general.

A khan and his wife on a throne, with ladies seated to their left, from a Mongol-era Persian manuscript.

9.1 Ting: When I arrived in the grassland, they had set up the Golden Tent, I think because they wanted to make an impressive show for an envoy who had been personally deputed by our dynasty's emperor. When the earlier convoy[30] of envoy Zou came such a tent had not been set up, nor had they erected one when the later convoy of ambassador Cheng

---

30. "Convoy" (Ch. *gāng* 綱) refers in Song-era Chinese to a group moving together on government business. See Yuan et al. 1997, 102. We would like to thank Prof. Ma Xiaolin and Dr. Qiu Zhirong for their assistance on this point.

or the still later convoy of envoy Zhou arrived.[31] The Golden Tent's structure is typical of large felt tents in the middle of the grassland. It is wrapped on the top and sides with felts. In the center [of the roof] there is a round opening of interwoven willow-wood that lets in the light, and it is pulled together firmly with more than a thousand ells. The threshold and sideposts of the entrance are all wrapped in gold foil, hence its name. It can hold several hundred people. The folding chair on which the Tatar ruler sits in the middle of the tent looks like the lecture seat in a Dhyana Buddhist monastery, and is also ornamented with gold. The empress and concubines seated in their successive ranks look rather like [performers in] a cabaret.[32] The yurts are of two kinds: the style in Yanjing uses willow-wood for the frame, which, like the screens[33] in the Southland, may be folded up or opened out. As one enters the door, the frame on top is like that of an umbrella, at the peak of which they leave an aperture, which they call a "sky window." It is all wrapped with felt, and can be loaded onto horses. The style on the steppe interweaves willow-wood to form a stiff and permanent enclosure, across which felt is beaten into place. This type cannot be folded up or opened out and must be loaded onto carts.[34] When the grass and water are exhausted, then they move, setting out on no fixed day.

10. Their food is meat, not grain. They get it by hunting animals, such as rabbit, elk, wild boar, ground squirrel, ibex (its backbones can be made into ladles), gazelle (its back is yellow, and its tail is as big as a fan), wild horses (with an

---

31. As Li Wentian and Wang Guowei established in their earlier commentary, Zou Shenzhi was appointed as envoy to the Mongols by the Southern Song official Shǐ Songzhi to the Mongols in Shaoding 5, XII (i.e., January–February 1233) in response to the Mongol embassy's request that the two countries coordinate the destruction of the Jin. Zou was sent again, with a larger party, on January 17, 1235, in response to the arrival of another Mongol envoy, Wang Ji, on January 5. Cheng Fei, defense commissioner of Hezhou, was appointed as a goodwill ambassador to the Mongols in the first moon of Duanping 2 (January–February 1235). And in Jiaxi 2, III (March–April 1238), Zhou Ciyue was appointed as goodwill envoy. See Xu 2014, 23–24.

32. Ch. *gòulán* 构欄(~闌). This term (or more commonly *gōulán* 勾欄) referred originally to places of entertainment or theater, but later came to be used for brothels (Long 1985, 155). "Cabaret" captures this somewhat risqué implication of Xu Ting's comparison. We would like to thank Prof. Ma Xiaolin, Dr. Qiu Zhirong, and Reader A for their assistance with this passage. The seating and appurtenances of Mongol courts are set out in detail based on visual and textual evidence in Matsuda 2021.

33. "Screen" is Ch. *guàsī* 罣罳; this term has often been misunderstood as "sieve," but it was actually a bamboo lattice work fitted with a cloth. The term is found with several phonetic variants and may have actually been borrowed from Kitan or Jurchen usage. See Yang Zhishui 2014, 71–72, fig. 19-1, 19-2; Yang Zhishui 2015. We would like to thank Prof. Ma Xiaolin and Dr. Qiu Zhirong for their assistance on this point.

34. Of these two styles, the "Yanjing style" is the one used today for the Mongolian *ger* or yurt. The "steppe style" has been preserved to the present only in a modified form in the tents used in the cult of Chinggis Khan. See Andrews 1999, I, 394–402; Kriukov and Kurylev 1992.

appearance like an ass),[35] and fish at the river heads (when the ground freezes such fishing is still possible). The animal most often pastured for cooking is the sheep, and next are cattle. Unless it is for a great banquet, they do not slaughter horses. They prepare nineteen containers of broiled, and twelve or thirteen containers of boiled food; [the principals] eat first after the meat is sliced; then the rest is fed to others.

> 10.1. Ting: I lived in the steppe for more than a month and never observed the Tatars killing a cow for food.

11. They drink horse's milk and kefir made from sheep and cow.[36] When they begin to pour, A must drink first, serving himself. After that it is B's turn, but before B drinks, he offers it to A, while C and D groan. This they call "clever persuasion." A does not drink, but hands it over to C. When C has finished drinking, he takes a ladle of drink and toasts B, who again does not drink, but has D drink. D shows the same courtesies toward B as C had. When B at last finishes drinking, he takes a ladle and toasts A, and A in turn takes a ladle and toasts C and D. This they call "exchanging chalices." Originally it was a precaution against poisoning, but through regular practice it became normal.

12. They use only one condiment, salt.

> 12.1. Ting: When I had gone out through Juyong Pass, surmounted Yehu Ridge, and passed through more than 350 miles,[37] I entered the steppe at a place called Ghaili Lake,[38] whose waters overflow its banks and leave a deposit of salt during the night. Visitors come and exchange rice for it, amounting to several thousand piculs a year.[39] Entering further into the steppe, I saw a kind of salt which the Tatars eat, which they called "jug salt." Its color is whiter than snow, its consistency is harder than ivory, and its bottom is more even than a jug's, so they call it "jug salt." It is the most superb of salt.[40] The farther one goes northward, the earth becomes more alkaline, and the grass is good for horses.

13. To cook, they burn steppe charcoal (cattle and horse dung).

---

35. These "wild horses" (Ch. *yěmǎ* 野馬) are kulan, that is, the Mongolian wild ass (*Equus hemionus*). See the citations in Xu 2014, 31.

36. "Milk" here is *rǔ* 乳, the usual term for human breast milk; "kefir" is *lào* 酪 or curdled milk.

37. Lit., "more than 1,000 *lǐ*." See the tables of weights and measures in Appendix §2.7 (p. 192). Ghaili Lake is about 60 miles beyond Yehu Ridge; Xu must be measuring the distance from Yanjing (Beijing), although even from there it is only about 210 miles.

38. *Ghaili* in Mongolian means "tax; customs payment" referring to the lake's purpose as part of the government revenue. This lake is Hashiyatu Nuur in southern Taipusi Banner. The lake is also described by Li Zhichang in his record of the famous Daoist master Changchun's travels. It is not to be confused with the nearby salt-lake visited by Zhang Dehui. See Li/Waley 1979, 63; Li/Wang, 17r/259.

39. A picul (Ch. *dàn*) was about 167.5 pounds. See Appendix §2.7 (p. 192).

40. This kind of rock salt is found in Mongolia today as well; it is called *jamts* salt.

14. Their lanterns have steppe charcoal as the core and sheep's lard as the oil.

15. It is their custom to hunt with bow and arrow. Whenever their ruler goes on a battue hunt,[41] they always gather in great numbers and dig pits, in which are stuck pieces of wood for markers. These are strung together with ropes made of fine animal hair, which are draped with felt "wings." The Han know a similar way to catch rabbits with nets, but the Tatars string their lines out for thirty-five to seventy miles.[42] The wind makes the "wings" flutter in the air, scaring the animals so that they do not dare to flee [outside the marked area]. Thereupon, [the hunters] contract the circle to attack and seize the game.

> 15.1. Ting: I observed how they collected animal-hair rope and felt from the lower-ranking Tatar households, and how it caused considerable hardship. Along my route, the station horses that I rode mostly had their manes sheared. When asked about this, they said it was for rope, which they deliver up to the *ordo* to be used in hunts. The hunting grounds are open from moon IX up to moon II when they close. Whenever they have hunts, they regularly eat the game they have caught and so slaughter fewer sheep.

16. As for headgear, the men have disheveled hair and a small mallet-shaped bun.[43] They wear caps in the winter and conical hats in summer, while the females top their heads with the *gùgū.*[44]

> 16.1. Ting: I observed the making of their *gùgū.* For the frame they use painted wood, wrapped with red-colored raw silk and gold silk, and on the very top, they use a four- or five-foot-long willow branch or else iron beaten into a branch-shaped wand and wrapped with black-green felt. Those of relatively high rank decorate these with either our court's baubles made of kingfisher feathers or strips of five-colored silk, which give a fluttering motion, while those of lower rank use pheasant down. The women are lovely and use wolf dung to powder their faces.

17. Their robes overlap to the right and have a square-angled collar.[45] Older ones are made of felt, furs, and leather, while newer ones are made of ramie and

---

41. Ch. *dǎwéi.*

42. Lit., "one or two hundred *lǐ.*" See Appendix §2.7 (p. 192).

43. Ch. *pīfà* 被髮, "disheveled hair," is a stock attribute of barbarians, hermits, and madmen in Chinese folklore. The description here seems self-contradictory but appears to mean that they let most of their hair fall loosely, while collecting some at the back in a mallet-shaped bun (*chuíjì* 椎髻).

44. *Gùgū* 故姑 was the standard Chinese term for the distinctive Mongolian married woman's hat. See Zhao Gong's "Memorandum," p. 90, and the image on p. 91.

45. This phrase, *yòurèn ér fānglǐng* 右衽而方領, plays off traditional phrases describing refinement, or the lack of, in clothing. *Zuǒrèn* 左衽, lit., "to overlap on the left," stereotypically describes barbarian clothing; the Mongols, however, button their clothes to the right. *Fānglǐng jǔbù* 方領矩步,

A Mongol lady with attendants and a handbag, from a Timurid-era Persian manuscript.

silk with gold thread.[46] Colors are red, purple, maroon, and green; and they are embellished with sun, moon, dragon, and phoenix patterns.[47] They do not distinguish noble and base ranks by their clothing.

> 17.1. Ting: I have investigated this, and indeed it is exactly like the cut of our ancient "long garment."[48] Basically, there is only the flat collar, which is very like our dynasty's Daoist garb and therefore is called the "square-angled collar." As for the "four-angled standing collar," it too is something the Han people devised, but the Tatar rulers and men of

---

lit., "an angled collar and a measured step," may be rendered idiomatically as "dressed in scholarly clothes and showing refined manners." Similarly, in the family rituals compiled by the famous Song philosopher Zhu Xi, the "square-angled neckline" (*fānglǐng*) is described as part of the scholars' semiformal "long garment" (Ebrey 1991, 23, fig. 5). Peng's point is, therefore, that the Tatars' clothing seems strangely refined for their otherwise barbaric condition.

46. Ch. *zhùsī* 紵絲 and *jīnxiàn* 金線, respectively. Ramie is made from the Chinese nettle (*Boehmeria nivea*). Its fibers are similar to linen but somewhat less durable.

47. The Chinese *fèng* 鳳, or male phoenix, is a legendary bird rather different from the phoenix of the Mediterranean world, but "an emblem of joy and happiness." On these designs, see Allsen 1997, 107–8.

48. Ch. *shēnyī* 深衣, lit., "deep robe," designates the dignified but informal Chinese scholar's robe, as found in the ancient classic *Records of Rituals* and describes in Song-era ritual works like Zhu Xi's *Family Rituals* (Ebrey 1991, 21–23). See Hu 2016.

A Mongol-era bianxian (braided waist) robe.

high rank such as in the Secretariat have never worn it.[49] At the midriff are closely sewn fine plaits of fabric, of undetermined number. If with the "long garment" there were at least twelve plaits of cloth, the Tatars' has more than that. They also twist reddish purple silk to make a cord worn horizontally around the midriff, which thus is called a "threaded cummerbund."[50] Probably they desire it because when the wearer is on horseback with this waistband tied tightly, the appearance is striking, colorful, and good-looking.

18. Their language has sounds but no graphs. They mostly borrow graphs of similar phonetic value to represent the sounds and thereby translate and communicate the meaning.[51] [Those who do this] are called "interpreter-clerks."[52]

19. They call one another by names given in childhood and do not use surnames or sobriquets. If someone feels uncomfortable with his name, then he changes it.

---

49. "Four-angled collar" is *sìfāng shànglǐng* 四方上領, lit., "four-corner standing collar." Despite Xu Ting's claim that Mongols never wore it, the portrait of Öködei Khan shows him wearing exactly such a collar.

50. Ch. *yāoxiàn* 腰線. On this part of Mongolian clothing, and a comparison of this passage with extant examples, see Shea 2020, 49–50.

51. Peng is of course incorrect in saying that Mongolian had no writing; in fact, he describes the Uyghur-Mongolian alphabet below. Peng here is referring not to translation from Mongolian script to Chinese, but rather to the transcription of Mongolian-language texts into Chinese graphs, syllable by syllable, using Chinese graphs purely for their sound value. This system for transcription continued into the Ming dynasty, when it was used to transcribe and preserve Mongolian-language books such as the *Secret History of the Mongols* and documents in the "Sino-Barbarian Vocabularies" (*Hua-Yi yiyu*).

52. Ch. *tōngshì* 通事. This term was used in earlier dynasties for administrative positions in the Secretariat. It was first used for interpreters in the Liao and Jin dynasty, and Peng was evidently unfamiliar with its usage. See Hucker 1985, §7503.

19.1. Ting: I observed how, from highest to lowest, they use only childhood names—that is, they never use surnames—nor do they call one another by official titles. Those who handle documents are called *bichi'echi*; those who administer the commoners are called *darughachi*; imperial guardsmen are called *qorchi*.[53] Regarding the grand councilors, that is, Chucai and his sort, they call themselves Lord Ministers of the Secretariat. As for Wang Ji, he refers to himself by such titles as Grand Master for Glorious Happiness with Silver Seal and Blue Ribbon, Censor-in-Chief, Pacification Commissioner, and Ambassador to the [Song] Court, which are not offices to which the Tatar ruler originally appointed him.[54]

20. Their courtesy upon meeting is to embrace rather than bowing with the hands clasped in front,[55] and to kneel on the left knee to do obeisance.

Men practicing ritual kneeling, from a Mongol-era illustrated encyclopedia.

---

53. These terms and their explanations are all basically correct: *bichi'echi* is a scribe; the *darughachi* is an overseer who supervises local authorities or communities who have surrendered to Mongol rule; and a *qorchi* is a quiver bearer, of whom there were 1,000 in the 10,000-man strong bodyguard of Chinggis Khan.

54. Wang Ji, from Fengxiangfu (near Xi'an in Shaanxi province), fought for the Jin but on being defeated was won over to Mongol service by Chinggis who admired his loyalty. From 1214 onward he served on many campaigns against the Jin and accompanied Chinggis against the Xia, and Öködei against the Jin armies at Fengxiangfu, and in Kaifengfu. He was a devoted patron of the Daoist master Changchun. In 1233 he was made an ambassador to the Southern Song court. He died in the South while on a diplomatic mission, and the Southern Song returned his body for burial in Yanjing. See his biography in *YS* 153.3611–13. As an ambassador, he had frequent conversations with Xu Ting. The *Yuanshi* biography records his receiving from Chinggis Khan a gold *paiza*, the title of "Pacification Commissioner," and management of the Mobile Secretariat and the Six Ministries, but not the other titles mentioned by Xu Ting. The title of "Grand Master for Glorious Happiness with Silver Seal and Blue Ribbon" was first held by Yan Shi in reward for leading 300,000 people in submission to Muqali in the autumn of 1220. Later Qutugha also held this title; he was the son of the Kitan official Hiêmdêibu (see his biographical notice in *YS* 150.3557).

55. Bowing with the hands clasped was the traditional Chinese manner. See Wilkinson 2000, 105–8.

20.1. Ting: I observed their embracing upon meeting, and indeed they do put their arms around each other.

21. For them, the center is the honored position, the right is next, and the left is the lowest.[56]

22. Their official calendar formerly used the animal correlates of the twelve branches (for example, the *zǐ* branch they called the mouse year, and so on), but now they use the full cycle of six *jiǎs* (for example, they say the first day or thirtieth day of the first moon of the *jiǎ/zǐ* year).[57] All this was taught them by Han people, Kitans, and Jurchens. In original Tatar customs, there was no understanding [of this system]; they could only take the greening of the grass as one year, and when a new moon first appeared, it meant one month had passed. If asked their age in years, then they would count on their fingers how many times the grass had greened.

22.1. Ting: When I was in Yanjing's Xuandezhou Prefecture,[58] I saw a calendar that was even printed and bound. Upon inquiry, it turned out that it had been personally calculated, printed, and distributed by Ila Chucai, without even the Tatar ruler's knowledge. Chucai has ability in astronomy, poetry, the zither,[59] and Zen meditation.[60] His moustache and beard are dark black and hang down to his knees. He usually twines this facial hair into horns and strikes a very tall and robust figure.

23. They chose days to do things or not by observing the wax and wane of the moon (periods before the crescent moon and after the last quarter are both avoided), and when they see the new moon, they always do obeisance.

24. Their affairs they write down with a wooden stick, with marks that look like the wriggling of a frightened snake, or like the "heavenly writing" script on amulets[61]

---

56. In Chinese-style government offices, the one on the left was always senior to the one on the right.

57. Here Peng refers to the difference between the twelve-year animal cycle and the sixty-year or sexagenary cycle. See also Zhao Gong's "Memorandum," pp. 73, 75–76; and the Introduction, pp. 31–32.

58. This is modern Xuanhua, northwest of Beijing, in Hebei province.

59. Ch. *qín* 琴. A fretless board zither with seven strings, today called the *guqin*, particularly favored by scholars of taste and distinction.

60. Ch. *cānchán* 參禪, referring to Buddhist meditation. Zen is the Chinese word *chán* in Japanese pronunciation. Both terms are originally transcriptions of the Sanskrit word *dhyāna*, "meditation, mind training."

61. "Heavenly writing" (Ch. *tiānshù* 天書) refers to eight graphs spoken by Heaven in the beginning of the world according to Daoist scriptures. They were written on amulets (Ch. *fúzhuàn* 符篆) worn for protection.

or else like the notes *wŭ, fán, gōng*, and *chĕ* of musical notation[62]—a very close relative of the Western letters.[63]

24.1. Ting: I have investigated this. The Tatars originally had no writing, but now there are three sorts in use: that which circulates in the Tatars' own country is incised on the four corners of four- or five-inch pieces of wood.[64] If ten horses are to be dispatched, then they carve ten marks, in general carving only their number. Their ways are pure and their hearts undivided so what they say is not contradictory. By their law, those who speak lies are to die, and so none dare practice falsehood. So even though they have no writing, they have been able to found a kingdom by themselves, their small pieces of wood serving in the same way as ancient wooden tallies. Among the Westerners, they use the Western writing under Chinqai's direction. The Western script has only twenty-one letters, with the rest simply being added like [elements] to the side and top

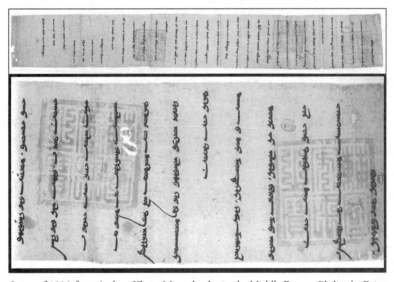

Letter of 1289 from Arghun Khan, Mongol ruler in the Middle East, to Philip the Fair, king of France (full text above, detail below).

62. *Wŭ* 五, *fán* 凡, *gong* 工, and *chĕ* 尺 represent four of the ten graphs used to record musical notes in the Gongche system of musical notation. As may be seen, their graphs are simple and, when written in cursive form, bear a certain chance similarity to some of the letters in the Uyghur-Mongolian script. On this passage, see Cleaves 1951, 499–500 n. 17.

63. "Western letters" here refers to the medieval Uyghur alphabet, written vertically in columns from left to right. It was derived from the Sogdian alphabet, which in turn was borrowed from the Aramaic script. It was adopted with very little change to the Mongolian script, and Peng is correct that they are "very close relatives."

64. Lit., three to four *cùn*. See the tables of weights and measures in Appendix §2.7 (p. 192).

of radicals.[65] Among the various vanquished kingdoms—Han, Kitan, and Jurchen—they employ only Chinese graphs, under the direction of Ila Chucai. Yet at the end [of each such Chinese-language document], before the date, Chinqai personally writes in the Western script to whom it is to be delivered. This is probably a special precaution against Chucai [acting on his own authority]: the document must be verified in the Western script, without which it cannot be considered a genuine document. Perhaps, as well, they want everything he writes to go through Chinqai to create as well a mutual check between them. The schools in Yanjing mostly teach Western writing and translating for the Tatars. Only after pupils learn to translate are they apprenticed to interpreters and allowed to follow the Tatars around. They put on the airs of power and wealth, wangling *saugha*[66] and demanding things to eat.[67] The Kitans and Jurchens have their own scripts, but the Tatars use neither of them.

25. Their seal says "Treasured Token for Issuing Commands"[68] in a folding style of script, square and over three inches in width. Chinqai controls it, and there is no sealed case to prevent its misuse. All affairs, major or minor, are supposedly decided by their bogus chief himself, yet Chucai, Cungšai, and Chinqai jointly wield the handle of Tatar power. Thus, throughout the country some affairs are not under the Tatar ruler's command, and power over life and death, reward and confiscation, has already moved into the hands of those who apply the seals.

25.1. Ting: I have investigated this, and if we consider just the handling of documents, it is probably the case that Chucai and Chinqai are able to act according to their own ideas because the Tatar ruler is actually illiterate.[69] But in such major matters as mobilizing the army and deploying

---

65. Xu Ting here is describing the Uyghur alphabet that was the basis of the Uyghur-Mongolian script. He makes an analogy with Chinese graphs. Just as compound Chinese graphs are made by combining a certain radical—which usually suggests the meaning and is placed on the left or sometimes above or below, with one or more additional elements that usually suggest the pronunciation—so too words are made up in the Uyghur alphabetical script by combining letters in a line.

66. Peng Daya later defines this Mongolian term *saugha* as *mì* 覓, "to seek" or "to look after something," hence similar to "long sought" (see p. 114). The term is also found in a number of Chinese and Mongolian sources, such as the *Secret History of the Mongols* (§§114, 135), where it refers to children either given to Chinggis Khan as companions or orphans found on the battlefield. See Pelliot 1936; Xu 2014, 65–66. However, the graphs used to transcribe it in Chinese, *sǎhuā*, literally mean "scatter flowers," and idiomatically refer to congratulatory gifts. In practice it seems that there has been some confusion, and Chinese writers use *saugha* in ways that actually more closely resemble Mongolian *tangsuq*, "delights, precious things" or rare gifts, which were used to establish social relations.

67. Here we follow Xu in reading *wùshì chī* 物事喫; two later manuscripts omit the last graph.

68. Ch. *xuānmìng zhī bǎo* 宣命之寶.

69. This is incorrect; Chinggis Khan had all his sons trained in Uyghur-Mongolian writing by the Uyghur scribe Tatar-Tong'a. See *YS* 124.3048. They could not, however, read Chinese.

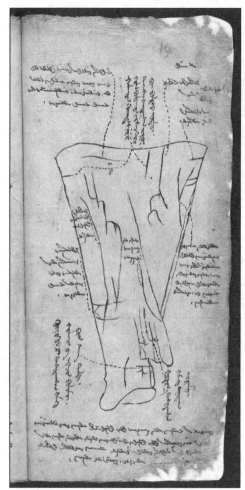

forces, the Tatar ruler alone makes the decision, or further consults with his close blood relations, not with any Han fellows and non-kin. Every Tatar is addressed as "a bone of my own body." However petty a lawsuit may be, they presume on *saugha* to bring the matter before the Tatar ruler, though in the end, who knows if they will receive a decision from him?

26. Their divination method is to burn the shoulder blades[70] of sheep and then examine the oppositions and confluences in the resulting patterns of cracks to discern what is good- or ill-omened. They strongly believe that what Heaven rejects or what Heaven grants is absolutely determined by this so-called burning the lute.[71] There is no affair that is too minor to be divined upon, and they will divine on a matter several times before desisting.

26.1. Ting: When I accompanied one embassy to the grasslands, the Tatar lord several times "burned the lute" to divine whether the embassy should be dismissed or retained. They thought that in the "lute" it read that the embassy should return,

Diagram on interpreting cracks in sheep shoulder blades for divination, from an early twentieth-century Mongolian manuscript.

so we were sent back. "Burning the lute" is just like the ancient practice of boring holes in tortoise shells [with a heated rod].[72]

---

70. Ch. *xiānzi gǔ* 杴子骨, lit., "shovel-shaped bones."

71. Ch. *shāo pípa* 燒琵琶. This refers to the practice of divination by scapulimancy, or placing shoulder blades in the fire and reading the cracks. This phrase derives from the resemblance between the shape of the lute and the shape of the sheep's shoulder blades used in this scapulimancy.

72. Despite Xu Ting's comparison, Mongolian and Siberian diviners do not use heated rods, but instead place the entire scapula in the fire (Bawden 1958, 9–11; Birtalan 1993). The difference is due to the thinness of sheep scapulae, which make them easier to crack than turtle shells.

27. In their everyday speech, they always say, "Relying on the strength of immortal Heaven and the fortunate protection of the emperor."[73] In all affairs that they desire to undertake, they say, "Heaven wants it like that." Regarding anything that people have already done, they say "Heaven is aware."[74] There is no affair that is not attributed to Heaven; from the lord of the Tatars to his common people, it is thus.

28. Their taxes are called "household requisitions."[75] They depend on horses for milk and sheep for food; both are levied according to the greater or lesser head of livestock herded by the commoner households, just like the tribute taxes in Han-style law.[76] The method of establishing the *jam*,[77] is left to the leading chieftains. The Han civilians who have long lived close to the routes of the messengers and envoys, except for the smiths and carpenters but without distinction of male or female, are each assessed. Town dwellers pay 25 *liǎng* of silk plus 50 *liǎng* of "cow and sheep silk" per year (that is, silver from the Westerners to pay for the food and expenses of the ambassadorial missions who travel through, depending on the number of men per party), while each person in the farming villages pays 100 *liǎng* of silk.[78] Grain is not levied according to the acreage of fields that are tilled; rather each household pays four piculs[79] per year. The silver

---

73. Ch. *Tuōzhu Chángshēng Tiāndi qìlì, Huángdìdi fúyìn* 托著長生天底氣力, 皇帝底福蔭. This was the official Chinese translation of the Mongolian phrase, attested in many Mongolian letters and inscriptions: *Möngke tngri-yin küchün-dur, yeke su jali-yin ibe'en-dür* (the second phrase is sometimes *qa'an-u su-dur*). This phrase may be rendered literally as "By the power of eternal Heaven/God, by the protection of the great fortune and blessing" (or more idiomatically, "by the imperial fortune").

74. These two phrases, *Tiān jiào nènde* 天教恁地 and *Tiān shízhu* 天識著, are both in the Yuan translation-style vernacular, in which, for example, *zhu* represents the present continuous tense. We would like to thank Prof. Ma Xiaolin and Dr. Qiu Zhirong for their assistance on this point.

75. Ch. *chāifā* 差發. In bilingual Sino-Mongolian inscriptions of the Yuan dynasty, Chinese *chāifā* translates Mongolian *alba ghubchiri*, "requisitions and contributions." This tax is mentioned also in Song Zizhen's "Spirit-Path Stele" under year 1238.

76. "Tribute taxes," or *shànggòng* 上供, lit., "gifts/tribute to be submitted," was a term from the classic taxation system of the Tang dynasty (618–907). It designated the portion of taxes that was forwarded to the central government, as opposed to the portions kept in the county, or forwarded only up to the prefectural level. See Twitchett 1970, 41–42.

77. *Jam*: Mongolian post-road system.

78. Peng Daya's description is somewhat confused, but combining it with Xu Ting's description below, it seems to be stating that in well-traveled areas, all people paid 50 taels (*liǎng*) of silver each year, as a commuted silk tax to pay for army and messenger provisions, and that urban households paid 25 and rural households paid 100 taels in addition. Xu Ting seems to think that all of these silk payments were commuted to silver, while Peng Daya indicates that only the 50 tael "cow and sheep" payment was so commuted. The *Yuanshi* states that only silk was paid (it is evidently mistaken on this point). It further gives the amount as 1 catty (Ch. *jīn*), or about 1.4 pounds, for every two households, together with local threads and dyes for those households paying taxes to the central treasury, and 1 catty per household for the appanage households subject to the Mongol princes and princesses. See *YS* 93.2361; Schurmann 1967, 88, 98.

79. The picul (Ch. *dàn*) as a dry measure is estimated at 1.90 bushels for the Song and 2.70 bushels for the Mongol Yuan dynasty. See the tables of weights and measures in Appendix §2.7 (p. 192).

shipped in convoy,[80] when added together for all routes, is 20,000 *dìng*[81] each year. The roundabout, convoluted ways in which their taxes are implemented defy description.

28.1. Ting: The desert land through which I passed had all been delimited into regions for the Tatar lord, the bogus "empresses," "crown-princes," "princesses," their kinsmen, and on downward. Within these regions, the commoner households all supply cattle, horses, cart-handlers, mutton, and mare's milk as requisitions. The Tatars have divided up the grass-lands, each separately gathering requisitions; surely no one, whether noble or base, is exempted. And there is another category under which everyone pays requisitions: it is to meet the needs of the regional *jam*, and here again there is one system from top to bottom. These then are the grassland requisitions. With regard to requisitions in the Han lands, apart from each household and each taxpayer having to convert silk and cotton cloth into silver, wherever the emissaries pass through, the people must send army remounts, provisions, equipment, and all other things needed for official purposes; moreover, from time to time they calculate the total amounts of these to be used and make a general assessment on the civilian households. The people of the conquered kingdoms find the levies extremely harsh. Their hatred and resentment penetrates to Heaven, yet in the end, there is nothing they can do. The lord of the Tatars occasionally dispatches officials from the grasslands to go out to the Han lands and set the level of requisitions. When I was in Yanjing, I saw that Grand Councilor Hu had been dispatched, but his indulgence in extortion was even more frightful than normal.[82] Everyone, from the literati to the beggars, had to pay silver for his requisitions. The educated in Yanjing had the following poem:

> Scholar-teachers every one, must in silver pay.
> Pupils few, they suffer in the "poor but righteous" way.

---

80. Ch. *cáoyùn* 漕運, "to transport grain to the capital by water." The implication, therefore, is that this silver is being transported as a commuted tax. The use of the term for waterborne shipping might indicate that the silver was going no farther than Yanjing, but we know from other sources that much silver was shipped to Qara-Qorum. Peng Daya is simply using an analogy to the Chinese system to refer to that portion of the revenues sent to the capital, as distinct from those portions retained for expenditures on the local or regional level.

81. About 88,000 pounds of silver; see the tables of weights and measures in Appendix §2.7 (p. 192).

82. Ch. *Hú Chéngxiàng* 胡丞相. *Hú* here refers to the first syllable of the official's name Qutu-ghu (nicknamed "Shiki" in Mongolian), but the whole could also be understood in Chinese as "Grand Councilor Barbarian." Qutughu was appointed chief judge (*jarghuchi*) for the Chinese districts in the seventh moon of 1234; he arrived at Yanjing and conducted census registration for tax purposes in 1235–1236. For a very different judgment on his tenure in office, see Zhang Dehui's "Notes," p. 174.

Gold Horse Gate and Jade Hall[83] for Lu Jingshan,
But just moonbeams and a clear breeze[84] for our Mr. Fan.
They only let Li She on paragons give answers;
Zhang Zhai by luck enjoys the rain-ritual dancers.[85]
Bigwigs charge Grand Councilor Hu of sin,
But he just got off scott-free—*nai sayin!*[86]

From this one may see their method of levying taxes.

29. They trade in sheep, horses, gold, silver, and fine silks.

30. In commercial trading, from the lord of the Tatars on through the bogus "princes," bogus "crown princes," bogus "princesses," and so on, all give silver on commission to Westerners. Or they lend it out to common people at inflated interest rates—one *ding* of principal, after circulating for ten years, will earn interest of 1,024 *ding*. Sometimes they purchase market goods and eagerly move them [to profit off the resale],[87] and sometimes they collude with night-burglars and then accuse other people to make them pay restitution.

30.1. Ting: My observation is that [among] the Tatars there is only *saugha*; not one of them understands how to be a merchant. From the Tatar lord on down, they just give their silver to the Westerners, having them carry on trade themselves and pay interest. The Westerners in turn lend the silver to common people, or they themselves travel widely as merchants, or they falsely claim to have been robbed and make accusations, forcing the civilian households of the districts to pay them restitution. In general, the Tatars only want satins, iron vessels, various sorts of timber, and household items; they do not go beyond satisfying their needs for

---

83. *Jīn mǎ (mén)* 金馬 門, or "gold horse (gate)," is a common allocution for the Hanlin Academy, while *yùtáng* 玉堂, "jade hall," designates its members.

84. Ch. *qīngfēng* 清風, lit., "soothing breezes," also refers to someone poor and virtuous even in retirement.

85. Ch. *wǔyú rén* 舞雩人, lit., "dancing-rain sacrifice people." In this ancient sacrifice for rain, female mediums danced around an altar, hence the name. The names Lu Jingshan, Mr. Fan, Li She, and Zhang Zhai are not otherwise known. They appear to be just stock names for ordinary people, like "John Doe" or "Jack and Jill," but may be particular scholars at the time.

86. Peng Daya below defines *nai sayin* (Ch. *nà shāyīn*) as Mongolian for "good." *Shāyīn* is obviously Mongolian *sayin* (modern *sain*) "good." *Nà* represents Mongolian *nai*, which appears once in the *Secret History of the Mongols* in the phrase *nai jöb* "very right" (see §126). Although *nà shāyīn* would be the standard pronunciation in both the Mongol era and today, there are Chinese dialects in which these graphs would be read *nai sayin* and that is evidently the sound intended here. The whole phrase, of course, is sarcastic.

87. Ch. *màoqiān* 懋遷, lit., "urge (someone) to transport (especially goods for sale)." This is an allusion to the canonical *Exalted Documents*, where Yu the Great, one of the ancient Chinese culture heroes, described how he helped rebuild the economy after floods: "I urged them further to exchange what they had for what they had not, and to dispose of their accumulated stores" (Legge [1865] 1991, 78). Despite this classical allusion, Peng Daya clearly views this behavior negatively as profiteering off of local gluts and scarcities.

food and clothing.[88] When Han fellows, Westerners, and other people go into the grasslands, the Tatars trade their highly valued sheep with them. The Tatar ways are so honest that they truly do not pick up things found on the road.[89] They do have some robberies, but only people from the conquered kingdoms commit them. The Westerners also plant goods in uninhabited places and keep keen watch on them from far away. Only when someone touches the goods do they come rushing over to make obfuscating false accusations. The Westerners' cunningness of mind is something frightful. On top of that, most of them are ingenious and able to speak the languages of many countries—frankly quite remarkable.[90]

31. As for their official titles, some usurp "Prince of State" while others make expedient use of "Emperor," as well as "Commandery Prince," and "herald." The fugitive captives from the various conquered kingdoms call themselves "Grand Councilor of the Secretariat," "General," "Vice-Director," "Pacification" or "Transport Commissioner," stealing titles however they please. Originally, the Tatars did not issue proclamations at court of important appointments.

31.1. Ting: I have investigated this. The Tatars originally did not use a system of official appointments and emoluments, nor did the Tatar lord understand the significance of official titles. The Tatars had only the tiger's-head gold paiza, the plain gold *paiza*, or the plain silver *paiza*. If someone has performed a service and presents his own gold or silver, asking the lord of the Tatars for one, then he may be permitted to make his own, on which could be engraved Western graphs, not going beyond such phrases as "By the strength of immortal Heaven."[91] Apart from that, there are gentlemen of the vanquished Jin who have managed one way or another to take up a variety of duties, falling as low as butchers and petty traders, or departing to become yellow-capped priests,[92] but still addressing each other by their old titles. The family of Pacification Commissioner Wang has several cart-pushers who are called "Transport Commissioner" or "Vice-Director." Those in the [Daoist] Palace of Eternal Spring[93] are mostly gentlemen of the defeated Jin court, who

---

88. Here I follow Ma Xiaolin's suggestion and interpret *dòngshǐ* 動使 as "utensils; household utensils"; see Long 1985, 291.

89. This is an ancient Chinese cliché meaning that people have a natural sense of right and wrong, which guides their behavior without laws or punishments.

90. Many of the stratagems and the suffering they caused mentioned by Peng and Xu here in §30 and §30.1 are also described in Song Zizhen's "Spirit-Path Stele" under year 1236 (p. 146).

91. Ch. *Chángshēng Tiāndi qìlì* 長生天底氣力. This passage describes the *paizas* denoting official position. Later in the empire, Chinese was replaced by Mongolian, and many *paiza* of various ranks with this formula in Mongolian have been discovered and published. See Dang 2001; Dang 2003.

92. Ch. *huángguān* 黃冠 ("yellow caps"), a term for Daoist clergy.

93. The Palace of Eternal Spring (Changchun Gong) in Yanjing was the center of the Quanzhen Daoist religion during the Mongol era. It was mostly destroyed in the mid-fourteenth century

avoid shaving their heads in the *bájiāo* style,[94] are exempted from tax and corvée, and also receive clothing and food. It is a most sorrowful and distressing sight.

32. In their system of commoner households, control over ten men is exercised by a *paiza* chief. Ten of these units of ten form a hundred-man unit, and ten hundreds form a thousand-man unit, and ten thousands make up a ten-thousand-man unit, each with a headman.

33. As for prohibitions in their country: those who break ground while the grass is growing, or who neglect a fire and burn up the grass, are executed with their families; those who take stray items, or tread on a threshold, or whip a horse on its face, or who have illicit relations and flee together, are executed individually. Those who choke while eating, or who bleed from the mouth or nose, are faulted for having impure hearts. Those who let an axle [get tangled?] outside its felt curtain are reprimanded for binding the Tatar lord's throat in their hearts.[95] Passing on the left when riding toward one another is called mutual accord, but when a person is offered meat and receives it with the left hand, then it is called mutual discord. Those who, when pouring out milk or kefir, empty the vessel completely are said to be cutting off their descendants. Those who encounter thunder and lightning abandon all their goods and their livestock and flee, returning only after a full year.

> 33.1. Ting: I have seen that whenever a Tatar hears a peal of thunder, he will always cover his ears and crouch down on the ground, as though hiding from something.

34. As for their rewards and punishments, the undertaking of tasks is commonly seen as expected and they dare not claim merit. In their mutual admonitions, they always say that if their lord sends them into fire or water, then all should go into it together. When they talk about hunger, cold, and other hardships, they call it *dai* (a word for "not good").[96] Thus when their country is at peace there are no rewards. Only soldiers who are victorious in war are rewarded with horses, gold or silver *paiza*s, or lengths of ramie or silk. When a city is captured, then they are set free to plunder lads and lasses, jade and silk. In this plundering, merit is apportioned by relative speed: the first to arrive sticks an arrow in the doorway, and those who arrive later do not dare enter. Those who commit transgressions are put to death,

---

but was rebuilt and exists today under the name of the White Cloud Temple (Baiyun Guan) in southwestern Beijing.

94. This *bájiāo* 跋焦 is a reference to the distinctive Mongolian way of shaving their head also described in Zhao Gong's "Memorandum," p. 79, where it is called *pójiāo*.

95. This passage has long baffled commentators; our translation is tentative.

96. Actually, as Peng correctly notes below, the Mongolian word for "bad" or "not good" is *ma'u* (Ch. *màowū*; modern Mongolian *muu*). Peng was perhaps confused by the fact that *dǎi* 觮 in Chinese also means "bad, wicked, depraved."

which is called *aldaqui*.[97] If the transgressor is not killed, then he is punished with service in the *ba'atur* army (similar to the suicide warriors of the Han people), and only after he has survived three or four times is he absolved.[98] Those whose crime is lightest are punished by confiscation of half their property.

> 34.1. Ting: The best law of theirs that I have seen is that those who tell lies are put to death.

35. Those who commit robbery are put to death, and their wives and children, livestock and property are confiscated and delivered to the household of the person robbed. If the slave of A steals the goods of B, or steals the goods of B's slave, in either case the wives, children, livestock, and property of A and his slave are confiscated and the slave as well as A is put to death. This they call "sentencing the case's principal." When someone sees and consequently covets something of someone else it is called *saugha*. If the owner gives it to him, they say "*nai sayin,*" which in the Tatar language means "good," but if he does not, then they say "*ma'u,*" which in the Tatar language means "not good."[99] *Saugha* in the Chinese language is "long sought."[100]

36. In horsemanship and archery, babies are tied with cords onto plats which then are fastened onto horses' backs, so they can go about with their mothers. Three-year-old toddlers[101] are secured to the saddle with rope and given something to grasp with their hands so they can follow along as the rest dash about on horseback. In their fourth and fifth years, they carry under one arm a small bow and short arrows; and when grown, they occupy themselves during all four seasons with hunting game. When they ride at a gallop, they always stand in the stirrups rather than sit in the saddle, so that eight or nine parts of their strength comes from the instep and just one or two parts from the buttocks. They are swift as the onrush of a gale and strong as the weight of a mountain. Wheeling left and cutting right like wings in flight, they thus can look left and shoot right, though they seldom shoot across the crupper. When they shoot on foot, then they stand like the graph *bā*,[102] with a wide stance and the midriff in a crouch. Thus, they shoot with power enough to pierce armor.

---

97. This Mongolian term, lit., "to lose; to lose control, to make a slip," was used in Mongolian legal phraseology to mean "to be punished."

98. These *ba'atur* (from written Mongolian *baghatur* "hero," "knight") armies were attached to the center or *ghol* of the military formations, and used in the forefront of attacks.

99. On *saugha* and *nai sayin*, see notes 66 and 86. *Ma'u* (Ch. *màowū*) is a good rendering of Mongolian *ma'u*, "bad."

100. *Mì* 覓, lit., "seek out, look for, hunt up," but here the meaning seems to be "something I have been looking for for a long time, and finally have found it with you."

101. All ages given here are in Chinese *sùi* 歲, which includes one year for time in the womb and advances by one year at the lunar New Year. Thus, a child born in December can be two *sùi* within one or two months of birth.

102. This Chinese graph, meaning "eight," consists of two lines diverging top to bottom: 八.

36.1. Ting: I saw an old Tatar lady, when she had finished giving birth to a baby in the wilderness. She used sheep's wool to wipe off the child, then used a sheepskin for swaddling clothes. Binding the baby up in a little cart, four or five feet long and one foot wide, the old lady thereupon tucked the cart crosswise under her arm and straightaway rode off on horseback.[103]

37. Their horses are pastured in the wild, without any hay or grains. In moon VI, they eat their fill of green grass and begin to fatten. When the males reach four years, then they are gelded, so they are stout and powerful yet gentle and yielding, not temperamental. Able to endure wind and cold, they are long-lived. If they are not castrated, it is the opposite of this; moreover, they readily neigh and get spooked, making them useless for ambushes. The horses' hooves are cut close to the quick, making them nervous about stony places, so they add a thin plate made from iron or a wooden board, calling it "hoof cleats."[104] Whenever they are riding about, they do not let the horses eat to the full, and whenever they take off the saddle, they inspect the beast carefully and look up at its head. They wait for the horse's breath to return to equilibrium and for its four hooves to become cold. Only then do they release it to water and pasture. Those who herd them are called *ula'achi*[105]; Westerners make up 30 percent of them, and Han men make up 70 percent.

37.1. Ting: I once investigated the Tatars' method of raising horses. From early spring, after they call off the campaigns, all good horses that have been on campaign are released to enjoy water and pasture without being ridden or driven, until the west wind is about to come. The horses then are caught, bridled, and tied up near the tents. They are given only a little water and grass until a month has gone by and their

---

103. Despite some unclarity, what is being described here is obviously the practice of tying the infant on to a cradleboard as a portable carrier. This practice is known among the Mongols as well as among many American Indian nations, the Saami, and elsewhere. What is less comprehensible is why the cradleboard is referred to as a "cart," as if it had wheels, and why it is so long (four or five *chǐ* or Chinese feet).

104. That is, horseshoes (Ch. *jiǎosè* 腳澀). While Peng Daya seems unfamiliar with them, the existing Chinese name indicates horseshoes were not completely unknown. In fact, a note in Ouyang Xiu's *Historical Records of the Five Dynasties*, in its chapter on the "Four Barbarians," records how an ambassador to Khotan heard that the Uyghurs of Ganzhou (modern Gansu) had taught the envoys of China's Latter Jin dynasty (936–947) about horseshoes ("wooden cleats for horses' hooves"). They were made of wood drilled with holes; four corresponding holes were bored in the horse's hooves for attaching the shoe. See Ouyang 2016, 1038; and the discussion in Xu 2014, 120–22.

105. *Ula'achi* does not mean simply herdsman, but rather one serving at a post-road station (*ula'a*). Peng's claim—that 30 percent are Westerners (Uyghurs, Tajiks, and other oasis dwellers) and 70 percent Han Chinese—may be true of those on the post-road stations, but it could hardly be true of horse-herders in Mongolia in general. Zhang Dehui also noticed a large number of non-Han farmers in Mongolia; see "Notes," p. 167.

fat has dropped. When ridden fully several hundred *lǐ*,[106] they naturally do not sweat, and thus they can endure the long distances of going on campaign. Usually when right on the road, the horses are not allowed to eat grass or drink water, for if they do so while under duress, far from putting on weight, they tend to get sick. These are excellent methods for raising horses. Southerners do the opposite, so many of their horses get sick. In husbanding their horses, they reserve the fully robust *ila*[107] stock, and mostly geld the rest, so all the horses are strong and vigorous. The *ila*, stallions that have not been gelded, are placed exclusively in control of the herds of mares and are not allowed in the herds of geldings, geldings and mares each having their separate herds. Ordinarily the horses, mostly in herds of four to five hundred head, are herded by only two *ula'achi*, who wield pendant-shaped iron crops,[108] used as whips to flog them. When the horses see it, they are afraid. Every morning and evening, each *ula'achi* leads the horses under their supervision to make a circle around the front of the master's tent,[109] and after a moment they all disperse. Whenever they water the horses, because their well holes can only serve four or five horses at a time, the beasts all come by themselves one after another in their natural order; when one has drunk its fill and gone away, the next one comes in turn. If one jumps the line, the *ula'achi* brandishes his iron whip from a distance and the horse bows its head and halts its steps. Not one beast dares act up. Most orderly are the mare herds. Each *ila* horse controls fifty or sixty mares. If a mare should stray from the herd, the *ila* horse will certainly bite and kick her, forcing her back. If an *ila* horse of some different herd should trespass, the *ila* horse of this herd will certainly bite and kick him. That they are sociable yet make distinctions is quite obvious.

38. Their saddles and bridles are light and simple, weighing less than seven or eight catties[110] to facilitate swift riding. The "goose-wings" of the saddle are upright in the front and flat in the back so that turns can be executed without injury to

---

106. A *lǐ* is about a little over a third of a mile or half a kilometer; see the tables of weights and measures in Appendix §2.7 (p. 192).

107. As Igor de Rachewiltz (1974; cf. Xu 2014, 125–26) points out, this word *ila* (Ch. *yǐlà*), meaning "stallion," is not actually Mongolian, but a Kitan word widely used in North China at the time. A Sino-Mongolian vocabulary from the time of Qubilai Khan actually gives *ila* in its Chinese form *yǐlà* as a Chinese term with the Mongolian definition as *ajirghai* "stallion"; see Kara 1990, 282.

108. Ch. *jīxīn tiězhuā* 鷄心鐵檛, lit., a "chicken-heart iron horsewhip." (The iron knob at its head presumably had a shape and size like a chicken's heart.) This type of iron crop was also called the *gǔduǒ* 骨朵 (also read as *gǔduǒ* 骨檕, *gǔdōu* 骨都, or even *guāzhūn* 胍肫), under which name it was also borne by guardsmen at the Southern Song, Mongol, and other imperial courts as a way of keeping order. See Xu 2014, 127; Matsuda 2021, 189–91, with fig. 6.6–6.8.

109. Ch. *zhǔrén zhàng* 主人帳. This was presumably the manager of the post-road station where the *ula'achi* worked and who probably also owned a good percentage of the herd.

110. Ch. *jīn*, about 1.4 pounds; see the tables of weights and measures in Appendix §2.7 (p. 192).

the horse's shoulder.[111] The sides of the stirrups are round so that one's feet can be planted in the middle without inclining to one side. The bottom is wide so one's boots slip in easily. The leather piece attaching the stirrup is massaged by hand, not tanned, and is soaked with sheep fat, so it is not ruined by rain. Its width barely exceeds one inch and its length does not reach four fists[112] in all, making it very convenient for turning one's body while standing astride the horse.

39. Their army is simply those commoners aged fifteen and older, and is all cavalrymen without any infantry. The men ride in groups of two to three or six to seven,[113] and fifty horsemen they call a *jiŭ*[114] (that is, a company). Military chiefs and able-bodied slaves voluntarily gather into five-man units, which specially guard the commanding generals on left and right. They call these *ba'atur* troops. In the past, when they attacked Hexi, the Jurchens, and other kingdoms, the Tatars drove those kingdoms' own people to attack their own cities.

> 39.1. Ting: In my travels back and forth over the steppe, I never once saw a person going on foot. When the troops set out, the leader rides one horse with five or six to three or four other horses following along. They regularly prepare thus for an emergency, and even without [so many backups] a man must have at least one or two extra mounts.

40. Their weapons and armor consist of scale armor, chain mail (with leather six layers deep),[115] tough sheep-horn bows (in which the horn interlaces with the handle for three feet), sounding (that is, whistling) arrows, camel-bone arrows, and "needle-propelling"[116] arrows. They whittle wood for the shafts and take down birds of prey for the feathers. Their scimitars follow the Westerners' style, light and sharp, with hilts that are small and narrow, making them easy to wield. They

---

111. "Goose-wings" (Ch. *yànchì* 雁翅) refers to the wooden base of Mongolian or Chinese saddles; see *IMEA* 1987, 35, where we have Chinese *ānchì* 鞍翅 "saddle-wings" and Mongolian *qabtasu*.

112. "Inch" is Ch. *cùn*, about 1.23 inches (see Appendix §2.7 [p. 192]). "Fist" is *zŏng* 總; for the reading of the graph and its interpretation we follow Xu Quansheng 2014, 129.

113. Or possibly, "Every man has from two or three or six or seven mounts."

114. The MSS here have two variants, *jiū* 糾 or *tŏu* 斜. *Tŏu* has neither an appropriate meaning ("silk-yellow") nor any identifiable use as a phonetic representation of a Mongolian or Kitan term. *Jiū*, however, is frequently confused with Chinese *jiŭ*, which designated the Jiün or border cavalry under the Kitan Liao and Jurchen Jin dynasties, as described by Zhao Gong in §10 of his "Complete Record of the Mong-Tatars" and mentioned elsewhere by him and Li Xinchuan. This term appears to derive from Kitan *tiur~tiuriñ*, "assemblage; gathering of people," which matches the meaning here. We thus follow Li Wentian in taking *Jiū* as a mistake for *Jiŭ* as the correct reading. See Xu 2014, 130–31.

115. "Scale armor" is *liŭyè jiǎ* 柳葉甲, lit., "willow-leaf armor," while "chain mail" is *luóquān jiǎ* 羅圈甲, lit., "ring-net armor" (the more ordinary Chinese term is *suŏzi jiǎ* 鎖子甲, lit., "interlocking armor"). Scale armor, along with plate armor, was typical during the Ming, while chain mail and plate armor, but not scale armor, was typical in the Song. At the beginning of the Ming, fine scale armor was made with the following components: neck guard piece: 30 scales; body piece: 209 scales; separate heart piece: 17 scales; limb-guards: 20 scales each. See Zhou 1984, 440, 315.

116. Ch. *pīzhēn* 批針. It is unclear what sort of arrow this is.

have long and short spears on which the tips are like drills, so that what is speared does not slip off, and they can penetrate heavy armor. They have defensive shields of short-stemmed bamboo, or else of willow, tied with leather; these are thirty-five inches in breadth[117] and twice as long as the breadth. Half of them have circular shields[118] which the vanguard in particular carry on their shoulders as they dismount from their horses and shoot—especially in breaking enemy lines. They also have circular shields made of iron that can substitute for helmets and are convenient when turning around in formation. And they have crutch-type shields,[119] used to avoid artillery fire in assaulting city walls. Every great chieftain and leader has a banner that is marked on only one side (lesser men are not allowed to raise them). These are normally kept rolled up and put away; when the commander directs military operations then his banner is unfurled and afterward furled again. In assaulting city walls, they have catapults, the catapults have sheds, and the sheds are covered in nets of rope, to screen those who are hauling the mechanism's ropes. When they prepared to attack Fengxiangfu,[120] they concentrated 400 catapults on one corner of the city wall. None of the rest of their weaponry is worth discussing. They are most skilled with bow and arrow, and secondarily with the scimitar.

40.1. Ting: I have investigated this. The Tatars in the beginning were primitively ignorant[121] and lacked even a single of the known crafts. In their whole country, apart from breeding livestock, what could they produce? Their people were plain and simple; how could they have any abilities? They only made saddle bridges from birch wood, shoes from sheepskin, and stirrups by gouging pieces of wood. Their arrowheads were of bone; they had nowhere to get iron. Only later when they conquered the Westerners did they begin to have products, craftsmen, and mechanisms. Now, the craftsmanship of the Westerners is extremely refined; especially fine are their instruments of siege warfare. After destroying the Jin caitiffs, the Tatars' skill in every sort of craftsmanship became complete.

41. Their army is provisioned with sheep and milking horses (squeezing the teats with the hands is called "milking"[122]). When a horse begins to lactate, they let the

---

117. Lit., "thirty *cùn* wide." See the tables of weights and measures in Appendix §2.7 (p. 192).

118. Previous editors and translators have read *cháng zé bèi yú kuò zhī bàn* 長則倍於闊之半 as one phrase. Literally, this would be "twice as long as half the width," which seems an absurdly roundabout way to say its length is the same as its breadth. We place a sentence break between *kuò* and *zhī bàn*, thus giving the reading here.

119. Ch. *guǎizi mùpái* 拐子木牌.

120. The siege of Fengxiangfu took place in the second moon of 1231, under Emperor Ögödei's personal command.

121. Ch. *cǎomèi* 草昧.

122. Ch. *jǐ* 泲, a rare word, lit., "to seep or ooze through something," as in straining through a cloth. In this section, it should be remembered that the Chinese never drank milk and the very idea of milking animals by hand was virtually unknown to them.

foals feed on it, only gathering the mares for milking at night. They store the milk in leather receptacles, churn it for several nights, and drink it only when the taste is a little sour. They call this "mare's milk." Only when invading other lands must they engage in seizure and plunder. This is just as the military master Sunzi said, "Rely on seizing provisions from the enemy."[123]

41.1. Ting: I have often observed them milking mare's milk during the day, and I also asked them about it once. At first there was no restriction to morning or evening. Their method of expressing is to first allow the foals to drink and open up the flow of milk, but then to drive the foals away. The people then use their own hands to express the milk into leather pails, after which, however, they pour it into leather sacks and beat it. Ordinarily people drink it after only a few nights. When I first went to the Golden Tent, the mare's milk drunk by the Tatar lord was clear in color and sweet to the taste; it was very different from the ordinary drink with its thick, white color and sour, rank taste. They call it "black horse's milk," perhaps because the clearness seems black to them.[124] When I asked, then they said that it is actually beaten for seven or eight days. The more it is beaten the clearer it gets, and when it is clear, it has no rankness. I was only able to drink it this once; I never saw it anywhere else. The fine foodstuffs presented as tribute are like this. Also twice when I was at the Golden Tent, grape wine was sent in. The wine had been poured into glass bottles, from each of which one could get more than ten small cups. Its color is that of the South's persimmon varnish,[125] its taste is extremely sweet, and I heard that if one drinks a lot then one will indeed get drunk. But anyway, I had no chance to drink a lot of it, since it was a tribute gift from a Western kingdom.

42. In their military deployments they have always feared attack from ambush. Even flank units must first send out crack cavalry, dispersing in all four directions, climbing high hills and looking far into the distance. Making deep patrols covering one or two hundred *li*, they ambush and detain residents and travelers, in order to reconnoiter the actual situation to the right, left, front, and rear, considering, for instance: by what road they can advance, what cities there are to attack, in what area they can give battle, in what places they can camp, in what direction

123. This very widely cited aphorism comes from Sunzi, II.9: "One who excels in employing the military does not conscript the people twice or transport provisions a third time. If you obtain your equipment from within the state and rely on seizing provisions from the enemy, then the army's foodstuffs will be sufficient." See Sawyer and Sawyer 1993, 159–60.

124. In Mongolian, clear liquids are generally termed "black," while in Chinese they are generally termed "white." So plain boiled water, without tea, is called *bái kāishǔi*, "white, boiled water," in modern Chinese and *khar us*, "black water," in modern Mongolian.

125. Ch. *shìqī* 柿漆. This is the juice obtained by mashing persimmon branches, which was used as a water repellant application. By "the South," Ting presumably means his own country of the Southern Song.

enemy soldiers may lie, or where fodder and provisions are available. The whole responsibility for discerning this rests on the reports of the mounted scouts when they return. If there is a great press of men and horses combining strength in a large-scale undertaking, then they will first "burn the lute" and settle their choice upon one man to command the units.

> 42.1. Ting: In my observations, I have never seen the Tatars station substantial numbers of troops inside city walls. In the districts I passed through, both in Henan and Hebei, there was not a single soldier within the cities. Only outside the cities, in the villages, were there mounted scouts scattered like constellations, managing things. If they suddenly are alerted to something untoward, the mounted scouts respond by investigating in all directions. If they are able to find out the actual situation, they will urgently report it to their leaders and to the main force of soldiers and horses.

43. For their camps they always choose a high mound, and the tent of the commanding general must face southeast. In front of that, they station the cavalry patrols—*taulawchi*[126] in Tatar—who guard the area in shifts (only to their front do no soldiers camp). To the left, right, and rear of the general's tent, the soldiers and horses of the units all bivouac in order under their leaders. In the camps they also place a premium on widely distributing tasks to facilitate haying and foddering. In each camp two horses are kept saddled at night to guard against the unexpected. The camp-head's name is the night password. If one camp has an alarm, then the nearby camps have horses at the ready, awaiting any need to pursue or attack; the rest of the camps all keep themselves in order without stirring. Only the camp of the mounted scouts is different from this: the commander stays in the middle, surrounded by soldiers on all four sides. They pass along a carved piece of wood when changing the night patrol (like Han armies' method of passing along arrows). Foddering the horses within the camp keeps the animals from bolting or getting lost. Even before sunset the camp prepares a fire—this is called a "fire for show."[127] After nightfall, they move to a place where others cannot see them, to guard against a night raid, though the "fire for show" is left in the original camp and not touched until daybreak.

> 43.1. Ting: I observed them frequently using these deceptive placements,[128] and also that as soon as they set camp, right away they would give thought to scouting out the surrounding conditions.

---

126. Ch. *tuōluòchì*. The medieval pronunciation of the Chinese would have been something like *tau-lau-chi*. We have taken it to be a *nomen actoris* in *-qchi* formed from the verb *ta'ul-*, "to hand over, deliver [information or things]."

127. Ch. *huǒpū* 火鋪. This term is not Mongolian and the practice is described for Chinese armies in the tenth century. See Xu 2014, 154.

128. Ch. *gǒupū* 狗鋪, lit., "dog for show"; this was the usual Song Chinese term for such deceptive signals, as can be seen in the citations assembled by Xu 2014, 154–55.

44. Their battle array is suited to wilderness warfare; if they do not see an advantage, they do not advance. Between bouts of activity and non-activity, they learn the enemy's strengths and weaknesses. A hundred cavalrymen circling around can contain a host of ten thousand; a thousand cavalrymen, breaking up and fanning out, can occupy a hundred *lĭ*. For breaking hardened troops and destroying enemy formations, they rely wholly on the armored vanguard that numbers 30 percent of the attack force. Whenever they approach an enemy formation, they break up into groups of three, four, or five, never clustering together to be surrounded by the enemy. As a general rule, infantry ought to keep rank, and the cavalry ought to split up. If the enemy splits up, one should also split up; if the enemy gathers, one should also gather. Just so, their cavalry charges—whether from near or far, whether there be many or few, whether close serried or spread out, whether upfront or stealthy—come on like the sky falling and depart like the disappearance of lightning. It is called "raven troops in a scattered-star battle array."[129] In splitting up from a gathered formation, they watch the directions pointed by the horsewhip [of their leader], and in gathering again from a dispersed array, they listen for the sound of the *gugui*.[130] By self-signaling, they transmit messages from near to far, reaching a thousand *lĭ* in almost no time. When they want to gather for the night, they look for the smoke from a large fire to know the meeting place. For them the best time for battle is when it is extremely cold with no snow. They then rub a stone and pray to Heaven.[131]

44.1. Ting: I have observed the Tatars in their military operations and they just charge in recklessly without even looking first.[132] They too are men, so how is it that they do not fear death? It is just that from the day when they mobilized their armies and encroached southward, they have only rarely suffered a loss. Therefore, their gall[133] increases and they dare to do anything. The Tatars' rations are truly just the sheep and horses that accompany them. They do not need to transport provisions. Yet in a given army, they prefer to have only so many Tatars; all the rest of them are preferably men from the defeated kingdoms. The sheep and horses that follow them are never sufficient; moreover, the men from the defeated kingdoms need grain rations to

---

129. Again, this term is not one Peng learned from the Mongols, but an old Chinese term for exceptionally stealthy and decentralized troops formations. See the citations in Xu 2014, 157.

130. Ch. *gūgŭi* 姑詭. Scholars have linked this to Mongolian *kö'erge*, "drum, tambourine." In China, drums signaled advance, and gongs retreat. However, the parallels from Kitan practice that scholars have drawn suggest, rather, that a horn is intended; see Xu 2014, 158. This *gugui* thus may be a transcription of the Kitan word for horn.

131. This is the famous weather magic of shamans, who use *jada* (Mongolian) or *yai* (Turkish) stones to produce snowfalls. This technique played a key role in the great Battle of Mount Sanfeng that destroyed the last major Jin field army in 1232. See Molnár 1994 and Boldbaatar 2008.

132. Here we follow the suggestion of Reader A and read *mán* not as an ethnic term for "savages," but as a colloquial term meaning "reckless; rash."

133. As in Greek medicine, the Chinese located courage in the gallbladder (*dǎn* 膽).

eat. From this one should know that we cannot just exaggerate the Tatars' strength while forgetting the principle of being responsible to strengthen ourselves.

45. To defeat the enemy, they climb high hills and look far into the distance, first examining the terrain and scoping out what is true and false about the enemy. They especially focus on exploiting any confusion. Thus, when the vanguard first engages, they always rush the enemy lines with a sharp, sudden, oblique attack before moving their main force. Then regardless of whether they be few or many, the Tatars charge straight in. Even an enemy numbering 100,000 cannot sustain such an attack. But if the enemy is not shaken, then the frontline unit passes to the side and the next rank of troops hits them again. If the enemy's ranks still are not broken, then the rear unit tries the same attack. When they are about to strike the enemy, they may also delay for a while, redistributing their troops left, right, and behind according to strategies. When their soldiers have come together from the four directions, then the last to arrive sounds the *gugui* and they all respond en masse, rousing their strength for another collective strike.

Apart from that plan, those with round shoulder shields may dismount and shoot on foot. As soon as they hit a target, the enemies on either side will buckle. Once buckled, they will certainly fall into confusion. Once the enemy is in confusion, the Tatars swiftly advance. The enemy may perceive that it is opportune for their cavalry to press those on foot, but then the cavalry units positioned behind the men on foot will gallop out and meet the enemy head on. If the enemy puts up a strong wall that all of the Tatars' plans fail to penetrate, then they will surely drive cattle at them or lash wild horses toward them, using animals to disturb the enemy's ranks; seldom does it fail to defeat them. Should the enemy set a forest of halberds in a line pointing outward to ward off the horses and stop their charge, then the surrounding cavalrymen and scattered scouts occasionally shoot single arrows, causing the enemy to continually make some effort. After the Tatars keep this up for quite a while, the enemy inevitably runs out of food or lacks firewood or water and has no choice but to make a move. Then the Tatars advance their troops and close in. Sometimes, though, if the enemy's line has been shaken, the Tatars will not attack right away, but instead wait until the enemy has become weary, and only then charge in.

When their own troops are few, sometimes the Tatars will first scatter dirt and then drag branches, making dust rise to the heavens and leading the enemy to suspect that their troops are many, thus inducing self-disintegration every time. Enemy forces that don't disintegrate are charged, their defeat being virtually certain. Sometimes the Tatars drive forth surrendered captives, let them be defeated in battle, and then take advantage of the enemy's exhaustion to attack them with crack troops. Or else they merely cross swords [with the enemy] and then fleeing in defeat, deceitfully abandon their military supplies and deliberately throw away gold and silver. The enemy may well consider this a real defeat and pursue the defeated without stopping—until they clash with the Tatars' hidden cavalry, often being completely wiped out. The difference between rejoicing one's way to defeat and seizing victory with a clever plan lies in the competing strategies.[134] The Tatars do things that are not addressed in the ancient techniques. When victorious, they dog the enemy's tail until the last man is killed, not permitting any to escape. If they are the ones defeated, they scatter in all four directions, beyond pursuit.

46. The commanders of their cavalry army were previously called the "seventeen leaders"[135]:

1. Temujin (or Chinggis; since his death, Ukudei's mother has personally led his cavalry army);[136]

2. Bogus senior "crown prince" Jochi (already killed);

3. Bogus second "crown prince" Chaghadai (he has been dispatched to garrison the Western kingdoms);

4. Bogus third "crown prince" Ukudei (that is, the present Tatar lord);

5. Bogus fourth "crown prince" Tolun (died of disease after returning from Henan; the above four are the true sons of Temujin);[137]

6. Temuge Otchin (also called Otčin, also called Great Prince Utshing [138]; he is Temujin's younger brother);

7. Alchidai (Temujin's fraternal nephew, Ukudei's younger paternal cousin);[139]

8. Imperial Son-in-Law Botu[140] (Temujin's son-in-law);

9. Baisma (alias Baisbu, the bogus "crown prince" of the White Tatars, Temujin's son-in-law, and the former husband of the bogus "princess" Alaqan);[141]

---

134. Ch. *bǐzōng cǐhéng* 彼縱此橫, lit., "that one is vertical, this one is horizontal." This refers to the "vertical" and "horizontal" alliances of the Warring States period in ancient Chinese history. These were two competing strategies of alliance for preventing the rise of the Qin kingdom in the west.

135. Actually, there are only sixteen; unless Öködei's mother (that is, Börte) is meant as a separate leader then one is missing. A numbering of "seventeen leaders" seems to have been a fixed phrase in use around the time of the Mongol conquest of the Jin rump state in Henan; see *JS* 117.2562; Xu Youren 2004, 483; cf. Xu 2014, 169–70.

136. Temüjin passed away in 1227. Öködei's mother was Chinggis Khan's first and primary wife, Börte. However, she is last mentioned in the sources around 1210, and it is possible that Peng Daya has confused her with one of Chinggis Khan's three other primary wives, each of whom controlled a palace-tent or *ordo* and its associated troops.

137. Tolun's name is more usually found as Tolui (-*i* and -*n* frequently alternate in Mongolian names).

138. We follow Wang Guowei in seeing the text's *niǎo* 裊 as a corruption of *wū* 烏; "Utshing" appears to be a dialect version of Otchin.

139. Alchidai was the son of Chinggis Khan's younger brother Qachi'un, and supposedly was his favorite nephew. He was mentioned in §4 and §4.1 (p. 94). On Alchidai, see Rashiduddin 1998/1999, 281, although the translator misreads his name in that source as "Elji'itäi.

140. Botu was an imperial son-in-law of the Ikires house. See his biography in *YS* 118.2921–23. Here the text mistakenly omits the *fù* in *fùmǎ* 駙馬, "imperial sons-in-law."

141. This figure is mentioned by Li Xinchuan and Zhao Gong as well, under the name Baisbo or Baisbu. His Chinese name was Zhenguo, which was locally pronounced as Chingui or Shingui.

10. Prince of State Muqali (a Black Tatar; he is[142] Bo'ol's father and Chala'un's grandfather);[143]

11. Commandery Prince Kete (a Black Tatar);[144]

12. Lady Xiao (a Kitan; she herself manages the catapult carts among her subordinate households);[145]

13. Aqai (a Kitan, originally in Dexingfu);

14. Tugha (that is, Aqai's younger brother; originally in Xuandezhou);[146]

15. Ming'an (a Kitan; the present-day Big Brother of the Mobile Secretariat of Yanjing, Hiêmdêibu, is his son);[147]

16. Liu Bolin (the top-ranking myriarch among the Han people).[148]

---

142. We follow Xu's reading of *nǎi* 乃, "is," for the text's *dāo* 刀, "knife." See Xu 2014, 169.

143. Muqali was the Cha'a'at branch of the Jalayir house; his official position and personality are sketched by Zhao Gong. By this time both he and Bo'ol had passed away and Chala'un (also known as Tash) had inherited his position.

144. This is the son of Jürchedei, a close companion of Chinggis Khan who is mentioned many times in the *Secret History of the Mongols*. His name is also written Ketei or Ke'etei.

145. The title "Lady" (Ch. *fūrén* 夫人), was granted to wives of nobles. Previous commentators have not satisfactorily identified this figure. Shen Cengzhi disregarded the surname and tried to identify her with the lady *née* Yaoli, the widow of Yêrud (Yelü) Liuke, the Kitan warlord in Manchuria. Xu Quansheng wished to emend *fūrén*, "lady," to *dàifu* 大夫, "sir," and identify him with the Kitan cavalry commander Xiao (or Šimei) Esen. See Xu 2014, 174–75. A better solution than either is to identify this Lady Xiao with the surviving wife of Xiao (Šimei) Chounu, a Kitan military official of the Jin dynasty who was one of the first to surrender to Chinggis Khan and served him on several of his campaigns. Xiao Chounu eventually received the rank of marshal of the Tanzhou Soldiery (in the mountains north of Yanjing) and supervised the craftsmen responsible for catching and housing birds for falconry. During Chinggis's Western Expedition, Chounu's men also supplied ten thousand arrows, bows, crossbows, and bowstrings, showing that they were involved in a wide variety of military technologies. Chounu died during the Western Expedition; his younger brother, Laowa, succeeded him as military commissioner of Tanzhou but also died in battle early in Öködei's reign, around 1230. Chounu's son, Qingshan, succeeded to Chounu's myriarchy in 1260, but between Laowa's death and Qingshan's succession, Chounu's wife must have succeeded him in his duties. See the brief biography in *YS* 179.4156. As Peng Daya's note indicates, during this time she must have branched out from small arms manufacture into larger-scale artillery craftsmanship.

146. Both Aqai and his brother Tugha were Kitans from Huanzhou Prefecture, on the southern edge of the Mongolian plateau. They were of the Kitans' imperial Ila surname and spoke fluent Chinese and Mongolian. See *YS* 150.3548–49 on Aqai and *YS* 149.3532 on Tugha. Dexingfu (modern Zhuolu) and Xuandezhou (modern Xuanhua) were the two main prefectures in the mountains north of Yanjing (Beijing). Zhang Dehui passed through both of them; see "Notes," p. 165.

147. Ming'an was a Kitan of the Šimei family, descended from one of the consort families of the Kitan Liao dynasty. Like Aqai and Tugha, he was from Huanzhou in Inner Mongolia. His son Hiêmdêibu's name is rendered in Chinese in a variety of ways. See their biography in *YS* 150.3555–57. The title "Big Brother of the Mobile Secretariat" is Ch. *Dàgē xíngshěng* 大哥行省; Hiêmdêibu was called that because he was Ming'an's eldest son, just as Shǐ Tianze was called "Shǐ the Third" or "Third Brother Shǐ" (see p. 126) because he was a third son. Zhao Gong (see p. 80) erroneously took "Big Brother," *Dàgē*, as Hiêmdêibu's name.

148. See Liu's biography in *YS* 149.3515–16. Born in Ji'nanfu in Shandong, he was assigned by the Jin dynasty to be a commander of a thousand in Inner Mongolia, where he deserted to

The number of their troops, whether greater or lesser, is unknowable. One man has several wives and one wife may have several sons, their formerly scarce number is now a multitude; they increase without diminishing. Also unknown is how many leaders there are. More than half of the old chiefs and veteran generals have died. Even so, those who formerly met the Jin caitiffs in battle between Tongguan Pass and the Yellow River,[149] such as Subu'edei, Temudei,[150] Ta'achar (now named Bunchan),[151] and Alchar,[152] still are healthy. As the battles do not cease, it seems they have no shortage of successors who are able at war.

> 46.1. Ting: I observed their custom of each husband having several tens of wives or even more than a hundred wives. A single wife's fertility is very rich. When Chinggis established the marriage law he was solely concerned to propagate the sons and grandsons of his own kind, so womanly jealousy was not permitted. The present Tatar lord Ukudei was born in the *bĭng/wŭ* year [1186], and has grown a beard. Most Black Tatars have scant whiskers, so a heavy beard is always honored. When I, Ting, was in front of the Golden Tent, I suddenly saw the Tatar lord come out of the tent together with one or two other men and shoot his bow. The Tatar lord alone personally shot four or five arrows for a distance up to 350 yards.[153] When he finished shooting, he reentered the Golden Tent.

47. The disposition of their leaders' forces is as follows:

1. Otchin's soldiers are in Liaodong;
2. Chaghadai's soldiers are spread out among the Westerners;
3. Imperial Son-in-Law Botu's soldiers are in Hexi.

All of them have to watch their backs. Under none of the Black Tatars' eight myriarchs do the men number ten thousand, but the soldiers under the myriarchs' senior and younger paternal uncles, elder and younger brothers, sons and paternal nephews, and other relatives are not counted as part of the ten thousand. There are four myriarchs in Han lands. They are:

Chinggis Khan. "Myriarch" is the conventional translation for a commander of a ten-thousand-household unit.

149. The battles between Tongguan Pass and the Yellow River took place from 1230 to 1234.

150. A commander of the Jalayir house, Temüdei has a brief biography in *YS* 131.3190.

151. Ta'achar, of the Hü'üshin family, was a grandnephew of Boroghul, one of Chinggis Khan's "four steeds." Ta'achar served in the *Keshikten* as a quiver-bearer (*qorchi*) and had his appanage in Guanshan Mountain in Inner Mongolia. He won merit in Tolui's campaign against the Jin in Henan. See *YS* 119.2952–53. His Mongolian nickname, Bunchan, comes from Jurchen *funcan*, "excess, extras."

152. Probably a member of the Tangut imperial family, which traced its ancestry to the ancient Tabghach house, he joined the Mongol camp in 1216, as did several other Tangut commanders. After playing a major role in Muqali's pacification of North China, he was eventually given command over the Pingyangfu area (modern Linfen in Shanxi). See *YS* 122.3006–7.

153. Lit., 200 *bù*. See the tables of weights and measures in Appendix §2.7 (p. 192).

1. Yan Shi in Yùnzhou (this is present-day Dongpingfu) has Shandong soldiers[154];

2. Shĭ Tianyi (or Shĭ the Third) in Zhendingfu, has Hedong and Hebei soldiers[155];

3. Zhang Rou in Mancheng (a county in Baozhou Prefecture), has the troops south of Yanjing[156]; and

4. Liu Heima (Bolin's son) in Tiancheng, has troops from behind the Yan-jing-Jìzhou Mountains.[157]

Although there are others who command substantial troops, none has the great numbers or powers of these four myriarchs. Besides the Han myriarchs, there are the troops in Liaodong, Hexi, and the Western kingdoms.

47.1. Ting: When I was on the steppe, I saw the commoner households under their chiefs, wagons loaded with supplies, their aged ones, young-sters, and livestock, traveling with their entire possessions for several days without cease. Also, there were many thirteen- and fourteen-year-olds among them. When I asked about this, they replied that all of them were Tatars being transferred to campaign against a Western kingdom. Since they would spend three years on the road, those who were now aged thir-teen or fourteen would, when they got there, turn seventeen or eighteen and all, thus, would be capable of serving as soldiers. The various races of Westerners have already all been made subjects. Only this one race of Westerners, who live just opposite the back passes to Western Sichuan,[158]

---

154. On Yan Shi, see his biography in the *YS* 148.3505–7. Dongpingfu Prefecture is modern-day Dongping in Shandong. Yùnzhou Prefecture was the city's name under the Song; the Jin dynasty had changed the name to Dongpingfu Prefecture.

155. Shĭ Tianyi appears in the *Yuanshi* as Shĭ Tianze, and was the younger brother of Shĭ Tianni and the third son of Shĭ Bingzhi, hence his nickname. See his biography in *YS* 155.3657–63. Zhendingfu is modern Zhengding, just north of Shijiazhuang.

156. On Zhang Rou, see his biography in the *YS* 147.3471–76.

157. On Liu Heima, see his biography in the *YS* 149.3516–18. "Behind the Yanjing-Jìzhou Moun-tains," refers to the areas north and northwest of the ridges north of present-day Beijing and Jìx-ian, thus the present-day Datong-Zhangjiakou area and the adjacent parts of Inner Mongolia. Tiancheng is modern-day Tianzhen in northern Shanxi province.

158. This "one race of Westerners . . . just opposite the back passes to Western Sichuan" has been interpreted differently by commentators. Li Wentian took it to be Samarqand on the basis of a general similarity in the description. However, Samarqand had long been pacified at this time and would not have been "three years" away. Peter Olbricht and Elisabeth Pinks, followed by Xu Quansheng, took it to be the Qipchaq country, probably on the basis of it being still in rebellion (Olbricht and Pinks 1980, 207–8; Xu 2014, 194). Yet the description does not match the Qipchaq lands at all. Moreover, these interpretations implicitly or explicitly take the *Xīchuān* 西川 of all the manuscripts to be not Western Sichuan, but a generic "Western River" (e.g., the *Weststromes* of Olbricht and Pinks 1980, 202–3), interpreted as either the Amu Darya near Samarqand or the Volga of the Qipchaq lands. Yet the same term is used by Xu Ting in §48.1 (p. 129) to mean specifically Western Sichuan. The same meaning should be intended here. Xu Ting saw a large expedition being readied while at Öködei's court in 1235–1236, as reinforce-ments for a previous dispatched expedition. This previously dispatched expedition cannot be the

with a city wall over a hundred miles long[159] and products in abundance, whose land is warm and grows the five grains, fruit trees, and big melons two men's arm spans in circumference, has until now been unwilling to submit. Chaghadai has been campaigning against them for several years, so these are reinforcements.

48. The kingdoms they have ruthlessly despoiled and which have already been defeated and no longer struggle, are: in the southeast, the White Tatars and the Jin caitiffs (the Jurchens); in the northwest, the Nayman (also called the Naiman), the Yughurs,[160] the Sultan,[161] the Sartaq,[162] the Qangli[163] (names of Western kingdoms); directly north, the Datar[164] (a race of the Ursut),[165] the Merkit; and directly south, the Western Xia. Those which still resist and are not yet finished are: in the east, Korea, and Wu'anu in Liaodong (that is, the Jurchens' Great Zhen kingdom; his Grand Councilor, Wang Xianzuo, is more than ninety years old and has vision into the future);[166] in the northeast, the Nibshu,[167] the Noqai-Irgen (that is, Dog Country. Their faces are like a crude lump[168] but their breasts are hairy. They can

---

great Western one against the Qipchaqs because the description of the destination does not fit at all. But there was also a large ongoing expedition against India via Afghanistan during Öködei's reign (Boyle 1963; Aubin 1969; May 2021, 276–81). The route from Sichuan through the Dali kingdom and Bengal into India was well-known at this time (Yang 2004; 2012), and this would explain why the object of the expedition is placed "opposite the back passes to Western Sichuan."

159. Lit., 300 *lǐ* long; see the tables of weights and measures in Appendix §2.7 (p. 192).

160. Ch. *Wǔyù*. This refers to the Uyghurs in the narrow sense and is simply a transcription of a common dialectal pronunciation of the word.

161. The Chinese has only *Sùlǐ* 速里, but these are the first two graphs used in the Chinese translation of the title "Sultan" in the *Campaigns of Chinggis Khan*. The third graph, *tán* 壇, has been inadvertently omitted.

162. Sartaq is the general Mongolian word for "Westerners," equivalent to the Chinese *Húihúi*. Although it is commonly translated as "Muslim," it actually includes what we would see as Middle Easterners of all religions. Rashid al-Din translates it as "Tajik" (Rashiduddin 1998/1999, 78).

163. The Qangli were nomadic, Turkic-speaking people in present-day central Kazakhstan. Qangli ladies, commanders, and soldiers played a major role in the Khwarazmian Empire.

164. "Datar" appears to be a variant spelling of "Tatar."

165. The Ursut (singular Urus) were a sub-ethnic group, of Sarmatian origin, found among several Turkic kingdoms: the Khazars, Qipchaqs, and Yenisey Qirgiz. In the *SHM* §239, the *Campaigns of Chinggis Khan*, and Rashid al-Din, the Ursut are found as one of the peoples in the Yenisey River basin (the area of modern Khakassia in Central Siberia). See Golden 1990.

166. Wu'anu was a Jurchen commander of the Fusen surname. In autumn 1216, he revolted against the Jin dynasty to establish his own regime in Manchuria. Within months of Peng Daya's visit to the Mongol court, an expedition was dispatched and captured him in October 1233. He also appears in *SHM* §253.

167. Ch. *Nīshū*. Xu Quansheng tries to identify this with the ethnonym Nivkh. We find more persuasive identification with *Nibcu*, the Manchu name of the Nercha River and the Nerchinsk settlement along it. Sound changes of *ch* to *sh* (*č* > *š*) were a feature of eastern Inner Mongolian dialects then and now.

168. Ch. *quánkuài* 拳塊, or lit., "fist-lump." We would like to thank the members of the Facebook "Sinologists" group for their helpful comments on this passage on June 26, 2020.

run fast enough to catch a fleeing horse, and the females are beautiful),[169] and the Husu-Irgen[170] (that is, Water Tatars); in the southwest,[171] the Mubo[172] (belongs to the western ethnic tribes; they do not have any monarch); in the northwest, the Kibsha'ut[173] (a Western kingdom, that is, a race of the Uyghurs)[174]—at first they were obedient to the Tatars but later they rebelled against them, blocking water sources to resist. While he was alive, Temujin often said: "Without ten years of toil, we could not finish the task of subduing them, and if we wait until that is finished, then the remnants of the Jin stock will have prospered again. Better to have Chaghadai set up garrisons to contain them and first eliminate the Jin remnants. Thereafter we can do something about the Kibsha'ut." In the year *gŭi/sì* [1233], Chaghadai was plundered by their crown prince.[175] In the northwest: the

---

169. This account combines the stories of men with the form of dogs and men with the hooves of cows who could outrun horses that were current among Central Eurasian nomads since at least the eighth century. These stories apparently stemmed from Siberian dog sledding and skiing. See Pelliot 1959, vol. 2, 685–87; Venturi 2008, 30, 31–32; and Ye Longli 2014, *Qidan guozhi*, 25.268. Both Giovanni del Piano Carpini and the Armenian king Hethum, in the descriptions of their visits to the Mongolian court, mention the Dog Country; see Dawson 1955, 23; Kirakos Gandzakets'i 1986, 307 (English), 370 (Armenian). Kirakos associates this kingdom with an "island" in the northeast from which "fish teeth," which grew in the manner of a tree, were sourced. These "fish teeth" were walrus ivory, and the "island" must be Kamchatka Peninsula. People from the Noqai-Irgen or Dog Country, along with the Ku'ui or Ainu of Sakhalin Island, raided the Gilemi or Nivkh-speaking Water Tatars who had submitted to the Mongols in 1264. In the spring of 1284, at the same time as campaigns to conquer Sakhalin, Qubilai Khan ordered a hundred ships built along the Sungari River to garrison the "Dog Country." On the "Dog People" and the trade of Arctic ivory to the Tang and Mongol empires, see Atwood 2019.

170. In context, Husu ought to be Mongolian *usu*, "water," but the *h*- in Chinese *husu* is difficult to account for. The transcription would make perfect sense as Middle Mongolian *hüsü*, "hair," in which case Peng may have confused "Water People" (*Usu-Irgen*) with "Hairy People" (*Hüsü-Irgen*). These Husu-Irgen may well thus be a confusion of the well-known Usu-Irgen "Water People" (a general term for the Hejen-Nanai and Nivkh peoples of the lower Amur) with the legendary "Country of Hairy People" (Ch. *Máorén guó*), which in turn seems to refer to the Ainu of Hokkaido and the southern Sakhalin and Kurile islands; Pelliot 1959, vol. 2, 687.

171. The original text places the phrase "in the southwest" before the Husu-Irgen; we follow Xu Quansheng (2014, 195) in his emendation of the text based on geographical plausibility.

172. "Western ethnic[s]" (Ch. *Xīfān* 西蕃) refers to the Qiang, Tibetan, and other peoples along the eastern edge of the Tibetan plateau, west of China's Gansu and Sichuan provinces. "Mubo" is identified with the Tibetan term *dBon-po* "fraternal nephew; official." The Mubo surrendered to the Mongols during the invasion of Sichuan under Prince Köten; see Atwood 2014a, 27, 37.

173. These are the Qipchaq Turkic nomads of the western Eurasian steppe. The Chinese *Kēbíshāo* must derive from an eastern dialect pronunciation of the Mongolian plural *Kibcha'ut*, "Qipchaqs," which has -*sh*- in place of -*ch*-.

174. Peng Daya uses here for the only time the Chinese term *Húihé*, which during the Tang dynasty designated the historic Uyghur Empire (742–847).

175. No commentator has been able to suggest an explanation of this "plundering" of Chaghadai, who is not recorded as campaigning against the Qipchaqs at this time; see Olbricht and Pinks 1980, 218. But it may presumably refer to some reverse in the poorly documented campaigns in the Volga-Ural area early in Öködei's reign and the rise of the Qipchaq prince Bachman; see Allsen 1983, 14–18.

Hindu (Black Westerners; there is no rain in their land, and they sell water to fund the state). Directly to the north are the Qara-Khitai (Black Kitans, one name for them is "Kitan," another name is "Great Dan," that is, Daiši Lemya's kingdom).[176] Either by whittling down their territory, or by making their people prisoners, those like the Koreans, the Wu'anu, the Dog Country, the Water Tatars, and the Mubo can be handled without any question. Only the Kibsha'ut kingdom is somewhat warlike. Their remaining cinders having not been stamped out, there is worry that those cinders might flame as before. This is something the Tatars must certainly contend with.

48.1. Ting: I was told by Wang Ji: "I followed Chinggis all through his attack on the Western Xia. In the custom of the Western Xia kingdom, all from its ruler on down honor and serve the State Preceptor.[177] Anyone who had a daughter would first offer her to the State Preceptor and only afterward dare marry her to someone else. Once Chinggis had wiped out their country, he first put to death by slicing the State Preceptor, who was a *bhikshu* or monk. Later I followed Chinggis when he attacked Fengxiangfu in the Jin kingdom, but Chinggis died before the walls were broken. The succeeding ruler, Ukudei, holding in his grief, said, 'The Jin kingdom securely guards Tongguan Pass and the Yellow River and that defense simply cannot be broken. I calculate that Fengxiangfu gives access to Western Sichuan,[178] and from Western Sichuan heading south there must be a route by which one can reach the Yellow River.' Later they proceeded from Western Sichuan by circuitous routes into Jinzhou and Fangzhou,[179] coming out by floating lightly [over the Hanjiang][180] and cutting straight across to the [lands] within the Yellow River. Indeed, they did wipe out the Jin kingdom." In general, the Tatars specially seek out practical routes for horses. But when he was about to set out from the grasslands, Chucai said to our ambassador, "You are relying only on the Great River, but if the horse hooves of our dynasty need to go up to the heavens, they will go up to the heavens; if under the seas, they will go under the seas."

---

176. The text here is rather corrupt, but Xu Quansheng's critical edition unravels the various difficulties; see Xu 2014, 195. In "Daiši Lemya's Kingdom," *daiši* and *lemya* are both titles of the empire's founder whose personal name seems unknown. *Daiši* is the Kitan version of "Grand Preceptor" and *lemya* is the Kitan word for secretary, both offices he held early in his career; Pelliot 1959, 222; Biran 2005, 19–20; Kane 2009, 49, 66.

177. Ch. *Guóshī* 國師. This title was accorded to clerics in the Western Xia. They were of a wide variety of ethnic origins, including Han, Tangut, and Tibetan. See Dunnell 1992, 2009.

178. Ch. *Xīchuān* "Western Sichuan" is the western part of Sichuan Province, centered on the city of Chengdu. See p. 126.

179. Present-day Ankang (Shaanxi) and Fangxian (Hubei).

180. The Mongol forces forded the river in their traditional fashion, swimming with their goods in leather bundles tied to their horses' tails.

49. For those who die in the army, they have the corpse hauled[181] home; otherwise they exhaust their treasure and resources to bury it.

> 49.1. Ting: I observed of some who died in the army, that if a slave or servant could haul his dead master's head home, then they gave him all his master's livestock. But if some other person[182] delivered it, then that man would take possession of all the deceased's wives, slaves, and livestock.

50. Their graves have no high mound; they trample them with horses, making them like flat land. As for Temujin's grave, they have planted arrows to make a fence (more than ten miles[183] wide), and cavalrymen patrol it as guards.

> 50.1. Ting: I saw Temujin's grave beside the Lugou River[184]; the mountain and the waters surround it. A story goes that Temujin was born there, and therefore in death was buried there. I do not know if it is true or false.

50.2. Concluding Note from Ting: When I first returned from the grasslands, I prepared a narrative of the local habits and customs there. When I reached Ezhu Islet,[185] I unexpectedly met the official who wrote the descriptions in the main entries above, Peng Daya. After some mutual explanation, we showed what we had written to one another for comparison, and indeed found that we had no great gaps or discrepancies. I took what Peng had compiled as the basic text, and wherever there was a difference I added a note. Yet this only relates the generalities; for my detailed record, please see what I have titled *Diary of the Northern Campaign*.[186]

Signed: Xu Ting, courtesy name, Changru, of Yongjia,[187] Summer, I, 1, *dīng/yǒu* year of Jiaxi [April 27, 1237].

---

181. Ch. *tuó* 駝, which should be "camel." But this is used below again for the dead master's head; one would hardly need a camel to transport a head. We take this as a variant graph form for *tuō* 拖, "drag, tow."

182. Implying a free man.

183. Lit., more than thirty *lǐ*; see the tables of weights and measures in Appendix §2.7 (p. 192).

184. This is the traditional Chinese name for the Kelüren (Kherlen) River in Mongolia. At the time it was pronounced almost identically to the Lüju used by Zhang Dehui; see "Notes," p. 167.

185. Originally designating a long island in the Yangtze River, the name Ezhu Islet was the origin of Ezhou Prefecture, the modern Wuchang portion of the vast triple city Wuhan in Hubei Province of central China.

186. This work has not survived.

187. Yongjia County, the seat of Wenzhou Prefecture, in present-day Zhejiang Province.

Spirit-Path Stele for His Honor Yelü, Director of the Secretariat

By Song Zizhen of the Great Mongol Empire

This "Spirit-Path Stele" for Yelü Chucai is a classic example of the Chinese biographical genre. In Chinese practice, when a distinguished official passed away, the family would be expected to produce several different descriptions of his life. An "account of conduct" (xíngzhuàng) *for the deceased would be submitted to the government; on it would be based any posthumous honors for the deceased, honors that could also substantially benefit his descendants. A "funerary epitaph"* (mùzhì) *would be carved on a stone block to be placed in the deceased's tomb. A "spirit-path stele"* (shéndào bēi) *would be erected above ground near the approach to the tomb of the deceased. Finally, a "sacrificial address"* (jìwén) *would be recited to honor the deceased during the rituals of ancestor worship.*

These genres have been called "social biographies," because they were commissioned by the deceased's family and were authored by persons in their private capacity as friends, family, or admirers of the deceased. Commissioning and writing such social biographies was a chance for prominent scholar-officials to express their friendship and admiration for deceased members of their ranks, but also to maintain connections with his family. Some highly regarded writers would even be paid to write such biographies. Texts in these genres were proudly included in the authors' collected works, and the "accounts of conduct" were also preserved by the government. Thus preserved, these "social biographies" would become first drafts for later "historical biographies," which would be commissioned for historical projects such as biographical collections, dynastic histories, and local gazetteers.[1]

Given the origin of these works in circles of mutual esteem, one might question how reliable they are as historical sources. Certainly, social biographies were written on the assumption that the object of the biography was an admirable man. Moreover, the dominant role of public service in validating social status meant that such admiration was directed above all toward the performance of particular roles in public service. The authors thus aimed more at providing a portrait of an ideal man of affairs, censor, financial specialist, military officer, or academician than at highlighting that man's individual personality. Yet modern historians have noted countervailing forces that encouraged accuracy as well. The existence of government records against which the biographies could be checked, the embeddedness of these biographies in social networks, the concern of the authors for their own reputations as truthful writers, and the

---

1. The distinction of "social" and "historical" biographies was first drawn in a seminal article by Peter Olbricht (1957).

general congruence between the authors' categories of judgement and the subjects' own ideals of conduct all worked to keep the biographies from departing too far from the consensus on a subject's life. The problem was not so much that any one biography would be full of fictitious praise as it was that only certain categories of people, that is, those participating in the circles of social esteem created by a Confucian education, would likely receive biographies at all.[2]

Ila (Yelü) Chucai (1190–1244) was the kind of person whose virtues the "social biography" genre was ideally poised to capture. By origin, he was a scion of the former imperial Kitan lineage, but his family served the Jurchen Jin for three generations. After he entered Mongol service with the fall of the Jin's Central Capital or Yanjing (present-day Beijing) in 1215, all the Song border officials noted his abilities; even the rather hostile Xu Ting admitted that he was tall, impressive, and a master of astronomy, poetry, the zither, and Buddhist meditation. But as the title of this stele inscription indicates, its focus is on his life and work as director of the Secretariat, that is, as the top civil official in North China under the Mongols. Portraying him as an impressive embodiment of the Chinese scholar-official ideal thus did not involve any great distortion of reality. One may notice, however, that this spirit-path stele completely ignores the likelihood, underlined by Xu Ting, that the Mongols themselves did not really pay much attention to his attempts to rebuild the government on Confucian lines.

The text for this spirit-path stele was written in 1268 by Song Zizhen (1188–1268), a scholar from Zhangzi County in southeastern Shanxi.[3] *His birthplace was part of Jin-ruled North China and, like many scholar-officials, he followed the Jin court south to Henan, but unusually, he soon returned to his war-torn homeland north of the Yellow River. He joined the pro-Song dynasty rebel Peng Yibin but then passed into the entourage of the pro-Mongol warlord Yan Shi when Peng Yibin was defeated and killed in 1225. Song Zizhen stayed in the service of Yan Shi and his sons until the enthronement of Qubilai Khan in 1260, when he was first appointed to office in the Mongol central government. Although he served briefly as Manager in the Secretariat before his retirement in 1265, his role was always more advisory than executive. As a local official, Song Zizhen had little contact with Ila Chucai during the heyday of his power in the 1230s, although Song did urge his warlord patron, Yan Shi, to cooperate with Chucai's demilitarizing measures. After joining the central government, Song became a close associate of Chucai's son, Yelü Zhu, however; they served together briefly in the local administration of Shandong in 1264.*

Song Zizhen's ties to Yelü Zhu were undoubtedly why he was chosen to write the spirit-path stele for Zhu's father, Chucai. The latter had passed away in Qara-Qorum in Mongolia in 1244, and in 1261, after Qubilai moved the capital from Mongolia

---

2. In addition to Olbricht above, see Schneewind (2009) and Twitchett (1992, 62–83; and 1962) on the strengths and weaknesses of Chinese social biographies and the historical biographies based on them.

3. Details of his life, as summarized in his own social biographies, are given in Su Tianjue (1996, 10.199–203), and *YS* 159.3735–37. The date of his death is often given as Zhiyuan 3 (1266) because that is the last year mentioned in his *Yuanshi* biography. Su Tianjue's biography, however, explicitly states that he died in Zhiyuan 5 (1268), the only death-date that is compatible with his known authorship of the Chucai memorial inscription in 1268.

to North China, he was interred according to his wishes in the Wengshan Hill cemetery north of Yanjing, on the outskirts of present-day Beijing. Probably in that year, Zhao Yan, a scholar in Zhu's entourage, compiled an "Account of Conduct" for Chucai, while Li Wei compiled his funerary epitaph. Unfortunately, neither of these two works is preserved, but from surviving citations of them, it seems that Song Zizhen drew heavily on Li Wei's previous social biography and likely on Zhao Yan's as well.

Ila Chucai was of the former imperial Kitan lineage, which, as is explained in more detail in the Introduction, p. 44, had two alternative surnames, Ila (Ch. Yila) and Yërud (Ch. Yelü). We know from his writings that Chucai used the form "Ila" throughout his life. However, after his death, his son Zhu preferred the form "Yelü" and had that used in all of his father's social biographies.

Spirit-path steles were bound by many conventions, visible in this example. The title, carved in large graphs in the actual inscription, gave the subject's surname, highest office, and honorific title, if any, but omitted his given name.[4] The impersonal tone was preserved by referring to the subject throughout as gōng, which we translate as "His Honor."[5] The text begins with some general comments, then covers the subject's ancestry, his birth and education, and then his official career chronologically, with most events dated to the year or to the year and moon. The biographical account finishes with his death (dated to the day) and a few anecdotes particularly illustrative of the subject's personality. Then follows a description of the occasion for the spirit-path stele to be written, a prose summary of the person's significance, and an ode extolling his character and public service.

The text of this spirit-path stele was printed in the Yuan wenlei, an anthology of the most distinguished writings of the Yuan dynasty, compiled by Su Tianjue in 1334 and blockprinted two years later. Since it was published during the Mongol Yuan dynasty, it observes the conventions protecting the sanctity of that dynasty. The personal names of the Yuan emperors are uniformly tabooed and replaced with the titles used in the ancestral temple, even though all the events took place long before any ancestral temples were created. References to emperors and to the dynasty itself are set off either by starting on a new line or by leaving a blank space above the name. Precisely because this is such a characteristic part of imperial rhetoric and of this genre, and because it is preserved only in this text among the five,[6] we have tried in our translation to re-create it by placing such emphasized words in SMALL CAPITALS.

Song Zizhen's text was intended to be an honest portrait of a widely admired man, who in his life had encountered much opposition. Yet it was also undoubtedly intended to speak to the time in which it was written. In 1268, the early hopes of Chinese

---

4. Since Mongols and Uyghurs did not use their family or clan names in the Chinese fashion, their surnames were simply omitted and only their title given.

5. For those of princely rank, the title *wáng*, "prince," would be substituted.

6. Since Zhao Gong's "Memorandum" and Peng and Xu's "Sketch" were entirely about foreign, non-Song rulers, there would, of course, be no occasion for them to show such respect. Li Xinchuan's history and Zhang Dehui's "Notes" in their original form presumably followed such conventions for their own Song and Mongol rulers, respectively. However, the oldest surviving texts of both of them postdate their original dynasty and, as commonly occurred when such works were reprinted in later dynasties, eliminated all such honorific features.

literati for Qubilai Khan were already withering, as the khan tired of their rigidity (as he saw it) and had begun to turn toward immigrant officials from the West. Chucai's son, Yelü Zhu, had just been reinstated as "Grand Councilor"—by 1271 he would be dismissed again—and Song Zizhen himself was in the last year of his life. The spirit-path stele was thus both a public exposition of the Confucian program for the peaceful evolution of the Mongol dynasty and a warning against the malignant forces already at work to derail that evolution.

Spirit-Path Stele for His Honor Yelü, Director of the Secretariat

In the rise of our dynasty, its foundations were laid in the North. Because the Emperor Great Founder[7] received the mandate with law-giving efficacy and reverently executed the heavenly chastisements, no kingdom could stand when his horse's head turned against it. The Great Ancestor[8] succeeded him and embraced all eight directions before stabilizing the Central Plains;[9] on this side and beyond the Bars Lake,[10] none did not yield humble vassalage. Thereupon he established the great government and ascended the imperial throne, building a new palace to call the regional lords[11] to court. His intent was to plant a foundation that could not be uprooted and pass down a unity that could be continued.

And His Honor, a man of talents that commanded the age, met with the trend of the sovereign's rise, serving as his mainstay among the ablest men of the court,[12] and assisting him with his comprehensive learning. He assured the continuity of two reigns, aiding the establishment of two courts. He approved guidelines for the emerging age and unified institutions for the aftermath of pacification. He took

---

7. Ch. *Tàizǔ*, the posthumous temple name of Chinggis Khan (r. 1206–1227).

8. Ch. *Tàizōng*, the posthumous temple name of Chinggis Khan's second son, Öködei or Ögedei Khan (r. 1229–1241).

9. Ch. *Zhōngyuán*; these are the plains along both sides of the Yellow River in the Henan area and by extension the entire heartland of North China.

10. Ch. *Púlèi*. This is the modern Barsköl or "Leopard Lake" in the Barköl Kazakh Autonomous County in Xinjiang. The Chinese name used here dates from the Han dynasty's campaigns in the region over a millennium before the Mongol era.

11. The "new palace to call the regional lords to court" evidently refers to Öködei building Qara-Qorum. "Regional lords" translates Ch. *zhūhóu* 諸侯, lit., "the many lords." Often translated as "feudal lords," this phrase stems from China's classical age, the Zhou dynasty (1046–256 BC), when the Zhou king ruled their newly conquered dominions through a system of autonomous, hereditary lordships; Li 2003; Pines 2020. As it broke down into "Warring States" in fifth to third centuries BC, this decentralized but peaceful early Zhou system was viewed nostalgically as a time of perfect sage rule. Even after China transitioned into an enduring system of bureaucratic rule through appointed functionaries, the idea of the emperor ruling through *zhūhóu* or hereditary regional lords continued from time to time to be part of both the idealized image and the reality of rulership. Here it has been repurposed to give an air of classical antiquity to the Mongol system of princely appanages.

12. Ch. *kuòmiào* 廓廟, understood here as a synonym of, or perhaps an error for, *lángmiào* 廊廟.

upon himself the weight of the civilized world (*tiānxià*), towering like a mountainous pillar in the midstream flow. For using all possible means to save living beings, he was inferior to no man in all past time.

His Honor's personal name was Chucai, his courtesy name was Jinqing, and his surname was of the Yelü clan; he was an eighth-generation descendant of Tuyu, the Prince of Dongdan under the Liao dynasty.[13] The prince begat Louguo, Viceroy and Director of Administration in Yanjing,[14] the Viceroy begat the general Guin, the general begat Grand Preceptor Qalu, Qalu begat Grand Preceptor Qudugh, Qudugh begat Dingyuan General Nuilgha, and the Dingyuan General begat Deyuan, Grand Master for Glorious Happiness and the Military Commissioner for the Xingping Army; he was the first of his lineage to give his allegiance to the Jin dynasty.

Deyuan's younger brother Yulu begat Lü, whom the commissioner for the Xingping Army took as a foster son and later treated as his own descendant.[15] Emperor Shizong[16] recognized Lü's literary ability and righteous conduct, and he was thus appointed first as Academician Awaiting Instruction before being transferred to serve as Vice Director in the Board of Rites. When Emperor Zhangzong[17] ascended the throne, Lü won merit for his strategies that stabilized the situation and was promoted to Vice Grand Councilor for the Board of Rites in the Department of State Affairs, passing away as Assistant Director of the Right in the Department of State Affairs, with the posthumous title "Duke of Civil Preferment."[18] He was His Honor's father. His mother's surname was Yang; she was posthumously enfeoffed as Lady of the Qishui Fief.[19]

His Honor was born on Mingchang 1, VI, 20 [July 24, 1190]. His father was a master of numerology and was especially advanced in the Supreme Mystery.[20]

---

13. On Tuyu (Ch. Bei; 900–937), see his biography in *LS* 72.1209–11.

14. On Louguo (d. 952), see the brief biographical notice in *LS* 102.1501.

15. On Ila Lü (1131–1191), see his biography in *JS* 95.2099–101.

16. The Jin emperor Yong (Jurchen name Uru); his posthumous temple title Shizong means "Renovating Ancestor" (r. 1161–1189). Note that by using these temple names, Song Zizhen was implicitly agreeing with Ila Chucai's own sentiment that the Jin dynasty had been the legitimate dynasty in its own time, until it was superseded by the Mongol Empire.

17. The Jin emperor Jing (Jurchen name Madaka); his posthumous temple title Zhangzong means "Model Ancestor" (r. 1189–1208).

18. "Civil Preferment" is Chinese *wénxiàn* 文獻. This title was later used by Chucai himself. On the bureaucratic and hereditary titles mentioned here, see the Introduction, pp. 32–33, 34.

19. Qishui is a river in present-day Shaanxi province, west of Xi'an. However, such titles were purely honorary and did not necessarily have anything to do with the place. Indeed, the title Prince of Qishui was quite common in the Liao dynasty, which never ruled that area at all.

20. Ch. *Tàixuán* 太玄, referring both to the book, *Taixuan jing* ("Canon of the Supreme Mystery"), by the Han-period Confucian Yang Xiong (53 BC–AD 18), and to the method of divination expounded in that work. This divination was modeled on the more ancient divination text, the *Yijing* (or *I Ching*), the "Classic of Changes." It organized the possible outcomes of divination according to stacks of four lines, each either unbroken, broken once, or broken twice. See the translation and study of the work in Nylan 1993.

He privately told those who were intimate with him, "I am sixty years old, yet now I have begotten this boy, who is a fleet-footed foal of our family able to run a thousand *lĭ*.[21] Someday he certainly will become a man of great ability; moreover, I predict he will serve a different dynasty." Therefore, he chose the personal and courtesy names for this son based on a quotation from Master Zuo: "The talents are Chu's but the use of them is Jin's."[22]

Three years after His Honor was born, he was orphaned. His mother, the lady *née* Yang, was thorough in rearing and educating him, and by the time he was a little older, he knew to study diligently. At seventeen, there was no book he did not read, and in writing he already had an authorial style.

Under the Jin system, the grand councilors' sons had the privilege of taking examinations for supplementary appointments as secretarial clerks.[23] His Honor did not do this, so Emperor Zhangzong specially ordered him to sit without prior qualification for the regular exam, in which he received the highest ranking. Having passed a performance review,[24] he was appointed as Vice-Prefect in Kaizhou Prefecture. In Zhenyou's *jiǎ/xū* year [1214], Emperor Xuanzong[25] left and crossed south over the Yellow River while the Grand Councilor, Wongian Chenghui,[26] remained as viceroy in Yanjing. As the man handling the Department of State Affairs, he recommended His Honor to be Vice Director of that department's Left and Right Offices. The next year the capital city fell, and so he became subject to OUR DYNASTY.

The GREAT FOUNDER[27] always had the ambition to swallow up the civilized world. At one point he sought out the surviving kinsmen of the Liao imperial family and summoned them to his traveling camp. At the audience, HIS MAJESTY said to His Honor, "The Liao and the Jin were rivals for generations. I have just taken vengeance on the Jin for you!" His Honor said, "Since the passing of my father

---

21. A *lĭ* is a little over half a kilometer or a third of a mile.

22. From the "Zuo Commentary" or *Zuozhuan*, Xianggong chapter, year 26; cf. Legge [1872] 1991, 521 (text), 526 (translation). Yelü Chucai's name, *Chŭcái*, means "talent (or material) of Chu," and his courtesy name, *Jìnqīng*, means "liege of Jin." Chu (modern Hunan and Hubei along the Middle Yangtze) and Jin (modern Shanxi) were two rival states in the Springs and Autumns period (722–484 BC); the *Zuozhuan* is the main source for the history of that period.

23. Such examinations were not as competitive as the regular exams and thus provided an easy way to get a first step into the official ranks.

24. Regular performance reviews were conducted for those holding office every three years. This implies that Ila Chucai held some minor post, in which he did well, before being appointed as vice-prefect.

25. The Jin emperor Xun (Jurchen name, Udubu); his posthumous temple title Xuanzong means "Comprehensive Ancestor" (r. 1213–1224).

26. Chenghui's Jurchen name was Fuking; he appears in Li Xinchuan's history exclusively as Wongian Fuking. Yelü Chucai's biography in the *Yuanshi* adds that the one handling the Department of State Affairs was Wongian Chenghui/Fuking; see *YS* 146.3455.

27. That is, Chinggis Khan.

and grandfather, in all things your servant has borne allegiance to[28] and served the Jin. As the son of a Jin vassal, how could I dare repay him by harboring divided loyalties and regard his ruler-father as my enemy?" HIS MAJESTY respected his words and kept him by his side, available for any consultation or inquiry.

Thus, in the summer, moon VI, of year *jǐ/mǎo* [1219], the imperial army launched an expedition to the west. On occasion of the sacrifices to the battle-standards, snow fell to a depth of three feet. HIS MAJESTY was worried by it, but His Honor said, "This is a sign that the enemy will be conquered." And in the winter of *gēng/chén* [1220–1221] there was a great thunder. HIS MAJESTY asked His Honor about it, and he said, "It should mean that a soltan has died in the middle of a wilderness," and indeed it turned out to be so. "Soltan" is a title of Turkestani kings.[29]

A man of the Xia, Chang Bajin, became well-known for his bow-making. So, surprised at His Honor's non-martial role, he spoke to him, saying, "Our dynasty esteems the military, yet Your Honor, an enlightened man, wishes to advance with civil skills. Is not that the wrong way to go about it?" His Honor said, "Even assembling a bow properly requires a bowyer. How can one assemble the civilized world without a craftsman skilled in assembling the civilized world?"[30] HIS MAJESTY, hearing this, was extremely pleased and from then on employed His Honor at increasingly confidential tasks.

At the beginning of the dynasty, there was no calendrical science. The Turkestanis memorialized[31] that on the night of the fifteenth day of moon V there would be a lunar eclipse. His Honor said there would not be an eclipse, and indeed, at the time indicated there was no eclipse. The next year, His Honor memorialized that on the night of the fifteenth day of moon X there would be a lunar eclipse,

---

28. Lit., "faced north." Rulers in China always held court facing south; to face north was thus to show submission and allegiance.

29. Based on differing Arabic or Persian dialectal forms, Chinese sources transcribe this title sometimes as *sultan* and sometimes as *soltan*. "Turkestani" here is Ch. *Húihú*. Originally meaning the Uyghur Empire in Mongolia, it later evolved into *Húihúi*, meaning "Muslim." Here we translate it as "Turkestani"; see the Introduction, p. 27.

30. The Chinese here uses the same verb (*zhì* 治) for assembling or "governing" a bow, as a bowyer or bow-maker would do, and "assembling" or governing the civilized world. Our English translation follows the need to find a single verb that would make the analogy plain. Analogies of Confucian governance with craftsmanship or medical practice were common in the Mongol Empire; see "Notes," p. 172; Shinno 2016, 30. These analogies were particularly apt because in the Mongol administrative system artisans and physicians had high-level tax exemptions that exemplified the Mongol rulers' appreciation of their skills. On this system of tax exemptions and Confucians' role within it, see Shinno 2016, 40–41; Atwood 2016, 279; Atwood 2004, 249–50, 281–82; Endicott-West 1999; Allsen 1987, 120, 159, 210–16; Dardess 1983, 14–19.

31. In the Chinese bureaucratic system, all policy initiatives were supposed to be first submitted in writing by high officials to the emperor, who would then accept, modify, or reject them, again in writing. Such "formal policy statements submitted to the ruler" (Kroll 2015, s.v. *zòu*, 632b) and the process of submitting them were both designated in Chinese as *zòu* 奏, conventionally translated as "memorial" or "to memorialize." This term is thus used for all of Chucai's communications with the Mongol emperors.

and the Turkestanis said there would not be. That night, the moon was eclipsed by 80 percent. HIS MAJESTY was greatly amazed by this and said, "There is nothing you do not understand about affairs in the heavens. How much more must you understand about affairs among men!"

In the summer of year *rén/wŭ*, moon V [June 1222], a comet was seen in the western quarter. HIS MAJESTY asked His Honor about this, and His Honor said, "It should mean that the Jurchen kingdom will change its ruler!" Over the course of the year, the Jin ruler died. From this point, whenever generals went out on campaign, His Honor was always ordered to divine omens of fortune and misfortune beforehand. HIS MAJESTY also burned sheep's thigh bones[32] to corroborate them.

Pitching camp at Iron Gate Pass in the country of East India,[33] men in the imperial guard saw a beast with the form of a deer and the tail of a horse, green in color with a single horn. It could speak like a man, and said, "Your lord should return soon." HIS MAJESTY thought this was uncanny and asked His Honor who said, "This beast is called *jiǎoduān* ("horn-end"). In one day it can travel 18,000 *lǐ* and can understand the languages of the barbarians in all four directions. This is a sign of the abhorrence of killing; Heaven must have sent it to warn YOUR HIGHNESS. Would that by taking up Heaven's heart and sparing human lives in these several countries, YOUR HIGHNESS's boundless blessings could be fulfilled!" That very day HIS MAJESTY issued an edict to withdraw the armies.

In the winter of year *bǐng/xū*, moon XI [November–December 1226], when Lingwu fell, the generals all vied with one another to capture lads, lasses, goods, and money.[34] His Honor took only several volumes of books and two camel-loads of rhubarb, nothing more. Later, when the officers and soldiers fell victim to an epidemic, only those who obtained rhubarb recovered. Those whom he kept alive numbered several ten-thousand.

---

32. As was described by Peng Daya and Xu Ting ("Sketch," p. 108), Mongolian diviners usually used shoulder blades of sheep and not thighbones. It is unclear if this is just Song Zizhen's mistake or if other bones were also sometimes used.

33. The background and subsequent history of this famous incident in later Chinese and Mongolian histories is explored in de Rachewiltz 2018 and Ho 2010. One should note, however, that its geography was confused by a misunderstanding of the originally Mongolian indications of direction. In Mongolian, the most common directional system is based on facing south, so that "left" also means "east." However, there is another directional system attested in the Mongol Empire based on facing east. In this system, "left" means "north." Based on the historical context, Chinggis Khan must have been attempting to return home via the mountain route along the Indus River up to Khotan in the Tarim Basin, and thence back to Mongolia. Thus, he camped in the "left" or "northern" part of India, not the eastern part. It is also worth noting that there are many passes called "Iron Gates" in Chinese and Mongolian sources; this must be one in what is now northern Pakistan, where rhinoceroses were found until the Mughal era.

34. This was the final campaign against the Tangut kingdom, the Western Xia. Chinggis Khan died in 1227 during this campaign.

After that, Yanjing had many bandits, who even drove carts to conduct their robberies; the local authorities could not stop them. The PERCEPTIVE ANCESTOR,[35] who then was serving as Regent,[36] ordered an imperial commissioner to accompany His Honor to go there posthaste particularly to settle the issue. After arriving, they made separate arrests and found that the robbers were all sons of influential families. Sundry family members came to give bribes and have them pardoned. The imperial commissioner was misled by them and wanted to memorialize against their punishment, but His Honor staunchly held that to do so would be unacceptable, saying, "Xin'an[37] is not far away and still has not fallen. If we do not enforce discipline, I fear anarchy could result." Sixteen men were then executed. The capital city became calm, and everyone could sleep securely.[38]

In the year of *jĭ/chŏu* [1229], the GREAT ANCESTOR[39] ascended the throne, and His Honor planned the proceedings and set up rules of propriety. The order was for the imperial clansmen and honored commanders to all form into ranks and prostrate themselves. Indeed, the honored commanders' practice of the ceremony of prostration began from this time. Most of those who came to the court from the tributary states ended up liable to death due to violating taboos, but His Honor said, "YOUR HIGHNESS has newly ascended the throne. May he not stain the white path." His opinion was approved. Now, the reason for this expression is that the dynastic customs exalt white and treat white as auspicious.

At the time, the civilized world had just been settled and was still without regulations. The senior clerks[40] in office all had the power to spare or kill entirely on their own authority. If anyone had defiant thoughts, then swords and rasps

---

35. Ch. Ruizong, the posthumous temple title of Chinggis Khan's youngest son, Tolui.

36. "Regent" translates the Chinese title *jiānguó* 監國. It is unclear, however, what Tolui's actual title, if any, was at the time. After Tolui's sons, first Möngke and then Qubilai, seized power from Öködei's family and ascended the throne, Tolui's role in the period between Chinggis Khan's death and Öködei's enthronement was exaggerated as a way of supplying a precedent for their own seizure of power.

37. A county town in Bazhou Prefecture, about ninety kilometers south of Yanjing; it was situated along the Juma River and suppliable by boat from the ocean. As is mentioned by Li Xinchuan, this town still remained under Jin dynasty control throughout the reign of Chinggis Khan; in fact it did not surrender to Mongol control until 1230.

38. In the *Yuashi*, the biographies of Yelü Chucai, Prince Tolui, and the imperial commissioner, Ta'achar, all discuss this incident. Ta'achar, of the Hüüshin surname, was an officer of the quiver-bearers (*qorchi*) in the imperial guard and a grandnephew of Boroghul (who had been one of Chinggis Khan's "four steeds"). After the conquest of North China, Ta'achar was given new pasturelands at Guanshan Mountain in Inner Mongolia. See *YS* 146.3457, 115.2885, and 119.2952.

39. Öködei or Ögedei Khan (r. 1229–1241).

40. Ch. *zhănglì* 長吏. In Chinese, "clerk" was both a neutral term for any official who was not part of the regular, centrally appointed officialdom, and a derogatory name for those officials who had not received Confucian training, and hence were not Yelü Chucai's "craftsman skilled in assembling [i.e., governing] the civilized world." Since the officials of the Mongol Empire before Qubilai had neither a regular process of selection nor widespread Confucian training, they were all mere clerks in Confucian eyes. As we will see, these "senior clerks" actually included powerful officials like the Kitan Šimei Hiêmdêibu. He was far from a mere "clerk" and referring to him

followed, such that whole households were massacred without even babes in arms being spared. And in this prefecture or that district soldiers rose on the slightest pretext and attacked each other. His Honor was the first to raise this issue; all such actions were prohibited and eliminated.

From the GREAT FOUNDER's western campaign onward, the granaries and public storehouses had not a peck of grain or a roll of silk. Thus, the imperial commissioner Bekter[41] and others all said, "Although we have conquered the Han men, they are really of no use. It would be better to get rid of them all and let the vegetation flourish to make pasture grounds." His Honor promptly came forward and said, "So large is the civilized world, and so rich are the lands within the four seas, that there is nothing you might seek that you cannot obtain. But you simply do not seek it. On what grounds do you call them useless?" Thereupon, he memorialized about how the land tax, the commercial tax, and profits from monopolies on liquor, vinegar, salt, iron, and products of the mountains and swamps could raise 500,000 taels of silver,[42] 80,000 bolts of raw silk, and 400,000 piculs[43] of grain annually. HIS MAJESTY said, "If it is truly as Our liege says, then this would be more than enough for the empire's use. Our liege, try to make it happen." Subsequently he memorialized to set up tax offices on ten routes, each with a commissioner and a vice-commissioner. He filled all the positions with Confucians,[44] such as Chen Shike in Yanjing and Liu Zhong on the Xuandezhou Route, all of whom were the pick of the civilized world. Following on this, from time to time he would advance the teachings of the Zhou dynasty and of Confucius,[45] stating, moreover, that "although the world may be won on horseback, it cannot be governed on horseback."[46] HIS MAJESTY concurred deeply. The dynasty's use of civil ministers was thus due to His Honor's initiative.

---

as such reflects Yelü Chucai (and Song Zizhen's) Confucian professional pride rather than an accurate view of his actual power.

41. This official's name is not securely identified, but he may be the same as the Tuqluq-Bekter who appears as a *darughachi*, or overseer, of the Yanjing area eleven years hence in late 1240; see Zhao and Yu [1330] 2020, 446.

42. A tael measured 1.4 ounces; 500,000 taels equaled 10,000 *ding* or *balish*, the standard ingot of the empire. See the tables of weights and measures in Appendix §2.7 (p. 192).

43. The Chinese picul or *dàn* as a dry measure of grain was variously standardized at 1.9 bushels under the Song, and at 2.7 under the Yuan. It is unclear which measure is in use here.

44. "Confucians" (Ch. *rúzhě* 儒者) were officially recognized in the Mongol period, but as an administrative profession, not as the clergy of a religion like Buddhism or Daoism.

45. The Confucian classics consisted of two parts. The first was the Five Canons (*Canon of Changes, Exalted Documents, The Canon of Odes, Records of Rituals,* and *Springs and Autumns Annals*), said to have been composed or edited under the Zhou dynasty (founded in 1046 BC). The second comprised the works of Confucius (551–479 BC) and his disciples (particularly the *Analects* of Confucius, and the *Mencius*, by his disciple of that name). Thus, Confucian doctrines may be summed up as the teachings of the Zhou and Confucius.

46. Yelü Chucai is here quoting from the biography of Lu Jia in chapter 97 of the *Shiji*, the *Records of the Grand Historian* written by Sima Qian (ca. 190–145 BC) of the Former Han dynasty. When

Before this, the senior clerks on the routes concurrently held command over both the armies and the civilian land tax. They often relied on their wealth and power to arbitraily act lawlessly. His Honor memorialized that the senior clerks should exclusively administer civilian affairs, the myriarchs manage the armies, and the land taxes should be managed by the tax offices, with none of them exercising control over the other. This was then made the official system.[47]

Yet certain influential officials could not accept this. Šimei Hiêmdêibu[48] stirred the Imperial Uncles[49] into a rage, such that they sent a special messenger with a memorial claiming that His Honor "is entirely employing men formerly of the Southern dynasty;[50] moreover, many of his kinsmen are among them, so we fear that he has subversive intent. He should not be employed in important positions." Beyond that, they played on dynastic sensitivities to falsely accuse him in a hundred ways, determined to have him put to death. The issues came to implicate the executive administrators.

At the time, Chinqai and Niêmha Cungšai held the same rank as His Honor;[51] put in a cold sweat by the accusations, they said, "Why was it necessary to change things so forcefully? We thought something like today's controversy would happen!" His Honor said, "From the founding of the dynastic court until now, every

---

Lu Jia began to expound the *Canon of Odes* and the *Exalted Documents*, the "Supreme Founder" of the Han (Han Gaozu, r. 202–194 BC) began to shout:

> "All I possess I have won on horseback! Why should I bother with the *Odes* and the *Documents*?"
>
> "Your Majesty may have won it on horseback, but can you rule it on horseback?" asked Master Lu. "Kings Tang and Wu in ancient times won possession of the empire through the principle of revolt, but it was by the principle of obedience that they assured the continuance of their dynasties. To pay due attention to both civil and military matters is the way for a dynasty to achieve long life. In the past, King Fuchai of Wu and Zhi Bo, minister of Jin, both perished because they paid too much attention to military affairs. Qin [the dynasty just before the Han] entrusted its future solely to punishments and laws, without changing with the times, and thus eventually brought about the destruction of its ruling family. If after it had united the world under its rule, Qin had practiced benevolence and righteousness and modeled its ways upon the sages of antiquity, how would Your Majesty ever have been able to win possession of the empire?" The emperor grew embarrassed and uneasy.

See Sima Qian/Watson 1993, 226–27, with a few modifications for consistency.

47. In fact, this division of civil, military, and fiscal offices was not fully implemented until decades later under Qubilai Khan.

48. Šimei Hiêmdêibu was the son of one of the first Kitans to go over to Chinggis Khan's cause, Šimei Ming'an. (See Zhao, "Memorandum," p. 80 and n. 58; Peng and Xu, "Sketch," p. 124.) The latter became the chief official in Yanjing after its fall to the Mongols in 1215, and he passed that authority onto his son Hiêmdêibu.

49. That is, Chinggis Khan's younger brothers (the uncles of Öködei), who held important fiefs in North China and Manchuria.

50. At this point, "the Southern dynasty" refers to the Jin, who were still holding out in Henan. Only after the annihilation of the Jin in 1234 would "the South" begin to mean the Southern Song dynasty.

51. As is mentioned by Peng Daya and Xu Ting ("Sketch," pp. 94–95), these were the three chief administrators in the Secretariat in Yanjing with roughly equal rank.

issue has been handled by me. What have you, sirs, had to do with it? If there are to be any criminal charges, I alone will bear them, and I certainly will not involve you." HIS MAJESTY investigated the slanders and angrily drove away the messengers who had come to the court.

Within a few months, it happened that someone made an accusation against Hiêmdêibu. HIS MAJESTY, knowing that there was no collusion with His Honor, specially ordered him to handle the interrogation. His Honor memorialized, "This man [Hiêmdêibu] is haughty, without manners, and consorts with a petty-minded crowd; he easily invites defamation. But just now there is business with the South, so if this could be handled some other day, it would still not be too late." HIS MAJESTY was a little unhappy but later said to his attendant officials, "This is a real gentleman; you all ought to imitate him."

In the autumn of year *xīn/mǎo*, moon VIII [September 1231], HIS MAJESTY arrived in Yunzhong.[52] The registers for the scheduled taxes in silver and cloth as well as grain stored in the granaries were all set out before him, and they completely matched the numbers His Honor had originally proposed. HIS MAJESTY laughed and said, "Our liege never left Our side, so how was he able he get money and grain to flow in like this? I wonder if the southern kingdom has a minister who can compare?" His Honor said, "Very many of my colleagues are more worthy. It is because your liege has no talent that he was left behind at Yanjing."[53] HIS MAJESTY personally poured him a great goblet of wine[54] to honor him. That very day, he granted him the Secretariat seal and authorized him to administer its affairs. All, whether large or small, were entrusted to him alone.[55]

The senior official of Xuandezhou Route, Grand Mentor Tugha, let more than 10,000 piculs[56] of official grain disappear. Relying on his past accomplishments, he secretly memorialized the throne seeking a pardon. HIS MAJESTY asked Tugha whether the Secretariat knew about this or not, and he replied, "They do not know." HIS MAJESTY grabbed a whistling arrow and several times made as though to shoot Tugha before finally, after some time, yelling at him to get out. He ordered Tugha to report the matter to the Secretariat and make restitution. Further, he issued an imperial order that, from then on, all business be first reported to the Secretariat and only afterward memorialized for the attention of the throne.

---

52. The county-seat name of modern Datong, in northern Shanxi. In the early Mongol era, it was also known as the Western Capital, or Xijing, from its Liao and Jin designation.

53. That is, in 1214–1215, when the Jin court fled to Henan, and Yanjing was taken by the Mongol armies.

54. Ch. *jiǔ* 酒. This would be a grain-based brew, similar to Japanese sake. See Zhao Gong's "Memorandum," p. 87 n. 54.

55. As may be seen from Peng Daya and Xu Ting's account, the reality was rather more complicated.

56. Ch. *dàn*. A *dàn* was a measure of weight. For dry grain, a picul in the Yuan was roughly 76 kilograms or 95 liters under Mongol rule; 10,000 *dàn* thus equaled about 760 metric tons or over 25,000 bushels of grain.

The eunuch Kümüs-Buqa[57] memorialized to set aside a full 10,000 households for mining and smelting precious metals and growing grapes. His Honor said, "The GREAT FOUNDER decreed that there would be no difference between the common folk behind the mountains and the people of our dynasty[58] in that the soldiers and taxes they produce should be reserved for emergencies. It would be better to substitute for these tasks the remnant civilians of Henan,[59] and not execute them. Moreover, the region beyond the mountains could be solidified."[60] HIS MAJESTY said, "What Our liege says is right." He also memorialized that the civilian households in the routes had been depleted by a pestilence, so the Mongols, Turkestanis, and Hexi people dwelling locally should pay taxes and perform corvée the same as the other civilians living there.[61] These proposals were all put into practice.

In the spring of year *rén/chén* [1232],[62] the emperor proceeded to Henan. An imperial decree was issued to people in Shanzhou, Luoyang, Qinzhou, and Guozhou who had fled into hiding in the mountain forests and caverns, that if they welcomed the army and came to surrender, they would be spared from massacre. Some said that this sort only came to allegiance when compelled, that if pressure were lessened they would just go back to helping the enemy. His Honor memorialized that several hundred banners calling all refugees to return home should be deployed in the districts that had already surrendered. The number whose lives he saved was incalculable.

According to the institutions of the dynasty, enemies who resisted the command to surrender and cast so much as a single arrow or stone would then be killed without pardon. When Bianjing[63] was about to surrender, the chief general

---

57. Eunuch here is *zhōnggùi* 中貴, lit., "[one] honored in the central [palace]." However, Kümüs-Buqa ("silver bull") is a Turkic name and there is no other reference to Turkic eunuchs in the Mongol court, so it is possible that here the term is to be taken literally as meaning simply an honored palace attendant and not as a eunuch.

58. "Common folk behind the mountains" refers to Han, that is, ethnic Chinese, civilians living in the Datong-Zhangjiakou area and the adjacent areas of Inner Mongolia; these areas were so-called because they were north of mountain ranges shielding Beijing to the northwest. The "people of our dynasty" are ethnic Mongols. The biography of Yelü Chucai in the *Yuanshi* adds that initially the emperor Öködei ordered that men from Yunzhong and Xuandezhou be chosen for these special households. It also notes that the cultivation of grapes was a still-recent import from "the West" (*Xīyù*), that is, the Middle East. See *YS* 146.3458.

59. Henan or "South of the (Yellow) River," was the last redoubt of the Jin dynasty. It was conquered in 1232–1234 and its inhabitants deported north of the Yellow River. It is unclear if this exchange took place after Henan had already been conquered, or if Yelü Chucai is looking forward to the future disposition of the Henan people after they were conquered.

60. Silver mines in the mountains northwest of Beijing are mentioned by Marco Polo (2016, §74, 63) and in the *Yuanshi*, in the area of Yúnzhou: See *YS* 5.86, 16.335, 352–53, 18.391; Schurmann 1967, 149.

61. This sentence is excerpted from an eighteen-item memorial which Yelü Chucai had presented to Öködei. See *YS* 146.3457. Hexi people are the Tanguts of Western Xia.

62. Adding *chūn* 春, "spring," following the text in *Yuanchao mingchen shilue* (Su 1996, 5.78).

63. This is modern Kaifeng, the Southern Capital of the Jurchen Jin dynasty.

Subu'edei dispatched a man to come and report, adding that since this city's defenders had resisted for many days and had killed or wounded many officers and soldiers, he intended to massacre them all. His Honor hastily forwarded a memorial saying, "The generals and soldiers, in exposing themselves to hardship for these many decades, have been fighting simply for land and people. If they get land without people, then what use will it be?" HIS MAJESTY was in doubt and made no decision, so His Honor again memorialized, saying, "All the craftsmen of bows, arrows, armor, weapons, gold, jade, and the rest, along with the wealthy families, both officials and commoners, have crowded into that city. If you kill them, then you get nothing from them, and your effort will be all in vain." HIS MAJESTY then began to agree. He issued an edict that, apart from the whole Wongian clan,[64] all the rest should be spared. At the time, those in Bianjing who had fled there from the warfare numbered 1,470,000 households. His Honor further memorialized that those in the classes of artisans, craftsmen, Confucian scholars, Buddhist monks, Daoist priests, physicians, and diviners should be resettled throughout Hebei with assistance from official funds. Thereafter, when the cities along the Huaihe and Hanjiang rivers were seized, this procedure was followed as an established precedent.

Previously, when Bianjing had not yet fallen, His Honor memorialized to dispatch a messenger into the city to search for and find the fifty-first generation descendant of Confucius, Kong Yuancuo, and reaffirm his enfeoffment as Duke Who Propagates the Sage.[65] He ordered ritualists and musicians who were scattered as refugees to be gathered together and many famous Confucian scholars such as Liang Zhi to be taken into protective custody. In Yanjing he set up an editorial office and in Pingyangfu[66] a canonical texts office in order to initiate civil administration.[67]

When Henan had first been conquered, the number of those taken prisoner was incalculable, but then when they heard that the great army was returning north, 80 to 90 percent of them fled away. An imperial edict was issued that anyone who took in or helped fugitive civilians by giving them food or drink would be killed. Whether in a walled city or a rural village, if one family violated this order, then the others, too, would all be implicated in the guilt. As a result, the common folk were dreadfully afraid, and even fathers and sons or elder and younger brothers, once any had become prisoners, did not dare to look each other in the

---

64. The Wongian clan was the imperial family of the Jin dynasty.

65. Ch. Yansheng Gong. This title had been regularly granted to the most senior descendant of Confucius and the senior of his descendants clan living in Qufu (Shandong Province) since the Song dynasty in 1055. The title continued to be granted until 1935.

66. Present-day Linfen, in south-central Shanxi Province. It had been a center of high-quality printing of popular texts, especially drama, under the Jin dynasty; see Zhang 2014.

67. These offices are said to have primarily compiled histories and canonical texts; Ila (Yelü) Chucai staffed them with Confucians (*YS* 2.34). However, it is a testament to the power of Daoists at this time that the main project of the Pingyangfu office was actually an edition of the Daoist canon. See Wang 2014; Wang 2018, 74–77. "Civil administration" (Ch. *wénzhì* 文治) here could also be understood as "literary or cultural administration."

eye. The fugitives had no way to get food and collapsed and died on the roads, one upon another. His Honor calmly entered the audience hall and, explaining the situation, said, "The reason why we have spared and succored the common people for over a decade is so they can be useful to us. When victory and defeat are undecided, one must consider that people may ally with the enemy. But now the rival empire has been destroyed. If its people run away, where can they go? How can several hundred people be faulted on account of a single escaped prisoner?" HIS MAJESTY realized the wisdom of this and suspended the order.

Though the Jin dynasty had fallen, a mere twenty or so prefectures in the Qinzhou-Gongzhou region still had not submitted for several years. His Honor memorialized, "Our people who fell afoul of the law and fled to the Jin kingdom have all congregated there. They fight so hard simply because they fear death. If you grant that they not be killed, then they will surrender on their own without any attack." The edict was issued, and all opened their city gates and surrendered. Within a month, everywhere west of the mountains[68] was pacified.

In the year *jiǎ/wǔ* [1234], by imperial edict, there was a census of households and the powerful vassal Qutughu was put in charge of it. At the beginning of the dynasty, the focus was on capturing territory, so any place that surrendered was simply left to those who surrendered. Each single hamlet and person had its own ruler with no general administration over them. It was only from this period that they came under the jurisdictions of prefectures and counties.

The court ministers as a body wanted to count every adult male as head of a separate household. His Honor alone thought this was unacceptable. Everyone said, "Whether it be our dynasty or the kingdoms in the West,[69] there is none that does not take each adult male as head of a separate household. How can you reject the great dynasty's laws and instead follow the policies of the fallen dynasty?" His Honor said, "Since ancient times, those in possession of the Central Plains have never once taken each adult male as head of a separate household. If you actually do that, then you could collect a single year of taxes, but afterward people will scatter in flight!" In the end, His Honor's opinion was adopted.

At that time, the slaves that the great princes and vassals, as well as the generals and officers, had taken as prisoners were usually lodged in the various districts, making up almost half of the whole population (*tiānxià*). His Honor therefore memorialized that in conducting the census of households they all be classified as registered civilians.[70]

---

68. These are the Longshan Mountains marking the border between present-day Shaanxi and Gansu Province. "West of the mountains" is thus present-day southern Gansu.

69. As always in Mongol-era texts, the West (*Xīyù*) here indicates Central Asia and the Middle East, i.e., all those sedentary kingdoms accessible to Chinese through caravan trade to the West.

70. As Matsuda Kōichi (2014) has shown, this estimate that almost half of the population of North China had been made prisoners of war to private commanders is confirmed in the surviving records of Dongpingfu in Shandong, where 113,000 households of "new civilians," that is, former enslaved prisoners, were added into the 115,000 households of "old civilians."

In the year *yĭ/wèi* [1235], the court proposed that Turkestanis go on campaign against the South while Han men campaign in the West. This was thought to be a winning strategy.[71] His Honor absolutely opposed it, saying "The Han lands and the Western regions are several thousand *lĭ* distant from each other. By the time the units would get to the land of the enemy, the transferred horses and men would be exhausted and unfit for service. Moreover, the living environment is different from what they are adapted to and would certainly breed epidemic diseases. It would be better for each to be sent on campaign in their own lands, which would seem to have double benefits." The debate lasted more than ten days before the original proposal finally was put to rest.

In year *bĭng/shēn* [1236], HIS MAJESTY assembled the princes and honored vassals and, personally offering a goblet of wine, toasted His Honor, "The reason why We have so sincerely trusted Our liege is that the LATE EMPEROR commanded it. Without Our liege, then the civilized world would not have seen this day. We rest high and peaceful on Our pillow due to the efforts of Our liege." It is the case that in the GREAT FOUNDER's last years he several times instructed[72] HIS MAJESTY, saying, "This man is Heaven's gift to our family; some day, you should entrust all the affairs of the empire to him."[73]

That autumn, in moon VII, Qutughu came to present the census results to the throne. He proposed that the prefectures be divided up and bestowed on the princes and aristocratic families as appanages for their household expenses.[74] His Honor said, "Big tails can't be wagged; this could easily produce conflict. It would be better to give them additional gold and silk, enough to show your benevolence." HIS MAJESTY said, "Patrimonies have already been conferred on them." His Honor went on, "If civil officials are set up and always follow orders from the court, and if they are not allowed to arbitrarily levy taxes apart from the regular quotas, the difference [for the court's interests] would be sustainable in the long term." This was approved. That year, the civilized world's taxes were fixed for the first time. Every two households would pay one catty of silk to supply official needs, while every five households would pay one catty of silk for the family to whom they had been granted. For each *mŭ*,[75] high-grade fields would pay a grain

---

71. "The South" here refers to the Southern Song dynasty in South China, while the "West" refers to the Qipchaq, Ruthenian, and other Eastern European kingdoms.

72. Ch. *zhŭ* 屬.

73. The very formal phrasing here and the departure from narrative order in referring to Chinggis Khan's legacy is rather unusual and suggests an apocryphal glorification of Chucai. It is notable that Su Tianjue, in excerpting the spirit-path stele for his own biography of Chucai, omits this passage. Perhaps he doubted its authenticity.

74. "Appanages for household expenses" is Chinese *tāngmù yì* 湯沐邑, lit., "town for hot bathing water." This traditional phrase designates a district set aside for the private expenses of a member of the imperial family. See Hucker 1985, §6301; Farquhar 1981, 46 n. 167.

75. A *mŭ* equaled about one-seventh of an acre or one-seventeenth of a hectare. See the tables of weights and measures in Appendix §2.7 (p. 192).

tax of three and one-half *dŏu*,[76] middle-grade fields would pay three *dŏu*, low-grade fields two and one-half *dŏu*, and irrigated fields five *dŏu*.[77] Commercial taxes were set at one part per thirty, and salt was set at forty catties per tael of silver. All the above were made perpetual rates. The dynasty's ministers all said the taxes were too light, but His Honor said, "In the future, interest certainly will be collected [on tax arrears],[78] and then the exactions already will be heavy."

At the beginning of the dynasty, robbers and bandits were so rife that merchants and traders could not travel. Thus, an order was issued that wherever there were losses due to robbers who escaped, if the main culprits were not apprehended within a full year, then the civilians of that route would have to pay compensation for the stolen goods. Over time, the accumulated fines reached a vast number. As for the local civil officials, they would have to borrow silver from Turkestanis, and the amount owed each year would double.[79] The next year, with the interest added, it would double again. This was called the "lamb profit." Such debts accumulated without end, often destroying families and scattering clans, to the point where wives and children had to be pawned; yet in the end they could not be paid off. His Honor made a request of HIS MAJESTY, and all the debts were repaid in silver with official funds, totaling 76,000 *dìng*. He memorialized as well that, from then on, no matter how many months or years have passed, when the interest on a loan has come to equal the principal, then the loan will no longer bear interest. This then became a set rule.[80]

The aide Toghan memorialized about the selection of virgins,[81] and by imperial order the Secretariat was to promulgate an edict for circulation. His Honor

---

76. The Chinese text here has *shēng*, or "pint," a measure of about .95 liters. This amount is absurdly low, and we follow the editors who suggest replacing *shēng* with *dŏu*, "peck" (ten *shēng* make a *dŏu*). See Schurmann 1967, 82 n. 9. This puzzle is probably due to confusion between the Uyghur-Mongolian measure *šim*, which was equivalent in value to the *dŏu*, but which sounded like the Chinese *shēng*.

77. Land yields in North China in the mid-eighteenth century for millet, probably the main crop, ranged from around five or six up to twelve or thirteen *dŏu* per *mŭ*. Occasional reports of up to twenty-five or even thirty *dŏu* per *mŭ* were achieved, but only with exceptionally good rains or irrigation. See Li 2007, 102–4.

78. This appears to be a reference to the practice, described below, of merchants extending loans to local governments to meet their tax quotas.

79. Although it is not directly stated why local officials were borrowing silver, it may have been due in part to the need to defray mandated expenses such as compensation for merchant losses, as mentioned just before. But the larger part probably was the need to pay taxes in silver. Chinese currency was based on copper coinage; precious metals had played only a small part in tax revenues. The institution of a broad-based silver tax thus created a severe shortage of silver, which local officials could only fill by borrowing from merchants with access to outside supplies; von Glahn 1996, 56–57.

80. Many policies and the suffering they caused, mentioned here and in the previous paragraphs, are also noted by Peng and Xu in "Sketch," pp. 109–111.

81. The drafting of virgins to serve in the palace, potentially to be selected as imperial concubines, was a standard practice of Chinese courts. Those selected would be ranked with a small number being directly chosen for the imperial bedchamber, others as palace women, and others kept in

received the order but did not send it on downward. HIS MAJESTY was angry and summoned him to explain. His Honor said, "There are still twenty-eight virgins in Yanjing from the previous round of elimination, more than enough to meet orders from the northern palace. Yet Toghan has transmitted a decree wishing to implement yet another general selection. Your liege fears that this will be a severe disturbance for the common folk and was just about to memorialize advocating reversal." HIS MAJESTY thought about this for a long while and said, "All right." The decree was then canceled.

[Toghan] also wanted to requisition selected mares from the Han lands. His Honor said, "What the Han lands have is only silkworm threads and the five grains; it is not a place that produces horses. If this is carried out today, then later it certainly will become a precedent. This would be to burden the civilized world for no good reason." So his request to stop the requisition was followed.

In the year of *dīng/yǒu* [1237], there was a vetting of specialists in the Three Teachings. Buddhist monks and Daoist priests were examined in the scriptures. Those who were proficient were given certificates of ordination and permission to dwell in monasteries or temples. The selected Confucian scholars were returned to their homes.[82] Previously His Honor had said, "Among Buddhist monks and Daoist priests many are just evading corvée; a qualifying examination should be held." At this point it was first implemented.

At the time,[83] the princes and aristocratic in-laws could use the post-road horses as they pleased, and the envoys were awfully numerous. Horses everywhere were in short supply, so civilians' horses would be seized high-handedly as mounts, raising commotions on the the roads between cities. When such travelers reached the next station, they would demand a hundred things, and if the food service were a little slow, then the staff would be horsewhipped; the people working in the hostels could not stand it.[84] His Honor memorialized that *paizas* and authorization

---

reserve as noted here. The age of the selectees varied from fifteen to twenty years of age in the Han dynasty to thirteen to sixteen in the last Manchu Qing dynasty (1644–1912). Usually girls were selected from easily accessible regions or tightly controlled status groups, such as military households. Girls within the groups to be selected were not allowed to be married before being inspected for potential palace service, but evasion was widespread. See Cutter and Crowell 1999, 13–14; Soulliere 1987, 263–85; Hsieh 1999; Wang 2004; Wang 2008. In the Mongol Empire, Marco Polo describes how women were chosen from the favored Qonggirat people; according to him, the Qonggirat men were eager to have their daughters chosen. See Polo 2016, §82 (pp. 72–73); cf. the additional passages in Polo 1976, 205–6. But often the practice led to resistance in which daughters were quickly married off before the selection; such resistance was met with draconian punishments. See Juvaini 1958, I, 235–36; *YS* 2.35, 20.442.

82. While Buddhist and Daoist clergy were expected to live celibate lives, Confucians were considered a class of professionals, like physicians and diviners, who would live in families, but with a distinct household status.

83. Following Su Tianjue's citation (Su 1996, 5.81) with "at the time" (*shí* 時), for the "originally" (*shǐ* 始) of the *Yuan wenlei* text.

84. Many of these abuses are described in Zhao Gong's "Memorandum," p. 89.

letters[85] should be given together with regulations on rations of food and drink to be established, so that the evils of the system were first reformed.

He followed up by setting forth ten proposals for tasks of the time,[86] to wit: 1) making rewards and punishments reliable; 2) correcting divisions of status; 3) issuing official salaries; 4) enfeoffing meritorious vassals;[87] 5) judging censures and commendations; 6) determining material resources;[88] 7) testing craftsmen; 8) promoting agriculture and sericulture; 9) fixing local tribute gifts; and 10) setting up water transport. Although HIS MAJESTY could not implement them all, still he made use of them at times.

A Turkestani man, Asan-Amish,[89] charged His Honor with using 1,000 *dìng*[90] of official silver for private purposes. HIS MAJESTY summoned His Honor and asked him about this. His Honor said, "Your Highness, try to think carefully about this. Has there been an edict to pay out some silver?" HIS MAJESTY answered, "We too recall that there was an order for repairs to this palace that used 1,000 *dìng* of silver." His Honor said, "That was it." Several days later, HIS MAJESTY held an audience at Wan'an Hall[91] and summoned Asan-Amish for questioning. He admitted making a false accusation.

An indictment of the tax clerks of Taiyuanfu Route for embezzlement was reported to the throne, and HIS MAJESTY chided His Honor: "Our liege says that the teachings of Confucius can be put into practice and that Confucian scholars are all good men, so how do we have this sort?" His Honor replied, "This vassal-son hardly would wish to defame as unrighteous the teaching of [subjects' honor to] the ruler-father. Yet sometimes there are unrighteous people. Wherever there is a kingdom or a family, all have followed the teaching of the Three Fundamental Bonds and Five Constant Virtues without exception,[92] just as Heaven has the sun, moon, and stars. How could the Way that has been continuously practiced in all

---

85. Ch. *páizhá* 牌劄, or lit., "tablet and letter," the equivalent of the "*paiza* and *yarligh*" found throughout the Persian histories (e.g., Juvaini 1958, vol. 1, 255). On these *paiza* (Mo. *gerege*), see Zhao Gong's "Memorandum," p. 86, and Xu Ting in the "Sketch," p. 112.

86. The full text of this memorial has not been preserved. However, its summary in *YS* 146.3462 occasionally gives a clearer picture of its contents.

87. "Meritorious vassals" or *gōngchén* 功臣 refers particularly to those commanders and officials who played a distinguished role in the imperial founding. In the *YS*, 146.3462, this item is summarized as "Appointing meritorious vassals as officials." Zhang Dehui, in the conversations with the young prince Qubilai, also emphasized the role of "meritorious elders"; see "Notes," p. 174.

88. In the *Yuanshi* summary (*YS* 146.3462), this is given as "equalizing the household requisitions" (*kēchāi* 科差).

89. Nothing else is known about him apart from what we see here, but from his name, he was a Turkic speaker and likely of Qipchaq or Qangli origin; see Rásonyi and Baski 2007, 79, 64.

90. Reading *dìng* 錠, "ingot," for the text's *dìng* 定, "settle, establish." A *dìng* was the Chinese name for the standard monetary unit of the Mongol Empire, called *balish* in Persian, *yastuq* in Uyghur, and *süke* in Mongolian. See the tables of weights and measures in Appendix §2.7 (p. 192).

91. This was the central hall at the Mongol capital of Qara-Qorum.

92. The "Three Fundamental Bonds" were the bonds between father and son, ruler and vassal, and husband and wife; the "Five Constant Virtues" were benevolence, righteousness, propriety,

ages be abandoned by our dynasty alone simply on account of one man's fault?" HIS MAJESTY's misgivings were thus allayed.

In the year of *wù/xū* [1238] there were severe drought and locust losses in the civilized world. HIS MAJESTY asked His Honor about methods to protect against these. His Honor said, "Your liege begs that this year's tax collections be temporarily stopped." HIS MAJESTY said, "We fear that there will not be enough for the needs of the state." His Honor said, "At present the granaries have enough to sustain us for ten years." It was permitted.

At the start, registration of the households in the civilized world yielded 1,040,000, but by this time, 40 to 50 percent had absconded. Still, taxes were levied by the old quotas, and the whole society was plagued by this. His Honor memorialized to remove 350,000 fugitive households from the rolls. The people depended on this for their peace.

Yanjing's Liu Quduma[93] secretly linked up with powerful personages and bought the commission on the civilized world's household requisitions[94] with a bid of 500,000 taels. Sheref ad-Din bought the commission on [collecting of rents from] the civilized world's government-owned corridor housing,[95] land foundations, irrigation systems, and pigs and chickens with a bid of 250,000 taels. Liu Tingyu bought the commission to manage the liquor monopoly in Yanjing with a bid of 50,000 taels. There was also a Turkestani who bought the commission to manage the civilized world's salt monopoly with a bid of 1,000,000 taels. It got to the point where even the civilized world's river moorages, bridges, and fords were all sold on commission. His Honor said, "These men are all crooks, swindling those below them and deceiving those above them. The damage they are doing is very great." He memorialized to get rid of all of them.[96] He once said, "Initiating one advantage is not as good as eliminating one harm; generating some measure is not

wisdom, and trustworthiness. This summary of Confucian ethics dates to Dongzhong Shu (197–104 BC) of the Han dynasty and was much used by later Confucians. See Knapp 2009.

93. This is an example of the common practice in the Yuan of people with Chinese surnames adopting Turco-Mongol given names.

94. Ch. *chāifā* translates the Mo. *alba ghubchiri*, designated a silver tax levied on households that purportedly was a commutation of occasional in-kind contributions to the Mongol armies and envoys. See Peng Daya's description in "Sketch," p. 109.

95. Ch. *lángfáng* 廊房: housing near the corners of walled cities built and owned by the government for security reasons and rented in times of peace to civilians.

96. This passage illustrates the practice of tax farming, whereby merchants would bid for the right to collect a given type of tax on behalf of the state. Tax farmers guaranteed the delivery to the state of the contracted amount and were allowed to collect a specified amount on top of that as their profit. In practice, tax farmers, such as the "publicans" of the New Testament who farmed taxes in Judaea on behalf of the Roman Empire, would try to outbid each other, as here; and in any case, they could easily collect far above the contracted amount and as a result had an evil reputation. The farming of direct taxes was a regular practice of many regimes, such as the Roman Empire, medieval Islamic empires, Jacobite England, Bourbon France, and colonial Southeast Asia. But it was more or less unknown in China, where tax farming was restricted to the indirect monopoly taxes, hence the sense of outrage in this passage. Note that Liu Quduma's bid for the household requisitions of 500,000 taels is actually the original quota for the silver tax

as good as eliminating some measure. Men today all think Ban Chao's words are just clichés, but since earliest antiquity this has been the final word."[97]

HIS MAJESTY was always fond of liquor, and in his later years this was especially the case, as he spent his days drinking his fill with the great vassals. His Honor repeatedly remonstrated with him but was not heeded. So, he held the metal mouth of the liquor spout and said, "This iron has been corroded by the liquor. If that is the effect even on this, how indeed could a man's internal organs not be damaged?" HIS MAJESTY was pleased and bestowed on him gold and silks, while also ordering that his attendants send in no more than three *zhōng* a day.[98] At this time, there were no worries in any direction, and HIS MAJESTY became rather negligent in attending to government affairs. Corrupt and twisted men took advantage of this interval to gain entry.

From the year *gēng/yín* [1230], His Honor had fixed the tax quota at 10,000 *dìng*; once Henan had fallen and the number of households had multiplied, then it was increased to 22,000 *dìng*. But the Turkestani translator An Tianhe arrived from Bianliang[99] and spared no effort to serve His Honor, hoping to be recommended employment. Although His Honor praised and encouraged him, in the end his ambitions were not satisfied. So he ran to visit Chinqai and used a hundred stratagems to play one man against the other.

The first thing he did was to induce the Turkestani Abduraqman[100] to bid for the commission on scheduled taxes to be increased to 44,000 *dìng*. His Honor

---

back when Ila Chucai was setting up the system. Evidently his system involved tax farmers like Liu Quduma from the beginning, although it is not mentioned until now.

97. Chucai here alludes to an episode in *Jianchu* ("Recommencing the Origin") 14 (AD 102) of the Latter Han dynasty. Ban Chao had reconquered for the dynasty the Tarim Basin (southern Xinjiang), an area inhabited by non-Chinese city-states and garrisoned by Han exiles. On relieving him, the harsh and impetuous Ren Shang asked Ban Chao what his strategy was, and the older general tried in vain to warn him:

> "The officials and clerks beyond the frontiers are fundamentally not filial sons or obedient grandsons; they are all convicts banished to support the border garrisons. Moreover, the savages and barbarians here all harbor hearts of birds and beasts, so it is hard to maintain our position and easy to be defeated. Now, My Lord's personality is strict and impatient. But if the water is too pure there will not be any big fish, and if you administer them too meticulously there will not be any peace under you. You should rest quietly like a lake and be simple and easy with them, tolerating small faults and only paying attention to the big picture." After Chao left, Shang privately said to his household, "I thought Lord Ban must have some marvelous strategy, but what he said just now was merely a bunch of clichés." Shang stayed for several years until the West broke out in rebellion and anarchy, and he was transferred under criminal charges, just as Chao had warned him (Fan Ye, *Hou Hanshu*, 47.1586).

98. A *zhōng* 鍾 was a vessel of liquor containing 34 *dǒu* 斗, a measure standardized in the Mongol Yuan at roughly 9.5 liters. Three *zhōng* was thus something like 969 liters a day. This should be understood as applying to liquor for all the court feasting with the emperor.

99. This city was earlier referred to as Bianjing; it is present-day Kaifeng, south of the Yellow River, and the Southern Capital of the Jurchen Jin dynasty.

100. Mongolian version of the Arabic name 'Abd al-Rahman. One may thus assume he was of Muslim background, but nothing else is known of his origin.

said, "Even though 440,000 could actually be raised, it would only be by applying strict laws and restrictions and would just be a covert seizure of the people's gain. Desperate people becoming robbers would not be good fortune for the state." Yet the intimate attendants and aides were enticed. HIS MAJESTY, too, was rather beguiled by the group opinion and wanted to order that the increase be implemented on a trial basis. His Honor contested it, arguing this way and that, his voice and expression both growing stern. HIS MAJESTY said, "Do you really want a fistfight over this?" His Honor's efforts could not carry the day, and with a great sigh he said, "Since the auctioning of tax profits has become ascendant, there certainly will be people who follow in these men's footsteps and arrogate their powers. Poverty and misery for the people will originate in this, and government authority will become diffused among many parties."[101]

His Honor stood firm at court with a serious countenance and was unbending in any way, as he desired to sacrifice his own body for the civilized world. Whenever he expounded on what brought advantage or disadvantage to the dynasty or joy or sorrow to the people, his manner of expression was sincere and his diligence ceaseless. HIS MAJESTY would say, "Are you going to start crying for the common folk again?" Nonetheless, he treated His Honor with ever greater respect. His Honor managed the state for a long time, and whatever salary or bonus he received, he distributed among his clansmen, never using his office or title for private advantage.

Someone urged him to take present opportunities to "widely spread the family tree"[102] as a method to secure his own base.[103] His Honor said, "Giving them money is enough to make their lives happy. Supposing I put them in government posts, then if there were unworthy ones who violated the regular statutes, I could not abandon the public laws and succumb to private feeling for them. 'A crafty rabbit has three burrows'—that is not a motto I live by."

In the spring of year *xīn/chǒu*, moon II [March/April 1241], HIS MAJESTY became seriously ill, such that his pulse stopped. Medicines were not able to cure him.[104] The Empress did not know the reason and summoned His Honor and asked him about it. At the time, the corrupt ministers had usurped the government, peddling justice and selling office. They had ordered that all the kingdoms

---

101. Ch. *zhèng chū duōmén* 政出多門, lit., "government goes out from many gates." His fear seems to be less the immediate result of the doubling of the quota, but the resulting diffusion of authority in which the exactions of imposters and profiteers would far exceed even the higher official quotas.

102. Ch. *guǎngbù zhīyè* 廣布枝葉.

103. The person who thus urged him is identified as Liu Min in *YS* 146.3463. Liu Min (1201–1259) was a man of Xuandezhou, northwest of Beijing, who was taken as a hostage into Chinggis Khan's *keshikten* (bodyguard) early in the Mongol conquests. Unlike Chucai, he was willing to work with Western officials, and so in the reshuffling of positions just before Öködei's death, he was placed in charge of the Yanjing Secretariat along with the Khwarazmian Mahmud Yalavach. See *YS* 153.3609–10, based on the spirit-path stele written for him by Yuan Haowen in *Quan Yuan wen*, vol. 1, 39.630–33.

104. Adding *zhūyào bùnéng liáo* 諸藥不能療 based on Su 1996, 5.83.

be put under the control of Turkestanis.[105] So His Honor replied to the Empress, "The imperial court now employs the wrong men, and the civilized world's prisoners certainly include many who have been falsely charged. Therefore disturbances in the heavens frequently occur. An amnesty should be proclaimed throughout the civilized world." When he drew for proof on how Duke Jing of the ancient Song state had gotten the planet Mars to leave his state's constellation,[106] the Empress became anxious to implement the measure. His Honor said, "Without the lord's command it cannot be done." Shortly afterwards, HIS MAJESTY revived a bit and the Empress memorialized about it. Unable to speak, HIS MAJESTY simply nodded his approval. When the amnesty was issued, his pulse again became active.

By moon XI (December 1241), HIS MAJESTY had long stopped taking medicine. His Honor several times divined by the Great Monad[107] that he should not hunt game, memorializing about it several times. His attendants all said, "If he does not ride and shoot, how will he enjoy himself?" HIS MAJESTY went hunting for five days and passed away.[108]

---

105. These two sentences (from "At the time. . . . under the control of Turkestanis") have been added from the text of the *Yuanchao mingchen shilue* (Su 1996, 5.83): *Shí jiānchén qiè zhèng, yùyù màiguān, zhuān líng Húihú kòngzhì zhūguó* 時姦臣竊政，鬻獄賣官，專令回鶻控治諸國.

106. This story appears in the *Shiji*, or *Records of the Grand Historian*, by the Han dynasty historian Sima Qian:

> In year 37 [of King Jing of the Zhou dynasty, that is 484 BC] . . . Mars remained stationary in the constellation Heart for a long time. Heart was the field of the Song state. Duke Jing [of the Song] was worried about this and the Director of Astronomy, Ziwei, said, "It could be deflected onto the ministers of state," but Duke Jing said, "The ministers are my arms and legs." He said, "It could be deflected onto the common people," but Duke Jing said, "A lord should treat the common people well." Ziwei said, "It could be deflected onto the harvest." Duke Jing said, "If the harvest fails, the common people will be hard-pressed. Would there be anyone left for me to be lord of?" Ziwei said, "Heaven is high, yet hears those who are low. Three times my lord has said what was right for a lord. Mars should show some movement." As a result, they waited and indeed it shifted three degrees (Sima Qian, *Shiji*, 38.1631).

The "constellation Heart" (Ch. *Xīn* 心) was one of the twenty-eight Lunar Lodgings in Chinese astronomy. It comprises the stars σ, α, and τ Scorpionis of West Eurasian astronomy. Each of the Chinese Lunar Lodgings was assigned to a state or direction and Mars's approach to a constellation was always a harbinger of disaster for the place associated with that constellation.

107. Ch. *Tàiyī* 太一. This refers simultaneously to the great Way, Dao, or prime spirit that in Chinese cosmology rules the ten-thousand things, and also to a dim star between the West Eurasian Ursa Major and Ursa Minor whose brightness is an indicator of the future. As the *Jìnshu* writes:

> The star *Tàiyī* ('Great Monad') is south of and near *Tiānyī* 天一 ("Celestial Monad"). It is also the spirit of the Celestial Emperor, controlling sixteen other spirits, and knowing the incidences of wind and rain, flood and drought, weapons and armaments, hunger and famine, diseases and epidemics, and the harm of calamities (*Jìnshu*, 11.290; Ho 1966, 71).

Given the wealth of astrological episodes in these last years of Öködei's life, an astrological reference seems more likely. The eighteenth-century Qianlong edition, however, reads the text here as *Tàiyǐ* 太乙 or "Great Binary," which could only refer to a method of divination.

108. In Chen Jing 2010, 23.18v, this final sentence is somewhat longer: "His Majesty listened to them and went out to hunt for five days before returning. Reaching Ötegü-Qulan Mountain,

In the year *gŭi/măo* [1243], the Empress asked His Honor about an heir and the succession. His Honor said, "This is not something which a minister of a different lineage should discuss. Of course, there is the testamentary edict of the LATE EMPEROR. Following it would be a great blessing to the altars of state."[109]

As Abduraqman had just seized power at court through bribery, everyone else with power toadied to him. He feared only that His Honor would block his doings. So he tried to bribe His Honor with 50,000 taels of silver. But His Honor would not accept it, and whenever Abduraqman's policies were harmful to the people, he immediately put a stop to them.

At the time, the Empress had already assumed the regency and she delivered to Abduraqman blank sheets with the imperial seal affixed, with the order to have them filled in with writing, as he liked. His Honor memorialized, saying, "The civilized world is the LATE EMPEROR'S world.[110] Laws and institutions, rules and regulations: all issued from the LATE EMPEROR. One must hope that it will continue to be thus, so your liege dares not receive this directive." Soon after there was another edict ordering that, since Abduraqman's memorials accord with reason, any scribe who would not write in his views on those sheets would have a hand cut off. His Honor said, "The LATE EMPEROR entrusted all affairs of army and state to this old vassal. What is the point of giving orders to scribes? If the policies are reasonable, then naturally I will honor them, but if they are unreasonable, then I will not hide even from death in my resistance. How could I care about a severed hand?" He thereupon said in a severe tone, "This old vassal served the GREAT FOUNDER and the GREAT ANCESTOR for more than thirty years and has certainly never turned his back on this dynasty. Even an Empress Dowager cannot kill a minister who has been without fault." Although the Empress resented his defiance of her, because he was a senior meritorious minister from the previous reigns, she bent to him out of respect and awe.

---

he drank with Abduraqman and the next day he passed away." This passage, which mentions Abduraqman's encouragement of the emperor's dissipation, and which thus alludes to the charge that the emperor was actually killed with poisoned liquor, may come from the lost grave epitaph composed by Li Wei, and was perhaps eliminated by Song Zizhen due to an unwillingness to countenance such speculation. Or else it may have been lost inadvertently in the copying of Song Zizhen's text. (Since the passage in question is bracketed by two instances of *rì* 日, or "day," the copyist's eye could easily slip from one *rì* to the next, thus omitting the intervening text. This is a process that textual scholars call "parablepsis" or oversight.) In any case, the fuller original text was the source of the account in *YS* 2.37.

109. Su Tianjue quotes this episode from the grave epitaph composed by Li Wei with a virtually identical text, but dated instead to the spring of *rén/yín* (1242). It is unclear which date is correct.

110. In the honorific spacing given these phrases about the "Late Emperor," one may see the influence of the Mongolian custom of exalted references to deceased emperors. Unfortunately, the Chinese does not distinguish singular or plural here, so it is impossible to tell if Ila Chucai here is speaking just of Öködei or of Öködei and Chinggis together. Our surmise that only Öködei is being referred to here is thus hypothetical.

In that year, His Honor grew sick and passed away in office on V, 14 [June 20, 1244], after enjoying fifty-five years of life.[111] All Mongols cried for him as if they were mourning a relative, the Qorum markets closed in respect for him, and music and entertainment ceased for several days. Among the scholar-officials of the civilized world, there were none who did not weep sorely and mutually mourn him. On Zhongtong 2, X, 20 [November 14, 1261], he was interred on the sunlit side of Wengshan Hill, east of Yuquan,[112] in accord with his last testament.

He was buried with his deceased wife, the lady *née* Su, of the Qishui Fief.[113] He had previously married a lady of the Liang family, from whom he was separated by the chaos of war, and who died in Fangcheng, Henan.[114] She had given birth to a son, Xuan, who was supervisor of the granaries in Kaipingfu before he passed away.[115] The lady *née* Su was the daughter of Su Gongbi, the prefect of Wēizhou and a fourth-generation descendant of Master Su Dongpo.[116] Her son was Zhu, who is now serving as the Grand Councilor on the Left of the Central Secretariat. There are eleven grandsons, named Xizhi, Xibo, Xiliang, Xikuan, Xisu, Xizhou,

---

111. Although the "Spirit-Path Stele" implies that his death was in the same *gǔi/mǎo* year (1243) as the previous incidents, other sources show that he actually passed away in the following *jiǎ/chén* year (1244). See Yelü Chucai/Xie Fang 1986, 372–73. Note that in the traditional East Asian reckoning, the time in the womb counted as one year and birthdays are conventionally reckoned on the Lunar New Year, so that ages are one or sometimes even two years greater than they would be in Western reckoning. Although it is not directly stated, he appears to have died while traveling with the empress dowager's camp in Mongolia.

112. This Wengshan Hill is the present-day Wanshou or Longevity Hill in the Summer Palace (Yihe Yuan) in the northwest of Beijing; see Yelü Chucai/Xie Fang 1986, 2–3. The spirit-path and temple dedicated to him were renovated under the Qing dynasty, but were destroyed in 1966 by Red Guards during the wave of vandalism that began the Cultural Revolution. Probably when he died in Mongolia, his family was unable immediately to follow his wishes and transport the body to Wengshan Hill for burial because they were poor and out of favor. His remains may have been temporarily buried or else embalmed and kept sealed in a coffin; seventeen years later, Qubilai Khan came to power and must have issued funds to transport Chucai's remains and inter them near Beijing according to his wishes.

113. This was the same honorific title borne by Chucai's mother, "the lady *née* Yang" (see p. 135).

114. Fangcheng is a county of the same name today in south-central Henan Province. This brief mention is all that is left of what must have been a tragic story of family separation. Evidently, his wife left Yanjing during the siege of 1214–1215 and, perhaps with her natal family, joined the mass exodus of Jin officials and scholars southward to Henan. There she presumably was killed in the fall of Fangcheng to Mongol forces under Tolui in 1232. Thus from 1215 to 1232, while Chucai was serving the Mongol campaigns against the Jin, he was presumably aware of the possibility that his former wife and in-laws were among those in the enemy camp.

115. Kaipingfu is the later Shangdu, the famous summer capital of Qubilai Khan. The city bore the name Kaipingfu from 1260 to 1268, and one may surmise that Xuan passed away during that period. Xuan was never recognized as Chucai's heir, perhaps due to the fact that his mother left her husband in Yanjing and fled to Kaifengfu.

116. Dongpo was the pen name of Su Shi (1037–1101), an official under the Song and one of China's most famous literary and artistic figures.

Xiguang, Xiyi, and so on.[117] There are five granddaughters, who have been married into noble families.

His Honor's natural endowment was exceedingly gallant, in every way going beyond the ordinary human measure. Though official correspondence filled his desk, he would grant this and reply to that on left and right, in everything fitting the case at hand. Also he was able to discipline himself with loyal dedication, once calculating the civilized world's nine-year tax revenue without a hair's breadth of discrepancy by staying up all night working on it sleeplessly.

Ordinarily he would not laugh or talk nonsense, and one might suspect he was cool and aloof, yet once he engaged with someone, his warm cordiality was unforgettable. He was not a regular drinker, and while only occasionally gathering for entertainment with friends and guests, he went from morning to evening sitting upright.[118] Throughout his life he paid no attention to making a living[119] and never once asked about the income and expenditures of his family finances. When he died, someone slandered him, saying "His Honor served as Grand Councilor for twenty years, during which the tribute and presents of the civilized world flowed into his private coffers." The Empress dispatched a man of the imperial body-guard[120] to inspect his place. Only a few fine zithers[121] and a few hundred rubbings of old inscriptions were found.[122]

---

117. The *YS* 146.3465 confirms that all of these grandsons were the sons of Yelü Zhu; it seems that Xuan died childless. Three additional grandsons are indicated, but their full names are partially blank in the "Spirit-Path Stele." One of Yelü Zhu's other sons, Xitu, is mentioned elsewhere and must be one of these other three (see Yelü Chucai/Xie Fang 1986, 373).

118. This sentence is not found in the *Yuan wenlei* text and has been added from the citation in *Yuanchao mingchen shilue* (Su 1996, 5.84). His biography in the *YS* 146.3461 adds a charming anecdote about one of these episodes of entertainment:

> Chucai was once feasting with the princes and fell asleep drunk in the middle of his cart. The emperor, surveying the open fields, saw him and drove his camp-tent straight there. Going up to the cart he shook him with his hand. Chucai was sound asleep and did not wake up, but then he got angry at being disturbed and suddenly opened his eyes. Only then did he realize that the emperor had arrived, and he jumped up in alarm and began making apologies. The emperor said, "So you get drunk drinking alone, but you will not enjoy yourself together with Us?" and departed with a laugh. Chucai, too flustered to put on his court cap and gown, rushed up to the traveling palace. The emperor served wine and they enjoyed themselves tremendously before calling a halt.

119. Ch. *bùzhì shēngchǎn* 不治生産. This phrase, used to show distance from mundane concern for family wealth, is a literary cliché, although that does not make it untrue in any particular case.

120. This man is named Marcha in the *YS* 146.3464; this information probably derives from the Li Wei version of the epitaph. This name is today found among the Turkic peoples of Siberia, which may be his origin.

121. Ch. *qín* 琴. See "Sketch," p. 105 n. 59.

122. The text in Su Tianjue's *Yuanchao mingchen shilue* (Su 1996, 5.84), and the *YS* 146.3464 both speak of "several tens" of zithers and "several thousands" of scrolls, which ironically diminishes the claim of Chucai's exemplary frugality. It is likely that the text originally had the higher number, but a later copy revised it to the lower number.

Poem by Ila Chucai in his own calligraphy, addressed to the local official Liu Man upon the
official's departure from office.

He was zealous in his love of study, which he did not dispense with morning
or night. He once admonished his children, saying, "No matter how numerous
your official duties, the days may belong to the office, but the nights belong to
yourselves and you can always study then." In his learning, he aimed for com-
prehensiveness. Astronomy and calendrics, medicine and divination, mathematics
and mental computation,[123] musical pitch, Confucianism and Buddhism, and the
scripts of various countries—there was none he did not grasp thoroughly. Once
he said that the understanding of the five planets is more precise in the Western
calendar than in the Chinese one,[124] and so he made the *Martabah* Calendar, which
should be the Turkestani name for calendar.[125] Moreover, when he found that their

---

123. Ch. *zásuàn, nèisuàn* 雜算, 內算. These terms are not found in reference works, and our translation of *nèisuàn*, in particular, is tentative.

124. "Chinese" here is *Zhōngguó*. This passage on the calendar systems is the only place in the
whole inscription where Song Zizhen uses that term.

125. This term, given in Chinese transcription as *mádābā* is not, as is implied, the Arabic or Persian word for calendar, which is rather *taqwīm* or *sālnāmah*. We read it as Perso-Arabic *martabah*,
"step, stair; watch-tower; office, employment; height; dignity, rank; time, instance," probably in
the sense of a tower where astronomical observations could be undertaken.

measurements of solar eclipse progression differed from the Chinese because of accumulated discrepancies in the Daming Calendar,[126] he set the "Duke of Civil Preferment's *Yi/wèi* [1235] Almanac"[127] and promulgated it throughout the world.

His Honor having been interred for seven years,[128] the Grand Councilor[129] brought to me the "Account of Conduct" composed by the Presented Scholar Zhao Yan[130] and entrusted me with writing a stele inscription and ode based on it. The dynasty inherited a state of great chaos, in which Heaven's bonds were ruptured, Earth's axis was broken, and human principles were eclipsed. What is called re-creating the bonds of husband and wife and reestablishing the relation of father and son—truly there was such a need![131] In addition, the regimes of the North and South[132] in all things were recalcitrant toward each other. Those who came and went making use of the situation were all from different countries, with mutually unintelligible languages and incongruent aims. Yet just at that time, His

---

126. This calendar was created in AD 462 by the Chinese mathematician and astronomer Zu Chongzhi (425–500) and was the first Chinese calendar to account for the precession of the equinoxes. It was formally adopted by the Southern Chinese Liang dynasty in 510.

127. This is the almanac mentioned by Xu Ting in the "Sketch," p. 105. "Civil Preferment" is Chinese *wénxiàn*. This title was, it may be recalled, the posthumous title of Chucai's father, and Chucai here seems to be using it in honor of his father.

128. Thus, in year 1268, seven years after Chucai's interment in Wengshan Hill in 1261. This was the last year of Song Zizhen's life.

129. Ila (Yelü) Chucai's son Zhu, had just been reinstated as "Grand Councilor on the Left" and would be dismissed two years later in 1270 (see *YS* 146.3465, 7.127, 126.3092; as modern *Yuanshi* editors note, the listing in *YS* 112.2797 is inaccurate).

130. Zhao Yan, from the small town of Beiping (present-day Shunping County in Hebei province), won his degree as "Presented Scholar" under the Jin regime. At the time of Chucai's death, he was in the entourage of Chucai's son Zhu, and was tutor for Chucai's grandson Xiliang; see Su Tianjue 1996, 5.82; *YS* 180.4159.

131. Song Zizhen here alludes to a passage in Ban Gu's "Rhapsody on the Two Capitals" (*Liangdu fu*), describing the situation at the end of the sectarian rebellions and civil war that overthrew the usurper Wang Mang's short-lived Xin dynasty (AD 9–23) and reestablished the Han dynasty:

> In the first year of Established Might [AD 25],
> Heaven and Earth changed the mandate.
> Within the Four Seas
> They created anew the relation of husband and wife,
> And there was now distinction between father and son.
> The positions of ruler and subject were now established,
> And the system of human relations began.
> It was this then on which [the primordial culture hero] Fu Xi based his august virtue.
> (Translation from Xiao/Knechtges 1982, 151, text in Fan Ye's *Hou Hanshu*, 40B.1360–61.)

We would like to thank the Reader A for bringing this allusion to our attention and correcting our translation of Song Zizhen's passage.

132. It is hard to tell if the "regimes in the North and South" here are the Jin and the Southern Song, or the Mongols and the Jin. Perhaps the ambiguity is intentional, and a covert criticism not just of the Mongol and Jin regimes' mutual intransigence, but also of Qubilai's Mongols and the Southern Song.

Honor, as a single student standing alone at the head of the court, still desired to practice what he had learned—how impossibly difficult it was! Fortunately, relying on an enlightened SON OF HEAVEN ascending the throne, his admonitions were heeded and his words were heard. He shook out his sleeves and strode straight ahead, vigorously pressing on with no regrets. Even though not more than two or three out of ten of his policies saw implementation, nonetheless the men of the civilized world have all shared equally in the blessings they conferred. If, at a time like this, His Honor had not existed, then no one knows indeed what would have become of the human race.

The ode reads:[133]

> The rise of noble kings
> Depends on worthy men.
> But who will take that role
> Cannot be known ahead.
> Aheng came back to Shang,[134]
> Shangfu returned to Zhou:[135]
> They rose like clouds in just a day,
> And hist'ry made for endless years.
> The scarlet mists announced his rise;
> A dragon flew in wint'ry steppes.
> Commanders marshaled righteous troops
> To pacify the civ'lized world.
> Confucians came in their due time
> And stitched again opposing sides.
> In earnest effort he excelled—
> Just him, Director in the Court.
> And what would be His Honor's way?
> To harmonize his ruler's realm.
> The foal of royal tutor's line,

---

133. This ode is written in unrhymed couplets each of four lines. We have translated this into English iambic quatrameter, also unrhymed.

134. Aheng was the title of Yi Yin who in legend served the first Shang king Tang and helped him conquer the last, bad king of the legendary first dynasty, the Xia. After King Tang's death, he was famous for putting Tang's grandson and heir under house arrest when he showed bad morals, not releasing him until three years later, when the new king was properly penitent. Yi Yin thus became a model and charter for powerful ministers dominating the monarch in the name of Confucian rectitude. (There is no evidence of Tang or Yi Yin outside of later legendary sources as yet, but if this legend has a historical basis it might be placed ca. 1600 BC.) In the Warring States period, many apocryphal speeches by Yi Yin were included in the *Exalted Documents* (Legge [1865] 1991, 191–219).

135. Shangfu is the courtesy name of the adviser surnamed Jiang who served kings Wen and Wu of the Zhou dynasty, helping them conquer the bad, last king of the Shang dynasty. This event and the two kings are historical and may be dated to 1046 BC. As grand duke, Jiang was titled Taigong, and the Warring State military classic "Taigong's Six Secret Teachings" was attributed to him; see Sawyer and Sawyer 1993, 21–105.

The duke who honored culture's son.
The flawless jade was grand, how grand,
A splendor that secured the state!
The monarch said, "Behold the man
Bestowed by Heav'n upon our clan!"
A double fire cohering flashed:[136]
The Mandate now has been transferred.[137]
The Heavens spin and Earth will turn[138]
As though to start all things anew.
In court and country all affairs
Entrusted were to his wise care
Our state, our people all as one.
"You effect and you shall act!"[139]
His Honor knelt and bowed his head,
"How dare I not to try?" he said.
Beginning with the thearchs' texts,
He raised up humane principles.[140]
The mighty men across the realm,
Took killing as their wanton sport.
Covertly they robbed the folk,
And played with soldiers all around.[141]

---

136. The idea of double fire cohering is an allusion to the trigrams and hexagrams of the *Yijing* (or *I Ching*), the *Canon of Changes*. *Lí* 離 here, symbolizing fire, is the seventh of the Eight Trigrams; two *lí* 離 trigrams together form the hexagram no. 30, also called *lí*, and which symbolizes "radiance" and "cohesion."

137. "Mandate" is *mìng* 命, "changed" or "transferred" is *gé* 革; "changing the mandate" is the classical way to refer to a change in dynasties and was later adapted to mean "revolution."

138. "Heaven" here is *qián* 乾 and "Earth" is *kūn* 坤, the trigrams that double to form the first and second hexagrams, respectively, of the *Yijing*. They represent the Heavenly or male principle and the Earthly or female principle in *Yijing* divination.

139. An allusion of the words of legendary Emperor Shun to his prospective new chief minister, the future Yu the Great, in the Confucian canon, *Exalted Documents*: "I wish to help and support my people—you give effect to my wishes. I wish to spread the influence of my government through the four quarters—you are my agents" (Legge [1865] 1991, 79–80). Song Zizhen thus draws a parallel between Öködei's employment of Ila (Yelü) Chucai and the affinity between two of China's greatest sage emperors of antiquity.

140. Thearchs (*dì* 帝) were mythical ideal rulers, who in Chinese mythology dating to the Warring States period, ruled between the time of the divine creators and the first, legendary, Xia dynasty (ca. 2070–1600 BC). The five thearchs included the Yao, Shun, Yu the Great, and other paragons of rule. The "thearchs' texts" (*dìfén* 帝墳) refer to the apocryphal documents attributed to them in the Confucian canonical collection, the *Exalted Documents*; see the translation in Legge [1865] 1991, 1–151.

141. This line and the one above both allude to the description the Han dynasty official Gong Sui gave of the conditions in the far northeast of the empire under the Han emperor Xuan (73–49 BC): "The seashores are distant and remote, not touched by the Sage Emperor's culture. The commoners suffer hunger and cold, but the officials show no concern. Thus, Your Highness's

But once his noble cry went out,
It traveled faster than a gale.
He took command of summoned braves
To pen and cage the bloody beasts.
The wise and good had hidden well,
Behind stout passes, holding out.[142]
In deep disguise went noble men
To seek to live amongst the weeds.
Yet choosing each to fit the task
He richly built the house of state.
He cast his net in every clime
To snare the rarest treasured game.[143]
To fill the stores with good supply
And issue wide the silk and grain,
His Honor was for just this time
Like Xiao He in the keep of Han.[144]
To form anew the halls of power[145]
And burnish bright the legal norms,
His Honor was for just this time
Like Xuanling of the halcyon Tang.[146]

---

folk are forced to rob, and Your Highness's soldiers are thrown away like playthings" (see Ban Gu's *Hanshu* 89.3639).

142. These two lines allude to a letter by the Tang Confucian Han Yu (768–824) to a late Tang dynasty official, Li Bo (773–831). In it he laments, "Now is a moment when something can be done, but [everyone else] hides in the deep mountains, locking their gates and refusing to let anyone in; their way of defense is different from the truly benevolent and righteous!" The official was convinced by Han Yu's argument and began to serve at court. See the biography of Li Bo in *Xin Tangshu*, 118.4282, by Ouyang Xiu and Song Qi. We would like to thank Reviewer A for drawing our attention to the allusion, and Prof. Sixiang Wang for his assistance on translating the passage.

143. Lit., "he hunted unicorns and searched for phoenixes." The unicorn (*lín* 麟) and phoenix (*fèng* 鳳) were classic animals that appear in times of good government. Here they are used as symbols of the great human talent that the court of a true monarch is expected to welcome and employ.

144. Xiao He (d. 193 BC) was the grand councilor for the first emperor of the Han dynasty, Liu Bang (r. 202–195 BC, as Han Gaozu). He was famous for organizing the home front in the Shaanxi area around Chang'an (modern Xi'an) with such efficiency that the emperor was always well supplied in his campaigns to unify the empire. Even so, the people were not oppressed with high taxes.

145. This is an allusion to the biography of the Tang official Du Ruhui (585–630) who was the close partner of Fang Xuanling (see note 146) in serving as dual chief ministers to the Tang emperor Taizong: "Right when they were serving as chief minister, the civilized world was newly stabilized; whether arranging measures in the halls of governance, or the regulation of finances and adjustments to the statutes, he followed what these two men [Du Ruhui and Fang Xuanling] reformed through discussion" (Ouyang Xiu and Song Qi, *Xin Tangshu*, 96.3859).

146. Fang Xuanling (579–648) was one of the famous officials under the first two Tang dynasty emperors, Tang Gaozu (r. 618–626) and his much more famous son, Tang Taizong (r. 626–649).

With captives chained in endless lines,
The lands were strewn with corpses stiff.[147]
We had been warm but now were cold;
We had been full but now were starved.
In cities tense with dreadful siege
Each breath was breathed on borrowed time.
The captives' bonds we then untied,
And brought the dying back to life.
The living multiplied and thrived,
Instructed well on nurturance.
And to today, each family
Receives the blessings of his care.
While Heaven high above us lies
What happens here is clearly known.
So bless'd is now the primal heir[148]
To grasp again the hinge of state.
His Honor's merit's well archived;
His name lights up dynastic tales.
The mighty, rich, and full of years
Will mourn and celebrate him here.
How lush, how lush this new grave-path
With surge, with surge will flow the spring.[149]
Immortal is his noble name,
For myriad years his verdant fame.

During Zhenguan, as Tang Taizong's year-slogan was called, Fang headed the administration as senior grand councilor, organized the imperial archives, drafted histories of the previous dynasties, and revised the Tang law code, which became the model for all subsequent Chinese codes.

147. This sentence begins a section on the campaign in Henan and how Chucai was instrumental in sparing those besieged in Bianjing and elsewhere in Henan.

148. "Primal heir" is an allusion to Qubilai Khan, whose year slogan from 1264 on was "Ultimate Primacy" (Zhiyuan).

149. "The path" or *qiān* 阡 is specifically the path to the tomb, along which this inscription would be carved. The "spring" (*quán* 泉) may be a spring within the cemetery area, but water flowing vastly from a source symbolizes the beneficial influences flowing vastly from Chucai's example.

Notes on a Journey

By Zhang Dehui of the Great Mongol Empire

Zhang Dehui (1194–1274, courtesy name Yaoqing) was born a subject of the Jin dynasty in Jiaocheng County, southwest of Taiyuanfu, in the Hedong region (modern Shanxi). He was a studious youth and when his family was devastated by the wars in the Zhenyou years (1213–1216), his brothers secured an entry-level position for him at the new Jin capital as a clerk in the censorate (assigned to review official actions and ferret out corruption and incompetence). The Jin court had moved its capital south to Kaifengfu in Henan. He and several other men from the Hedong, Zhendingfu, and Yunzhong regions, who earned degrees or entered the bureaucracy at that time—Lei Yuan, Li Ye, Yuan Haowen, and Bai Hua—formed a group of able young Confucians. Early on, Zhang Dehui won fame for reopening a robbery case, acquitting a Buddhist monk who had falsely confessed to the robbery because he feared torture, and then arresting the real culprit.

After the final destruction of the Jin, he went north to Hebei and served as a registrar in the Zhendingfu prefectural office of Shǐ Tianze, one of the leading Chinese commanders on the Mongol side. In 1247, and again in 1252 (this time with Yuan Haowen), he was summoned north by Qubilai, then a prince, to discuss the Confucian way of rule. After Qubilai was enthroned as Great Khan in 1260, Zhang Dehui served as the Hedong Circuit pacification commissioner, where he earned both a wide reputation and significant hostility as an independent-minded defender of the common farmers' interests.

In 1266 he was made an adviser to the Secretariat (the main policy-making body), and in 1268 he was nominated as one of two attendant censors, one of the highest offices in the censorate, but declined the nomination. When asked to draw up regulations for the censorate, he again demurred, saying that in the absence of an officially promulgated legal code it would be impossible to draw up rules. When the emperor pressed him, he refused again on grounds of age. In the end, the emperor asked only that he nominate suitable persons, which he did. The following is Zhang Dehui's record of his first meeting with Qubilai.

Notes on a Journey

1. On *dīng/wèi*, VI, 1 [July 4, 1247], we proceeded north in response to the summons, setting out from Zhenyang.[1] The envoys stayed the night when passing through Zhongshanfu, during which time it was densely cloudy without raining. There was a moment when the sky began to clear, and one could see in the west

---

1. Zhenyang was an alternate name of Zhenzhou, the Tang-era name for Zhendingfu. We would like to thank Reader A for this information.

the lofty summit of Hengshan Mountain (Note: This is the so-called sacred peak)[2] rising up like a green canopy. Then, one after another, the surrounding peaks could be counted, so I turned my head and addressed my traveling companions, saying, "In this journey of ours, will we not have a speedy return? This is the felicitous omen of Tuizhi's Hengshan."[3]

2. The next day we left Baosai,[4] crossing the bridge over the Xuhe River. To the west, Langshan Mountain could be seen, its forests like swords and halberds in luxuriant green.[5] Then, as we went from Liangmen Gate and Dingxing to reach Zhuojun Commandery,[6] in the east the Lousang Temple of the Former Lord of Shu[7] could

---

2. This is one of a small number of notes added into the text in smaller type; it is nowhere explicitly stated, but these appear to be annotations by Zhang Dehui's younger contemporary Wang Yun, which he added when he entered this text into his anthology, "Praiseworthy Conversations from the Jade Hall."

3. Tuizhi is the courtesy name (*zi*) of the Tang Confucian Han Yu (768–824), famous for his opposition to the imperial court's patronage of Buddhism, an opposition that began the revival of Confucianism. Zhang Dehui alludes to Han Yu's famous poem, "Stopping at a Temple on Hengshan Mountain, I Inscribed This Poem in the Gate Tower," which begins:

> The Five Holy Mountains have the rank of the Three Dukes;
> The other four make a ring with the Song Mountain midmost.
> To this one, in the fire-ruled south, where evil signs are rife,
> Heaven gave divine power, ordaining it a peer.
> All the clouds and hazes are hidden in its girdle,
> And its forehead is beheld only by a few.
> . . . I came here in autumn during the rainy season
> When the sky was overcast and clear wind gone.
> I quieted my mind and prayed for an answer,
> For surely righteous thinking reaches to high heaven.
> And soon all the mountain peaks were showing me their faces.
> (Adapted from a translation by Bynner and Kiang 1972, 31)

Han Yu wrote this poem after visiting Hengshan Mountain in Hunan Province of southern China. The fact that Hengshan in Hunan and Hengshan in Hebei are homonyms undoubtedly added to the significance of the parallel for Zhang Dehui.

4. Zhang Dehui uses the older Song-era name for the seat of Baozhou Prefecture.

5. Ch. *cōngcuì kěyì* 葱翠可挹.

6. The Han dynasty (206 BC–AD 220) name of what in Zhang Dehui's day was Zhuozhou Prefecture (modern Zhuoxian County).

7. "The Former Lord of Shu" is Liu Bei, who from AD 180 onward upheld the cause of the Han dynasty's imperial Liu family, of which he was a very distant relative. The temple that Zhang Dehui saw was built in his birthplace. When rebellions shook the Han dynasty and the warlord Cao Cao reunified North China under his new Wèi regime, Liu Bei built a Han government in exile in Shu, that is, Sichuan. Liu Bei's struggle, aided by his brilliant and loyal grand councilor, Zhuge Liang, became an exemplar of loyalty and resistance to evil ambition, particularly invoked by southerners against northerners. Yet other scholars, such as Sima Guang (1019–1086), considered that the Han was finished and that the Cao family's Wèi dynasty was its legitimate successor. Liu Bei's official temple name was Han Zhaoliedi ("Luminous and Majestic Emperor of the Han"), but his son, who eventually lost the kingdom, received the temple name "Latter Lord."

be seen; by passing through Liangxiang and crossing Lugou Bridge,[8] we arrived at Yanjing.

Setting off again after a ten-day stay there, going north we passed Shuangtabao Fort and Xindian Courier Station,[9] entered Nankou Gap, and crossed Juyong Pass. We exited that pass by the Beikou Gap, and then went west through Yulin Courier Station, Leijiadian Inn, reaching Huailai County. East of the county seat was a bridge, in the middle of which were horizontal wood planks, with stonework both above and below. West of the bridge was a settlement where people lived, but the county seat's outer wall was crumbling and neglected.[10] Going westward we passed along the southern side of Mount Jiming; there was a lodging house called Pingyu, and on its summit a dwelling for monks had been built.[11] Holding to the west side of the mountain, we went northward and then followed the Sanggan River upstream. The river had a stone bridge, which we took westward onto the road for Dexingfu Prefecture. Heading northward, we passed an inn called Dingfang, crossed the river at Shitizi,[12] and reached Xuandezhou Prefecture. Traveling again to the northwest, we passed Shalingzi Gap and Xuanping County Courier Station; setting out through Desheng Gap, we arrived at Ehu Ridge.[13]

3. Below, there was a courier station named Boro. From this place northward, the courier stations were all divided up under the lordships of various Mongol tribes and clans; each station was named after the one ruling it. Going upward over Ehu Ridge and traveling northeastward, we first saw fleece-bordered felt-carts,[14] the occupants of which were simply following the water and grass to herd their livestock. We were no longer in the local conditions[15] of the Central Plains.

By using the title "Former Lord of the Shu" rather than his full temple name, Zhang implicitly affirms the view of Sima Guang that Liu Bei's attempt to restore the Han was doomed.

8. This bridge still exists. It was described by Marco Polo and hence it is often called "Marco Polo Bridge" in Western sources. See Polo 2016, §105 (93).

9. "Courier Station" is the Chinese name for what under the Mongols were called *jam*, the famous Mongol post-road system. As the guest of a Mongol prince, Zhang Dehui would have had the right to use these stations free of charge.

10. One of the conditions of surrender to the Mongols was to tear down city walls that could impede rural-based Mongol cavalry from entering if the city should rebel again.

11. This is the Yongning Monastery built in 1023 under the Liao dynasty.

12. That is, "Stone Ladder." The river here is the modern Yanghe, a tributary of the Sanggan River, just south of present-day Xuanhua. In fact, although Zhang Dehui says they crossed a stone bridge over the Sanggan, that bridge, too, was over the Yanghe River.

13. That is, "Barbarian-Quelling" Ridge. The usual name for this pass is Yehu or "Wild Fox" Ridge; see Li Xinchuan, n. 44, pp. 52–53; Peng Daya, "Sketch," n. 19, p. 96. Zhang Dehui's *Èhú* 扼胡, "Barbarian-Quelling," would have been pronounced virtually identically to *Yěhú* 野狐, "Wild Fox," in medieval Chinese. Zhang Dehui appears confused about the location of Desheng Gap; other sources place it to the east of Juyong Pass.

14. Ch. *cùfú zhānchē* 毳幞氈車. "Felt carts," or *zhānchē*, refers to the yurts described by Xu Ting as the "steppe style" ("Sketch," p. 99) and placed permanently on carts. The idea of a bordering with fleece (*cùfú*), however, is unique to Zhang's description.

15. Ch. *fēngtǔ* 風土. This refers to both the social and environmental conditions, seen as a unit. See the discussion of *fēngsú*, "traditional customs," in the Introduction, p. 22.

Soon after, we passed through Fuzhou, where only deserted city walls were left. Heading north, we entered Changzhou Prefecture, where the residents were barely a hundred families. In the middle of it was a government building erected by the Prince of State;[16] there also was a granary under the control of the prefecture's salt office. East of the prefecture was a salt lake at least thirty-five miles[17] around, which the local people called Dog Lake because of its similar shape.[18] Going more than a hundred *lǐ* north of the prefecture, we found an ancient rampart, almost hidden now, connected all the way to a mountain ravine. South of the rampart was a small, abandoned walled town. When we asked those who lived there, they said that it was a guard post built by the previous dynasty. The settlement is inhabited by the guards stationed there.

From the guard post we went through four courier stations before entering the sand hills.[19] In the whole extent of the hills, there were no rocks or an inch of soil. From afar there seemed to be ridges or mounds, but upon approach, it was all deep sand. As for trees, it was suitable only for elms and willows; moreover, they all grew in forlorn clusters. Its water was all brackish and alkaline. We passed through six courier stations in all before exiting the hills.

4. Again turning northwest for one station, we passed Fish Lake.[20] This is actually two lakes, more than thirty-five miles around, but with a land road in the middle running between the northern and southern shores. On the eastern waterfront was the summer palace of a princess, around which was a wall almost one rod[21] high and about seven-tenths of mile square.[22] In the middle was built a sleeping chamber wedged between two halls, with a turtle-shaped promenade[23] behind it, and two corridors ranged beside that. In front, a lookout tower stood like a

---

16. "Prince of State" (*Guówáng* 國王) was the title of Muqali and his descendants who served as viceroys in North China when Chinggis Khan left for the invasion of Central Asia; see Zhao Gong's "Memorandum," p. 78.

17. Lit., 100 *lǐ*; see the tables of weights and measures in Appendix §2.7 (p. 192).

18. "Dog Lake" is Chinese *Gǒupō* 狗泊. This lake, present-day Jiuliancheng Lake (Urtu Nuur in modern Mongolian), was one of the seven major salt production areas of the Jin dynasty (*JS* 24.567, 49.1094–95). The shape is very long and narrow.

19. Ch. *shātuó* 沙陀. This term designates what Chinese geographers today call "sandy lands" and what in North America are called sandhills. They differ from the shifting dunes of true deserts in being fixed and having, as Zhang notes, quite a bit of vegetation. The medieval Chinese name for this terrain was applied to the Shatuo, ancestors in part to the "White Tatars" much discussed by Li Xinchuan and Zhao Gong. The sandy lands Zhang passed through are called the Hunshandak in Chinese, a name of unclear origin. On the origins and ecology of this and other Inner Mongolian sandy lands, see Yang et al. 2015; Zhang and Gillis 2002.

20. Ch. *Yúpō* 魚兒泊. As identified by Shiraishi (2012), this is the Khür-Chaghan Lake of Abagha Banner, Inner Mongolia. Khür-Chaghan is a double lake divided by a sandbar or spit of land, visible except when the water level is at its highest.

21. Lit., more than one *zhàng* high. See the tables of weights and measures in Appendix §2.7 (p. 192).

22. Lit., about two *lǐ* square. See Appendix §2.7 (p. 192).

23. Ch. *guīxuān* 龜軒, lit., "turtle balustrade." This term designates a short promenade with a high walkway in the middle and two low walkways in front and behind.

mountain; climbing it quite enhanced one's vision. To the east of the palace were the residences of commoners and craftsmen, gathered together somewhat to make a village. Among those was a building with a placard that read, "Welcoming the Sunshine." Traveling northwest from the lake for four courier stations, we encountered the crumbling ruins of a great wall that could be seen to stretch infinitely. This, too, was built by the previous dynasty as their outermost fortification.

5. Traveling fifteen courier stations on from this outer fortification, we reached a river, which in depth and width was about one third of the Hutuo River.[24] In the northern tongue they call it Hiluren; in Chinese it is called the Lüju River.[25] Close by the banks are many willow stands, and the river flowing eastward is very swift and turbulent. The residents said that the fish in it can grow as long as three or four feet.[26] If one tries to catch them in spring, summer, or autumn, one will never succeed, but when winter comes, then by boring through the ice they can be caught. The people living by the water's edge were a mixture of ethnics[27] and Han, some of whom had houses, all plastered with earth. In addition, quite a few knew the arts of cultivation, but only for hemp and wheat. North of the river there is a big mountain called Kurawu,[28] or in Chinese, "Black Mountain." Seen from one of the homes it appeared dark, as though it had a flourishing forest, but given a closer look it was all dark green mossy rocks, probably so because the predominantly cloudy and misty weather covers them with it.[29]

6. We traveled southwest from the southern slopes of the Black Mountain, through nine courier stations, until we again approached a river, about one third as deep

---

24. The Hutuo River rises in the sacred Buddhist mountain of Wutai and flows west through the Taihang Mountains, past Zhendingfu (Zhang Dehui's Zhenyang) and across the North China plain, merging with the Sanggan shortly before emptying into the Bohai Gulf. Since Zhang Dehui was living in Zhendingfu, he took it as a familiar measure of width.

25. This is the present-day Kherlen River in present-day Mongolia ("Outer Mongolia"). Zhang's version of it as "Hiluren," with the spirant *h* and not the harder *k* of Middle Mongolian *Kelüren*, may represent the Jurchen pronunciation. For unclear reasons, imperial Chinese writers historically referred to this river as Lüju or Lugou (the two were pronounced very similarly in the thirteenth century), a word that was a homonym of the "Marco Polo Bridge's" Lugou River south of Beijing. See for example, "Sketch," p. 130.

26. This fish is the taimen or Siberian salmon (*Hucho taimen*), known as the *tul* in Mongolian.

27. "Ethnics" here translates *fan*, and the term is quite as vague in Chinese as it is English. But it probably refers not to Mongols but to Uyghurs, Turkestanis, and other people from the West; see Peng Daya and Xu Ting's "Sketch," p. 115.

28. We follow Yao Congwu in emending the *sù* of the text's *Kūsùwú* 窟速吾 to *là* 剌. Unlike Yao and Erdemtü, however, we see this as a version not of Mo. *Qara A'ula*, "Black Mountain," but of *Qara'u(n)*, "dark, shadowy," a term that appears frequently in Middle Mongolian toponymy. Since Zhang Dehui shows familiarity with Jurchen, he may have misheard *Qara'u* as *Kurawu* due to confusion with *huru~kuru*, "rise, high place," attested in Jurchen and Manchu.

29. This is the present-day Kherlen Toono Uul massif. With its highest peak at 1,578 meters above sea level, it is by several hundred meters the highest point on the northern banks of the Kherlen River and is currently a nature preserve in Mongolia. To its west is the Awraga site, which was the site of Chinggis Khan's great base camp (*a'uruq*); see Shiraishi 2013.

and broad as the Hiluren. The fish are as large as those in the Hiluren and the method of catching them is similar. Where its current first flows west, it is too deep and rushing to ford. In the northern tongue it is called Hun-Tula; in Chinese it is called Tur.[30]

Following that river westward and traveling one station, there is an ancient town built by the Kitans; it is a mile square,[31] backing onto a mountain and facing the river.[32] From this point on, the river flows northward. Going northwest from the ancient town for three courier stations, we passed Bitehetu,[33] which is a colony of bowyers.[34] Traveling through another station, we passed a great lake, which is twenty to twenty-five miles around[35] and whose water is extremely clear and still; it is called in the northern tongue Ugei-Naur.[36] Going south from the lake, turning

---

30. That is, "Rabbit." As Jagchid Sechin recognized, Hun-Tula should be Mongolian Gün Tu'ula, or the "deep Tu'ula," the change from *g* to *h* perhaps attributable to the influence of Jurchen pronunciation. The Chinese *Tùr* or "Rabbit" is an unusual combination of both phonetic and semantic elements. Middle Mongolian for rabbit is *taulai*, modern *tuulai*, which to Chinese ears would sound close to both *Tu'ula* and the Chinese for "rabbit" (*tùr* or *tùzi*). The -*r* added to the Chinese can be either a colloquial dialect ending or else a rendering of the -*l*- in *Tu'ula* and *taulai*.

31. Lit., three *lǐ* square. See the tables of weights and measures in Appendix §2.7 (p. 192).

32. These ruins are known today as Khermen Denj, one of several Kitan garrison towns in the area. Khermen Denj is just north of the Tuul River. Its roughly rectangular wall is 1.9 kilometers or about 3 1/3 *lǐ* around. There is no mountain directly north of it, but there is a long spur of the Khentii to the east of it, and an isolated massif called Tömstei Mountain to the northwest of it. Probably the latter is meant. South of the Tuul is a much smaller ruins called Tsgaan Denj ("White Platform"), about 700 meters square, also dating from the Kitan period. See "Khermen Denj"; Ochir, Enkhtör, and Erdenebold 2005, 140–63; Kradin et al. 2012; Kradin and Ivliev 2014, 68, fig. 1, no. 37.

33. The *Bìlǐhédū* 畢里紇都 of the texts would read something like Mongolian *Biliktu*, "Wise One"; although common as a personal name, this term is unknown as a place name, here or anywhere else. If *lǐ* is emended to *tè* 忒, however, then the name may be matched with the *Bìtèqiètū* 必忒忲秃, also found in *YS* 31.698 in an itinerary passing exactly through this region, and which as Bitehetu "Having an Inscription," is a plausible Turco-Mongolian toponym. We have thus emended the text.

34. If Zhang Dehui's indications of distance are correct, and if the road from Khermen Denj to Ögii Nuur was roughly straight, as is the modern road, then this settlement of Bitehetu would be in present-day Gurwanbulag *Sum* (county), Bulgan Province. But no Mongol-era site there has been identified, and the distance between Khermen Denj and Ögii Nuur (about 150 kilometers) seems too short for four courier stations in sparsely settled Mongolia. It is likely that the post road was not as direct as the modern road.

35. Lit., sixty to seventy *lǐ* around; see the tables of weights and measures in Appendix §2.7 (p. 192).

36. This is present-day Ögii Nuur (Middle Mongolian *Ögei Na'ur*) in Mongolia's Northern Khangai (Arkhangai) Province. Today it is about twenty-two kilometers or about forty *lǐ* around and is indeed by far the largest lake in the area. But if Zhang Dehui's figure is accurate, it would mean that it was even larger then and that the marshy grounds and salt flats to the west of the current lakeshore were underwater during his time. The text here reads *Wúwùjié-Nǎor*, 吾惧竭·腦 兒, which would imply a Mongolian of Uwugei-Naur. However, the reduplication of two graphs reading virtually the same, *wú* and *wù*, is very likely the result of a scribe checking his base text against a second text and noting the variant form in the margin of the draft. The marginal note

westward are separate roads, diverging by thirty-five miles[37] or more, that lead into Qorum[38] city. Directly west of the lake there is a small ancient town which also was built by the Kitans.[39] Seen in all four directions around the town, the land is very open and flat for almost forty miles,[40] but beyond that are mountains. On the shady, northern side of the mountains, there are pine forests,[41] while along the waterfront there are only poplars and clustered willows. In the middle [of the mountains] is Qorum Steppe.[42] The residents mostly tend fields for which they all draw water [from the Orqan River] for irrigation, and some of them also have vegetable gardens.[43] At the time, it was the last part of the first moon of autumn [August 21–31], and the broomcorn millet and wheat had all withered. When the farmers were asked about it, they said there already had been three frosts!

7. Going northwest one courier station from that steppe, we passed Horse-Head Mountain, which the residents said was named for a large horse head on top of it.[44] From the north side of Horse-Head Mountain, we turned and again went

---

was then mistakenly incorporated into the main text producing a doublet. This is a common occurrence; we thus read the name with only the second, less expected, graph.

37. Lit., a hundred *lĭ*; see the tables of weights and measures in Appendix §2.7 (p. 192).

38. This is Qara-Qorum (also written Karakorum), the famous capital of the Mongol Empire.

39. Previous commentators have speculated that this small Kitan town might be the Khöshöö Tsaidam site, where the famous Old Turkic inscription of Bilge Qaghan (r. 717–734) was found, or the famous ruins of Ordu-Baliq, capital of the Uyghur Empire (742–847). But the latter is far from "small" and both are quite a distance south, not "directly west," of Ögii Nuur. The ruins here must be those of Chilen Owoo, six kilometers to the west of Ögii Nuur, and which excavations have shown to be of Kitan origin (Ochir, Enkhtör, and Erdenebold 2005, 163–72; Matsuda 2013, map 1).

40. Lit., a hundred *lĭ*; see the tables of weights and measures in Appendix §2.7 (p. 192).

41. "Shady, northern side" is Ch. *yīn*, of the famous pair *yīn-yáng*. This pair originally designated the shady northern side of a mountain and the sunny, southern side of the mountain, respectively. In Mongolia, this contrast is particularly clear as the shade on the northern side keeps moisture and allows trees to grow, while the southern, sunny side is dry and grassy.

42. Ch. *chuān* 川 would normally mean "stream" or "valley" in Chinese. In Chinese of the Mongol Yuan period, however, it was treated as the equivalent of Mongolian *ke'ere*, "steppe," and from the context this is how it is being understood here. Yao Congwu followed an inaccurate note in the *Yuanshi* (*YS* 58.1382) and claimed that Zhang is referring here to the so-called Qara-Qorum River after which the Mongol capital of Qara-Qorum was supposedly named. In reality, however, the main river through this plain is the Orqan (Orkhon) River and *qorum* is a Turkic word meaning "stony ground, boulders." The city and steppe were named after the boulders, not after the mythical "Qara-Qorum River." See Juvaini 1958, vol. 1, 236; Rashiduddin 1998/1999, vol. 1, 75.

43. This area of Qara-Qorum has been a major center of agriculture in Mongolia up to the present.

44. Skulls of beloved horses are frequently placed on mountaintop cairns (*owoo*) in Mongolia today. This is presumably a reference to the same custom. This mountain may be the Bor Azarga ("Brown Stallion") peak (1,899 meters above sea level) or the Ukhaa Azarga ("Light-Red Stallion") peak (2,011 meters above sea level), both north of the Tamir River in Northern Khangai province. Matsuda (2013, 1, 7) also places "Horse-Head Mountain" in this area.

Taikhar Rock in Ikh Tamir Sumu (county), Northern Khangai Province, Mongolia.

southwestward, passing Hula'an-Chikin, a place where commoners and artisans who have been drafted into servitude practice farming and crafts. A river called the Tamir waters it.[45]

Going northeast through another station, we passed a [naturally formed] stone beacon-tower. Standing beside the post road, it is a little more than three rods high and seventy yards around at the bottom.[46] Exactly square with four corners,

---

45. This is the present-day Khoid Tamir or "Rear Tamir" River. Matsuda (2013, 7, fig. 2) has identified this Hula'an-Chikin Mountain with the present-day peak Ulaan-Chikh, on the right bank of the Khoid Tamir, fourteen to fifteen kilometers northeast of Taikhar Rock. No archaeological traces of the Hula'an-Chikin settlement have yet been identified, however.

46. Lit., a little more than five *zhàng* high and forty *bù* around. However, the text as we have it speaks of it being 'a little more than five feet high' (*gāo wǔchǐ xǔ* 高五尺許). Such a height would not strike anyone in Mongolia as having a "wonderfully imposing appearance." We have

it towers above the level ground with a wonderfully imposing appearance. Seen from afar, it looks like a great beacon-tower, and therefore it is named that.[47] Traveling three courier stations southwestward from the beacon-tower, we passed a river called the Tangut, which is named because its source is in the Western Xia; its current too flows to the northeast.[48] West of that river there is a high ridge, whose stones all seem to be iron. On the northern side of the ridge is pine forest, and on its southern side is a tent-palace,[49] which is the summer residence.

We waited until after Mid-Autumn[50] before setting out to travel around. Going east along the courier-station route past the stone beacon-tower, we arrived northeast of Hula'an-Chikin and meandered by foot into a craggy mountain. From then on we sometimes traveled and sometimes stayed, traveling no farther than one stop at a time, and staying no longer than two nights. As we did not pass any famous mountains or great rivers, I have not recorded this exhaustively.

Here we follow Yao Congwu, who inserted into the text Zhang Dehui's conversation with Qubilai drawn from the "Account of Conduct," composed by Wang Yun after Zhang Dehui's death:

8. Once I had met him, the prince calmly asked, "It has been long since Confucius died, so where is his essence now?"[51] My reply was, "Sages[52] are as eternal as

---

followed Prof. Ma Xiaolin's suggestion to emend Zhang's text to read *gāo wǔzhàng xǔ* 高五丈許 'a little more than five *zhàng* high,' or about fifteen meters high.

47. Matsuda Kōichi (2013, 7–8) first made the correct identification of this "stone beacon-tower" with the famous natural rock formation Taikhar Rock. The rock stands across the Khoid Tamir River from the Zaankhoshuu, the center of Ikhtamir *Sum* (county). It is 68.9 meters around and 20 meters high. This rock has an ink inscription on it, reading "Autumn, VIII, *dīng/yǒu* [=August–September 1237], I was here. Signed: Shǐ Ge of Zhendingfu." This inscription refers to Shǐ Ge (1222–1279), the son of Zhang Dehui's patron Shǐ Tianze. In 1237, at age sixteen, he was summoned to the camp of Qubilai's mother, Sorghaqtani Beki, as a hostage for his father and left this graffiti as he passed where Zhang Dehui would pass about a decade later. See Matsuda 2013, 4–6. Since Qubilai and his mother were likely nomadizing together it is not surprising that visitors to their camp followed the same route. The identifications proposed by Matsuda and followed here supersede those attempted in Atwood 2015, 342–43.

48. There is no river named Tangut in the area today or mentioned in any other source. Perhaps Zhang Dehui misunderstood a statement that this river was on the road to the Tangut land. The Chuluut, or "Stony" River, may be the one intended; its headwaters rise near the Eg Pass, which gives access to the south-flowing waters of the Baidrag River on its way south to the Tangut lands.

49. "Tent-palace," or *zhàngdiàn* 帳殿, translates Mongolian *ordo* or "horde," the mobile palace of the Inner Asian nomads. See Peng Daya and Xu Ting's "Sketch," pp. 97, 101.

50. The fifteenth day of the eighth moon, the day of the East Asian Mid-Autumn, or Moon-Watching, Festival. In 1247, it fell on September 15, 1247.

51. "Essence" here translates Chinese *xìng* 性, meaning "one's inborn nature," "particular inherent quality," or "innate destiny" (Kroll 2015, s.v. *xìng₂* 510b).

52. Ch. *shèngrén* 聖人. We follow Sinological convention in translating this as "sage," but such a translation does not fully capture the political implications of the term. English "sage" may bring to mind an unworldly and secluded thinker, but in Chinese philosophy, a *shèngrén* was rather

Heaven and Earth; they are omnipresent. If Your Highness can follow the Way of the Sages,[53] you too will be a Sage, and Confucius's essence will be present in this tent-palace."

He also asked, "Some say 'The Liao was ruined by Buddhism, and the Jin was destroyed by Confucianism.' Is this so?" My reply was, "Your servant is not thoroughly familiar with Liao affairs, but he did personally experience the late Jin period. Although one or two Confucian ministers were employed among the state councilors,[54] the other officials were all military men and hereditary office-holders, and when they discussed important affairs of army and state, they did not allow the Confucians to know of it beforehand. Scholars who advanced to hold any office in court or province were but one out of thirty; they did nothing more than read record books, hear lawsuits, and manage finances. Responsibility for the survival or destruction of a state lies with those who are in charge of it; how then could it be the fault of the Confucians?" The prince was pleased. Following up, he asked me, "The laws and institutions of the ancestors[55] all still exist, but so many of them have not been implemented; what is to be done about this?" I then pointed at a silver plate before His Highness, and used it as a figure, saying, "To be the ruler who starts a great enterprise, is like making this utensil; having achieved it by handpicking pure silver and the best craftsmen and plans, then, when delivered to later generations, it will be transmitted without end. Now, you should seek out prudent and honest men to take charge of the matter so that what is crafted can be used as a prized heirloom forever. Otherwise, not only might it be damaged, one also fears that someone might snatch it away!"[56]

After quite a while, the prince said, "This truly is something my heart will not forget!"

---

someone who through receptivity to Heaven and the needs of age created the sociopolitical institutions that would justly govern the civilized world. Thus, every founder of a legitimate dynasty was, by definition, a *shèngrén*. Such "sages" played the role in Confucian tradition that "lawgivers" such as Moses, Lycurgus, Numa, or Muhammad played in the Western Eurasian traditions. Indeed, in Chinese Islam, Muhammad's role as the final prophet is translated as *zhìshèng* 至聖 or "ultimate sage, lawgiver, prophet." Confucius was the archetypal *shèngrén*, but for Confucian thinkers the great puzzle was why, if he was so receptive to Heaven, he was never able to reorder the world in accordance with his teachings.

53. The "Way of the Sages" (Ch. *Shèngrén zhī dào* 聖人之道) was a common term for Confucianism particularly associated with the "Neo-Confucian" school of Song dynasty onward.

54. Ch. *zǎizhí* 宰執: in the Song and Jin a general term for officials who had the right to participate in high-level, policy-making deliberations with the emperor. See the Introduction, pp. 32–33.

55. Ch. *zǔzōng* 祖宗. This term, redolent of sacrality, here refers to the founders of the dynasty. Qubilai is probably referring particularly to the measures issued by Öködei Khan under the influence of Ila Chucai which, as Song Zizhen emphasized in the "Spirit-Path Stele," were largely never implemented. As Ila Chucai says in the "Spirit-Path Stele": "Laws and institutions, rules and regulations: all issued from the LATE EMPEROR[S]."

56. Comparisons of Confucian governance with craftsmanship or medical practice were common in the Mongol era; see the anecdote about the Xia artisan, Chang Bajin, in Song Zizhen's "Spirit-Path Stele," p. 137.

He also inquired about talented men in China, and I thereupon recommended more than twenty men, including Wei Fan, Yuan Haowen, and Li Ye.[57] The prince counted their number on his fingers, and he was able to say the family name and given name of several of them.

The prince asked again, "[Aside from officials,] the farmers also toil hard, so why is their clothing and food never adequate?" I replied, "Farming and silk-making are the foundation of the world, whence comes clothing and food. Men farm and women weave diligently despite hardship the whole year through, and then they choose their finest and most beautiful things to submit to officials, reserving the coarse and ugly stuff to provide for their elders and children. But government clerks who are closest to the people make additional, irregular exactions that exhaust their resources, so rarely are there common people who do not go cold and hungry!"

9. When the Double Ninth arrived,[58] the prince led those under his banner to assemble at the great flag tent and sprinkle the milk of a white mare as a practice of seasonal offering. All the implements used were of birchwood; they do not use gold or silver to ornament their services, as part of their esteem of simplicity. Not until the middle of moon X [October 9–18] did they move to a mountain hollow[59] to avoid the worst of winter. The forest there was very thick and the waters all frozen solid, so the people were keen to collect fuel and store water, preparing to protect themselves from the cold.

They insist on making their clothes out of fur or leather. For their food they take mutton as their staple and grains like rice as a delicacy. Every year on New Year's Eve, they move their tents to different locations, which will be their place for exchanging visits on New Year's Day. On that day [January 28, 1248], there was a great entertainment for his whole appanage (*bù*) in front of the tents, and

---

57. Wei Fan: From Hongzhou in the Yunzhong area (present-day northern Shanxi), he received his metropolitan graduate degree in 1216 and served the Jin until its destruction when he returned north to his village. After Qubilai summoned him, he went to Qorum and recommended many other officials, before dying there (see the biography of his grandson Wei Chu in *YS* 164.3856–7). Yuan Haowen (1190–1257): From Taiyuanfu, he was the son of a distinguished local poet and himself one of the Jin dynasty's most noted authors of verse and prose. He served in various low-level positions in the Jin bureaucracy and retired from office after the fall of the dynasty, writing poetry, anthologizing the finest poetry of his contemporaries, and collecting historical materials. Many of his poetical works are extant. As far as is known, he did not accept any summons from Qubilai (see *JS* 126.3742–43). Li Ye (1192–1279): From Zhendingfu, he received his metropolitan graduate degree under the Jin and was serving the dynasty as the prefect of Junzhou in Henan when it was overrun by the Mongols in 1232. He went into retirement in his home town. Qubilai summoned him after Zhang Dehui's visit and the two discussed Confucian principles but Li Ye avoided office (see *YS* 160.3759–60). He was also a noted mathematician and one of the few Chinese proponents of a round earth.

58. Ninth day of the ninth moon, the day of the East Asian Double Ninth Festival. In 1247 it fell on October 8.

59. Ch. *yán* 崦, a literary term for mountain, derived from the legend of a mountain in northwest China into which the sun sets.

everyone from the prince on down wore pure white furs. After three days of this, they went to the great flag tent to extend congratulations as a ritual.[60] On the last day of moon I [February 25], we again traveled southwestward. In the middle of moon II [March 6–15], we reached Hula'an-Chikin and then traveled east until we reached Horse-Head Mountain, where we camped. The reason was to take advantage of the spring thaw for falconry.

The second conversation from Wang Yun's "Account of Conduct" of Zhang Dehui:

10. In the spring of *wù/shēn* [1248], a sacrifice was offered, and I presented its meat to the prince. The prince asked, "Why is there a ritual offering of food in the temples of Confucius?" I replied, "Confucius is the teacher of all true princes for ten-thousand generations. Heads of state honor him, and so they solemnize the temple services and practice seasonal offerings. Whether he is worshiped or not makes no difference to the Sage himself. It's just that from this may be seen the veneration of the scholar's way [i.e., Confucianism] in the current ruler's heart."

The prince said, "From now on, this ritual will not be abandoned."

The prince further asked, "Who does the people greater injury today, those who control the soldiers or those who govern the people?" I replied, "As for those who control the soldiers, the army is without discipline; no matter how cruel and heartless they are, what they succeed in getting is not worth what is destroyed. Their crimes certainly are grave. Regarding those who supervise the people, they poison the civilized world with their relentless taxes and afflict the descendants of the ancestor's[61] subjects as if they were treading in water or fire. The harm they do is especially great." The prince was silent for a long time before saying, "If so, then what can be done?" I said, "Best would be to choose anew a wise man of the clan, such as Kö'ün-Buqa, to handle the soldiers, and choose someone from the meritorious elders[62] like Qutughu to rule the civil administration. Then the whole civilized world would benefit."[63]

---

60. "Ritual," or *lǐ*, here and below means more than just a custom, but a practice that serves to train the performers in proper moral attitudes and sentiments.

61. Ch. *zǔzōng*. Again, it is the dynastic ancestors, the founders of the Mongol Empire, which are being referred to. As Ila Chucai says in the "Spirit-Path Stele": "The civilized world [*tiānxià*] is the LATE EMPEROR[s]' world."

62. "Meritorious elder" (Ch. *xūnjiù* 勳舊) has the same sense as the "meritorious vassals" whose role is also emphasized in a famous memorial of Ila Chucai. See Song Zizhen's "Spirit Path Stele" under year 1237, p. 149.

63. Kö'ün-Buqa was the second son of Chinggis's half brother Belgüdei. Qutughu is the Tatar foundling called Shiki Qutughu in the *Secret History of the Mongols*. Kö'ün-Buqa led campaigns against the Southern Song in the Huainan area from 1235 to 1237; Qutughu served as judge (*jarghuchi*) for the central prefectures during the same period. Xu Ting ("Sketch," pp. 110–11) charges that Qutughu's application of Mongol taxes caused great distress. Zhang's point may not be so much about the high quality of the administrators he mentions, but rather to have all of North China placed under a unified administration. It was the separate fiefs run by Mongol princes, empresses, and commanders as their private estates that were most notorious for exploitation and abuse.

11. On IV, 9, [May 3, 1248], the prince again led those under his banner to assemble at the great flag tent and sprinkle the milk of white mares; the utensils were also the same as before. Every year, this sacrifice is repeated only on the Double Ninth and on IV, 9. On no other holiday is this done. From that day, we began our return, going southwest again on the post road toward the summer camp site. In general, when summer comes around, then they go to a high, cool site, and when winter arrives, then they hasten to a sunny, warm place where fuel and water are easily obtained, to avoid each season's extremes. Passing that place, we continued on, traveling one day and staying the next, just following the water and grass for the sake of our animals. This is the appropriate thing to do under local conditions and generally summarizes their traditional customs.[64]

The final round of recommendations from Wang Yun's "Account of Conduct" of Zhang Dehui:

12. In the summer of that year, I was able to inform the prince that I was returning, and once again I recommended several men to him: Bai Wenju, Zheng Xianzhi, Zhao Yuande, Li Jinzhi, Gao Ming, Li Pan, and Li Tao.[65] Taking leave of the throne, I again spoke of venerating the virtues of the elders, appointing a few primary ministers, choosing men of talent, inspecting the situation among subor-

---

64. "Local conditions" and "traditional customs" are *fēngtǔ* 風土 and *xísú* 習俗, respectively. See the Introduction, p. 22.

65. Bai Wenju (legal name, Hua): From Yùzhou Prefecture (in Hedong), he received his metropolitan graduate degree in 1216 and served first as registrar and then as administrative assistant in the Jin Privy Council. As such, from 1226 on, he participated in increasingly desperate debates as the Jin fell, and became known, at least to his Confucian colleagues, as both a staunch Confucian and a man of good military judgment. At the end of the dynasty he was sent to the border city of Dengzhou on a futile mission; he briefly surrendered the city to the Southern Song and received official positions from them, but later when another Jin official rebelled and handed the city over to the Mongols, he returned north. He is not known to have accepted any summons from Qubilai (see *JS* 114.2503–14). Gao Ming (1209–1274): From Zhendingfu, he had acquired a literary reputation in his youth. Turning down other offers of patronage, he accepted a summons from Hüle'ü when a messenger returned a third time and set forth more than twenty stratagems for the Mongol prince's upcoming expedition against the Baghdad and the West. After 1260, he served Qubilai as an academician in the Hanlin Academy and as concurrent vice-minister in the Court of Imperial Sacrifices. From 1268 onward, he served as attendant censor in the new censorate. In 1270 his memorial played an important role in dissuading Qubilai from plans to revive the cumbersome three-departments organization of the central administration, which had not been genuinely in use since the Tang dynasty of 618–907 (see *YS* 160.3758–59). Li Pan: From Zhendingfu, he was employed by Qubilai's mother, Sorghoqtani Beki, as a tutor for her youngest son, Ariq-Böke, presumably as a result of Zhang Dehui's recommendation. Even so, Li Pan was imprisoned during Ariq-Böke's attempt to raise an army in North China and fight Qubilai for the throne. Later, Qubilai's part-Uyghur, part-Kitan advisor, Lian Xixian, brought his case to Qubilai's attention and he was released (see *YS* 126.3086). As for Li Jinzhi and Zhao Yuande, an anthology of poetry by Yuan Haowen includes a poem by Li Jinzhi, and another poem in the anthology is dedicated to Zhao Yuande. In it, Zhao is called a censor for the Jin. No other details are known of their lives, however. Zheng Xianzhi and Li Tao are otherwise unknown.

dinates, valuing consideration of both sides, drawing true gentlemen near, putting trust in rewards and punishments, and cutting down expenses levels—along these lines I admonished the prince. I was at the northern court for a full year, and whenever I had an audience, the prince inquired at length about the meaning of the Sage's Way and its virtue,[66] methods of self-cultivation and administering the state, and the sources of order and anarchy in ancient times and the present. Our discussions were clearly detailed and engagingly frank, and many were the things he began to comprehend. Thus, the prince called me by my name and allowed me to sit down in his presence; his magnanimous courtesy was truly great.

13. I, a humble servant, from when I first arrived until I returned home, roamed with the prince's court for more than ten moons. Whenever there was a feast or an audience, the prince made a point of receiving me with due ceremony. Considering his provision of a tent, bedding, clothing, food and drink, and medicine, not one expression of cordiality was lacking. From this one may understand the sincerity of his affectionate concern. Assaying my own decrepitude and lack of talent, how did I deserve this? The source of the prince's intention lay in his "loving goodness and forgetting his power," that is, in giving position to our Confucius's Way and restraining his own desires in order to attract the exemplary gentlemen of the civilized world. [67] How could I be worthy of this? Later there will certainly be other men worthier than Kui[68] who will go to him. For that reason, I recorded my mission from beginning to end and now have written a full account of it. Respectfully signed: Zhang Dehui of Taiyuanfu, in the summer of *wù/shēn*, VI, 15 [July 7, 1248].

---

66. That is, the Confucian Classical tradition.

67. The phrase "loving goodness and forgetting his power" is a quotation from the Warring States era Confucian thinker Mencius 7.viii.1 (cf. Legge [1895] 1970, 452).

68. This is an allusion to a story of the Warring States period told in chapter 34 of the *Shiji*, or the *Records of the Grand Historian*:

> King Zhāo of Yan [r. 311–279 BC], after the shattering defeat of the kingdom of Yan [by the rival kingdom of Qi], abased himself and gave rich rewards to show respect to the worthy. [His tutor] Guo Kui said to him, "As Your Majesty certainly desires to summon scholars, let him first begin with Kui. Then indeed why would ones worthier than Kui think even a thousand *lǐ* far to travel?" Thereupon King Zhao refurbished a hall in the palace for Kui and served him as a pupil serves his tutor. [The brilliant general] Yue Yi came from Wèi, [the famous *yin-yang* theorist] Zou Yan came from Qi, and Ju Xin came from Zhào; scholars raced to get to Yan. The King of Yan lamented the dead, inquired after the lonely, and in all things shared the weal and woe of the common people."

And indeed, then, in 284 BC, King Zhāo was able to ally with other kingdoms and crush the kingdom of Qi (Sima Qian, *Shiji*, 34.1558).

Appendix 1

Notes on the Texts

Chinese texts from the thirteenth century have come down to us through a variety of paths. Although printing by the blockprinting, or "xylograph," method was well known in the Song and Yuan eras, it was actually more expensive at that time than manuscript copying and hence was used primarily for pricier, prestige editions of major works, such as dynastic histories, canons, Buddhist scriptures, and collected works of major scholars. Blockprinting involved transferring a freshly inked manuscript version of the text onto a wooden block and then following the ink marks on the wood to carve away all of the block surface except for the black character strokes. Once carved, the wooden blocks could be preserved for decades or even centuries, but it was very difficult to make even minor corrections to the works later on.

Of the five works translated here, four were blockprinted relatively soon after their manuscripts were completed, but only in one of these four cases, that of the "Spirit-Path Stele," did a copy of that early blockprint survive that was legible enough to be the major source for modern versions of the text. In the other three cases, the currently used texts go back to Ming- or Qing-era manuscript copies taken from the now-lost early blockprints. In the case of Zhao Gong's "Memorandum," the text was not printed until centuries after it was written. The lack of early printed texts for Chinese works on the Mongols is quite frustrating. Mongolian words and terms were particularly prone to being misread and miscopied, since to the average Chinese scribe they were meaningless sequences of graphs. Thus, Chinese texts on Mongolian, or other foreign, topics are far more likely to contain error than those on topics in the mainstream of Chinese civilization.

The following review of the sources for the texts we have translated will allow the reader to follow the textual discussions in the notes.

Random Notes from Court and Country since the Jianyan Years, vol. 2

Li Xinchuan's *Random Notes* was a famous text. We know that a printed version of it was produced by the Xin family in Chengdu, the largest city in Li Xinchuan's home province of Sichuan. Unfortunately, however, this printed version has not survived.

We have based our translation on the version edited and punctuated by the modern scholar Xu Gui, and published by the Zhonghua shuju, China's most prestigious publisher of editions of premodern works. This edition is itself based, directly or indirectly, on two different eighteenth-century Qing dynasty printed editions. The first is the Wuyingdian or Wuying Palace's Juzhen print series (*Wŭyĭng-diàn Jùzhēn bănshū*), sponsored by the Qianlong ("Celestial Ascendancy") emperor (r. 1735–1796). The second is in the Hanhai series of blockprinted rare texts, sponsored by Li Diaoyuan of the Northeastern city of Jĭnzhou, also published during the Qianlong years. Presumably because their base manuscripts differed, these two editions vary substantially in the text of Li's second, later, compilation.[1] Compared to the Wuying Palace edition, the Hanhai edition has a different division into *juàn* (chapters), and the text omits the eleven "Border Defense" narratives (focused on the Sichuan frontier troubles with Tibetans, Qiang, and other tributary peoples), which should immediately follow the three sections touching on the Tatar incursions.

Although Xu Gui's edition is ultimately based on the two printed editions mentioned above, the Wuying Palace and Hanhai editions, he also consulted three other editions mostly based on them. All the editions used were from relatively late in the Qing dynasty:[2]

1. His base text was a 1914 imprint published by Zhang Junheng of Wuxing in his Shiyuan congshu series of scholarly texts. This edition itself was based on the Wuying Palace edition published during the Qianlong years, but it made a number of changes based on comparisons with unspecified manuscripts.

This base text was collated against four other texts:

2. The Guangxu 19 or *gŭi/sì* (1893) edition published by Xiao Lunong of Jingyan County (where Li Xinchuan was born). This took the Hanhai edition as its base text but collated it against the Wuying Palace edition and a Song manuscript. As a result of this collation, the division into *juàn* (chapters) in this Xiao edition differs only slightly from the Wuying Palace edition and the Shiyuan congshu edition based on it.

3. The Guangxu 20 or *jiă/wŭ* (1894) reprint of the Wuying Palace edition. In the appendix to this edition, the Fujian publisher added a list of divergent readings taken from a collation that Sun Xinghua of Guiji had done against a Song-era manuscript in the collection of Lu Xinyuan.

4. The *Siku quanshu* edition of the text, accessed in a photographic reproduction. (This edition was a manuscript edition sponsored by the Qianlong emperor.) The organization of the second volume is the same as in the Hanhai edition, but some further changes have been made in the first volume.

5. An imprint from the Hanhai blockprint.

---

1. On Li Xinchuan's two compilations, see the Preface to the translated selections from the *Random Notes*, p. 45.

2. On these editions, and Xu Gui's use of them, see Xu Gui 1991, 5–7.

Xu Gui's text is thus heavily dependent on the two Qianlong-era editions, as he had only indirect access to Song-era manuscripts through the Guangxu 19 and 20 editions. This is potentially a problem, since the Qianlong emperor went through older Chinese works replacing what he thought to be inaccurate or demeaning transcriptions of Manchu, Mongolian, and other non-Chinese words. Since his alterations had little philological basis, they generated lasting confusion. In the sections translated here, however, only two of the transcriptions, *Hābùr* and *Tĕmòjīn*, seem to date from the Qianlong years.

A Memorandum on the Mong-Tatars

Zhao Gong's work was preserved in an anthology of classic and recent texts assembled by Tao Zongyi (1316–1403) in the wake of the fall of Mongol rule in China in 1368. In this, his *Shuofu*, or "Purlieus of Exposition," Tao Zongyi assembled into 100 *juàn* (chapters) longer or shorter excerpts from 600 or so different works. Among those about border and foreign affairs, he included the text of Zhao Gong's "Memorandum on the Mong-Tatars." The *Shuofu* began as Tao Zongyi's own personal reading notes; it was not until seventy-five years or so after his death that it began to circulate in manuscript in various expanded or abridged recensions.[3] As it originally was just for Tao's own use, the copying was not done very carefully. As a result, his text has by far the most errors of any of those discussed here. He even mistook the author, assuming that the Gong of the text must be the famous general Meng Gong.

The first scholar to approach this problematical text in a serious way was Cao Yuanzhong (1865–1923) from Jiangsu's Wuxian. His edition, which solved many fundamental problems, was published in 1901 but remained extremely obscure and did not attempt to deal with the Mongolian-language terms. Moreover, Cao still considered Meng Gong to be the author. It was eventually the brilliant Wang Guowei, in his 1926 masterpiece *Menggu shiliao sizhong* ("Four Sources on the Mongols"), who brought the text fully into the light of scholarship.

Both Cao Yuanzhong and Wang Guowei relied primarily on the text as found in the first printing of the whole *Shuofu*, whose blocks were carved around 1615. Wang Guowei was able to supplement this with two very closely related manuscripts of the *Shuofu* text. Fortunately, comparison with the other manuscript versions shows that the original manuscript for the ca. 1615 blockprint version was quite close to the original. Still, in many cases, Wang Guowei was reduced to "divining" (the word textual critics use for "guessing") the right reading.

Since then, as part of our own research into the textual history of the *Shuofu* anthology and the *Shengwu qinzheng lu* (*Campaigns of Chinggis Khan*), which was also preserved in it, we have used many codices (manuscripts and printed texts) to confirm or suggest new readings of the text. Several of Wang Guowei's guesses have

---

3. On the *Shuofu* and its recensions, see Atwood 2017.

been confirmed by such sources, and improved readings not previously imagined by scholars have also emerged.

The codices we used, apart from Wang Guowei's modern edition, are listed below, by the recensions (or basic stages in the overall evolution) of the text:[4]

a) Manuscripts of the γ recension. This recension was put together around 1440, after Tao Zongyi's death. In it, Zhao Gong's work forms part of *juàn* 54. In 1927, a printed version of this recension was made, mixing readings from the Zhang and the Fu_3 manuscripts listed below:

   (1) Zhao: National Library of China, Beijing

   (2) Niu: National Library of China, Beijing

   (3) Zhang: National Library of China, Beijing

   (4) Fu_3: Shanghai Library

   (5) Uang: Zhejiang Library, Hangzhou

b) Manuscript of the ε recension. This recension was put together around 1550, on the basis of a *Shuofu* manuscript similar to that of the Fu_3 manuscript. In it, Zhao Gong's work is found in *juàn* 60:

   (6) Shen: Fung Ping Shan Library, University of Hong Kong

c) Blockprinted ζ recension. This blockprint was produced around 1615 by collating a number of manuscripts into a new recension. Fortunately, the manuscript chosen as base for the ζ recension's text of the Meng-Da beilu was independent of the γ and ε recensions. It is found in *juàn* 56 of the *Shuofu* anthology.

Detailed information on all these codices may be found in Atwood 2017, 40–52 and 32–35.

The text has been previously translated into Russian (Munkuev 1975), German (Olbricht and Pinks 1980, 1–84), and Mongolian, the latter in the vertical or Uyghur-Mongolian script (Möngkejayaġ-a 1985a).

---

4. The names of the manuscripts are mostly taken from the surname of the first collector to own the manuscript and derive ultimately from Jia Jingyan's study of the *Campaigns of Chinggis Khan*. The Fu manuscript is actually a composite manuscript, cobbled together from at least three different manuscripts of the vast *Shuofu* collection. These separate manuscripts are distinguished by subscript numbers. (Zhao's "Memorandum" is found in the third of these Fu MSS, hence Fu_3.) Since single or at most double letter abbreviations have to be used in the critical apparatus of MSS, at some points it is useful to distinguish semi-homophonous names through Yuen Ren Chao's system of "tonal spelling" (the system used to distinguish "Shaanxi" from "Shanxi," for example). Thus, *Wáng* 汪 is written as Uang and abbreviated as U to distinguish it from the more common *Wáng* 王 abbreviated as W.

A Sketch of the Black Tatars

The oldest known copy of this text, and apparently the basis for all currently known texts, is a copy made by Yao Zi in Jiajing ("Admirable Settlement") 21 (1542). This copy is now kept in the National Library of China. In his colophon, Yao Zi says he copied the text from a Song-era blockprint owned by Wang Mao-zhong. Yao Zi's copy remained little studied, however, until the late Qing dynasty. At that point, as interest grew in the history of Mongolia, Xinjiang, and other Inner Asian possessions of China, scholars like Li Wentian and Shen Cengzhi began to excavate the history of China and the Mongols through old manuscripts.

In the mid-nineteenth century, the bibliophile Zhang Rongjing acquired a manuscript that had been copied from Yao Zi's manuscript. The colophon, however, dated Yao Zi's copy not to Jiajing 21, but to Jiajing 36 (1557); it is not clear what its relationship is to the extant Jiajing 21 copy, although the two have very few differences. After Zhang's death, the Jiajing 36 manuscript surfaced on the Beijing book market; that copy was eventually purchased by the scholar Li Wentian. Another copy of Zhang's manuscript must have been made by the booksellers, because the scholar Miao Quansun also obtained a copy. Li Wentian, Miao Quansun, and Miao's friend Shen Cengzhi all made copies, with some preliminary scholarly commentary, in Guangxu 16 (1890).[5]

Twentieth-century scholarly editions, of which Wang Guowei's was the most significant, were all based on these manuscripts. Xu Quansheng's 2014 edition is the only one to directly consult Yao Zi's surviving 1542 manuscript and has now become the standard. In reality, however, it seems that since all the manuscripts derive from the two Jiajing-era copies mentioned earlier, the variations are extremely few and are attributable to random lapses and occasional scholarly speculation. They do not supply independent witness to any text predating Yao Zi's 1542 copy of the now lost blockprint.

The text has been previously translated into German (Olbricht and Pinks 1980, 85–226) and into Mongolian in the vertical or Uyghur-Mongolian script (Möngkejayaġ-a 1985b).

Spirit-Path Stele for His Honor Yelü, Director of the Secretariat

The textual history of this source, in a way, is very simple. The text was completed in 1268, to be carved into the tomb-site where Ila (Yelü) Chucai was interred at Wengshan Hill, northwest of the Mongol capital of Daidu. The text was soon recognized as a classic and was included by Su Tianjue (1294–1352) in his anthology of the best Chinese literature of the Mongol Yuan dynasty, completed in 1334. As an emblem of the dynasty's claim to embody the best values of Chinese culture,

---

5. On the textual history of the "Sketch of the Black Tatars," see the notes in Xu Quansheng 2014, iii–vii, 1–2, and 234–38.

Su's *Anthology of the Yuan* (*Yuan wenlei*)[6] was blockprinted in 1336. Copies of this 1336 edition have survived to the present and are the basis of all modern editions, of which there are many. Some are photographic reproductions of the original imprint, while others are reset in modern type or punctuated. Editions we have consulted are listed in the bibliography under the author's name, Song Zizhen.

Yet, there are citations to the spirit-path stele that seem to diverge from the 1336 imprints in ways that suggest the presence of small but significant errors in that original printing. Su Tianjue cumulatively cited most of the text in his history, *Eminent Vassals of the Yuan Dynasty* (*Yuanchao mingchen shilue*),[7] explicitly stating the source of each of his passages; it is thus an invaluable source for checking the texts of the works he cites. This history too was blockprinted in 1335, and that imprint survived to form the basis for all modern editions (see the entries under Su Tianjue in the bibliography). In several cases, Su Tianjue's excerpts as cited in *Eminent Vassals* differ, however, from those in his *Anthology*, usually in being slightly longer. Presumably, in his haste to copy content into the much larger *Anthology*, sentences were accidentally omitted.

There are a few other texts which certainly cite the "Spirit-Path Stele," but which do not mark their sources for each passage, as did Su Tianjue in his *Eminent Vassals*. One such work is Chen Jing's annalistic history *Continuation of the Comprehensive Mirror* (*Tongjian xubian*; 1350), a continuation of the monumental *Comprehensive Mirror* by Sima Guang (1019–1086). This history, too, was blockprinted and the imprint survives; for the reign of Öködei its primary source was Song Zizhen's "Spirit-Path Stele." Another is the *History of the Yuan Dynasty* (*Yuanshi*), compiled in 1370 by a committee under the new Ming dynasty to mark its victory over and replacement of the Mongol Yuan. Its chapter 146 is a biography based closely on the social biographies of Ila (Yelü) Chucai; a few other passages in the "Basic Annals" of the emperors also match the "Spirit-Path Stele" closely. In a few passages that we have identified in the footnotes above, it seems the Chen Jing and the *Yuanshi* compilers are citing passages that were accidentally omitted in Su Tianjue's copy of the "Spirit-Path Stele." Unfortunately, it is hard to be sure, since they may be citing, rather, Li Wei's "Account of Conduct," which was Song Zizhen's source for his spirit-path stele and which was probably known to Chen Jing and the *Yuanshi* compilers. In any case, these passages, which were possibly or probably found in the original "Spirit-Path Stele," have been included, with annotation, in our footnotes.

This text has been previously translated into Russian (Munkuev 1965), and the Russian further has been translated into Cyrillic-script Mongolian (Munkuev 2005).

---

6. The original title was *Anthology of Our Dynasty* (*Guochao wenlei*), but the work's title was generally changed after the fall of the Mongol Yuan in 1368.

7. The original title was *Eminent Vassals of Our Dynasty* (*Guochao mingchen shilue*), but the work's title was generally changed after the fall of the Mongol Yuan in 1368.

Notes on a Journey

Zhang Dehui's "Notes on a Journey" was preserved by Wang Yun, one of the leading classically trained literati at Qubilai's court. Wang Yun included the text in his *Yutang jiahua* ("Praiseworthy Conversations from the Jade Hall"), an anthology of anecdotes, conversations, and citations from his own experiences as an official and from the precedents of previous dynasties.[8] The anthology was completed in 1288 but remained in manuscript until Wang Yun's death in 1304. His family wished to publish his complete works but lacked the funds until a subvention from the court was issued. A blockprint was finally carved and printed in the Mongol Yuan dynasty's Zhizhi ("Ultimate Governance") 1 (1321), but few copies were printed and the three remaining copies found today are in relatively poor condition, with many graphs illegible or pages missing.

During the succeeding Ming dynasty, an official serving in Wang Yun's home province of Henan wished to burnish Wang Yun's reputation. Copies of the Zhizhi 1 imprint were already scarce, so he sponsored a new printing, completed in Hongzhi ("Broad Governance") 11 (1497). The Hongzhi 11 edition in most places closely matches the earlier blockprint, but it does contain some text not found in the Zhizhi 1 edition, so it must have also used some other manuscript to fill certain lacunae. The Ming edition was printed in many copies and became by far the most widely used edition.

A modern landmark in the study of this text was the edition of Yao Congwu, first published in 1962. Produced with the aid of the Inner Mongolian Mongolist Jagchid Sechin, this was the first study to decipher the Mongolian terms and geography of the "Notes." Yao's edition also began the tradition of including, at relevant points, the conversations with Qubilai Khan, taken from Zhang Dehui's biography. Jia Jingyan's commentary, published posthumously in 2004, adds to our understanding of the referenced geography, but does not go beyond Yao Congwu's text. The most recent edition of the text, that in Yang Liang and Zhong Yanfei's 2013 edition of Wang Yun's complete works, also makes use of the *Siku quanshu* edition. This edition in turn was based on one manuscript kept by the Yu family, and one kept by the official Song Binwang. The former was probably based on the Ming imprint, but the latter appears to be based on the Yuan imprint and hence is relatively valuable.

Following the example of Yao Congwu's edition, we have also inserted into the translated text at the relevant points the record of Zhang Dehui's conversations with the prince Qubilai. This record is cited from the "Account of Conduct" (*xíngzhuàng*) of Zhang Dehui, which Wang Yun wrote for Zhang's family after he died in Zhiyuan 11 (1274). This "Account of Conduct" was not included in Wang Yun's collected works, but it was excerpted at length in Su Tianjue's biography of Zhang Dehui. This biography was part of Su Tianjue's

---

8. "Jade Hall" was a common poetic way to refer to the Hanlin Academy, of which Wang Yun was a member. On the textual history of Wang Yun's collected works, including the *Yutang jiahua*, see Yang Liang 2013, 4–8; Yang Xiaochun 2006.

prosopographical history, *Eminent Vassals of the Yuan Dynasty* (*Yuanchao mingchen shi-lue*), which was printed in 1335. This blockprint is the basis for those portions of the text translated here.

The only previous scholarly translation of this text is that by Erdemtü (1994), which follows Yao Congwu's text closely.

Appendix 2

Tables and Charts

1. Table of Dynasties and Personalities in China, Mongolia, and Manchuria

China		Mongolia		Manchuria	
South	North	South	North	North	South
Mythic Thearchs: Yao, Shun, Yu the Great					
XIA (ca. 2070?–1600? BC)					
SHANG (ca. 1600–1046 BC)		*Deer Stones,*			
King Tang, Yi Yin (Aheng)					
ZHOU (1046–256 BC)		*Kheregsuuri tombs*			
Kings Wen and Wu, Jiang Shangfu (Taigong)				"Sushen"	
Canons of Changes, Odes, Documents					
Confucius, Springs and Autumns Annals					
Warring States, Zhuangzi, Mencius					
QIN (221–206 BC)					
HAN (206 BC–AD 220)		XIONGNU EMPIRE (ca. 209 BC–AD 89)		"Yilou"	
Liu Bang (Han Gaozu), Lu Jia, Xiao He					Goguryeo
Sima Qian and his Shiji		*Terrace Tombs*			(from ca. BC 37)
Wang Mang and his short-lived XIN dynasty (9–23 AD)					
Yang Xiong and his Taixuan jing					
Ban Gu and his Hanshu *and "Rhapsody"*		Xianbei		Murkit	
Ban Chao's campaigns in the West					

Three Kingdoms (ca. 180–280) *Cao Cao, Liu Bei of Shu, Zhuge Liang*				
Southern Dynasties (317–589)	*Tabghach Wèi (386–534)	Rou-Ran Empire (ca. 330–555)		
	*N. Qi and *N. Zhou (550–581)	1st And 2nd Türk Empires (552–630 and 682–744)	Marghat	Goguryeo (to 668)
Sui (581–618)				
Tang (618–907) *Tang Taizong, Fang Xuanling, Du Ruhui*		Orkhon Inscriptions	Marghat	Balhae (698–926)
Han Yu		Uyghur Empire (742–847) *Ordu-Baliq*		
Huang Chao Rebellion		Tatars		
*Five Dynasties (907–960) *Shatuo regimes*		Kitan Liao (907–1125)		
Song (960–1127)	*Tangut Xia (982–1227)	*Kitan Liao *Walls, forts in Mongolia*		Kitan Liao Jurchen
Southern Song (1127–1279)	*Jurchen Jin (1115–1234)	White Tatars	Black Tatars	Jurchen Jin
Li Xinchuan	*Ila Chucai*	Mongol Empire (1206 on) *Chinggis Khan*		
Peng Daya Xu Ting	*Song Zizhen*	*Öködei Khan*		
	Zhang Dehui	Secret History of the Mongols		
	*Mongol Yuan (1206/1271–1369)			
	Qubilai Khan			Jurchen
Ming (1368–1644)		*Conversion to Buddhism*	Jurchen	
*Manchu Qing (1644–1912)				

Note: *Indicates non-Han regime ruling in China. SMALL CAPITALS indicate regime that united all of China or Mongolia.

2. Emperors of the Jin Dynasty

Jurchen Name	Chinese Name	Posthumous Temple Title	Translation	Reign Dates
Akûdai(i)	Min 旻	Taizu 太祖	Great Founder	1115–1123
Ukima(i)	Sheng 晟	Taizong 太宗	Great Ancestor	1123–1135
Hara(ma)	Dan 亶	Xizong 熙宗	Radiant Ancestor	1135–1149
Di'unai	Liang 亮	Hailing Wang 海陵王	Prince of Hailing	1149–1161
Uru	Yong 雍	Shizong 世宗	Renovating Ancestor	1161–1189
Madaka	Jing 璟	Zhangzong 章宗	Model Ancestor	1189–1209
Kimšan	Yunji 允濟	Donghaijun Hou 東海郡侯 *or* Wei Shaowang 衛紹王	Commandery Marquis of Donghai *or* Prince Shao of Wei	1209–1213
Udubu	Xun 珣	Xuanzong 宣宗	Comprehensive Ancestor	1213–1224
Ninggiasu	Shouxu 守緒	Aizong 哀宗	Lamented Ancestor	1224–1234

3. Emperors of the Early Mongol Empire

Name (Reign Title)	Posthumous Temple Title	Translation	Reign Dates
Temüjin (Chinggis)	Taizu 太祖	Great Founder	1206–1227
Regent: Tolui	Ruizong 睿宗	Perceptive Ancestor	1228–1229
Öködei (Qa'an)	Taizong 太宗	Great Ancestor	1229–1241
Regent: Töregene			1242–1246
Güyük	Dingzong 定宗	Decisive Ancestor	1246–1248
Regent: Oghul-Qaimish			1248–1251
Möngke	Xianzong 憲宗	Exemplary Ancestor	1251–1259
Qubilai	Shizu 世祖	Renovating Founder	1260–1294

4. Genealogy of the Jin Dynasty

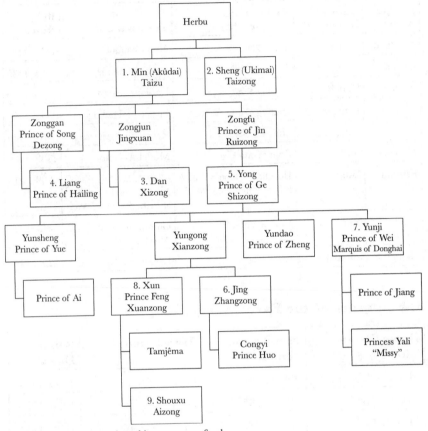

Note: Emperors are numbered in sequence of rule.

5. Genealogy of the Mongol Dynasty

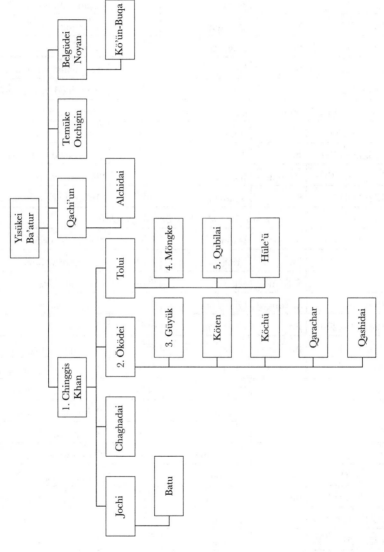

Note: Emperors are numbered in sequence of rule.

6. Relevant Song and Jin Year Slogans

Years	Dynasty	Pronunciation	Characters	Meaning
1101	Song	Jianzhong-Jingguo	建中靖國	"Reviving Centrality and Settling the Empire"
1102–1106	Song	Chongning	崇寧	"Exalting Calm"
1107–1110	Song	Daguan	大觀	"Great Regard"
1111–1117	Song	Zhenghe	政和	"Regulated Harmony"
1118–1122	Jin	Tianfu	天輔	"Sustained by Heaven"
1118, XI–1119, I	Song	Chonghe	重和	"Redoubled Harmony"
1119, I–1125	Song	Jingkang	靖康	"Settled Prosperity"
1123, IX–1137	Jin	Tianhui	天會	"Assembled by Heaven"
1127, V–1130	S. Song	Jianyan	建炎	"Recommencing the Flame"
1131–1162	S. Song	Shaoxing	紹興	"Inheriting Restoration"
Numerous Jin and S. Song Year Slogans Omitted				
1161, X–1189	Jin	Dading	大定	"Great Security"
1190–1196, XI	Jin	Mingchang	明昌	"Luminous Glory"
1190–1194	S. Song	Shaoxi	紹熙	"Inheriting Radiance"
1195–1200	S. Song	Qingyuan	慶元	"Felicitous Primacy"
1196, XI–1200	Jin	Cheng'an	承安	"Receiving Peace"
1201–1208	Jin	Taihe	泰和	"Tranquil Harmony"
1201–1204	S. Song	Jiatai	嘉泰	"Admirable Tranquility"
1205–1207	S. Song	Kaixi	開禧	"Inaugurating Jubilation"
1208–1224	S. Song	Jiading	嘉定	"Admirable Security"
1209, I–1211	Jin	Da'an	大安	"Great Peace"
1212–1213, IV	Jin	Chongqing	崇慶	"Exalting Felicity"
1213, V–IX	Jin	Zhining	至寧	"Ultimate Calm"
1213, IX–1217, IX	Jin	Zhenyou	貞祐	"Immaculate Blessing"
1217, IX–1222, VIII	Jin	Xingding	興定	"Restoring Security"
1222, VIII–1223	Jin	Yuanguang	元光	"Primal Radiance"
1224–1232, I	Jin	Zhengda	正大	"Correct Greatness"
1225–1227	Song	Baoqing	寶慶	"Precious Felicity"
1228–1233	Song	Shaoding	紹定	"Inheriting Security"

1232, I–IV	Jin	Kaixing	開興	"Inaugurating Restoration"
1232, IV–1234, I	Jin	Tianxing	天興	"Restored by Heaven"
1234–1236	Song	Duanping	端平	"Proper Stability"
1237–1240	Song	Jiaxi	嘉熙	"Admirable Radiance"
Numerous S. Song Year Slogans Omitted				
1260–1263	Yuan	Zhongtong	中統	"Central Unification"
1260–1294	Yuan	Zhiyuan	至元	"Ultimate Primacy"

Note: Where the slogan changed in the middle of the year, the moon when it changed is indicated by a Roman numeral; otherwise, changes were proclaimed on the Lunar New Year.

7. Weights and Measures in Yuan Dynasty

Length

Unit and Subunit	Metric Equivalent	English or Customary Equivalent
1 *lǐ* 里 = 360 *bù* 步	1 *lǐ* 里 = 0.56 kilometers	*lǐ* 里 = 0.35 miles
1 *zhàng* 丈 = 10 *chǐ* 尺	1 *zhàng* 丈 = 3.12 meters	*zhàng* 丈 = 0.62 rods
1 *bù* 步 = 5 *chǐ* 尺	1 *bù* 步 = 1.56 meters	*bù* 步 = 1.71 yards
1 *chǐ* 尺 = 10 *cùn* 寸	1 *chǐ* 尺 = 31.2 centimeters	*chǐ* 尺 = 1.023 feet
	1 *cùn* 寸 = 3.12 centimeters	*cùn* 寸 = 1.23 inches

Area

1 *qǐng* 頃 = 100 *mǔ* 畝	1 *qǐng* 頃 = 5.84 hectares	1 *qǐng* 頃 = 14.43 acres
	1 *mǔ* 畝 = 584 meters² or 0.058 hectares	1 *mǔ* 畝 = 0.14 acres

Dry measure

1 *dàn* 石 = 2 *hú* 斛	1 *dàn* 石 = 95 liters	*dàn* 石 or picul = 2.7 bushels (US)
1 *hú* 斛 = 5 *dǒu* 斗	1 *hú* 斛 = 47.5 liters	*hú* 斛 = 1.35 bushels (US)
1 *dǒu* 斗 = 10 *shēng* 升	1 *dǒu* 斗 = 9.5 liters	*dǒu* 斗 = 1.08 pecks (US)
	1 *shēng* 升 = 0.95 liters	*shēng* 升 = 2.01 pints

Weight

1 *dàn* 石 = 120 *jīn* 斤	1 *dàn* 石 = 76 kilograms	*dàn* 石 or picul = 167.46 pounds
1 *jīn* 斤 = 16 *liǎng* 兩	1 *jīn* 斤 = 0.633 kilograms	*jīn* 斤 or catty = 1.4 pounds
	1 *liǎng* 兩 = 40 grams	*liǎng* 兩 or tael = 1.4 oz

Currency[9]

1 *dìng* 錠 (silver) = 50 *liǎng* 兩	1 *dìng* 錠 = 2.01 kilograms	*dìng* 錠 = 4.43 lbs
	1 *liǎng* 兩 (silver) = 40.2 grams	*liǎng* 兩 or tael (silver) = 1.42 ounces
1 *liǎng* 兩 (cloth) = 40 *chǐ* 尺	1 *liǎng* 兩 (cloth) = 12.48 × 0.52 meters = 6.49 meters²	*liǎng* 兩 or bolt = 7.76 square yards

---

9. For Jin-Yuan silver ingot sizes, see Li and Xiao 1989, 93–94, 140, 142; *liǎng* weights of surviving ingots range from 40.2 to 37.9 grams. Bolt widths are from Wang and Wang 2013, based on the Tang-era standard.

Appendix 3

Glossary of Chinese and Transcribed Terms

1. Chinese Names and Terms

Name	Graph
Aheng	阿衡
Ai, Prince of	愛王
An Tianhe	安天合
Anci	安次
Bai Hua (Wenju)	白華 (文舉)
Bai Lun	白倫
Bailu Lake	白鹿湖
Ban Chao	班超
Baosai	保塞
Baozhou	保州
Bazhou	霸州
Beikou	北口
Bianjing	汴京
Bianliang	汴梁
bìxià	陛下
bù (appanage)	部
Cai Jing	蔡京
cānzhèng	參政
Chang Bajin	常八斤
Chang'an	長安
Changbai	長白山
Changchun Gong	長春宮
Changzhou	昌州
Chanyu	單于

Name	Graph
chén	臣
Chen Shike	陳時可
Chenghui (Wongian)	承暉
chéngxiàng	丞相
Chu	楚
Chucai (Ila)	楚材
Chumiaogang	褚廟壋
Congyi	從彝
Cuiping Gap	翠屏口
Dádá	韃靼
Dage	大葛
Dai	代
Daming Calendar	大明曆
Damingfu	大名府
Dan (Kitan name)	丹
Dangchang Fort	宕昌寨
Dashengdian	大勝甸
Daxingfu	大興府
Desheng Gap	得勝口
Dexingfu	德興府
Deyuan	德元
Dí	狄
Dingfang	定防
Dingxing	定興

Name	Graph	Name	Graph
Dingyuan	定遠	Han Yu (Tuizhi)	韓愈 (退之)
dìzhī	地支	*Hàndì*	漢地
Dong Renfu	董仁父	Hanjiang	漢江
Dongdan, Prince of	東丹王	*hào*	號
Donghai	東海	Hao the Eighth	郝八
Donghuamen Gate	東華門	Hao Yi	郝儀
Dongpingfu	東平府	Haozhou	濠州
Ehu Ridge	扼胡嶺	Hedong	河東
Ezhu	鄂渚	Hengshan (Hunan)	衡山
fān	蕃	Hengshan (Shanxi)	恒山
Fan, Mr.	范子仁	Hexi	河西
Fangcheng	方城	*Hóngǎo*	紅襖
Fangzhou	房州	Hongxian	虹縣
Feng, Prince	豐王	*hú*	胡
Fengshengzhou	奉聖州	*Huá*	華
fēngsú	風俗	Huaihe River	淮河
Fengxiangfu	鳳翔府	Huailai	懷來
fǔ	府	Huanzhou	桓州
Fu Yi	傅翊	Huihe River	灰河
Fuhai (Wongian)	福海	*Húihé*	回紇
Fuzhou	撫州	*Húihú*	回鶻
Gao Ming	高鳴	*Húihúi*	回回
Ge, Prince of	葛王	Huntong River	混同江
gōng ("His Honor")	公	Huo, Prince	霍王
Gu'an	固安	Hutuo	滹沱
Guangding	光定	*jiǎ*	甲
Guanshan	官山	*jiǎ/zǐ*	甲子
Guanxi	關西	Jiang, Prince of	蔣王
Guo Zhong	郭忠	*jiǎoduān*	角端
Guozhou	虢州	*jiéqi*	節氣
Haizhou	海州	Jiming, Mt.	雞鳴山
Han (dynasty, ethnicity)	漢	Jin (dynasty, "gold")	金

Name	Graph
Jìn (dynasty, region)	晉
Ji'nanfu	濟南府
Jǐng (Jin monarch)	璟
Jingzhou	淨州
Jining	集寧
Jinqing (Ila)	晉卿
Jinshan	縉山
Jinshou	金壽
Jinzhou	金州
Jiǔ	𢆉(酒)or 糺
jìwén	祭文
Jizhou	薊州
Juyong Pass	居庸關
Kaifengfu	開封府
Kaipingfu	開平府
Kaizhou	開州
Kong Yuancuo	孔元措
Langshan	琅山
Leijiadian	雷家店
lǐ (ritual)	禮
Li, Palace Gateman	李黃門
Li, Supervisor	李監丞
Li Daliang	李大諒
Li Jinzhi	李進之
Li Jiqian	李繼遷
Li Pan	李槃
Li Quan	李全
Li She	李舍
Li Tao	李濤
Li Wei	李微
Li Xinchuan (Weizhi)	李心傳 (微之)
Li Xing	李興

Name	Graph
Li Ye	李冶
Li Zao	李藻
Liang	梁
Liang (Wongian)	亮
Liang Shi	梁實
Liangmen Gate	良門
Liangxiang	良鄉
Liao	遼
Liaodong	遼東
ling	令
Lingwu	靈武
Lingzhou	靈州
Linhuangfu	臨潢府
Liu, Miss (*Liú Xiǎojiě*)	劉小姐
Liu Bolin	劉伯林
Liu Erzu	劉二祖
Liu Heima	劉黑馬
Liu Tingyu	劉庭玉
Liu Yu	劉豫
Liu Zhong	劉中
liúshǒu	留守
Lizemen Gate	麗澤門
Louguo	婁國
Lousang Temple	樓桑廟
Lü (Yelü)	履
lù	路
lǔ, lǔrén	虜, 虜人
Lu Jingshan	盧景善
Lugou	瀘溝
Lüju	驢駒
Luoyang	洛陽
Ma, Secretary	馬錄事

Name	Graph
Mán	蠻
Mancheng	滿城
Ménxià shěng	門下省
miàohào	廟號
Min (Wongian)	旻
míng	名
Mozhou	莫州
Mubo	木波
mùzhì	墓誌
Nankou Gap	南口
Nanping (Tukdan)	南平
niánhào	年號
Peng Daya	彭大雅
Pingyangfu	平陽府
Pingyu	平輿
píngzhāng	平章
Pizhou	邳州
Pusan Qijin (Duan)	僕散七斤 (端)
Qi (kingdom, dynasty)	齊
Qianshun	乾順
qīng	卿
Qingtang	青唐
Qingzhou	青州
Qinzhou	秦州
Qishui	漆水
Róng	戎
Ruzhou	汝州
Sān Gōng	三公
sān shěng	三省
Sanggan	桑乾
Sanmen	三門
Shajing	沙井

Name	Graph
Shalingzi Gap	沙嶺子口
Shang	商
Shangfu (Jiang)	尚父 (姜)
Shangjing	上京
Shàngshū shěng	尚書省
Shanzhou	陝州
shāo pípa	燒琵琶
Shatuo	沙陀
Shen, Prince	申王
shéndào bēi	神道碑
Sheng (Wongian)	晟
shěng	省
Shenzong	神宗
shì (posthumous title)	謚
shì (surname)	氏
Shǐ Tianni	史天倪
Shǐ Tianyi	史天翼
Shitizi	石梯子
Shu	蜀
Shuangtabao	雙塔堡
Shūmì yuàn	樞密院
Shun	舜
Shuntian	順天
Shunzhou	順州
Sizhou	泗州
Song	宋
Song Zizhen	宋子貞
Songshan Mountains	嵩山
Su, Lady *née*	蘇氏
Su Dongpo	蘇東坡
Su Gongbi	蘇公弼
Sui	隋

Name	Graph
Sushen	肅慎
Taihang	太行
Tàishī	太師
Taiyuanfu	太原府
Taizong	太宗
Taizu	太祖
Tang (ancient king)	湯
Tang (dynasty)	唐
Tian	田
Tiancheng	天城
tiāngān	天干
Tianshan	天山
tiānxià	天下
Tianxing	天興
Tiānyī	天一
Tianzuo	天祚
Tong Guan	童貫
Tongguan	潼關
Tongzhou	通州
Tur	兔兒
Tuyu (Yelü)	突欲
Wan'an Hall	萬安殿
wáng	王
Wang Fu	王黼
Wang Ji	王概
Wang Xianzuo	王賢佐
Wanqing Yiyong	萬慶義勇
Wei, Prince of	衛王
wéi	偽
Wèi (kingdom, dynasty)	魏
Wei Fan	魏瑶
Wèizhou	魏州

Name	Graph
Wēizhou	威州
Wengshan	甕山
Wozhou	沃州
Wutuanpu	吳團鋪
wǔxíng	五行
Xia (dynasty)	夏
Xià ("Chinese")	夏
xiàn (county)	縣
xiànggōng	相公
Xiao He	蕭何
Xiao, Lady	蕭夫人
xiǎomíng	小名
Xibo (Yelü)	希勃
Xiguang (Yelü)	希光
Xihezhou	西和州
Xijin	析津
Xijing	西京
Xikuan (Yelü)	希款
Xiliang (Yelü)	希亮
Xin'an Military Prefecture	新安軍
Xindian	新店
xíng	行
Xinghuaying	杏花營
Xingping Army	興平軍
Xingzhou	興州
xíngzhuàng	行狀
Xinwèizhou	新衛州
Xiongzhou	雄州
Xisu (Yelü)	希素
Xitu (Yelü)	希圖
Xixia	西夏
Xiyi (Yelü)	希逸

Name	Graph
Xīyù	西域
Xizhi (Yelü)	希徵
Xizhou (Yelü)	希周
Xu Ding	胥鼎
Xu Ting (Changru)	徐霆 (長孺)
Xuan (Yelü)	鉉
xuǎn	選
Xuandezhou	宣德州
Xuanfeng, Fort	旋風寨
Xuānfǔshǐ	宣撫使
xuānmìng zhī bǎo	宣命之寶
Xuanping	宣平
Xuhe	徐河
Xun (Wongian)	珣
Yalu River	鴨綠水
Yan (region, kingdom)	燕
Yan Shi	嚴寔
Yang, Lady *née*	楊氏
Yang An'er	楊安兒
Yang Biao	楊彪
Yang Boyu	楊伯遇
Yang Zao	楊藻
Yanjing	燕京
Yanshan	燕山
Yansheng Gong	衍聖公
Yao	堯
Yehu Ridge	野狐領
Yēlǜ	耶律
Yelü Chucai	耶律楚材
Yelü Zhu	耶律鑄
yí (barbarian)	夷
Yílà	移剌

Name	Graph
Yila Chucai	移剌楚材
Yilou	挹婁
Yingtianmen Gate	應天門
Yinshan	陰山
Yí-Xià	夷夏
Yizhou	易州
Yong (Wongian)	雍
Yongjia	永嘉
Yongning	永寧
Yu Rong	余嶸
Yuan	元
Yuan Haowen	元好問
Yuan Wèi	元魏
Yue, Prince of	越王
Yulin	榆林
Yulu (Yelü)	聿魯
Yunji	允濟
Yunneizhou	雲內州
Yunzhong	雲中
Yúnzhou	雲州
Yùnzhou	鄆州
Yuquan	玉泉
Yùshǐtái	禦史台
Yuzhou	蔚州
Yùzhou	陝州
Zaohe	皂河
Ze, Prince of	澤王
Zhang Dehui (Yaoqing)	張德輝 (耀卿)
Zhang Fu	張甫
Zhang Jin	張進
Zhang Rou	張柔
Zhang Sanshen	張三深

Name	Graph	Name	Graph
Zhang Zhai	張齋	Zhongli	鐘離
Zhao Gong	趙珙	Zhongshanfu	中山府
Zhao Yan	趙衍	*Zhōngshū shěng*	中書省
Zhao Yuande	趙元德	*Zhōngyuán*	中原
Zhāotǎoshǐ	招討使	Zhou	周
Zhen, Great	大真	*zhōu*	州
zhèn	朕	Zhuojun	涿郡
Zhendingfu	真定府	Zhuozhou	涿州
Zheng, Prince of	鄭王	*zǐ*	子
Zheng Meng ji	征蒙記	*zì*	字
Zheng Xianzhi	鄭顯之	Zijing Pass	紫荊關
Zhenguo	鎮國	Zizhou	淄州
Zhenyang	鎮陽	*Zōng*	宗
Zhipu	指浦	*zǒng*	總
Zhizhong (Hû-Šire)	執中	Zongbi	宗弼
Zhongdu	中都	*zǔ*	祖
Zhōngguó	中國	*Zúliè-Duóhé*	卒坺·奪合

2. Non-Chinese Names and Terms

Name	Chinese Graphs	Historical Pronunciation (Yuan unless otherwise specified)	Modern Mandarin Pronunciation
Abduraqman	奧都剌合蠻	Au-du-la-hâ-man	Aòdūlàhémán
Akûdai	阿骨打	Â-gu-da	Āgǔdǎ
Alaqan	阿剌罕	Â-la-han	Ālàhǎn
Alchar	按察兒	An-ča-ři	Ànchár
Alchi Noyê	按赤那耶	An-či No-ye	Ànchì-Nuóyē
Alchidai	按只觷	An-ʒi-dai	Ànzhǐdǎi
aldaqui	按打奚	An-da-hi	*àndǎxī*
Aqai	阿海	Â-hai	Āhǎi
Ariq Bayin	阿里黑 ·百因	Â-li-hei Baiyin	Ālǐhēi-Bǎyīn
Asan-Amish	阿散 ·阿迷失	Â-san Â-mi-ši	Āsǎn-Āmíshī
ba'atur	八都	ba-du	*bādū*
Baekdu	白頭	(Korean)	Báitóu
Baisbo	白斯波	Bai-sï-buo	Báisībō
Baisbu	白四部 (Zhao)	Bai-sï-bu	Báisìbù
Baisbu	白厮卜 (Peng and Xu)	Bai-sï-bu	Básībǔ
Baisma	白厮馬	Bai-sï-ma	Básīmǎ
Balhae	渤海	(Korean)	Bóhǎi
Bars	蒲類	Ba-lus (Han)	Púlèi
Beki	必姬	Bi-gi	Bìjī
Bekter	別迭	Bie-die	Biédié
Belgudei Noyê	便古得 那耶	Bien-gu-dei No-ye	Biàngǔděi-Nuóyē
bhikshu	比丘	Pi-khiu (Tang)	Bǐqiū
bichi'echi	必徹徹	Bi-čie-čie	*Bìchèchè*
Bitehetu	畢忒紇都	Bi-tei-hu-du	Bìtèhédū
Biyin	比因	Bi-yin	Bǐyīn
Bo'ol	袍阿 (Zhao)	Pau-o	Páo'ē
Bo'ol	博窩 (Peng and Xu)	Bau-wo	Bówō
Boro	孛落	Bo-lo	Bèiluò

Name	Chinese Graphs	Historical Pronunciation (Yuan unless otherwise specified)	Modern Mandarin Pronunciation
Botu	撥都	Buo-du	Bōdū
Bunchan	俸盞	Bun-ǯan	Bènzhǎn
Chaghadai	茶合觹	Ča-hâ-dai	Cháhédǎi
Chala'un	察剌溫	Ča-la-un	Chálàwēn
Chinggis	成吉思	Čing-gi-sï	Chéngjísī
Chinqai	鎮海	Ǯin-hai	Zhènhǎi
Daiši Lemya	大石 林牙	Dai-ši Lim-ya	Dàshí Línyá
Daisun	帶孫	Dai-sun	Dàisūn
Darughachi	達魯花赤	da-lu-hua-či	Dálǔhuāchì
Datar	達塔	Da-ta	Dátǎ
Dhyana	禪	Dźan (Tang)	Chán
Gambo Babo	減波 把波	Giam-buo Ba-buo	Jiǎnbō-Bābō
Geuki (Juhung)	高乞	Gau-ki	Gāoqǐ
Ghaili	界里	Giai-li	Jièlǐ
Gie-leu	結婁	Gie-lėu	Jiélóu
Goguryeo	高句麗	(Korean)	Gāogōulí
Gugui	姑詭	gu-guei	*gūguǐ*
Guin	國隱	Guei-in	Guóyìn
Gui-Ong	歸王	Guei-wang	Gūiwáng
Haju	合住	Hâ-ǯü	Hézhù
Herbu	劾里鉢	Hei-li-buo	Hélǐbō
Hiêmdêibu	憨塔卜 (Peng and Xu)	Ham-ta-bu	Hāntǎbǔ
Hiêmdêibu	咸得不 (Song)	Hiam-dei-bu	Xiānděibù
Hiluren	翕陸連	Hi-lü-lien	Xīlùlián
Hindu	脛篤	Hing-du	Jìngdǔ
Hiuden	後典	Hėu-dien	Hòudiǎn
Hula'an-Chikin	忽蘭 赤斤	Hu-lan-či-gin	Hūlán-Chìjīn
Hun-Tula	渾 獨剌	Hun-Du-la	Hún-Dúlà
Hûša	胡沙	Hu-ša	Húshā
Hûšahû	胡沙虎 (*Jinshi*)	Hu-ša-hu	Húshāhǔ

Name	Chinese Graphs	Historical Pronunciation (Yuan unless otherwise specified)	Modern Mandarin Pronunciation
Hûšahû	忽殺虎 (Zhao)	Hu-ša-hu	Hūshāhǔ
Hû-Šire	紇 ·石烈	Hu-Ši-lie	Hé-Shíliè
Husu-Irgen	斛速 ·益律干	Hu-su I-lü-gan	Húsù-Yìlǜgān
Ila (stallion, surname)	移剌	I-la	Yílà
Iladu	耶剌都	Ye-la-du	Yélàdū
Jabar	札八	ǯa-ba	Zhábā
Jam	蘸	ǯam	*Zhàn*
Jebe	鷓博	ǯie-bau	Zhèbó
Jilar	紙蠟兒	ǯi-la-ři	Zhǐlàr
Jilger Noyê	汁里哥 ·那耶	ǯi-li-go No-ye	Zhīlīgē-Nuóyē
Jiün	纠 (Li)	?	Jiǔ
Jiün	纠 (Zhao)	?	Jiǔ
Jochi	拙職	ǯüä-ǯi	Zhuōzhí
Juhung	朮虎	ǯü-hu	Zhúhǔ
Jurchen	女真	Nü-ǯin	Nǚzhēn
Kete	紇忒	Ki-tei	Gētè
Kibsha'ut	克鼻梢	Kei-bu-šau	Kèbíshāo
Kitan	契丹	Khit-tan (Tang)	Qìdān
Kö'ün-Buqa	口溫 ·不花	Kėu-un Bu-hua	Kǒwēn-Bùhuā
Köchü	闊除	Kuo-čü	Kuòchú
Korea	高麗	Goryeo (Korean)	Gāolí
Köten	闊端	Kuo-don	Kuòduān
Kümüs-Buqa	苦木思 ·不花	Ku-mu-sï Bu-hua	Kǔmùsī-Bùhuā
Kurawu	窟剌吾	Ku-la-u	Kūlàwú
lemya	林牙	Lim-ya	*Línyá*
Marcha	麻里扎	Ma-li-ǯa	Málǐzhā
Marghat	靺鞨	Mar-γat (Tang)	Mòhé
Martabah	麻答把	Ma-da-ba	*Mádābā*
ma'u	冒烏	Mau-u	*màowū*

Name	Chinese Graphs	Historical Pronunciation (Yuan unless otherwise specified)	Modern Mandarin Pronunciation
Me	咩	?	Miē
Ming'an	明安	Ming-an	Míng'ān
Moge	抹歌	Muo-ko	Mògē
Mohulo	摩睺羅	Muo-ḣeu-lo	Móhóuluó
Mong	蒙	Mung	Měng
Monggu	萌骨	Mung-gu	Ménggǔ
Monggus	蒙古斯, 盲骨子, 萌骨子	Mung-gu-sï, Mung-gu-ʒï, Mung-gu-ʒï	Měnggǔsī, Mánggǔzǐ, Ménggǔzǐ
Mongol	蒙古	Mung-gu	Měnggǔ
Mong'u	蒙兀	Mong-u	Měngwù
Moqlei	没黑肋	Mu-hei-lei	Mòhēilèi
Muden	木典	Mu-dien	Mùdiǎn
Muqali	謀合理 (Zhao)	Mėu-hâ-li	Móuhélǐ
Muqali	暮花里 (Peng and Xu)	Mu-hua-li	Mùhuālǐ
Murkit	勿吉	Mur-kit (Tang)	Wùjí
nai sayin	捺殺因	Na ša-yin	*nà shāyīn*
Naiman	賴蠻 (Zhao)	Lai-man	Làimán
Naiman	乃滿 (Peng and Xu)	Nai-man	Nǎimán
Nayman	奈蠻	Nai-man	Nàimán
Nibshu	妮叔	Ni-šü	Nīshū
Niêmha Cungšai	粘合·重山	Niem-hâ Čung-šan	Niánhé-Chóngshān
Noqai-Irgen	那海·益律干	No-hai I-lü-gan	Nuóhǎi-Yìlǜgān
Nuilgha	内剌	Nui-la	Nèilà
Ojin Beki	阿真·鱉擨	O-ʒin Bie-gi	Āzhēn-Biējǐ
Okodai	阿可戴	O-ko-dai	Ākědài
Ordo	窝裏陀	Wo-li-tuo	*wōlǐtuó*
Otčin	窝陳	Wo-čin	Wōchén
Paiza	牌子	Pai-ʒï	*páizi*

Name	Chinese Graphs	Historical Pronunciation (Yuan unless otherwise specified)	Modern Mandarin Pronunciation
Pusan Siging	蒲散 七斤	Pu-san Ci-gin	Púsǎn-Qījīn
Pusen	蒲鮮	Pu-sien	Púxiān
Qai	奚	Hei (Tang)	Xī
Qalu	合魯	Hâ-lu	Hélǔ
Qamuli	合謀理	Hâ-mėu-li	Hémóulǐ
Qangli	抗里	Kang-li	Kànglǐ
Qarachi	合剌直	Hâ-la-ǧi	Hélàzhí
Qara-Khitai	呷辣 吸紿	Hia-la Hi-dai	Xiālà-Xīdài
Qashidai	河西鍴	Ho-si-dai	Héxīdǎi
qorchi	火魯赤	Huo-lu-či	*huǒlǔchì*
Qorum	和林	Huo-lim	Hélín
Qudugh	胡篤	Hu-du	Hú-dǔ
Quduma	忽篤馬	Hu-du-ma	Hūdǔmǎ
Qutugha	忽篤華	Hu-du-hua	Hūdǔhuá
Qutughu	忽覩虎	Hu-du-hu	Hūdǔhǔ
Sahal	撒罕勒	Sa-han-lei	Sāhǎnlè
Samuqa	撒没曷, 撒没喝	Sa-mu-hâ	Sāmòhé, Sāmòhē
Sartaq	撒里達	Sa-li-da	Sālǐdá
Saugha	撒花	Sa-hua	*sǎhuā*
Sayin	殺因	ša-yin	*shāyīn*
Sesui	攝叔	Šie-šü	Shèshū
Sheref ad-Din	涉獵發丁	Šie-lie-fa-ding	Shèlièfādīng
Siging	七金	Ci-gim	Qījīn
Silla	新羅	(Korean)	Xīnluó
Šimei	石抹	Ši-muo	Shímó
Soltan	梭里檀	Suo-li-tan	Suōlǐtán
Subqan	速不罕	Su-bu-han	Sùbùhǎn
Subu'edei	速不鍴	Su-bu-dai	Sùbùdǎi
Sultan	速里壇	Su-li-tan	Sùlǐtán

Name	Chinese Graphs	Historical Pronunciation (Yuan unless otherwise specified)	Modern Mandarin Pronunciation
Ta'achar	塔察兒	Ta-ča-ři	Tǎchár
Tabghach	拓跋	Thak-bat (Wèi)	Tuòbá
Tamir	塌米	Ta-mi	Tāmǐ
Tamjêma	譚哲馬	Tam-ʒie-ma	Tánzhémǎ
Tangut	唐古	Tang-gu	Tánggǔ
Tatar	韃靼	Dat-tar (Tang)	Dádá
taulawchi	托落赤	tau-lau-či	*tuōluòchì*
Telleu	天婁	Tien-lêu	Tiānlóu
Temüdei	忒沒艀	Tei-mu-dai	Tèmòdǎi
Temuge Otchin	忒沒哥·窩真 (Peng & Xu)	Tei-mu-go Wo-ʒin	Tèmògē-Wōzhēn
Temuge Otchin	忒沒葛·窩真 (Zhao)	Tei-mu-go Wo-ʒin	Tèmògě-Wōzhēn
Temujin	忒沒真 (Zhao, Peng and Xu)	Tei-mu-ʒin	Tèmòzhēn
Temujin	忒沒貞 (Li)	Tei-mu-ʒin	Tèmòzhēn
Temüjin	鐵木真	Tie-mu-ʒin	Tiěmùzhēn
Togha	脫合	Tuo-hâ	Tuōhé
Toghan	脫歡	Tuo-hon	Tuōhuān
Tolun	馳欒	To-lon	Tuóluán
Tugha	禿花 (Peng and Xu, Song)	Tu-hua	Tūhuā
Tugha	兔花 (Zhao)	Tu-hua	Tùhuā
Tukdan	徒單	Tu-dan	Túdān
Tuqluq-Bekter	禿魯·別迭兒	Tu-lu-bie-die-ři	Tūlǔ-Biédiér
Ugei Naur	悞竭·腦兒	U-gie Nau-ři	Wùjiénǎor
Uju	兀朮	U-ʒü	Wùzhú
Ukimai	吳乞買	U-ki-mai	Wúqǐmǎi
Ukudei	兀窟艀	U-ku-dai	Wùkūdǎi
ula'achi	兀剌赤	u-la-či	*wùlàchì*
Ursut	兀魯速	U-lu-su	Wùlǔsù
Utshing	烏聖	U-šing	Wūshèng

Name	Chinese Graphs	Historical Pronunciation (Yuan unless otherwise specified)	Modern Mandarin Pronunciation
Wongian Fuking	完顏 福興	On-yan Fu-hing	Wányán Fúxīng
Wongian Šanggian	完顏 善羊	On-yan Šien-yang	Wányán Shànyáng
Wu'anu	萬奴	Wan-nu	Wànnú
Yêrud	耶律	Ye-lü	Yēlǜ
Yochi	約直	Yo-ʒi	Yuēzhí
Yughur	烏鴒	U-yu	Wūyù

Note: The Yuan-era readings are based on Coblin 2007 and Yang 1981, with some modifications to match transcription usage. The most important is the use of *â* to mark when a vowel usually read as *o* was being used conventionally to represent a foreign *a* sound. (Yuan-era Chinese did not have any -*a* sound.) Han, Wèi, and Tang-era transcriptions are based on Coblin 1994, supplemented by Pulleyblank 1991 and Schuessler 2009.

Appendix 4

Image Details and Credits

Image 1, p. 2. Chinggis Khan, personally named Temüjin (1162?–1227). Album leaf, ink and color on silk, 59.1 cm × 46.8 cm. National Palace Museum, Taipei, Taiwan. C2A000324N-1. Public domain.

Image 2, p. 3. Öködei Khan (1186–1241), second emperor of the Mongol Empire. Album leaf, ink and color on silk, 59.4 cm × 47 cm. National Palace Museum, Taipei, Taiwan. C2A000324N-2. Public domain.

Image 3, p. 7. Kitan groom leading a horse, ca. late 11th century. A painting from the approach wall, east ramp, tomb 7, Khüree (Kulun) Banner, Inner Mongolia, height: 1.71 m. Photo credit: Nei Menggu Wenwu Kaogu Yanjiusuo and Zhelimumeng Bowuguan 1987, pl. 1.1.

Image 4, p. 11. Standing archer, showing classic Mongol hat, braids, cummerbund, boots, and accessories, from a Mongol-era illustrated encyclopedia. An illustration of methods of standing archery from the Xiyuan jingshe printing (Zhishun period or 1330–1333) of Chen Yuanjing's illustrated encyclopedia, *Shilin guangji*.

Image 5, p. 15. A court vassal, probably a Turkic bodyguard, at a Khwarazmian or Seljuk court, twelfth to early thirteenth century. Painted and gilded gypsum plaster. 143.5 cm × 51.5 cm × 25.4 cm. Metropolitan Museum of Art, accession no. 67.119. Photo credit: Metropolitan Museum of Art.

Image 6, p. 68. Temple scene from a mural in a Jin-era Buddhist monastery illustrating the most splendid architecture of the period. Line drawing taken from a mural on the south side of the east wall of the Yanshan Monastery (Fanshi County, Shanxi), attributed to Wan Kui and his workshop, 1167. Photo Credit: Fu 1982, 123.

Image 7, p. 82. Siege with engines and sappers from a Mongol-era Persian manuscript. Mahmud ibn Sebuktegin attacking the fortress of Zarang; from the Edinburgh illustrated Arabic manuscript of the *Compendium of Chronicles* by Rashid al-Din (1247–1318), AD 1314. Repository: Edinburgh Library, MS Or 20 f 124v. Photo Credit: Edinburgh Library.

Image 8, p. 86. An early *paiza* from Chinggis Khan's time with Chinese (left) and Kitan (right) inscriptions. Line drawing of a *paiza* originally found by a farmer in Yanshan County, Hebei, now in the National Museum of China. Silver with letters gilt in gold. Length 21.7 cm, width 6 cm, thickness 0.3 cm. Photo credit: Drawing by Elizabeth Wilson based on Shi 2000.

Image 9, p. 87. A girl (left) and a boy (right) showing Mongol hairstyles from a Mongol-era illustrated encyclopedia. An illustration of "the practice of respectful bowing" in an article on how children should be trained from the Xiyuan jingshe printing (Zhishun period or 1330–1333) of Chen Yuanjing's illustrated encyclopedia, *Shilin guangji*.

Image 10, p. 88. Wooden saddle-tree with gold plating, front and back, from a Mongol-era tomb. Front plate 21 cm high, back plate 11.1 cm high. Inner Mongolian Autonomous Region Museum, Höhhot. Photo credit: Gary Todd.

Image 11, p. 91. Empress Chabui (ca. 1225–1281), Qubilai Khan's principal wife, wearing a *boqto* hat. Album leaf, ink and color on silk, 61.5 cm × 47.6 cm. National Palace Museum, Taipei, Taiwan. C2A000325N-1. Photo credit: Wikimedia commons.

Image 12, p. 97. Two archaic-style yurts housing relics attributed to Chinggis Khan, Ejen-Khoroo Banner, Ordos, Inner Mongolia, 1932. Normally kept on the ground, these yurts are harnessed to carts drawn by white camels for special ritual purposes, thus being, as the photographer Owen Lattimore noted, the only occasions where yurts are still carried whole on carts (Lattimore 1941, 52). Credit line: Photograph by Owen Lattimore © President and Fellows of Harvard College, Peabody Museum of Archaeology and Ethnology, PM 2010.5.36199

Image 13, p. 98. A khan and his wife on a throne, with ladies seated to their left, from a Mongol-era Persian manuscript. Illuminated manuscript page from the *Jāmiʿ al-Tavārīkh* or *Compendium of Chronicles*, by Rashid al-Din (1247–1318). Iran, Tabriz, ca. AD 1330. Inv. Diez A fol. 70, S. 23 Nr. I. Oriental Division. Staatsbibliothek zu Berlin, Stiftung Preussischer Kulturbesitz, Berlin, Germany. Photo Credit: Art Resource, NY.

Image 14, p. 102. A Mongol lady with attendants and a handbag, from a Timurid-era Persian manuscript. Saray-Albums (Diez-Albums), fol. 72, S. 11, No. 2 - Mongolian Lady with her servants, AD 1400–1425. Tabriz(?), Iran. Artist: Muhammad ibn Mahmudshah al-Khayyam (fifteenth century). Two of the servants wear Mongolian feather caps. Miniature, 11.0 × 14.6 cm to 14.8 cm (irregular) Inv. Diez A Fol 72, S. 11, Nr. 2. Oriental Division. Photo Credit: Art Resource, NY.

Image 15, p. 103. A Mongol-era *bianxian* ("braided waist") robe. Silk tabby with supplementary wefts of gilt thread. China, Mongol period (thirteenth to mid-fourteenth century). Length (collar to hem): 202 cm; width (sleeve to sleeve): 117 cm. China National Silk Museum, Hangzhou. No. 1753. Photo Credit: China National Silk Museum, Hangzhou.

Image 16, p. 104. Men practicing ritual kneeling, from a Mongol-era illustrated encyclopedia. An illustration of "the practice of kneeling" from an article in the Xiyuan jingshe printing (Zhishun period or 1330–1333) of Chen Yuanjing's illustrated encyclopedia *Shilin guangji*.

Image 17, p. 106. Letter of 1289 from Arghun Khan, Mongol ruler in the Middle East, to Philip the Fair, king of France. Scroll on linen-based paper, written in black ink with a calamus and stamps in red ink. Overall dimensions: 183 cm × 25 cm. Archives Nationales, no. J.937 Paris. Public domain.

Image 18, p. 108. Diagram on interpreting cracks in sheep shoulder blades for divination, from an early twentieth-century Mongolian manuscript. Manuscript in Chinese-style binding on Chinese handmade paper, written with a brush in black ink. Pages 21 × 11.5 cm. Catalogue no. Mong. 125a. Photo Credit: The Royal Danish Library.

Image 19a-b, p. 157. Poem by Ila Chucai in his own calligraphy, addressed to the local official Liu Man upon his departure from office. The poem reads, "In Yunzhong and in Xuandezhou, half the commons fled their homes. Only your thousand folk guard their farms. The Heavenly Court has many able men, only your clear fame exceeds the peak of high Taishan." Date: *geng/zi*, X, 16 (November 1, 1240). Handscroll; ink on paper. Each image: 36.8 × 283.8 cm; overall dimensions with mounting: 38.1 × 1147.3 cm. Metropolitan Museum of Art, accession no. 1989.363.17. Photo Credit: Metropolitan Museum of Art.

Image 20, p. 170. Taikhar Rock in Ikh Tamir *Sumu* (county), Northern Khangai Province, Mongolia. Photo by Tugstenuun Luvsantseren, summer, 2015.

Bibliography

Chinese Sources

Ban Gu 班固, with notes by Yan Shigu 顏師古. 1962. *Hanshu* 漢書. Edited by Yang Jialuo 楊家駱. 12 vols. Beijing: Zhonghua shuju.

Chen Jing 陳樫. [1361] 2010. *Tongjian xubian* 通鑑續編. *Siku tiyao zhulu congshu. Shi bu* 四庫提要著錄叢書.史部, vol. 75, 1–441. Rpt. Beijing: Beijing Press.

Chen Yuanjing 陳元靚. *Xinbian zuantu zenglei qunshu leiyao Shilin guangji: Qianji shisan juan houji shisan juan; xuji can bajuan; bieji shiyi juan* 新編纂圖增類群書類要事林廣記. 前集十三卷後集十三卷續集殘八卷別集十一卷. Zhishun era [1330–1333]: Xiyuan jingshe 西園精舍刊本. Earlier compilation: 13 chapters; later compilation: 13 chapters; supplementary compilation: 8 chapters incomplete; extraneous compilation: 11 chapters.

Fan Ye 范曄, with notes by Li Xian 李賢. 1965. *Hou Hanshu* 後漢書. Edited by Yang Jialuo 楊家駱. 12 vols. Beijing: Zhonghua shuju.

Jia Jingyan 贾敬颜, ed. 2004. "Zhang Dehui 'Lingbei jixing' shuzheng gao" 张德辉《岭北纪行》疏证稿. In *Wudai Song Jin Yuan ren bianjiang xingji shisan zhong shuzheng gao* 五代宋金元人边疆行记十三种疏证稿, compiled by Jia Jingyan 贾敬颜 and edited by Cui Wenyin 崔文印, 333–53. Beijing: Zhonghua shuju.

JS: Jinshi 金史. 1975. Compiled by Tuotuo 脫脫 [Toqto'a] et al. and edited by Yang Jialuo 楊家駱. 8 vols. Beijing: Zhonghua shuju.

Jinshu 晉書. 1974. Compiled by Fang Xuanling 房玄齡 et al. and edited by Yang Jialuo 楊家駱. 10 vols. Beijing: Zhonghua shuju.

Li Xinchuan 李心傳. 2000. *Jianyan yilai chaoye zaji* 建炎以來朝野雜記. Edited by Xu Gui 徐規. Beijing: Zhonghua shuju.

[Li Zhichang 李志常] Wang Guowei 王國維, ed. 1962. "Changchun zhenren Xiyouji zhu 長春真人西游記注." In *Menggu shiliao sizhong* 蒙古史料四種, prefaces (221–26); Part I, 1r–59v (227–344); Part II, 1r–26r (345–96); appendices (397–404); and colophon (405–29). 1926; facsimile rpt. Taiwan: Cheng-chung Press.

LS: Liao shi 遼史. 1974. Compiled by Tuotuo 脫脫 [Toqto'a] et al. and edited by Yang Jialuo 楊家駱. 5 vols. Beijing: Zhonghua shuju.

Meng Gong 孟珙 [error for Zhao Gong 趙珙]. 1995. *Meng-Da beilu jiaozhu* 蒙韃備錄校注. Edited by Cao Yuanzhong 曹元忠. 1901; facsimile rpt. Shanghai: Shangahi Guji Press.

Ouyang Xiu 歐陽脩, with notes by Xu Wudang 徐無黨. 2016. *Xin Wudaishi* 新五代史. Edited by Chen Shangjun 陳尚君. Beijing: Zhonghua shuju.

Ouyang Xiu 歐陽修 and Song Qi 宋祁, eds. 1975. *Xin Tangshu* 新唐書. Edited by Yang Jialuo 楊家駱. 20 vols. Beijing: Zhonghua shuju.

Song Zizhen 宋子貞. 1958. "Zhongshuling Yelü gong shendao bei 中書令耶律公神道碑." In *Yuan wenlei* 元文類, edited by Su Tianjue 蘇天爵, punctuated, 57.830–38. Guoxue jiben congshu 國學基本叢書series. 1936; rpt. Beijing: Commercial Press, 1958.

Song Zizhen 宋子貞. 1962. "Zhongshuling Yelü gong shendao bei 中書令耶律公神道碑." In *Yuan wenlei* 元文類, edited by Su Tianjue 蘇天爵, 57.9r–24v. 1342; rpt. Taipei: Shih-chieh shu-chü.

Song Zizhen 宋子貞. 1986. "Zhongshuling Yelü gong shendao bei 中書令耶律公神道碑." In *Zhanran jushi wenji* 湛然居士文集, by Yelü Chucai 耶律楚材 and edited by Xie Fang 謝方, Appendix, 323–35. Beijing: Zhonghua shuju.

Song Zizhen 宋子貞. 1997. "Zhongshuling Yelü gong shendao bei 中書令耶律公神道碑." In *Quan Yuan wen* 全元文, edited by Li Xiusheng 李修生, vol. 1, 8.172–82. Nanjing: Phoenix Press.

SS: Songshi 宋史. 1985. Compiled by Tuotuo 脫脫 [Toqto'a] et al. and edited by Yang Jialuo 楊家駱. 40 vols. Beijing: Zhonghua shuju.

Su Tianjue 蘇天爵. [1335] 1962. *Yuanchao mingchen shilue* 元朝名臣事略. 1335; rpt. Beijing: Zhonghua shuju.

Su Tianjue 蘇天爵. 1996. *Yuanchao mingchen shilue* 元朝名臣事略. Edited by Yao Jing'an 姚景安. Beijing: Zhonghua shuju.

Wang Guowei 王國維. [1926] 1962. *Menggu shiliao sizhong* 蒙古史料四種. Facsimile rpt. Taiwan: Cheng-chung Press.

Xu Quansheng 許全胜, ed. 2014. *Hei-Da shilue jiaozhu* 黑韃事略校注. Lanzhou: Lanzhou University Press.

Xu Youren 許有壬. 2004. "Yuan gu youchengxiang Qielie gong shendao beiming (bingxu) 元故右丞相怯烈公神道碑銘并序." In *Quan Yuan wen* 全元文, edited by Li Xiusheng 李修生, vol. 38, 1200.482–84. Nanjing: Phoenix Press.

Yao Congwu 姚從吾. [1962] 1971. "Zhang Dehui 'Lingbei jixing' zuben jiaozhu 張德輝嶺北紀行足本校注." In *Yao Congwu xiansheng quanji* 姚從吾先生全集, edited by Zhaqi-Siqin 札奇斯钦 [Jaġcidsecen] and Chen Jiexian 陳捷先, vol. 7, 289–347. Taipei: Cheng-chung Press.

Ye Longli 葉隆禮. 2014. *Qidan guozhi* 契丹國志. Edited by Jia Jingyan 賈敬顏 and Lin Rong-gui 林榮貴. Beijing: Zhonghua shuju.

Yelü Chucai 耶律楚材. 1986. *Zhanran jushi* 湛然居士文集. Edited by Xie Fang 謝方. Beijing: Zhonghua shuju.

YS: Yuanshi 元史. 1976. Compiled by Song Lian 宋濂 et al. and edited by Yang Jialuo 楊家駱. Beijing: Zhonghua shuju.

Yuwen Maozhao 宇文懋昭. 2011. *Da Jin guozhi jiaozheng* 大金國志校證, 2nd edition. Edited by Cui Wenyin 崔文印. [1234]; rpt. Beijing: Zhonghua shuju.

Zhang Canyi Yaoqing 張參議曜卿 [Zhang Dehui]. 1922. "Jixing" 紀行. In *Qiujian xiansheng daquan wenji* 秋澗先生大全文集, by Wang Yun 王惲, 933b–935b. Hongzhi 弘治 era; rpt. Shanghai: Commercial Press.

Zhang Canyi Yaoqing 張參議曜卿 [Zhang Dehui]. 2006. "Jixing" 紀行. In *Yutang jiahua* 玉堂嘉話; *Shanju xinyu* 山居新語, by Wang Yun 王惲 and Yang Yu 楊瑀, and edited by Yang Xiaochun 楊曉春 and Yu Dajun 余大鈞, 174–76. Beijing: Zhonghua shuju.

Zhang Canyi Yaoqing 張參議耀卿 [Zhang Dehui]. 2013. "Jixing" 紀行. In *Wang Yun quanji huijiao* 王惲全集彙校, by Wang Yun 王惲 and edited by Yang Liang 楊亮 and Zhong Yan-fei 鍾彥飛, 100.3962–68. Beijing: Zhonghua shuju.

Zhang Shiyan 張師顏. 1996 [facsimile reprint]. *Nanqian lu* 南遷錄. *Siku quanshu cunmu congshu* 四庫全書存目叢書. Edited by Siku quanshu cunmu congshu bianzuan weiyuanhui 四庫全書存目叢書編纂委員會, *Shi Bu* 史部, vol. 45, 137–59. Ji'nan: Qilu Shushe.

[Zhao Gong 趙珙] Wang Guowei 王國維, ed. 1962. "Meng-Da beilu jianzheng 蒙韃備錄箋證." In *Menggu shiliao sizhong* 蒙古史料四種, 431–57 (1r–14v) + 459–64. 1926; facsimile rpt. Taiwan: Cheng-chung Press.

Zhao Shiyan 趙世延 and Yu Ji 虞集. 2020. *Jingshi dadian jijiao* 經世大典輯校. Edited by Zhou Shaochuan 周少川, Wei Xuntian 魏訓田, and Xie Hui 謝輝. 2 vols. Beijing: Zhonghua.

Secondary and Non-Chinese Sources

Abramson, Marc S. 2008. *Ethnic Identity in Tang China*. Philadelphia: University of Pennsylvania.

Allsen, Thomas T. 1983. "Prelude to the Western Campaigns: Mongol Military Operations in the Volga-Ural Region, 1217–1237." *Archivum Eurasiae Medii Aevi*, vol. 3: 5–24.

Allsen, Thomas T. 1987. *Mongol Imperialism: The Policies of Grand Qan Möngke in China, Russia, and the Islamic Lands, 1251–1259*. Berkeley: University of California Press.

Allsen, Thomas T. 1989. "Mongolian Princes and Their Merchant Partners." *Asia Major*, series 3, vol. 2: 83–126.

Allsen, Thomas T. 1997. *Commodity and Exchange in the Mongol Empire: A Cultural History of Islamic Textiles*. Cambridge: Cambridge University Press.

Allsen, Thomas T. 2006. *The Royal Hunt in Eurasian History*. Philadelphia: University of Pennsylvania Press.

Andrews, Peter Alford. 1999. *Felt Tents and Pavilions: The Nomadic Tradition and Its Interaction with Princely Tentage*. 2 vols. London: Melisende.

Atwood, Christopher P. 2004. "Validated by Holiness or Sovereignty: Religious Toleration as Political Theology in the Mongol World Empire of the Thirteenth Century." *International History Review*, vol. 26, no. 2: 237–56.

Atwood, Christopher P. 2010. "The Notion of Tribe in Medieval China: Ouyang Xiu and the Shatuo Dynastic Myth." In *Miscellanea Asiatica: Festschrift in Honour of Françoise Aubin*, edited by Denise Aigle, Isabelle Charleux, Vincent Goossaert, and Roberte Hamayon, 593–621. Sankt Augustin: Institute Monumenta Serica.

Atwood, Christopher P. 2014a. "The First Mongol Contacts with the Tibetans." In *Trails of the Tibetan Tradition: Papers for Elliot Sperling*, edited by Roberto Vitali with Gedun Rabsal and Nicole Willock. Special issue of *Revue d'Etudes Tibétaines*, no. 31: 21–45.

Atwood, Christopher P. 2014b. "Historiography and Transformation of Ethnic Identity in the Mongol Empire: The Öng'üt Case." *Asian Ethnicity*, vol. 15, no. 4: 514–34.

Atwood, Christopher P. 2014c. "Earliest European Reference to 'Korea.'" In *A Window onto the Other: Contributions on the Study of the Mongolian, Turkic, and Manchu-Tungusic Peoples, Languages and Cultures Dedicated to Jerzy Tulisow on the Occasion of His Seventieth Birthday*, edited by Agata Bareja-Starzyńska, Jan Rogala, and Filip Majkowski, 42–51. Warsaw: Warsaw University.

Atwood, Christopher P. 2014/2015. "Chikü *Küregen* and the Origins of the Xiningzhou Qonggirads." *Archivum Eurasiae Medii Aevi*, vol. 21: 7–26.

Atwood, Christopher P. 2015. "Imperial Itinerance and Mobile Pastoralism: The State and Mobility in Medieval Inner Asia." *Inner* Asia, vol. 17: 293–349.

Atwood, Christopher P. 2016. "Buddhists as Natives: Changing Positions in the Religious Ecology of the Mongol Yuan Dynasty." In *The Middle Kingdom and the Dharma Wheel: Aspects of the Relationship between the Buddhist Samgha and the State in Chinese History*, edited by Thomas Jülch, 278–321. Leiden: Brill.

Atwood, Christopher P. 2017. "The Textual History of Tao Zongyi's *Shuofu*: Preliminary Results of Stemmatic Research on the *Shengwu qinzheng lu*." *Sino-Platonic Papers*, no. 271 (June): 1–70.

Atwood, Christopher P. 2019. "Arctic Ivory and the Routes North from the Tang to the Mongol Empires." In *For the Centennial of Berthold Laufer's Classic Sino-Iranica (1919)*, edited by Alessandro Grossato. Special Issue of *Quaderni di Studi Indo-Mediterranei*, vol. 13: 453–84.

Aubin, Jean. 1969. "L'ethnogenese des Qaraunas." *Turcica*, vol. 1: 65–94.

Bawden, C. R. 1958. "On the Practice of Scapulimancy among the Mongols." *Central Asiatic Journal*, vol. 4, no. 1: 1–44.

Biran, Michal. 2005. *Empire of the Qara Khitai in Eurasian History*. Cambridge: Cambridge University Press.

Birtalan, Ágnes. 1993. "Scapulimancy and Purifying Ceremony (New Data on the Darqad Shamanism on the Basis of Materials Collected in 1992)." In *Proceedings of the 35th PIAC September 12–17, 1992 Taipei, China*, edited by Chieh-hsien Ch'en, 1–10. Taipei: National Taiwan University and Center for Chinese Studies Materials.

Boldbaatar, Aldar owogt Yündenbatyn. 2008. *Mongol nutag dakhĭ ertnii nüüdelchdiin zadny shütleg*. Ulaanbaatar: Node.

Boyle, John Andrew. 1963. "The Mongol Commanders in Afghanistan and India According to the *Ṭabaqāt-i Nāṣirī* of Jūzjānī," *Islamic Studies* (Islamabad), vol. 2: 235–47.

Buell, Paul. 1993. "Činqai (*ca.* 1169–1252)." In *In the Service of the Khan: Eminent Personalities of the Early Mongol-Yüan Period*, edited by Igor de Rachewiltz, Hok-lam Chan, Hsiao Ch'i-ch'ing, and Peter W. Geier, with May Wang, 95–111. Weisbaden: Harrassowitz.

Buell, Paul. 1994. "Činqai (*ca.* 1169–1252): Architect of Mongolian Empire." In *Opuscula Altaica: Essays Presented in Honor of Henry Schwarz*, edited by Edward H. Kaplan and Donald W. Whisenhunt, 168–86. Bellingham: Western Washington University.

Bynner, Witter, and Kang-Hu Kiang. 1972. *The Jade Mountain: A Chinese Anthology, Being Three Hundred Poems of the T'ang Dynasty, 618–906*. New York: Doubleday.

Chaffee, John W. 1993. "The Historian as Critic: Li Hsin-ch'uan and the Dilemmas of Statecraft in Southern Song China." In *Ordering the World: Approaches to State and Society in Sung Dynasty China*, edited by Robert P. Hymes and Conrad Schirokauer, 310–35. Berkeley: University of California Press.

Chen, Yuan Julian. 2018. "Frontier, Fortification, and Forestation: Defensive Woodland on the Song-Liao Border in the Long Eleventh Century." *Journal of Chinese History*, vol. 2: 313–34.

"Chingisu kōtei seishi haishi 成吉思皇帝聖旨牌子." On website *Sankokan Selection* 参考館セレクション sankokan.jp/selection/antiquities/paizi.html, hosted by Tenri University. Accessed October 23, 2020.

Chrysos, Evangelos K. 1978. "The Title Βασιλευσ in Early Byzantine International Relations." *Dumbarton Oaks Papers*, vol. 32: 29–75.

Cleaves, Francis Woodman. 1951. "A Chancellery Practice of the Mongols in the Thirteenth and Fourteenth Centuries." *Harvard Journal of Asiatic Studies*, 14: 493–526.

Coblin, W. South. 1994. *A Compendium of Phonetics in Northwest Chinese*. Journal of Chinese Linguistics Monograph Series No. 7.

Coblin, W. South. 2007. *A Handbook of 'Phags-pa Chinese*. Honolulu: University of Hawai'i.

Creel, H. G. 1964. "The Beginnings of Bureaucracy in China: The Origin of the Hsien." *The Journal of Asian Studies*, vol. 23, no. 2: 155–84.

Cutter, Robert Joe, and William Gordon Crowell, trans. and eds. 1999. *Empresses and Consorts: Selections from Chen Shou's Records of the Three States with Pei Songzhi's Commentary*. Honolulu: University of Hawai'i Press.

Dang Baohai. 2001. "The Paizi of the Mongol Empire." *Zentralasiatische Studien*, vol. 31: 31–62.

Dang Baohai. 2003. "The Paizi of the Mongol Empire (Continued)." *Zentralasiatische Studien*, vol. 32: 7–10.

Dardess, John W. 1983. *Confucianism and Autocracy: Professional Elites in the Founding of the Ming Dynasty*. Berkeley: University of California Press.

Dawson, Christopher, ed., and a nun of Stanbrook Abbey, trans. [1955] n.d. *The Mongol Mission: Narratives and Letters of the Franciscan Missionaries in Mongolia and China in the Thirteenth and Fourteenth Centuries*. Rpt. New York: AMS.

de Rachewiltz, Igor. 1962. "The Hsi-yu lu 西遊錄 by Yeh-lü Ch'u-ts'ai 耶律楚材." *Monumenta Serica*, vol. 21: 1–128.

de Rachewiltz, Igor. 1974. "Some Remarks on the Khitan Clan Name Yeh-lü ~ I-la." *Papers in Far Eastern History*, vol. 9: 187–204.

de Rachewiltz, Igor. [1982] 2018. "More About the Story of Cinggis-Qan and the Peace-Loving Rhinoceros." *East Asian History*, vol 42: 57–66.

Doljinsuren, Myagmar, and Chandima Gomes. 2015. "Lightning Incidents in Mongolia." *Geomatics, Natural Hazards and Risk*, vol. 6, no. 8: 686–701.

Dunnell, Ruth. 1992. "The Hsia Origins of the Yüan Institution of Imperial Preceptor." *Asia Major*, third series, 5.1: 85–111.

Dunnell, Ruth W. 2009. "Translating History from Tangut Buddhist Texts." *Asia Major*, third series, 22.1: 41–78.

Duturaeva, Dilnoza. 2018. "Qarakhanid Envoys to Song China." *Journal of Asian History*, vol. 52, no. 2: 179–208.

Ebrey, Patricia Buckley. 1991. *Chu Hsi's Family Rituals*. Princeton: Princeton University Press.

Elman, Benjamin A. 2000. *Cultural History of Civil Examinations in Late Imperial China*. Berkeley: University of California Press.

Endicott-West, Elizabeth. 1999. "Notes on Shamans, Fortune-Tellers and *Yin-Yang* Practitioners and Civil Administration in Yuan China." In *The Mongol Empire and Its Legacy*, edited by Reuven Amitai-Preiss and David O. Morgan, 224–39. Leiden: Brill.

Erdemtü, trans., and Cünn-a, ed. 1994. *Jang Dé Hüi-yin "Dabaġan aru-ber jiġulcilaġsan temdeglel."* Tongliao: Inner Mongolian Education Press.

Farquhar, David M. 1981. "Structure and Function in the Yuan Imperial Government." In *China under Mongol Rule*, edited by John D. Langlois Jr., 25–55. Princeton: Princeton University Press.

Franke, Herbert. 1974. "Siege and Defense of Towns in Medieval China." In *Chinese Ways in Warfare*, edited by Frank A. Kierman Jr. and John King Fairbank, 151–201. Cambridge: Harvard University Press.

Fu Xinian 傅熹年. 1982. "Shanxisheng Fanshixian Yanshansi Nandian Jindai bihuazhong suohui jianzhu de chubu fenxi 山西省繁峙县岩山寺南殿金代壁画中所绘建筑的初步分析." In *Jianzhu lishi yanjiu* 建筑历史研究, vol. 1, 119–51. Beijing: Chinese Academy of Building Research.

Garcia, Chad D. 2012. "A New Kind of Northerner: Initial Song Perceptions of the Mongols." *Journal of Song-Yuan Studies*, vol. 42: 309–42.

Golden, Peter B. 1990. "Cumanica III: Urusoba." In *Aspects of Altaic Civilization III*, edited by Denis Sinor, 33–46. Bloomington: Indiana University.

Haneda, Toru. 1936. "Une Tablette du Décret Sacré de L'empereur Genghis." *Memoirs of the Research Department of the Toyo Bunko (The Oriental Library)*, vol. 8: 85–91.

Ho, Kai-lung. 2010. "Jiaoduan, Yelü Chucai yu Liu Bingzhong: yi yaoyan lilun yanjiu chuanshuo liubian" 角端、耶律楚材與劉秉忠: 以謠言理論研究傳說流變. In *Yuanshi luncong* 元史論叢, vol. 13, 293–302. Tianjin: Tianjin Guji Press.

Ho Peng Yoke. 1966. *The Astronomical Chapters of the Chin Shu: With Amendments, Full Translation, and Annotations.* The Hague: Mouton & Co.

Hsieh, Bao Hua. 1999. "From Charwoman to Empress Dowager: Serving-Women in the Ming Palace." *Ming Studies*, vol. 42: 26–80.

Hu, Minghui. 2016. "The Scholar's Robe." *Frontiers of History in China*, vol. 11, no. 3: 339–75.

Hucker, Charles O. 1985. *A Dictionary of Official Titles in Imperial China.* Stanford: Stanford University Press.

IMEA: *Nei Menggu minzu wenwu* 内蒙古民族文物 / *Öbör Monggol-un ündüsüten-ü durasqaltu jüil.* 1987. Edited by Nei Menggu bowuguan 内蒙古博物馆 / Öbör Monggol-un müdzéi. Beijing: People's Art Press.

Irwin, Robert. 2018. *Ibn Khaldun: An Intellectual Biography.* Princeton: Princeton University Press.

Jackson, Peter. 2009. *The Mission of Friar William of Rubruck: His Journey to the Court of the Great Khan Möngke, 1253–1255.* Translated and edited by David Morgan. 1990 rpt. Indianapolis: Hackett Publishing.

Jagchid, Sechin. 1988. *Essays in Mongolian Studies.* Provo, Utah: Brigham Young University, 1988.

Juvaini, ʿAla-ad-Din ʿAta-Malik. 1958. *The History of the World Conqueror.* Translated by John Andrew Boyle. 2 vols. Cambridge: Harvard University Press.

[Jūzjānī], Minhāj-ud-Dīn, Abū-'Ūmar-i-'Uṣmān Siraj. [1881]; rpt. 1995. *Ṭabaḳāt-i-Nāṣirī: A General History of the Muhammadan Dynasties of Asia, Including Hindustan; from A.H. 194*

(810 A.D.) to A.H. 658 (1260 A.D.) and the Irruption of the Infidel Mughals into Islam. Translated by Major H. G. Raverty. Calcutta: Asiatic Society.

Kane, Daniel. 2009. *The Kitan Language and Script.* Leiden: Brill.

Kane, Daniel. 2013. "The Great Central Liao Kitan State." *Journal of Song-Yuan Studies,* vol. 43: 27–50.

Kara, György. 1990. "*Zhiyuan yiyu*: Index alphabétique des mots mongols." *Acta Orientalia Academiae Scientiarum Hung.,* vol. 44, no. 3: 279–344.

"Khermen Denj." On website *Mongol Tüükhiin Tailbar Tolĭ* mongoltoli.mn/history/h/314. Accessed May 30, 2020.

Kirakos Gandzakets'i, and Robert Bedrosian, trans. 1986. *History of the Armenians.* New York: Sources of the Armenian Tradition.

Knapp, Keith N. 2009. "Three Fundamental Bonds and Five Constant Virtues: *Sāngāng Wǔcháng* 三 纲 五 常." In *Berkshire Encyclopedia of China,* edited by Linsun Cheng, vol. 5, 2252–55. Great Barrington, MA: Berkshire Publishing Group.

Kradin, N. N., and A. L. Ivliev. 2014. *Istoriia Kidan'skoi imperii Liao.* Moscow: Nauka.

Kradin, N. N., et al. 2012. "Rezultaty issledovanii gorodosha Khermen-denzh v Mongolii v 2010–11 gg." In *Istoriia i kul'tura srednevekovykh narodov stepnoi Evrazii: Materialy II Mezhdunarodnogo kongressa srednovekovoi arkheologii Evraziiskikh stepei,* 168–71. Barnaul: Altai University Press.

Kriukov, Michael V., and Vadim P. Kurylev. 1992. "The Origins of the Yurt: Evidence from Chinese Sources of the Third Century B.C. to the Thirteenth Century A.D." In *Foundations of Empire: Archaeology and Art of the Eurasian Steppes,* edited by Gary Seaman, 143–56. Los Angeles: University of Southern California.

Kroll, Paul W. 2015. *A Student's Dictionary of Classical and Medieval Chinese.* Leiden: Brill.

Kuribayashi, Hitoshi 栗林均. 2012. "*Genchō hishi*" *bōyaku Kango sakuin* 「元朝秘史」傍訳漢語 索引. Sendai: Tohoku University.

Lattimore, Owen. 1941. *Mongol Journeys.* New York: Doubleday, Doran and Co.

Laufer, Berthold. 1916. "Supplementary Notes on Walrus and Narwhal Ivory." *T'oung Pao,* Second Series, vol. 17, no. 3: 348–89.

Legge, James, ed. and trans. [1895] 1970. *The Works of Mencius: Translated with Critical and Exegetical Notes, Prolegomena, and Copious Indexes.* Rpt. New York: Dover Publications.

Legge, James, ed. and trans. [1865] 1991. *Chinese Classics: With a Translation, Critical and Exegetical Notes, Prolegomena, and Copious Indices,* Vol. III: *The Shoo King.* Rpt. Taipei: SMC Publishing.

Legge, James, ed. and trans. [1871] 1991. *Chinese Classics: With a Translation, Critical and Exegetical Notes, Prolegomena, and Copious Indices,* Vol. IV: *The She King.* Rpt. Taipei: SMC Publishing.

Legge, James, ed. and trans. [1872] 1991. *Chinese Classics: With a Translation, Critical and Exegetical Notes, Prolegomena, and Copious Indices,* Vol. V: *The Ch'un Ts'ew with the Tso Chuen.* Rpt. Taipei: SMC Publishing.

Levin, M. G., and L. P. Potapov. 1964. *Peoples of Siberia.* Edited by Stephen Dunn. Chicago: University of Chicago Press.

Li Chih-ch'ang. [1931] 1979. *The Travels of an Alchemist.* Translated by Arthur Waley. Rpt. New York: AMS.

Li, Feng. 2003. "'Feudalism' and Western Zhou China: A Criticism." *Harvard Journal of Asiatic Studies*, vol. 63, no. 1: 115–44.

Li, Lillian M. 2007. *Fighting Famine in North China: State, Market, and Environmental Decline, 1690s–1990s.* Stanford: Stanford University Press.

Li Wei 李蔚. 2000. "Chengjisi Han wenwu 成吉思汗文物." *Renmin ribao haiwai ban* 《人民日報海外版》(2000年05月26日第九版).

Li Xia 李俠 and Xiao Feng 曉峰. 1989. *Zhongguo beifang minzu huobi shi* 中國北方民族貨幣史. Harbin: Heilongjiang People's Press.

Long, Qian'an 龙潜庵. 1985. *Song-Yuan yuyan cidian* 宋元语言词典. Shanghai: Shanghai Lexicographic Press.

Matsuda, Kōichi 松田孝一. 2013. "Mongorukoku hakken no Shi Kaku no sumi shoni tsuite モンゴル国発見の史格の墨書について." *13, 14 shiki Tō Ajiya shiryō tsūshin* 13、14世紀東アジア史料通信, no. 21: 1–8.

Matsuda, Kōichi 松田孝一. 2014. "Cong 'Dayuan mazheng ji' kan Dongpingfu huji bu 從《大元馬政記》看東平府戶籍簿." *Xiyu lishi yuyan yanjiu jikan* 西域歷史語言研究集刊, vol. 7: 169–85.

Matsuda, Kōichi. 2021. "Comparing the Depictions of the Mongol Courts Created in the Yuan and the Ilkhanate." In *New Approaches to the Ilkhans*, edited by Timothy May, Dashdondug Bayarsaikhan, and Christopher P. Atwood, 176–97. Leiden: Brill.

May, Timothy. 2021. "The Ilkhanate and Afghanistan." In *New Approaches to the Ilkhans*, edited by Timothy May, Dashdondug Bayarsaikhan, and Christopher P. Atwood, 272–320. Leiden: Brill.

Michell, Robert, and Nevill Forbes. 1914. *The Chronicle of Novgorod, 1016–1471.* London: Camden Society.

Miyazaki, Ichisada. 1981. *China's Examination Hell: The Civil Service Examinations of Imperial China.* Translated by Conrad Schirokauer. New Haven: Yale University Press.

Molnár, Ádám. 1994. *Weather-Magic in Inner Asia.* Bloomington: Indiana University.

Möngkejayaġ-a, trans. 1985a. "'Mongġol—Tatar-un tuqai bürin temdeglel'-un taiilburilan gerecilegsen bicig." In *Boġda Baġatur bey-e-ber dayilaġsan temdeglel*, edited by Ge. Asaraltu and Köke'öndör, 93–156. Höhhot: Inner Mongolia People's Press.

Möngkejayaġ-a, trans. 1985b. "'Qar-a Tatar-un tuqai kereg-ün tobci'-yin taiilburilan gerecilegsen bicig." In *Boġda Baġatur bey-e-ber dayilaġsan temdeglel*, edited by Ge. Asaraltu and Köke'öndör, 157–253. Höhhot: Inner Mongolia People's Press.

Mostaert, Antoine. 1977. *Le matériel mongol de* Houa i i iu 華夷譯語 *de Houng-ou (1389)*, Vol. I. Edited by Igor de Rachewiltz, with Anthony Schönbaum. Brussels: Institute belge des hautes études chinoises.

Munkuev, Nikolai Tsyrendorzhievich, trans. 1965. *Kitaiskii istochnik o pervykh mongol'skikh khanakh; nadgrobnaia nadpis na mogile Eliui Chu-Tsaia. Perevod i issledovanie.* Moscow: Nauka.

Munkuev, Nikolai Tsyrendorzhievich, trans. 1975. *Men-da bei-lu: "Polnoe opisanie Mongolo-Tatar": faksimile ksilografa.* Moscow: Nauka.

Munkuev, Nikolai Tsyrendorzhievich. 2005. *Mongolyn ankhny khaadyn tukhai Khyatad ekh surwalj.* Translated by Choizongiin Baatar. Ulaanbaatar: Monsudar.

Nei Menggu Wenwu Kaogu Yanjiusuo 内蒙古文物考古研究所 and Zhelimu Meng Bowu-guan 哲里木盟博物馆. (1987) "Nei Menggu Kulun qi, bahao Liaomu," 内 蒙 古 库 伦 旗 七 、 八 号 辽 墓. *Wenwu* 文物, no. 7 (1987): 74–84, 3 pls.

"Nivkh Fish Skin Robe." On website *Things That Talk . . . Exploring Humanities through the Life of Objects* thingsthattalk.net/t/ttt:TNTDex. Accessed June 14, 2020.

Nylan, Michael. 1993. *The Canon of Supreme Mystery by Yang Hsiung; a Translation with Commentary of the T'ai Hsüan Ching.* Albany: State University of New York Press.

Obolensky, Dimitri. 1971. *The Byzantine Commonwealth: Eastern Europe, 500–1453.* New York: Praeger Publishers.

Ochir, A., A. Enkhtör, and L. Erdenebold. 2005. *Khar bukh balgas ba Tuul golyn saw dakhĭ Khyatany üyeiin khot, suuringuud.* Ulaanbaatar: Mongolian National Museum and the Academy of Sciences.

Olbricht, Peter. 1957. "Die Biographie in China." *Saeculum*, vol. 8: 224–35.

Olbricht, Peter, and Elisabeth Pinks, trans., based on the draft of Erich Haenisch and Yao Ts'ung-wu. 1980. *Meng-Ta pei-lu und Hei-Ta shih-lüeh: chinesische Gesandtenberichte über die frühen Mongolen 1221 und 1237.* Wiesbaden: Otto Harrassowitz.

Ostrogorsky, George. 1959. "The Byzantine Empire in the World of the Seventh Century." *Dumbarton Oaks Papers*, vol. 13: 1–21.

Pelliot, Paul. 1936. "Sao-houa, sauɣa, sauɣat, saguate." *T'oung Pao*, vol. 32: 230–37.

Pelliot, Paul. 1944. "Les forms avec et sans q- (k-) initial en Turk et en Mongol." *T'oung Pao*, vol. 37, no. 3/4: 73–101.

Pelliot, Paul. 1959. *Notes on Marco Polo.* 2 vols. and index vol. with continuous pagination. Paris: Adrien-Maisonneuve.

Peng, Xinwei. 1994. *A Monetary History of China.* Translated by Edward H. Kaplan. 2 vols. Bellingham: Western Washington University.

Pines, Yuri. 2020. "Names and Titles in Eastern Zhou Texts." *T'oung Pao*, vol. 106: 714–720.

Polo, Marco. [1938] 1976. *The Description of the World.* Translated by A. C. Moule and Paul Pelliot. 2 vols. Rpt. New York: AMS Press.

Polo, Marco. 2016. *The Description of the World.* Translated by Sharon Kinoshita. Indianapolis: Hackett Publishing Co.

Pulleyblank, Edwin G. 1991. *Lexicon of Reconstructed Pronunciation in Early Middle Chinese, Late Middle Chinese, and Early Mandarin*, comp. Vancouver: UBC Press.

Pursey, Lance. 2019. "Tents, Towns and Topography: How Chinese-Language Liao Epitaphs Depicted the Moving Court." *Journal of Song-Yuan Studies*, vol. 48: 177–206.

Raaflaub, Kurt A. 1987. "Herodotus, Political Thought, and the Meaning of History." *Arethusa*, vol. 20, no. 1/2: 221–48.

Rásonyi, László, and Imre Baski. 2007. *Onomasticon Turcicum: Turkic Personal Names.* 2 vols. Bloomington: Indiana University.

Ratchnevsky, Paul. 1966. "Les Che-wei étaient-ils des Mongols?" In *Melanges de sinologie offerts à Monsieur Paul Demiéville*, vol. 1, 225–251. Paris: Presses universitaires de France.

Rashiduddin, Fazlullah. 1998/1999. *Jami'u't-Tawarikh: Compendium of Chronicles: A History of the Mongols.* Translated by W. M. Thackston. Cambridge: Harvard University Press.

Sawyer, Ralph D., with Mei-chün Sawyer, trans. 1993. *The Seven Military Classics of Ancient China*. New York: Basic Books.

Schneewind, Sarah. 2009. "Reduce, Re-use, Recycle: Imperial Autocracy and Scholar-Official Autonomy in the Background to the Ming History Biography of Early Ming Scholar-Official Fang Keqin (1326–1376)." *Oriens Extremus*, vol. 48: 103–52.

Schuessler, Axel. 2009. *Minimal Old Chinese and Latter Han Chinese: A Companion to* Grammata Serice Recensa. Honolulu: University of Hawai'i Press.

Schurmann, Herbert Franz. 1967. *Economic Structure of the Yüan Dynasty*. Cambridge: Harvard University Press.

Shea, Eiren. 2020. *Mongol Court Dress, Identity Formation, and Global Exchange*. Abingdon: Routledge.

Shelach-Lavi, Gideon, Ido Wachtel, Dan Golan, Otgonjargal Batzorig, Chunag Amartuvshin, Ronnie Ellenblum, and William Honeychurch. 2020. "Medieval Long-Wall Construction on the Mongolian Steppe during the Eleventh to Thirteenth Centuries AD." *Antiquity*, vol. 94 (375): 724–41.

Shelach-Lavi, Gideon, William Honeychurch, and Amartuvshin Chunag. 2020. "Does Extra-Large Equal Extra-Ordinary? The 'Wall of Chinggis Khan' from a Multidimensional Perspective." *Humanities and Social Sciences Communications*. https://doi.org/10.1057/s41599-020-0524-2.

Shi, Shuqing 史树青. 2000. "Chengjisi huangdi shengzhi jinpai kao 成吉思皇帝圣旨金牌考." *Shoucangjia* 收藏家, no. 4: 45–46.

Shimunek, Andrew. 2017. *Language of Ancient Southern Mongolia and North China*. Wiesbaden: Harrassowitz Verlag.

Shinno, Reiko. 2016. *The Politics of Chinese Medicine under Mongol Rule*. London: Routledge.

Shiraishi, Noriyuki 白石典之. 2012 "'Gyonihaku' saikō 「魚兒濼」再考." *Nihon Mongoru gakkai kiyō* 日本モンゴル学会紀要, no. 42: 23–38.

Shiraishi, Noriyuki. 2013. "Searching for Genghis: Excavations of the Ruins at Avraga." In *Genghis Khan and the Mongol Empire*, edited by William W. Fitzhugh, Morris Rossabi, and William Honeychurch, 132–35. Washington: Smithsonian Institution.

Sima, Qian. 1993. *Records of the Grand Historian, Vol. 2: Han Dynasty I*, revised edition. Translated by Burton Watson. New York: Columbia University Press.

"Skin Clothing Online—Nationalmuseet." On website *Nationalmuseet* skinddragter.natmus.dk/. Accessed June 14, 2020.

Soulliere, Ellen Felicia. 1987. *Palace Women in the Ming Dynasty: 1368–1644*. PhD diss., Princeton University.

Steinhardt, Nancy Shatzman. 2016. "The Pagoda in Kherlen-Bars: New Understandings of Khitan-Period Towering Pagodas." *Archives of Asian Art*, vol. 66, no. 2: 187–212.

Tackett, Nicolas. 2008. "The Great Wall and Conceptualizations of the Border under the Northern Song." *Journal of Song-Yuan Studies*, vol. 38: 99–138.

Twitchett, Denis. 1962. "Problems of Chinese Biography." In *Confucian Personalities*, ed. Arthur F. Wright and Denis Twitchett, 24–39. Stanford: Stanford University Press.

Twitchett, Denis. 1970. *Financial Administration under the T'ang Dynasty*. Cambridge: Cambridge University Press.

Twitchett, Denis. 1992. *The Writing of Official History under the T'ang.* Cambridge: Cambridge University Press.

Venturi, Federica. 2008. "An Old Tibetan Document on the Uighurs: A New Translation and Interpretation." *Journal of Asian History*, vol. 42, no. 1: 1–35.

Von Glahn, Richard. 1996. *Fountain of Fortune: Money and Monetary Policy in China, 1000–1700.* Berkeley: University of California Press.

Von Glahn, Richard. 2016. *The Economic History of China: From Antiquity to the Nineteenth Century.* Cambridge: Cambridge University Press.

Waley, Arthur. 1960. *The Book of Songs.* New York: Grove Press.

Wang, Binghua, and Helen Wang. 2013. "A Study of the Tang Dynasty Tax Textiles (*Yongdiao Bu*) from Turfan." *Journal of the Royal Asiatic Society*, vol. 23 no. 22: 263–80.

Wang, Jinping. 2014. "A Social History of the *Treasured Canon of the Mysterious Capital* in North China under Mongol-Yuan Rule." *East Asian Publishing and Society*, vol. 4: 1–35.

Wang, Jinping. 2018. *In the Wake of the Mongols: The Making of a New Social Order in North China, 1200–1600.* Cambridge: Harvard University Press.

Wang, Shuo. 2004. "The Selection of Women for the Qing Imperial Harem." *The Chinese Historical Review*, vol. 11, no. 2: 212–22.

Wang, Shuo. 2008. "Qing Imperial Women: Empresses, Concubines, and Aisin Gioro Daughters." In *Servants of the Dynasty: Palace Women in World History*, edited by Anne Walthall, 137–71. Berkeley: University of California Press.

Watson, Burton, trans. 1964. *Chuang Tzu: Basic Writings.* New York: Columbia University Press.

Whaley, Mark A. 2001. "An Account of the 13th Century Qubchir of the Mongol 'Great Courts.'" *Acta Orientalia Academiae Scientiarum Hungaricae*, vol. 54, no. 1: 1–84.

Wilkinson, Endymion. 2000. *Chinese History: A Manual*, revised and enlarged edition. Cambridge: Harvard University Press.

Wu, Pei-yi. 2002. "Yang Miaozhen: A Woman Warrior in Thirteenth-Century China." *Nan Nü*, vol. 4, no. 2: 137–69.

Xiao, Tong. 1982. *Wen Xuan or Selections of Refined Literature*, Vol. I: *Rhapsodies on Metropolises and Capitals.* Translated by David R. Knechtges. Princeton: Princeton University Press.

Xu, Gui 徐規. 1991. "Dianjiao shuoming" 點校説明. In *Jianyan yilai chaoye zaji* 建炎以來朝野雜記, by Li Xinchuan 李心傳 and edited by Xu Gui, 1–14. Beijing: Zhonghua shuju, 2000.

Yang, Bin. 2004. "Horses, Silver, and Cowries: Yunnan in Global Perspective." *Journal of World History*, vol. 15, no. 3: 281–322.

Yang, Bin. 2012. "The Bengal Connections in Yunnan." *China Report*, vol. 48: 125–45.

Yang, Liang 楊亮. 2013. "Qian yan 前言." In *Wang Yun quanji huijiao* 王惲全集彙校, by Wang Yun 王惲, edited by Yang Liang 楊亮 and Zhong Yanfei 鍾彥飛, 1–38. Beijing: Zhonghua shuju.

Yang, Naisi 楊耐思. 1981. *Zhongyuan yinyun yinxi* 中原音韵音系. Beijing: China Academy of Social Sciences Press.

Yang, Shao-yun. 2015. "'Their Lands Are Peripheral and Their Qi Is Blocked Up': The Uses of Environmental Determinism in Han (206 BCE–220 CE) and Tang (618–907

CE) Chinese Interpretations of the 'Barbarians.'" In *The Routledge Handbook of Identity and the Environment in the Classical and Medieval Worlds*, edited by Rebecca Futo Kennedy, and Molly Jones-Lewis, 390–412. Abingdon-on-Thames: Taylor and Francis.

Yang, Shao-yun. 2019. *The Way of the Barbarians: Redrawing Ethnic Boundaries in Tang and Song China*. Seattle: University of Washington Press.

Yang, Xiaochun 楊曉春. 2006. "Qian yan 前言." In *Yutang jiahua* 玉堂嘉話; *Shanju xinyu* 山居新語, by Wang Yun 王惲 and Yang Yu 楊瑀, edited by Yang Xiaochun 楊曉春 and Yu Dajun 余大鈞, 3–16. Beijing: Zhonghua shuju.

Yang, Xiaoping, et al. 2015. "Groundwater Sapping as the Cause of Irreversible Desertification of Hunshandake Sandy Lands, Inner Mongolia, Northern China." *Proceedings of the National Academy of Sciences*, vol. 112, no. 3: 702–6. https://www.pnas.org/content/112/3/702.

Yang, Zhishui 扬之水. 2014. "'Qianchun yong ru shi ri' Luzhou Song mu shike zhong de shenghuo gushi "千春永如是日": 泸州宋墓石刻中的生活故事." *Xingxiang shixue yanjiu* 形象史学研究, 60–81. Beijing: People's Press.

Yang, Zhishui 扬之水. 2015. "Guanyu 'Guasi' 关于'罣罳.'" *Xingxiang shixue yanjiu* 形象史学研究, no. 1: 159.

Yuan, Bin 袁宾, et al. 1997. *Song yuyan cidian* 宋语言词典. Shanghai: Shanghai Educational Press.

Zhang, Fan Jeremy. 2014. "Jin-Dynasty Pingyang and the Rise of Theatrical Pictures." *Artibus Asiae*, vol. 74, no. 2: 337–80.

Zhang, Ling. 2016. *The River, the Plain, and the State: An Environmental Drama in Northern Song China, 1048–1128*. Cambridge: Cambridge University Press.

Zhang, Weidong, and Martin Gillis, ed. 2002. *Notes on Elm in the Korqin Sandy Lands, Northeast China*. Project "Afforestation, Forestry Research, Planning and Development in the Three North-Region" (FAO/GCP/CPR/009/BEL). Accessed August 25, 2020. https://www.fao.org/3/AD110E00.htm.

Zheng, Lin-Lin, Sun Jian-Hua, and Wei Jie. 2010. "Thunder Events in China: 1980–2008." *Atmospheric and Oceanic Science Letters*, vol. 3, no. 4: 181–88.

Zhou, Xibao 周锡保. 1984. *Zhongguo gudai fushi shi* 中國古代服飾史. Beijing: China Theater Press.

Index

Abduraqman, 151, 154
Ai, (Jin) Prince of, 50
airag. See fermented mare's milk
Akûdai (Wongian Min), 8, 21, 47–49, 57
Alaqai (Alaqan, Princess or Lady Beki),
 72, 77–78, 123
Alchar, 125
Alchi Noyê (Imperial Maternal Uncle),
 78, 79
Alchidai, Prince, 94, 123
An Tianhe, 151
ancestors, dynastic, 39, 56, 172, 174
Anci County, 66
appanages, 146, 173
Aqai, 80–81, 124. *See also* Tugha
archery, 114, 122, 125. *See also* bows and
 arrows
Ariq Bayan, 77
Asan-Amish, 149

Bai Hua, 163
Baisbu (Baisbo, Baisma, Zhenguo), 64,
 77–78, 123
Balhae, 59
bandits, 61, 66–67, 112, 139, 147
bandit-suppression commissioners
 (*zhāotǎoshǐ*), 34–35, 58, 60, 63
banners, military, 88–89, 118
Baozhou Prefecture (Baosai), 56, 66, 126,
 164; Liangmen Gate, 164
"barbarians": attitudes toward, 16–17, 19,
 34, 151; clothing, 91, 101; Mongols as,
 75; terms for, 13, 24–26, 78, 165
Bars Lake (Barsköl), 134
battle-standards, 153
Bazhou Prefecture, 67. *See also* Xin'an
 Military Prefecture
beauty and ugliness: in architecture, 68;
 in men, 73, 127; in women, 91, 92,
 101, 128
Beijing. *See* Yanjing
Bekter (imperial commissioner), 140

Belgudei Noyê, 76–77. *See also*
 Kö'ün-Buqa
biographies, Chinese-style, 131–32,
 181–82, 183–84
Bitehetu, 168
blockprinting (xylograph), 133,
 177–83
Bo'ol, Prince of State, 79, 124
bodyguards: Turkic, 15; Jin, 33, 52,
 53, 54, 65, 85; Mongol, 78–79, 88,
 97, 138; *qorchi*, 104. *See also* Mongol
 military.
"bogus" (*wěi*), 19, 31, 40, 74
Botu, Imperial Son-in-Law, 77,
 123, 125
bows and arrows: characteristics, 60,
 89, 117–18, 124, 142; illustrated, 11;
 manufacture, 137, 144, 168
Buddhism: and Ila Chucai, 105, 157; and
 Liao, 172; monasteries, 99, 165, 207;
 monks, 144, 148, 163; State Preceptor,
 129

Cai Jing, 49
"caitiff" (*lǔ*), 25, 51, 58, 61, 74, 127
calendars: Daming: 158; Ila Chucai's
 almanac, 105, 157–58; imperial role,
 16–17, 29–30; Martabah 157–58;
 Mongols ignorant of, 30, 63, 73, 105;
 sexagenary cycle, 31–32, 73, 76, 105;
 twelve-animal cycle, 32, 75, 105
camels, 96
Cao Yuanzhong, 74n19, 179
capital punishment: *aldaqui*, 113–14;
 application of, 107, 143–45; crimes,
 113–14; death by slicing, 129
Censorate (*Yùshǐtái*), 33, 163
census, 145, 146, 150
Central Plains (*Zhōngyuán*), 28, 56, 65, 66,
 84, 134, 145, 165
Chaghadai, 123, 125, 127, 128
chairs, 88, 99